Authenticity

Also by the Authors

The Experience Economy:
Work Is Theatre & Every Business a Stage

Mass Customization:
The New Frontier in Business Competition

Authenticity
WHAT CONSUMERS *REALLY* WANT

JAMES H. GILMORE

B. JOSEPH PINE II

HARVARD BUSINESS SCHOOL PRESS
Boston, Massachusetts

No part of this publication may be reproduced, stored in or introduced into a retrieval system, or transmitted, in any form, or by any means (electronic, mechanical, photocopying, recording, or otherwise), without the prior permission of the publisher. Requests for permission should be directed to permissions@hbsp.harvard.edu, or mailed to Permissions, Harvard Business School Publishing, 60 Harvard Way, Boston, Massachusetts 02163.

Library of Congress Cataloging-in-Publication Data

Gilmore, James H., 1959–
    Authenticity : contending with the new consumer sensibility / James H. Gilmore, B. Joseph Pine II.
        p. cm.
    ISBN-13: 978-1-59139-145-6 (hardcover : alk. paper)
    ISBN-10: 1-59139-145-8
    1. Product management. 2. Consumer behavior. 3. Consumers' preferences. I. Pine, B. Joseph. II. Title.
    HF5415.15.G55 2007
    658.8'343—dc22

                                                                2007017287

The paper used in this publication meets the requirements of the American National Standard for Permanence of Paper for Publications and Documents in Libraries and Archives Z39.48-1992.

To those who

seek the real—and

find the truth.

CONTENTS

Preface   *xi*

1   **Authenticity**   1
The New Business Imperative
The Appeal of Real

2   **The Demand for Authenticity**   9
Why Now?
Drivers of the New Consumer Sensibility

3   **The Supply of Inauthenticity**   31
What's Going On?
Reality, Fakery, and Three Axioms of Authenticity

4   **Rendering Authenticity**   45
What to Do
Five Genres of Authenticity

5   **Fake, Fake, It's *All* Fake**   81
Why Offerings Are Inauthentic
Lessons from Philosophy

6   **The Real/Fake Reality**   95
How Offerings Become Authentic
Two Time-Honored Standards of Authenticity

7   Deconstructing Authenticity   115

How to Assess Your Business

Ten Elements of Authenticity

8   From Marketing to Placemaking   147

Being What You Say You Are

The Placemaking Portfolio

9   From Strategy to Decision Making   179

Being True to Self

Here-and-Now Space

10 Finding Authenticity   219

The Right Direction for You

Real/Fake Polarities

Notes   253
Acknowledgments   283
Index   287
About the Authors   301

Authenticity will be the buzzword of the twenty-first century. And what is authentic? Anything that is not devised and structured to make a profit. Anything that is not controlled by corporations. Anything that exists for its own sake, that assumes its own shape. The modern world is the corporate equivalent of a formal garden, where everything is planted and arranged for effect. Where nothing is untouched, where nothing is authentic.

—Robert Doniger, in Michael Crichton's *Timeline*

PREFACE

Raise the subject of authenticity today and many people eagerly talk about what is real and what is fake. The topic—whether concerning people, places, or things—triggers strong opinions and passionate disagreements even among close friends. What we deem real may not seem so real to you; you may even view it as downright fake. Yet underlying any difference of opinion about what constitutes authenticity is a shared belief that whatever is real is valued. On that we all agree.

In business today, executives recognize that their leadership skills hinge largely on their ability to gain a reputation among employees as real. Middle managers grow frustrated when corporate culture mandates collective acts of fakery. You've seen it: all heads nodding in agreement at the conclusion of a meeting, everyone dismissing the decision the moment they leave the conference room. Frontline workers feign certain desired behaviors, projecting a faked niceness that reflects poorly on the whole business. And when customers encounter real behavior, it's so often really bad.

This book does not focus on such matters of executive leadership, organizational culture, or employee empowerment, as important as they may be. Rather, our concern lies in helping you manage the perceptions of real or fake held by the consumers of your enterprise's output—because people increasingly make purchase decisions based on how real or fake they perceive various offerings. These perceptions flow directly from how well any particular offering conforms to the individual customer's self-image.

As such, any offering we cite as exemplifying authenticity automatically runs the risk of alienating readers who do not deem it real themselves (because their self-image necessarily varies from ours). We know this firsthand, for the two of us have disagreed over particular examples in writing this book. We learned that it takes concerted effort not to let one's own personal views intrude when making a professional assessment of authenticity in business—and so we urge you not to miss the core of our analysis of how offerings appeal to authenticity with others because certain exemplars do not work for you.

In our last book, *The Experience Economy*, we introduced a whole new vocabulary for what was already underway in business. Here, in *Authenticity*, we must contend with a word full of import and meaning, one that has already gained considerable currency in business circles. We sort through the verbal commotion, clarify the issues, and encourage business practices that as of yet few do. In essence, we strive to introduce a whole new management discipline. Think here of how Deming's thought served to elevate quality as a distinct management responsibility. In this regard, authenticity is the new quality.

Particularly in the field of philosophy, but also in the arts, the social sciences, various strains of cultural criticism, and more recently in business, much has already been expounded on this subject. We have sifted through this body of thought to articulate our own philosophy of authenticity in business, found in chapter 5 and serving as a fulcrum for the book. To make a clear statement of what authenticity is, and what it is not, we necessarily include this material; to omit it would leave our work hollow and leave readers to wonder just where we stand on fundamental matters—as well as leave you without a touchstone to guide your own thinking on this issue.

Our method, as when we previously addressed the concepts of Mass Customization and the Experience Economy, lies in observing what is happening in the world of business, identifying far-reaching changes that threaten accepted ways of thinking, and then developing new frameworks to help executives, managers, and workers see the world differently and thereby figure out what to do about it. We view the subjects of Mass Customization, the Experience Economy, and now Authenticity in business as not only interlinked but as flowing one into another to form a single, cohesive view of the economic landscape. We make reference throughout this book to our prior work in these fields, not to forcibly recast everything in terms of authenticity, but as a practical demonstration of the long-term structural changes taking place in advanced economies and the interplay between major forces not only affecting the world of business but influencing the world at large. If we've done our job, as we did in *The Experience Economy* and *Mass Customization* before it, this book will "have legs" and we'll not have to write another such tome for a number of years.

Despite the success of our previous books, not enough businesses have shifted to mass customizing their offerings or staging experiences. In particular, too many have latched onto that single word—experience—without changing core business practices. Too many companies say they're offering "experiences" without actually *staging* experiences. That alone contributes greatly to being perceived as fake, and drives demand for experiences people deem authentic. Now more than ever, the authentic is what consumers really want.

This book examines the authenticity of economic offerings, not the authenticity of individuals in personal relationships, something people also greatly desire but the subject of many other tomes. We do recognize that many individuals reject the label "consumer" in any context. However, we take here the viewpoint of businesses, whose customers—individuals or other businesses—consume their economic offerings, and so the term is appropriate in this context.

In addressing these consumer wants, we do not construct a specific set of components that constitute authenticity in the mind of customers, such as consistency, honesty, integrity, transparency, trust, and so forth. Frankly, understanding the desire for authenticity cannot be reduced to a simple checklist. Every customer is unique; dissecting self-image therefore proves a most complex, if not impossible, task. Yet we do construct frameworks, models, and heuristics throughout the book to help companies respond to this customer uniqueness; and we cite various exemplars, not as best practices in authenticity, but to bring clarity to best principles. Every business is unique, and only you can determine how to contend with the authenticity imperative in your enterprise.

We admittedly cite two exemplars more frequently than all others: Disney and Starbucks. Why? At least for academics and social critics, no company has more affected our collective view of what is real and what is not than the Walt Disney Company. Cinderella's Castle casts an unavoidable shadow over the subject of authenticity. And Starbucks? No company more explicitly manages its perception of authenticity, making direct appeals to authenticity in nearly every way we describe this new discipline. Moreover, most people in business have been to both a Disney theme park and a Starbucks café, and those who haven't certainly know them as cultural phenomena.

Finally, to be true to ourselves we must share one final observation: issues of Real and Fake are not the same as issues of True and False. Being *true to oneself* does not define *truth* itself. Examine, for example, *Young's Analytical Concordance to the Bible* and you will not find a single citation of "authentic" or "inauthentic," "real" or "fake," in the entire King James translation of the Old or New Testaments—the Authorized Version predating any contemporary conceptualization of authenticity. It is replete, however, with citations of "true" and "false." The question "What is Real?" is not the same as "What is Truth?" Indeed, the pursuit of authenticity should not be mistaken for the way to eternity.

James H. Gilmore   April 2007
Shaker Heights, Ohio

B. Joseph Pine II
Dellwood, Minnesota

Strategic Horizons LLP
PO Box 548
Aurora, OH 44202-0548 USA
+1 (330) 995-4680
Pine&Gilmore@StrategicHorizons.com

Authenticity

THE NEW BUSINESS IMPERATIVE

AKE. CONTRIVED. DISINGENUOUS. PHONY. *INAUTHENTIC*. DO your customers use any of those words to describe what you sell or how you sell it? That is exactly how more and more consumers view what companies offer them. People increasingly see the world in terms of real and fake, and want to buy something real from someone genuine, not a fake from some phony.

Why—and why now? Because of the shift to the Experience Economy. Goods and services are no longer enough; what consumers want today are experiences—memorable events that engage them in an inherently personal way. As paid-for experiences proliferate, people now decide *where* and *when* to spend their money and their time—the currency of experiences—as much if not more than they deliberate on *what* and *how* to buy (the purview of goods and services). But in a world increasingly filled with deliberately and sensationally staged experiences—an increasingly *unreal* world—consumers choose to buy or not buy based on how *real* they perceive an offering to be. Business today, therefore, is all about being real. Original. Genuine. Sincere. *Authentic*.

In any industry where experiences come to the fore, issues of authenticity follow closely behind. Think of Disneyland. No place before or since its opening in 1955 has provoked more debate on authenticity within modern culture, nor has any other business sparked more controversy on the effect of commercial activity on the reality of modern living than the Walt Disney Company.

Or think of coffee. Starbucks earns several dollars for every cup of coffee, over and above the few cents the beans are worth, precisely because it has learned to stage a distinctive coffee-drinking experience centered on the ambience of each place and the theatre of making each cup. Perhaps no other company in the world more earnestly and steadfastly seeks to render authenticity—resolutely shaping how real consumers perceive it to be. That task has become harder and harder, however, as Starbucks has grown from one shop in Seattle to over 13,000 venues around the world, for nothing kills authenticity like ubiquity. The success of Starbucks no longer depends on its operational prowess or taste superiority; it lies solely in sustaining coffee drinkers' perception of the Starbucks experience as authentic.

The New Consumer Sensibility

Now that the Experience Economy has reached full flower—supplanting the Service Economy as it had in turn overtaken the Industrial Economy, which itself had replaced the Agrarian Economy—such issues of authenticity now bear down on not only all experience offerings but across all of the economy. For in the course of economic progress, new consumer sensibilities arise, taking their cues from the dominant economic offering to affect the dynamic between sellers and buyers of commercial output. When such a sensibility—keen sensitiveness to particular perceptions[1]—appears, businesses must master some new discipline to ensure continued success.

Consider the last time a consumer sensibility emerged that required businesses to develop a fundamentally new competency. What is the one rock-hard imperative in business today that was nowhere to be found in management theory and practice, say, fifty years ago? Quality, of course. The need to improve quality was a newborn competency that replaced lowering costs as "Job 1" by not only the Ford Motor Company but every enterprise appealing to consumers' newfound desire for high-quality offerings. A complete suite of tools—books, software, workshops, methodologies, certifications, awards— emerged to help managers continuously improve their quality performance through a constantly growing set of techniques—Total Quality Management, *kaizen*, zero defects, Six Sigma, and so forth.

Why did quality become the dominant consumer sensibility, and bring with it the need for a whole new area of management expertise? Pundits tend to overlook one significant factor: the rise of the Service Economy. A world saturated with goods—thanks to the Industrial Revolution—became a world desperate for new services. First came those needed to specify, install, maintain, repair, and replace all those goods—service stations, repair shops, parts

distributors, product retailers, interior decorators, and the li
whole new categories of services that enhanced the goods, such as
tems, dry cleaners, landscapers, lawn specialists, security systems, and so
With so much money spent on services, quality increasingly became th
means by which businesses competed.

As consumers began to expect higher and higher quality goods and services, they stopped tolerating poor quality. Features and benefits had to be the right ones, in the right place, at the right time. Low cost and high quality fused as product plus process. Enhancing quality became *the* business imperative, supplanting cost control—the key imperative of the Industrial Economy—as it in turn had replaced the mere availability of supply required in the Agrarian Economy. This meant businesses had to create and embrace the entirely new discipline of understanding, managing, and excelling at quality improvement.

Before this time consumers would describe poorly perceived products as "junk." After businesses' long, successful journey of quality improvement, consumers today rarely use that term as a measure of dissatisfaction or derision. Instead, they tend to call such lowly offerings "fake."

So just as the rise of services helped to establish quality as a field worthy of deliberate management attention, the rise of experiences calls for a new arena of management expertise. Organizations today must learn to understand, manage, and excel at *rendering authenticity*. Indeed, "rendering authenticity" should one day roll trippingly off the tongue as easily as "controlling costs" and "improving quality," for rendering is precisely the right term for what's involved. To be blunt: your business offerings must get real. When consumers want what's real, the *management of the customer perception of authenticity* becomes the primary new source of competitive advantage—the new business imperative.

The Appeal of Real

We are not the first authors to detect authenticity as a new strain of consumer desire, although they've tended to limit its manifestation to a specific segment of consumers. David Lewis and Darren Bridger, in *The Soul of the New Consumer: Authenticity—What We Buy and Why in the New Economy*, rightly see the developed world having moved "from scarcity to abundance—from abundance to authenticity."[2] Although this is consistent with our own view of advancing sensibilities from availability [scarcity], to cost and quality [abundance], to authenticity, Lewis and Bridger associate this new-felt desire for authenticity only with one of two segments—New Consumers—whom they define as individualistic, involved, independent, and well informed in their tastes and behaviors, and

ng national boundaries, ages, ethnic groups, and in-
no surprise: Old Consumers.)

tive Class, Richard Florida likewise sees "the emer-
s" for which "the defining basis . . . is economic."[4] Any
on economics by definition represents a segmentation
Florida notes that those he places in this class "do not
lass" (perhaps because of the individualistic and inde-
ics Lewis and Bridger identified).[5] Florida describes how
what these ors of creativity" do for a living influences their choices of
what and how to buy, and even more so, where to live. In short, the Creative
Class desires "more active, authentic and participatory experiences" in "more
authentic, indigenous or organic venues."[6]

While Florida largely focuses on regional economic development (often
reading like the *Queer Eye for the Straight Guy* of urban planning guides), his
views have contributed greatly to cementing what psychologist Paul Ray earlier called "cultural creatives" as a discrete market segment in the minds of any
number of marketeers and their accomplice agencies. Ray, who advises companies to account for "The Authenticity Factor," partitions consumers into
three buckets: "Traditionals," "Moderns," and "Cultural Creatives."[7] The latter,
he asserts, "invented the current interest in personal authenticity in America."[8]
David Boyle, author of *Authenticity: Brands, Fakes, Spin and the Lust for Real
Life*, likens these cultural creatives to European "inner-directeds," together
constituting what he calls today's "New Realists." Boyle claims that these people, who represent "a little less than half the British population, and just under
a quarter of the American population," are the ones "driving the demand for
authenticity."[9]

Finally, Rob Dreher, author of *Crunchy Cons*, sees a much larger set of authenticity seekers, including both prototypical leftists as well as many conservatives. But he sees only certain conservatives as "big ones for authenticity"—
those who enjoy the crunchy granola to which his title refers, or as his subtitle attests, those who are "*Birkenstocked Burkeans, gun-loving organic gardeners, evangelical free-range farmers, hip homeschooling mamas, right-wing nature lovers, and
their diverse tribe of countercultural conservatives.*"[10]

Our fellow commentators offer many insights, but they tend to limit the
manifestation of authenticity to a specific segment of consumers, thereby
missing how universal is the appeal of real. Practically *all* consumers desire authenticity.[11] Every person is unique—intimately aware of and valuing his own
uniqueness. The consumer sensibility for authenticity evidences itself whenever informed individuals independently purchase *any* item with which they
are intensely involved. What differs is the combination of categories and times

underlying these purchases, the particular offerings they personally view as authentic or inauthentic, and the terms they use to describe their opinions.[12] This desire for authenticity exists as strongly in Fargo and Fresno as it does in such Richard Florida favorites as San Francisco and Seattle. It includes those who frequent Wal-Mart and those who boycott the big-box stores, all who love Starbucks and everyone sporting "Friends don't let friends drink at Starbucks" bumper stickers. In industry after industry, in customer after customer, authenticity has overtaken quality as the prevailing purchasing criterion, just as quality overtook cost, and as cost overtook availability.

Therefore, to availability of commodities, cost of goods, and quality of service, businesses now must add *authenticity of experience* as something to be managed. Let us now explicitly define these four successively dominant consumer sensibilities:

1. **Availability:** Purchasing on the basis of accessing a *reliable supply*

2. **Cost:** Purchasing on the basis of obtaining an *affordable price*

3. **Quality:** Purchasing on the basis of excelling in *product performance*

4. **Authenticity:** Purchasing on the basis of conforming to *self-image*

No longer content just with available, affordable, and excellent offerings, both consumers and business-to-business customers now purchase offerings based on how well those purchases conform to their own self-image. What they buy must reflect who they are and who they aspire to be in relation to how they perceive the world—with lightning-quick judgments of "real" or "fake" hanging in the balance.

Regina Bendix, in *In Search of Authenticity*, puts it quite well: *"Authenticity . . . is generated not from the bounded classification of an Other, but from the probing comparison between self and Other, as well as between external and internal states of being.* Invocations of authenticity are admissions of vulnerability, filtering the self's longings into the shaping of the subject."[13] Buyers view those Others—those economic offerings—that conform in both depiction and perception to their self-image—their perceived state of being, including aspects real, representational, and aspirational—as authentic. Those that do not match to a sufficient enough degree to generate a "sympathetic vibration" between the offering and the buyer will be viewed as inauthentic.

People no longer accept fake offerings from slickly marketed phonies; they want real offerings from genuinely transparent sources. Commodity traders, goods manufacturers, and service providers must grasp this authenticity imperative as much as experience stagers like Starbucks, the third place, or *Second*

FIGURE 1-1

Successive imperatives and sensibilities

Economic output	Commodities	Goods	Services	Experiences
Business imperative	Supply	Control	Improve	Render
Consumer sensibility	Availability	Cost	Quality	Authenticity

Life, the virtual world—for to compete with such experiences, authenticity must become the primary source of differentiation for commodities as well as commoditized goods and services. The real appeal of enterprises like Pike Place Fish Market, Build-a-Bear, and ING Direct Café attests to the ability to render fish commodities, teddy bear goods, and financial services more authentic. To succeed, managers across most all industries must add to their expertise in supply-chain management, cost containment, and quality enhancement an understanding of what their customers consider real and fake—or at least which elements influence such consumer perceptions—about their company's offerings. For, as shown in figure 1-1, each successive consumer sensibility comes paired with a specific business imperative: *supply* availability, *control* cost, *improve* quality, *render* authenticity.

One important note: while the imperative for authenticity may dominate managerial attention, it is not an absolute. Companies such as Kmart, United Airlines, or General Motors should not be focusing on rendering anything authentic or staging experiences when they are still flailing around for an effective supply chain, maintaining high cost structures, or providing lesser-quality products. Such companies should concentrate on the basics. Otherwise, they will limp along, occasionally making profits, while generating little customer loyalty, rarely inspiring employees, and seldom exciting investors.

Authenticity in Business

With this book, we venture with readers into the philosophical field of authenticity as it pertains to business. We look to provide a foundation for examining the subject further, as the vitality of advanced economies will flow directly from the individual and collective ability of businesses to master the discipline of authenticity.

This authenticity imperative intensifies as fakes saturate contemporary markets and product counterfeiting becomes more sophisticated and more global. In 2005, *BusinessWeek* called attention to the competitive threat posed by this illegal activity with a red-lettered headline shouting "FAKES!" On the cover were pictured two motorcycles: "One of these Honda CG125 motorcycles is a Chinese knockoff." Only by reading the fine print at the bottom would one have any hope of discerning "The real one is on the left."[14] The story surveyed numerous counterfeited items—auto parts, batteries, beer and liquor, cigarettes, clothing and footwear, golf clubs, medicines, power tools, purses, shoe polish, software, and watches—and outlined how counterfeiters now secure capital, reverse-engineer products, replicate packaging, and penetrate legitimate channels of distribution.

China is well known as the leading source of fake goods, counterfeit software, and pirated content.[15] But other nations also contribute to the supply of illegal knock-offs. *Inc.* magazine identified ten other countries and the primary counterfeit product for which they are known: Bulgaria (liquor), India (computer hardware), Malaysia (DVDs and CDs), Nigeria (computer gaming equipment), North Korea (U.S. currency), Pakistan (apparel, textiles), Philippines (cigarettes), Russia (pharmaceuticals), Taiwan (auto parts), and Thailand (golf clubs).[16]

Such counterfeiting threatens to decrease significantly the economic output of legitimate producers. *BusinessWeek* estimated that the worldwide trade in fakes represented over $512 billion in lost revenue in 2004.[17] Such a number raises the question: doesn't the buying of so many fakes fly in the face of the contention that people now desire authenticity? Not really—if consumers didn't care about the authenticity of the original articles, then the counterfeiters wouldn't have to pretend to *be* those originals; they could just supply cheap goods under their own brands. Moreover, most of these fakes find their way into the marketplace not via street vendors in Beijing, Hong Kong, or New York, but through corporate distribution centers and retail shelves. In most cases consumers have no idea that they are buying counterfeits. When they do knowingly buy fakes, they tend to do so as a lark, for the fun of it, or to impress their friends. (The latter motivation brands both buyer and seller as phonies.) In some cases consumers may even prefer imitations precisely because the quality of the original isn't great enough to offset the higher price. Consumers will pay a premium for authenticity, but there comes a point (which differs, depending on the individual) when they trade off the real for a more available, cheaper substitute with sufficient quality.

Long ago, American companies began to worry about the huge influx of cheap but low-quality goods from the Far East. Then they faced the greater problem of high-quality but cheap goods imported from that same region. Today, as the business press frequently points out, many companies must grapple with the region's tremendous production of fake but high-quality goods—what the *New York Times* has called its ability to "Manufaketure."[18] But watch out. As China in particular globalizes and develops its own brands, Western companies may soon face competition from a huge influx of high-quality, inexpensive, *real* goods. It would be foolish to bet against it. Thus, as Japan was once known for junk and is now known for quality, China is now known for fakes but may one day be known for authenticity.

While business leaders and policymakers should continue their efforts to protect intellectual property rights, stopping the production or the trading of the fake is no substitute for innovating the real. Yes, counterfeiting is a global problem. But the greater threat lies in managerial inaction when there is much to do. Worse, companies frequently behave in ways that render their own offerings inauthentic. By word or deed—via marketing activities or designed offerings—businesses all too often produce their own counterfeits.

We hope to help you avoid that fate. The rest of this book sets forth deliberate steps companies can take to overcome managerial inertia and fulfill consumer demand for the real.

2

The Demand for Authenticity

WHY NOW?

UTHENTIC WALT DISNEY WORLD EST. 71." SO READ THE
baseball cap purchased by dad on a Gilmore family vacation
in Orlando a few years ago. Authentic—Disney? En route to
Disney's Animal Kingdom later that day, six-year-old Evan asked, "Are they
real animals or just machines that move?" He had visited a zoo or two, learned
about animals at school, and attended a friend's birthday party that featured
the animal acts of "Jungle Terry." He had also previously experienced Disney's
Magic Kingdom. So after the Kilimanjaro Safari at Animal Kingdom—with its
Africa-themed savannahs, bathing elephants, lounging lions, and yawning hip-
popotami—Evan disappointedly blurted out, "When are we going to *real* Disney?"

This distinction between real and fake typifies the awareness of and demand
for authenticity among today's consumers, even those as young as Evan. Their
concerns extend beyond issues of natural versus artificial. To someone who had
been on safari in Africa, Disney's Kilimanjaro would seem entirely fake; to
someone who has experienced wild animals only at a zoo, Animal Kingdom
could seem quite real. To young Evan, however, something else factored into his
experience: this Disney offering was inauthentic not because it was artificial
(and Disney), but because it *wasn't* artificial (and Disney) enough.

People increasingly evaluate the world in terms of real and fake, based on
their own views of what is and is not authentic. Why? In this chapter, we examine five key drivers behind the demand for authenticity. First, we treat the

emergence of the Experience Economy as a backdrop and consider how staged experiences can leave consumers longing for less contrived encounters. We next look at how technology frustrates consumers when they interact with businesses. Third, we examine the rise of postmodern thought and how such views of society influence personal, and therefore consumer, behavior. Fourth, we probe the psychology of aging baby boomers and the influence of this particular generation's consumption decisions on us all. Finally, we examine how all this culminates in an eroding confidence in our major social institutions and the ever-growing perception of how their practices run afoul of their purposes—leaving wide room for businesses to offer alternatives that provide real value.

Emergence of Experiences: The Commercially Sold Reality

In today's Experience Economy we pay admission—whether an entry fee, event fee, per-play fee, initiation fee, membership fee, or some other access fee—to spend time in various experiences. The consumption of such experiences goes far beyond once-in-a-lifetime trips to Africa or once-every-four-years trips to Walt Disney World. Consider the range of paid-for experiences that comprise our everyday lives.

Every day, devoted customers line up to pay $3 or $4 for a cup of coffee—make that a coffee-drinking experience—at Starbucks. (To which many think, what ever happened to regular old office coffee?) Fifty years ago, going out for a meal at a restaurant was a rare treat, reserved for special occasions; today, Americans consume an average of over four meals per week away from home.[1] (Mom's homemade cooking isn't good enough?) Moreover, we often go out to eat at some theme restaurant like ESPN Zone, Dave & Buster's, or Chuck E. Cheese's, where part and parcel of the evening is buying tokens or charging up some debit cards to play arcade games, sports simulators, or virtual reality rides. (Food and conversation alone no longer suffice?)

At the behest of modern-day homeowners, builders construct experiential palaces to call home. Spacious kitchens come equipped with Internet access and industrial-grade appliances. (Who uses their professional Viking range for anything other than show?) Plasma TVs, surround-sound systems, cinema-style seating, and other home-theater accoutrements have turned many a basement or family room into a multisensory entertainment complex. (One can't just enjoy movies at the local cinema?) Of course, enjoying all this requires paying some cable operator or satellite dish company for at least basic programming, and many households also buy TiVos to customize their TV time. (Remember when we gathered around the set as a family to watch free network television?) Still others pay membership to Netflix in order to queue up their movie-watching experiences. (No more runs to Blockbuster to rent something next?) Add in an Xbox, Nintendo, or Sony PlayStation, and the ever more innovative interactive gaming they enable. Guitar Hero, anyone? (Hands-free air guitar is evidently passé.) And don't forget the millions who subscribe to satellite radio. (But can it ever beat your thrill as a kid tuning in faraway stations on a transistor radio under your blankets?)

People pay not only for high-tech experiences, but for high-touch ones as well. Witness the explosion of spa venues and treatments. *Spa Finder* magazine and Web guide divides the industry into nine spa categories: resort and hotel, destination, connoisseur, casino, day, wellness-medical, cosmetic-medical, dental, and mobile spas. (You can't just take a warm bath at home to unwind and relax?)

Music enthusiasts often pay a premium for concert experiences. Fervent followers of the Dave Matthews Band, for example, pay $40 per year to join the Warehouse—the band's official fan association—in order to gain early access to the best concert seats whenever DMB tours. (No more camping out all night—for free—at a nearby Ticketmaster outlet?) Untold sports fans pay thousands of dollars for a Professional Seat License, or PSL, that allows them to purchase season tickets to attend the home games of their local National Football League team. (Pay—and pay *again* for tickets?) Many also pay to participate in various online fantasy leagues. (The televised games no longer thrill?) More and more travelers even pay outfits like VocationVacations to *work* while on vacation. (You take some job *as* a vacation?) And a select few—both truly adventurous and incredibly wealthy—pay millions of dollars to Space Adventures or competing outfits to orbit our planet or walk in space. (It is a small world after all.)

It seems no part of life hasn't been touched by this shift to commercialized experiences. Consider that most precious of family traditions, celebrating a child's birthday. Parents today routinely spend hundreds of dollars for someone else to stage these birthday parties. We used to, as good parents, encourage our daughters to invite friends over to play with dolls and let our sons go out and play "pick up" ball games with neighborhood buddies. Now, we bustle our daughters to venues like the American Girl Place and turn our sons loose in indoor skateboarding venues like Vans Skateparks. We used to sit around the porch, parlor, or living room and talk. Now we pay access fees to frequent chat rooms or conduct instant messaging (IM) sessions, subscription fees to join online games like *EverQuest*, and admission fees to create avatars in virtual worlds like *Second Life* or *There.com* that stand in for our real selves.

Experience-based commerce represents a global shift in economic activity. South Korea, for example, leads in the creation and visitation of virtual worlds.

Hard Rock Cafe, the world's first theme restaurant, was founded in London back in 1971, where today Piccadilly Circus and its surrounding environs have become a hub of retail experiences. Japan specializes in recreating foreign places, including Huis Ten Bosch, a Dutch village in Nagasaki; Parque España, a Spanish-themed park in Shima City; The Italian Village in Nagoya; and, of course, Tokyo Disneyland. New Zealand offers Agrodome sheepshearing, tours of left-over sets from the *Lord of the Rings* movies, bungee jumping, bridge climbing, canyoning, and zorbing (which involves rolling down a hill inside a large ball).

There is ICEHOTEL in Jukkasjärvi, Sweden, the Haus der Musik in Vienna, and La Ciudad de los Niños in Mexico City (as well as its offshoot, Kidzania, in Japan and Jakarta). You can play James Bond with Munich-based adventure travel agency Mydays, fly MiGs over Moscow with Incredible Adventures, and explore the wreck of the *Titanic* with Deep Ocean Expeditions. Dubai has invested its oil money in a host of new experiences, including the magnificent Burj Al Arab hotel and Ski Dubai—an indoor ski slope kept at snow-producing temperatures amid 120-degree heat.

These so-often contrived and sometimes gratuitous experiences force us to consider: What is a real experience and what is not? What is really necessary and what is not? Why do we so readily hire outside companies—who are in it for a profit—to fabricate such experiences? We understandably question the authenticity of paid-for experiences as we participate more and more in the Experience Economy. Yet more people are buying not only travel and entertainment experiences but matchmaking, wedding, birthing, parenting, celebrating, and even death-and-dying experiences. Why? People may say they want such personal experiences to remain untouched by commerce, but if consumers want more efficiency (for cost reasons), more excellence (for quality reasons), or more sincerity (for authenticity reasons), then buying expertise and assistance often increases the real value of such life moments.

Bottom line: *Can businesses help render authenticity in a world they themselves saturate with paid-for experiences?* We think so, but it requires reconciling *what* companies offer with *why* people buy. Consumers will continue to purchase from others what they once did for themselves, and more of what they have never before experienced. In losing degrees of self-sufficiency, and perhaps innocence, people will seek something in return—specifically, a self more aligned with who one wants to be, a lived-in self conforming more to one's own self-image.

Rendering Commerce Less Commercial

All these staged experiences leave many consumers longing for less-contrived encounters. The most direct way to help individuals fashion their own self-image: let people define and even create their own offerings. When consumers design their own footwear online at miadidas.com or NIKEiD.com, style their own clothes at landsend.com, configure their own car at mini.com or scion .com, express themselves at cafepress.com or zazzle.com, or craft their own music playlists for their iPods, the output automatically qualifies as authentic for the consumer. It turns each individual into what Alvin Toffler calls a "prosumer," that is, a producing consumer.[2] Rendering authenticity through customization occurs beyond online or high-tech offerings. Intentionally low-tech Build-a-Bear Workshop enables customers to make their own plush animal—more real than off-the-shelf, mass-produced alternatives.

Consumer-controlled production, offering a prosumer platform rather than a finished product, shifts attention from the supplier's moneymaking motives to the buyer's self-defining pursuits. Supply still meets demand in a commercial sale, and the interests of both parties necessarily interplay, but the buyer feels less "sold" or manipulated. More significantly, direct customer involvement in this customer-unique output yields deeper insights into personal preferences and ultimately to a keener sense of self.

There is no need to avoid staging experiences, even virtual experiences, now that authenticity is the foremost consumer sensibility. Despite the fact that prosumption is inherent in experience offerings—because every experience happens *within* the individual person, in response to the events staged around that person—few companies allow people to define and create their own experiences. Some such offerings do exist; for example, Yahoo!'s LAUNCHCast or CBS's Last.fm, which customize broadband music stations; Harrah's Total Gold program, which matches experience rewards to player profiles; Disney, which uses RFID technology to enable "Pal Mickey," a talking Mickey Mouse doll, to respond to individual journeys through the Magic Kingdom. But even these are early stabs at making experiences more personal, and therefore more real.[3] Much opportunity lies ahead in helping people fashion their own experiences and thereby their own self-image.[4]

Automation of Services: The Technologically Mediated Reality

One clear result of the shift to an Experience Economy has been the increasing commoditization of services, just as the rise of the Service Economy in the latter half of the twentieth century resulted in the commoditization of goods. Service providers have thus resorted to automating labor—as was done earlier in manufacturing, and before that in agriculture. Computer automation replaced clerical work. Operational positions were lost to new process technologies.

More recently, customer interaction jobs such as bank tellers, call center representatives, and telephone operators have started to disappear.

As a result, consumers interact less with people and more with machines. Think of how the replacement of customer service representatives with voice response systems so frequently requires a descent into "voice mail hell," where you have no hope of reaching a human being.[5] Or how, when you encounter difficulty with a Web site, your request for help gets only automated nonresponses. So thoroughly has technology replaced personal interaction that we are delighted, even shocked, to get a human voice immediately after ringing a toll-free service number. No wonder a reporter for *USA Today* issued this challenge: "But go ahead: Just try to get human-to-human service in this service economy."[6]

Such low-authenticity service follows from high-quality and low-cost automation. Countless hours of computer programming and systems integration go into ensuring these telecommunications systems work exactly as planned, eliminating human error, wasted time on hold, and of course excess costs. But such quality excellence goes largely unrecognized because of the utter lack of authenticity in the resulting encounters. As David Wolfe, author of *Ageless Marketing*, recognizes, "A recording telling customers how much the company values them while they have to wait to talk to a live human being is disingenuous."[7] Paul English, cofounder and chief technology officer of Kayak.com, a travel search engine, became so fed up with automated customer service and the elusiveness of live contact that he set up a Web site, GetHuman.com, on which visitors posted exactly how to reach a human being—from simply hitting "0" or "*" repeatedly to keying in more convoluted sequences—for hundreds of companies.

Savvy companies stress human interaction with customers. For example, Geico Direct automobile insurance uses the campaign slogan, "Instead of Answering Machines, Humans with Answers." But, alas, call the advertised number and you must listen to a prerecorded message and then press several numbers to reach a human with answers.[8] Same with Allstate Insurance, whose recent advertisements cajole: "You dream of a relationship with a real person." Call the advertised number, however, and encounter—once again—a machine.[9] Automated services so dominate business practices that even companies that recognize the value of real conversations rarely give customers immediate access to a real person.

Would our ancestors have even needed to qualify the noun *person* with the adjective *real*? Certainly not. "Real person" is a retronym—a term qualified in a once unnecessary way (such as "acoustic guitar," "live performance," "scripted TV," and "real life") before new technologies and new behaviors created new entities ("electric guitar," "recorded performance," "Reality TV," and "virtual life"). Automated voice technologies have put "real person" on the list, and simulated visual and artificial intelligence technologies may soon create virtual customer service representatives requiring further qualification.

Because our daily dealings with companies increasingly rely on technology, we place greater value on person-to-person conversations (yet another retronym) when they do happen. But when we *do* reach some representative on the phone, we have no assurance that that person actually works for the company, lives in the country dialed, or goes by the name given.[10] How unreal is that?

We ourselves contribute to this rising unreality: many of us would rather leave a recorded message than talk to the actual people we're calling, at least some of the time. Robert Johansen of the Institute for the Future mapped out a two-by-two matrix to categorize our technology-mediated interactions: Same-Time/Different-Place, Different-Time/Same-Place, Different-Time/Different-Place, and Same-Time/Same-Place.[11] Remember when most of the connections we made with corporations happened in that last realm? Now my machine calls your machine.

In the *Los Angeles Times*, Gina Piccalo captured this epidemic infliction of technology: "In the blink of a satellite, modern life has become an endless high-speed connection. It's streaming 24/7 . . . you're always online—and on medication—checking e-mail, checking voicemail. What you crave is something more visceral . . . You want the stripped-down, lo-fi version of life, the kind that feels vintage, handmade or home grown. You want authenticity."[12] Mark Slouka takes on technology in his book *War of the Worlds*: "We stand on the threshold of turning life itself into computer code, of transforming the experience of living in the physical world—every sensation, every detail—into a product for our consumption . . . [C]omputer simulations may soon be so pervasive (and so realistic) that life itself will require some sort of mark of authenticity. Reality, in other words, may one day come with an asterisk."[13]

Bottom line: *Can businesses help render authenticity in a world of such technological intrusion?* Yes. While enterprises must continue to cut costs, *how* they employ cost-cutting technologies can counteract the loss of personal touch so evident in today's automated interactions, making them playful, fun, and even desirable.

Rendering Technology More Human

With voice systems, eliminate any features that hide how to reach a real person, or that make it difficult (or impossible) to navigate the system. Follow the GetHuman standard and let people press "0" to get a human being, perhaps making it the first option. Rather than automating human activity, humanize the automated activity.[14]

Consider the Geek Squad, whose very purpose is to help those tormented by technology run amuck. In designing the 24-Hour Computer Support Task Force, founder Robert Stephens humanized the task of installing and repairing computers—first with his own company and now as part of Best Buy—including the experience of the voice response system. Call Geek Squad Mission Control at 1-800-GEEK-SQUAD (that's 1-800-433-5778) and listen to how it conveys the company's ethos in the commanding voice of a Special Agent before connecting you with an "actual human." Every call manages to lay a human voice atop a technological interface.

Consider also Amtrak's "Julie," its affable "automated agent" at 1-800-USA-RAIL (1-800-872-7245) who "sounds and acts so lifelike that [many riders] did not immediately realize that she was just a computer program."[15] Behind the personable persona is the real Julie Stinneford, a professional voice actress whose recordings for Amtrak handle about five million calls annually, saving Amtrak some $13 million a year that it would otherwise spend on call center representatives.[16] The company thus manages to automate and humanize simultaneously.

Work, too, to humanize all other technologies that replace, displace, or otherwise prevent direct human interaction—such as ATMs, kiosks, credit card swipes, point-of-sale terminals, and Web sites. Many retailers and bankers have added "live chat" buttons to their Internet and intranet sites, using technology from such companies as LivePerson to let customers interact with other humans online.

Also be sure to focus your remaining live person-to-person interactions on turning every seemingly mundane encounter into an engaging experience. Amidst today's sea of technological mediation, handling this human remnant well sends a powerful message to your customers and should inform the design of all other interactions.

Finally, go beyond all technological intrusion to stage or sponsor events that bring together otherwise dispersed customers, such as the Harley-Davidson rally in Sturgis, South Dakota, or eBay Live!, which has rotated in its first five years from Anaheim to Orlando, New Orleans, San Jose, and Las Vegas. Gatherings like these provide a measure of the authentic social experiences enjoyed before life became so technologically alienating.

Prevalence of Postmodernism: The Socially Constructed Reality

One new technology that offers the hope of interpersonal experiences is so-called "social networking." At its core, however, social networking represents just the most recent medium through which to show off one's self. In *Life the Movie: How Entertainment Conquered Reality*, Neal Gabler reflects on how "life itself was gradually becoming a medium all its own, like television, radio, print and film, and that all of us were becoming at once performance artists in and audiences for a grand, ongoing show . . . In short, life was becoming a movie."[17] Life, camcorder, YouTube!

Thomas de Zengotita picks up on Gabler in *Mediated*, asserting, "From now on [people] will be constructing themselves and performing the constructions. They will never again just be." He suggests that TV, movies, and other such media now make our lives "an unprecedented fusion of the real and the represented" and are therefore "lives shaped by a culture of performance that constitutes a quality of being, a type of person—the mediated person."[18]

Social commentators have long recognized the shifting cultural conditions caused by the increasing influence of celebrity (Daniel Boorstin), media (Marshall McLuhan), simulacra (Jean Baudrillard), hyperrealism (Umberto Eco), and amusement (Neil Postman).[19] Each has observed how we increasingly take our everyday cues of how to behave from the commercial realm.[20] As a result, reality isn't what it used to be.

Actually, that's the title of Walter Truett Anderson's book on the subject, which posits that conflict arises today not from differing beliefs but from differences *about* belief.[21] For Anderson and other postmodernists, these beliefs are not objective truths about an objective world but rather socially constructed realities ("SCRs"). As one postmodernist puts it, "There is no stable, unchanging, and unitary Real against which our thoughts can be tested."[22]

Neither, apparently, is there a stable, unchanging, and unitary Self. Sherry Turkle, MIT professor and director of the university's Initiative on Technology and Self, shows in *Life on the Screen* how the Internet enables us to form a new identity—or, rather, multiple identities—online: "Today more than ever we blur the line between simulation and reality, between what exists on the computer and what is real."[23] Turkle primarily studied an early form of remote computer gaming available for free over the Internet—MUDs (Multi-User Domains). More recently, more realistic virtual worlds awkwardly called MMPORGs (massive multiplayer online role-playing games) have enabled even more flexible role-playing.

Linden Lab's *Second Life*, to take one example, enables people to make their own virtual places within its online world, such as the Neverland theme park. Linden founder Philip Rosedale says, "We think it's competitive with and in many ways better than real life."[24] Hundreds of people, mostly in underdeveloped countries, make their living via *Second Life*'s multimillion-dollar economy, designing clothes, buildings, even dance moves.[25] Edward Castronova of Indiana University estimated that the economies of all virtual worlds total over a billion dollars a year (a figure now several years old), spent by players to enhance their virtual experiences—mostly through acquiring gold, weapons, fighting skills, magic tricks, and virtual real estate for their avatars.[26] Call it *Second Life: The Movie Sequel.*

While these postmodernist views make for interesting (if often cryptic) reading, they go too far in claiming that unreality has assumed absolute control of our daily lives, to the detriment of objective truth within the socially constructed reality (after all, as Anderson readily admits, "the idea of the social construction of reality is itself an SCR"[27]). And yet they also don't go far enough—although the rise of the Experience Economy and technological mediation of services exacerbate the sense that objective reality has been lost, the evidence cited by most scholars who posit postmodernism has actually been around for ages.

We can trace this line of social commentary all the way back to Plato's "Allegory of the Cave." The philosopher describes ordinary people as prisoners in a cave, duped into believing that the shadows thrown onto the wall by a fire comprise all of reality.[28] As at least one commentator has noted, "If he were living today, Plato might replace his rather awkward cave metaphor with a movie theater . . ."[29] And, we add, the movie shown would have to be *The Matrix.* As we examine the consumer sensibility of authenticity, we cannot all take the blue pill and remain blissfully ignorant of our postmodern dilemma. Nor does the red pill of socially constructed reality yield a true view of reality.

Bottom line: *Can businesses help render authenticity in a world where reality itself seems socially constructed?* Certainly. But it means intentionally offsetting the lost sense of objective reality thrust on us by postmodernists with an understanding of the difference between what *is* real and what we *perceive* to be real. What James W. Carey said of media—"Reality is, above all, a scarce resource"—applies to business as well.[30] Because consumers hunger for this scarce resource, you must no longer restrict your commercial activities to managing traditional functions and features, uses and benefits, cues and sensations. Rather, actively engage customers not just individually but as a community of like-minded people, so that your offerings—and by extension your businesses—gain in stature as authentically constructed.

Rendering Society More Social

To do so, offer a platform for individual customers to collaborate with one another. Admittedly, it's yet another means of self-expression, but more importantly it's a way of sharing that self with others—yet is unlike customized offerings that cater strictly to individual desires. Let customers provide input to a collective process not only for their own pleasure but for the enjoyment of others. Not just any others, moreover, but specifically those others who have similar self-images. So as new customers introduce themselves to such "co-created" brands, they simultaneously introduce themselves to the brand's raving fans.

This benefit has fueled the success of social networks—YouTube, MySpace, Facebook, and so forth—that enable people to share what they find funny, sad, outrageous, patriotic, telling, compelling, and pretty much any other adjective that might apply to one's view of life.[31] People also spill their most personal thoughts, feelings, and opinions out onto blogs, reviews, social bookmarking sites, and pretty much any Web site with a published comment field, while also designing ads for others to vote on, produce, and see, such as Chevrolet, Doritos, and the NFL itself enabled for the 2007 Super Bowl.[32] This newfound ability is why *Time* magazine made "You" Person of the Year at the end of 2006—all these amateur contributors "have a kind of just-plain-folks authenticity that the professionals just can't match."[33]

Myriad companies now tap into this desire for social interaction. Jones Soda, for example, adorns the labels of all its soft-drink bottles with photographs taken by its customers. It uses these photos on its standard product, not for some one-time gimmick as some consumer goods manufacturers do. How? First, Jones Soda allows customers to post digital photographs via the company's Web site to an online gallery as mocked-up labels for other customers to view. (At the time of this writing, over 500,000 virtual labels were posted.) Visitors vote for their favorites, and Jones Soda personnel periodically select popular labels to use in production. Then, at the Web site, it makes available renditions of the actual print sheets sent to its outside label vendor.

Consider allowing customers to participate in making *your* offerings *theirs* through increased control and customization or some other collective, collaborative, or contributive process that directly affects the final output. Chicago-based Threadless, for example, turns over the design of all its T-shirt offerings to customers, who vote as a community to determine which designs go into actual production. Consider also the emerging use of iPods among bloggers to podcast audio tours of museums, art galleries, and the like. Some listeners find the user-generated results more genuine than official curator recordings. (Google "museum podcasts" and discover the richness of the unofficial audio expertise.) Nike lets customers post their homemade videos praising the shoes of its Converse division at conversegallery.com. Converse executive Erick Soderstrom remarks, "We're trying to blow the barrier between brand and consumer."[34] That barrier equally separates brand from authenticity.

Managers in business-to-business (B2B) relationships can take similar steps to remove that barrier. How would you describe the last trade show you attended—

slightly better than a trip to the Department of Motor Vehicles? Conventions need not be so conventional. Consider the Coverings expo held each year by National Trade Productions at the Orlando Convention Center, which features ceramic tile and stone floor covering exhibitors from over fifty countries. Show management assigns space by country and requires vendors to codesign the shared aisle carpeting and signage. Twelve of the largest vendor concentrations also design, construct, and operate an "International Pavilion"—with restaurants themed to their specific countries and offering indigenous cuisine—in addition to their individual booths. The collaboration not only draws more traffic but also renders the overall experience more authentic for the distributors, retailers, designers, builders, installers, and architects attending the show.

The crucial component of such social authenticity comes from letting customers construct a piece of your business. If customers create it themselves, then they will consider it real.

Rise of the Baby Boomers: The Generationally Inspired Reality

The concerns of baby boomers drive much of contemporary commerce. Noted gerontologist Ken Dychtwald declares, "At each stage of their lives, the needs and desires of the baby boomers have become the dominant concerns of American business and popular culture."[35] For almost twenty years, adults over the age of forty have represented a majority of the U.S. population, constituting the bulk of consumer demand. As David Wolfe points out, boomers "now rule the marketplace—in numbers, in spending, and in determining the rules for successful marketplace engagement." Moreover, "they choose brands they want to experience—not simply have or use" in order to employ those brands in the "processes of becoming or actualizing the real self—the *authentic self*."[36]

Boomers lead this trend but they certainly are not alone. Everyone cycles through periods where authenticity matters most, according to Margaret King and Jamie O'Boyle of the Center for Cultural Studies & Analysis.[37] Every twenty years or so people question and then redefine their personal identity. These life stages—Adolescence (15–20 years old), Evaluation (35–40), Re-evaluation (55–60), and Acceptance (75+)—yield successively nuanced versions of the same individual. O'Boyle shared with us, "As individuals enter these transformation stages, they examine their identities, their lives, and their relationships—everything that comprises their social whole—and reject that which they view as fake, holding dear to what they see as authentic."[38]

Every year in the United States, three or four million people transition through each of these phases (meaning thirty to forty million people are constantly in the Evaluation or Re-evaluation states), and we've been living through a period where the oldest boomers (born in 1946) turned fifty-five in 2001 and are now shifting into their sixties while the youngest (born in 1964) turned thirty-five in 1999. The baby boom generation now brackets King and O'Boyle's prime periods of authenticity-seeking—a stage of a heightened thirst for authenticity—making them an ever-present phenomenon, not a one-time demographic-based fad.[39]

Consider Joie de Vivre Hospitality. In 1986, its boomer founder, Chip Conley, entered the hospitality business by buying a cheap, rundown motel in San Francisco's Tenderloin district. Conley wanted to create a unique hotel experience for an identifiable set of customers, and decided to theme his Phoenix Hotel based on that iconic boomer magazine, *Rolling Stone.*

Conley pored over back issues of *Rolling Stone* to determine the five impressions that this rock 'n' roll rag imparted to its readers—coming up with adventurous, hip, funky, irreverent, and young-at-heart—then redesigned the entire place, harmonizing these impressions into a consistent, coherent, and compelling theme. The Phoenix Hotel became *the* place to stay in San Francisco for touring rock bands and their roadies—without ever explicitly announcing that it had anything to do with *Rolling Stone* or even rock music.[40]

Using this same pick-a-magazine theming technique for each of its properties, JDV Hospitality has grown into the Bay Area's leading purveyor of boutique experiences, with over thirty hotels—now reaching into the rest of California—as well as a number of restaurants, bars, and one day spa. In *The Rebel Rules: Daring to Be Yourself in Business*, Conley describes the economic value of his first hotel as "the identity refreshment the guests are seeking by visiting The Phoenix. By staying at The Phoenix, a guest might feel a little more adventurous or hip . . . People are willing to pay a premium for this experience." The approach, he explains, "is not based upon demographics—which describes what you see on the surface—but instead it's based upon psychographics, which describes what's going on underneath the surface for each of us—our passions, beliefs, and values." Conley concludes, "Rule number one for brands: the words that a loyal customer uses to describe her dream product tend to be the same words she would use to affectionately describe herself."[41] In other words, brands should conform to the self-image of loyal customers, and thereby become authentic to them.

All this codifies what Christopher Lasch described twenty-five years ago, in *The Culture of Narcissism*, in anticipating "the dogma of authenticity" according to which one must "'keep up with the kids,' to master their incomprehensible jargon, and even imitate their dress and manners in the hope of preserving a youthful appearance and outlook."[42] No wonder so much advertising fixates on Gen Xers; advertising managers and marketing executives know they and their fellow boomers want to be perceived as young, energetic, cool, and as real as they once were, and as they see Gen Xers today.

Gen Xers themselves also want to be as young, energetic, cool, and as real as possible. Jane Rinzler Buckingham, president of New York–based market research firm Youth Intelligence, points out, "Kids aged 18–30 [kids!] have an incredible need for authenticity. They are tired of artifice. They want the 'real deal.'"[43]

Bottom line: *Can businesses help render authenticity in a world with narcissistic tendencies unlike any other time before?* We think so, but it requires understanding that despite the loss of individual character subsumed within the concept, demographics are not destiny. Even the me-me-me generation eventually grows up to desire the real-real-real. Moreover, consumers' perception of what is and is not authentic changes over time, based on life stages, personal experiences, and changes in brands and offerings they habitually use. Businesses—particularly those responsible for enduring brands (think Tide, Coke, Levi's, and so forth)—must therefore manage the ongoing relevancy of their offerings for their ever-changing, always-aging (but so often de-maturing) set of customers. They must revive for each generation an appreciation of their brand's appeal to previous generations.

Rendering Generations More Cross-Generational

One centuries-old brand that thus far is maintaining its cross-generational relevancy is Guinness. Founded in 1759 when Sir Arthur Guinness signed a nine-thousand-year lease on the St. James Gate Brewery in Dublin, this brewer of exceptionally dark, heavy, creamy, slow-poured, and warm beer began to lose sales for the first time in 1999, most dramatically in Ireland, chiefly because younger consumers felt it did not fit their generation.[44] So Guinness (since 1997 a part of Diageo) tried a number of tactics. Neither the FastPour system for bars, which lowered pouring time from two minutes to less than thirty seconds, nor the brand extension Guinness Extra Cold did well, as consumers regarded them as inauthentic Guinness. While Extra Cold remains on store shelves (much to the ire of many longtime drinkers), FastPour is now defunct. But other innovations—such as the "rocket widget," which creates its signature creamy head in a can, and especially the Guinness Storehouse in Dublin—are succeeding by *extending* the authentic Guinness experience for a new generation.

Rising out of an abandoned fermentation plant, the Storehouse has become the number-one tourist attraction in Ireland.[45] For a €14 admission fee, guests enter and promptly receive "the pebble"—an actual globule of Guinness stout encased in Lucite. Encountering interactive exhibits, they slowly ascend through the building to the Gravity Bar, with its panoramic view of Dublin. Ralph Ardill, former director of marketing at designer Imagination, Ltd (and now CEO of the Brand Experience Consultancy in London), told us, "The Storehouse was designed to not only share the richness of Guinness heritage with brand 'loyalists' but to also experientially drive re-engagement with a new generation of brand 'rejecters'—both inside and outside of Ireland—who potentially grew up viewing Guinness stout as not for them."[46] If you get the lads, boomers are sure to follow. The general affluence of boomers makes cost generally irrelevant; if they want anything, they simply buy it. Quality no longer differentiates; authenticity does.

One very modern brand that similarly makes a cross-generational appeal is American Girl. It is adept at fostering conversations between parent and daughter, and sometimes across three generations to include grandmother. In particular, the company's American Girl Places in Chicago, New York, and Los Angeles create numerous possibilities for bonding—from talking about the historical context of the company's dolls to discussing issues raised by the "table talk" cards in each Café.

Think about what prompts you can provide your customers that would keep your brand relevant for each successive generation.

Failure of Institutions: The Obviously Ineffective Reality

The final driver of authenticity as the new consumer sensibility? The eroding reputation of our major social institutions. The most glaring example is the *deceit of corporations*. Corporate scandals have incalculably undermined the trust that girds the capitalist system. From Oxford Health Plans to Sunbeam to Cendant to Enron to Tyco to all those companies backdating options without disclosing them, each successive scandal exacerbates the problem. Despite the Private Securities Litigation Reform Act, legislation that made it more difficult for trial lawyers to file cases without evidence of specific fraudulent events, an average of almost 250 shareholders class action suits have been filed per year since its 1995 passage, with seven of the ten largest settlements ever awarded made in 2005 and 2006.[47] Who knows which company will be found out next?

Furthermore, grandiose statements of corporate social responsibility (CSR) too often ring hollow. William Clay Ford, the executive chairman of Ford

Motor Company, went to the fifth annual Greenpeace Business Conference in London in October 2000.[48] Ford agreed with the Greens, "We're at a crucial point in the world's history. Our oceans and forests are suffering, species are disappearing; the climate is changing." Then he declared his ultimate goal, to "end the 100-year reign of the internal combustion engine." The company also issued its first Corporate Citizenship Report, which recast founder Henry Ford's "legacy as an industrialist and conservationist" under the heading "Ninety-Six Years Commitment to Conservation and the Environment."[49]

Meanwhile, however, Ford bolstered its formidable lineup of gas-guzzling SUVs and trucks. In 2003, it reneged on its CEO's commitment to improve the gas mileage of SUVs by 2005.[50] Its launch of a new advertising campaign in 2004, "The Greening of the Blue Oval," and introduction of the Ford Escape Hybrid did little to improve the company's image. Jane Holtz Kay, author of the anti-automobile *Asphalt Nation*, said at the time of Ford's Greenpeace speech, "He's a car guy. He may actually believe that he's trying to become more ecologically sound and worker friendly, but it's basically greenwash. It comes off to me as a series of hypocritical gestures."[51] In an op-ed for the *Los Angeles Times*, Geoffrey Johnson of the greenwashing watchdog group Green Life opined, "Ford hopes to mold a public perception that Ford has gone green, that the company is a model of corporate responsibility," while diverting "our attention from the corporate-fueled environmental destruction taking place all around us."[52] When Ford announced in June 2006 that it wouldn't meet its goal of selling 250,000 hybrids a year by 2010—a goal announced less than a year earlier, after hurricane Katrina hit the oil-refining business—the Sierra Club said that Ford was "rapidly becoming the automaker that cried wolf."[53]

Even for companies without hollow CSR promises and financial scandals, common business practices—underfunded employee pensions, plant closings, headquarters layoffs, and increased outsourcing—contribute to the perception of businesses as untrustworthy. These actions inevitably tarnish the reputation of all in business, making it more difficult for any one to render authenticity.

Businesses are not the only institutions that fail the test of authenticity. The *inanity of educational institutions* also causes them to be seen as fake. Too many public schools are undeniably broken, unable to offer a real education for their children. Both parents and their kids understandably complain of too much homework (the time devoted to homework has increased over 50 percent since 1981[54]) and wonder: "What are they doing in school?" To make up for the inadequacies of public schooling many parents resort to buying tutorial services from companies like Educate, Score Learning Centers, or Sylvan Learning. Others homeschool; over a million U.S. children are taught today at home.[55]

Doubts exist about our colleges and universities as well. Many who matriculate aren't really there to learn but to get credentialed and/or have a good time; and there is a body of fiction, including Tom Wolfe's novel *I Am Charlotte Simmons*, that exposes the unseemly realities of many institutions of higher learning.[56] Many less-prestigious schools have become businesses—competing for students, marketing to gain sufficient enrollments to survive. Grade inflation—students receiving what they did not earn—is commonplace: Princeton awards A grades almost half the time; Harvard awards "honors" to an amazing 90 percent of its graduating students.[57]

In the meantime, plenty of campus tours for prospective students sugarcoat real college life—for example, "[s]ome institutions, like the University of Rochester, simply set up a model room, with two beds and two desks, but none of the detritus of real college students."[58] According to Jeff Kallay, "Experience Evangelist" at TargetX, who specializes in college recruiting experiences, "Most of these model rooms are furnished by Bed Bath & Beyond or similar retailer in return for promotion, and in no way represent what real campus dorms look like. In fact, most campus tours present most prospective students and their parents with such a stilted view—particularly of the party scene—that they have no idea what the place is really like."[59] Enter theU.com, offering "uncensored college videos" for some fifty major universities and over two thousand "totally honest college confessions" written by actual students. Says one testimonial, "The way you show real kids, real classrooms, real parties was great: this was the only site that allowed me to understand what going to college was actually going to be like."[60]

Graduate business schools are just as inauthentic. Henry Mintzberg, professor of management studies at McGill University, attacks prevailing pedagogical approaches, student and faculty composition, and the results of leading MBA programs. "Conventional MBA programs," he writes in *Managers Not MBAs: A Hard Look at the Soft Practice of Managing and Management Development*, "train the wrong people in the wrong way with the wrong consequences."[61] He claims B-schools have miseducated a generation of managers, and outlines an alternative MBA curriculum implemented at McGill, positioning the place as the authentic B-school.[62]

Warren G. Bennis and James O'Toole echo Mintzberg in their *Harvard Business Review* article "How Business Schools Lost Their Way," but believe "the curriculum is the effect, not the cause, of what ails the modern business school." They suggest that the ingrained culture of most B-schools accounts for the undue influence of a scientific/academic operating model over a more practical/professional one. How did this ethos emerge? Bennis and O'Toole contend that "professors like it that way."[63] Practical advice about changing this condition remains scant, leaving prospective students—as consumers—to conclude a real education about business occurs only in real business.

Consider too the *phoniness of politicians*. Columnist Kathleen Parker says that what matters today "is authenticity. There's no surer way to lose the public's confidence than to pretend to be something you're not."[64] Such pols run heavy risks of being found out; media pundits endlessly analyze their personalities, positions, decisions, and transgressions. Voters are left jaded by the present state of affairs and discouraged about the future.

Former Vice President Al Gore may well be the poster child for such disenchantment. On Gore's efforts to remake his image after losing the 2000 presidential election, philosophy professor Crispin Sartwell wrote, "It reached the point at which asking who Al Gore really is, deep inside, was like asking who [animated movie character] Shrek really is: He really is whatever he's programmed to be, whatever sells tickets. Now Gore regrets his lost authenticity, pines nostalgically for the time he actually existed. But it is too late. His authenticity is conceptually unrecoverable."[65] Sartwell's conclusion makes for an inconvenient truth about the whole lot of phony politicians: "Every attempt to regain authenticity only casts a new, infinitely repeated image through the hall of mirrors that is his political life and our media experience of that life."[66]

Following the Supreme Court–decided presidential contest of 2000, elections now often provoke lawsuits. The Democratic Party trained ten thousand lawyers for duty on Election Day in 2002 to guard against voter intimidation. Litigation soon followed, most notably in that year over New Jersey's Democratic nominee for U.S. Senate, and in 2004 over the governorship of Washington State.

Howard Dean's 2004 presidential campaign slogan was "Real Choice, Real Change." Yet *Time* magazine asked, "Who Is the Real Dean?"[67] To which Dean answered in Iowa: "Yeeeeeeeearrrrrrhhhhh!" The eventual Democratic nominee John Kerry ran with a self-proclaimed slogan, "The Real Deal." Of course voters reelected George W. Bush, despite his launching a real war with real casualties in Iraq over alleged weapons of mass destruction.

To promote their respective policies, both the Bush and Clinton administrations used video news releases (VNRs) that paid talent posing as journalists. Media critics called it "faux news" (with more than a wink to Fox News).[68] Citizens understandably wonder whom to trust. Thus Hillary Clinton embarks on her "listening tours" and Barack Obama holds up his youth and inexperience as a political virtue, while Republicans try to sort out who is a real conservative in the coming wake of President Bush. Tim Russert, host of NBC's *Meet the Press*, probably takes the pulse of the populace as well as any political analyst. He contends, "There's such a yearning in this country . . . I've been to Iowa, Florida, Ohio, California, everywhere. People are begging for authenticity."[69] In fact, journalist Paul Starobin asserts that for the 2008 Presidential election "the 'authenticity' standard" matters more than any other.[70]

There is also the *futility of nonprofit organizations*. They ostensibly seek to do a greater good, but have become so politicized (the Boy Scouts?), commercialized (the Girl Scouts?), or marginalized (PromiseKeepers?) that people wonder about their efficacy. As with their corporate brethren, financial inefficiencies and leadership scandals have eroded credibility (the Red Cross? the United Way?). Many foundations give away only 5 percent of their total capital holdings each year, the minimum required by law—with the remaining 95 percent operating as an investment portfolio for money managers. Donations increasingly come with strings attached.

A new generation of philanthropists, from eBay founder Pierre Omidyar to rapper Snoop Dogg, seek active involvement in the charities to which they give or foundations they establish, as much as a form of self-actualization as an act of selfless giving, or so it seems. Both the cars Oprah Winfrey gives away on her show and the overseas schools established in her name surely serve to attract viewers and further her business interests, in addition to helping others, to give just one example. Call it *narcithropy* rather than philanthropy. Giving something today usually comes with getting something, whether access, influence, or recognition.[71] How refreshing that Warren Buffett pledged his billions to a foundation—the Bill Gates Foundation—that will not bear his own name.

And have you seen the funnel devices at malls where people put a coin into a slot and watch it spiral around into a center hole? The charity's collection jar offers a coin-spiraling experience in return for your donation. Such a concern for "the donor experience" dominates many nonprofit institutions. As donors increasingly give with a consumer mentality and nonprofits correspondingly behave more like businesses, for-profit enterprises may feel pressure to act like charities as they struggle to pursue both profit and the perception of authenticity.

Finally, *turmoil within religious institutions* has diminished people's faith in their respective religious institutions and leadership while simultaneously stirring desire for authentic spirituality. Priests' molestation of youths in their care shook the faith of many Roman Catholics. The institutional cover-up—the denials, the moving of priests from parish to parish, the hush money—was even more harmful in damaging Catholicism's reputation with its own adherents.[72]

The actions of mainline Protestant denominations frustrate many members. These include not only the well-publicized debate over the ordination of homosexuals, but a wide spectrum of theological and ecclesiastical issues. A study by Ellison Research found that 40 percent of Protestant pastors hold beliefs that run counter to the official positions of their own denominations.

Methodist ministers are most likely to differ from governing bodies—only 33 percent contend their positions align—as they strive to reflect (or lead) the sentiments of local congregations.[73]

Evangelical Christians have created megachurches that resemble shopping malls, with bookstores, food courts and restaurants, cafés ("Holy Grounds" seems to be a popular name), skate parks, fitness centers, water parks, and hotels.[74] Sanctuaries resemble movie cinemas, with cup holders (for soda pop, not communion wine), rock bands (instead of choirs), and PowerPoint presentations on jumbo screens (in lieu of real preaching from pulpits).[75]

Within Judaism, fundamental questions are emerging about what constitutes the real faith. In *Jew vs. Jew*, Samuel Freedman examines the impact of intermarriage and other issues and imagines the day when American Jewry may reorganize into factions he calls Haredi, Conservadox, Reformative, and Just Jews.[76]

Global debate ensues about the real tenets of Islam. In Kazakhstan, just two weeks after the terrorist attacks on America, Pope John Paul II said, "I wish to reaffirm the Catholic Church's respect for Islam, for authentic Islam."[77] But what is authentic Islam? Is it "the Islam that prays, that is concerned for those in need," as the Pope declared?[78] Or is it the one that declared war on the West and that continues to terrorize innocent people throughout much of the world?

People find themselves spiritually confused, turning away from organized religion to find something to fill some void in their lives. Witness the explosion of New Age and New Age-ish variations of lifestyle spas, tranquility retreats, and wellness programs—as well as the weekend worship of recreation and sports to which so many people now turn to bring meaning to their lives.

Regarding the failure of all these institutions—religious, nonprofit, government, educational, and corporate—the bottom line is: *Can businesses help individuals find authenticity in a world where people no longer esteem our most basic social institutions?* Yes, but only if each kind of institution recognizes the loss of purpose at the core of their problems. Businesses in particular must accept greater responsibility and transparency in all activities—starting with maintaining basic accounting integrity—and then fully contend with this new consumer sensibility for authenticity. After all, business is the dominant social institution of our time. Business is where people (whether employees or customers) receive continued educational training, debate current affairs, donate to charities, and share their faith—all the more reason why business output must be managed so that consumers come to perceive it as authentic.

Rendering Institutions More Effective

While every kind of institution is "in business" in the sense of endeavoring in some rightful pursuit, only companies should be in the business of *commerce*—

buying and selling in the pursuit of personal and corporate profit. When educational, governmental, charitable, and church-based institutions engage in commerce, the genuineness of their motives readily comes into doubt.

To overcome the perception of being inauthentic, first abandon any incestuous business dealings that cloud your real purpose. Embrace your own raison d'être, and let that drive your every pursuit. While each particular enterprise must identify its own particular reason for being, nevertheless there is a general and time-honored raison d'être for each social institution, as shown in figure 2-1:

- **For business:** Unapologetically make a profit for the sake of your shareholders and employees.

- **For education:** Diligently advance knowledge in individuals and humankind.

- **For government:** Only preserve and protect the people of whom, by whom, and for whom you govern.

- **For charities:** Generously help neighbors near and far.

- **For church:** Simply proclaim truth to all who will hear.

Effectively rendering authenticity becomes more difficult the more an enterprise strays from the raison d'être associated with its kind of institution.

Second, return to the primary method of funding your enterprise befitting the nature of your institution. Becoming a business—by engaging in commerce—when not a business represents the most fundamental means by

FIGURE 2-1

The five social institutions

Social institution	Raison d'être	Method of funding
Business	Make a profit	Payments and fees
Education	Advance knowledge	Grants and tuitions
Government	Preserve and protect	Taxes and tariffs
Charity	Help neighbors	Donations and gifts
Church	Proclaim truth	Tithes and offerings

which enterprises stray from their raison d'être and render themselves inauthentic. Each kind of institution has an intrinsic method of raising money, again shown in figure 2-1:

- **For business:** Payments and fees from customers should comprise the sole source of revenue. (Government subsidies only serve to signal inauthenticity in the eyes of many.)

- **For education:** Grants and tuition should cover the costs of operating the school. (Gifts to general funds, including those from alumni, only preclude thinking about ongoing tuition for lifelong learning as well as grants targeted at specific student needs.)

- **For government:** Taxes and tariffs should fund the needs of the state. (Charges for business-like offerings only indicate where government has stomped on properly private-sector initiatives.)

- **For charities:** Donations and gifts should constitute the very existence and charter of any nonprofit. (Payments received from government agencies, business owners, education systems, and church denominations always come with strings attached; better to only accept money from individuals.)

- **For churches:** All activities should be financed solely through tithes and offerings. (Efforts to have only those who benefit from a particular ministry—say a couples retreat—pay for it renders the ministry a commercial offering and not a caring act of love.)

Many enterprises may find it a struggle to rely exclusively on the corresponding method of funding, but the more they depend on expedient but unfitting sources, the greater the likelihood that they will be seen as inauthentic. More significantly, they run the risk of forever losing touch with their raison d'être. If the impurity of your current financing practices makes you incapable of appreciating the underlying virtue in knowing your proper place, then you may be worse off, authenticity-wise, than you can even imagine.

3

The Supply of Inauthenticity

WHAT'S GOING ON?

AUTHENTICITY IS IN THE AIR. YOU SEE IT, FEEL IT, ALL around you. Most of what we experience in today's consumer-oriented society revolves around issues of what is real and what is fake. Postmodern theorists constantly write about the interplay and intermingling of the authentic and the inauthentic. But one need not be well-versed in Jean Baudrillard's concept of *simulacra*, familiar with Umberto Eco's musings about *hyperreality*, nor even comprehend the Wachowski brothers' philosophy in *The Matrix* to see what's going on. A single day of shopping will suffice.

One Unreal Day

The alarm goes off at 8:15 a.m. on Saturday morning, and Eddie hits the snooze button on the John Deere Tractor Alarm (with "Authentic John Deere Tractor and Barnyard Sounds!"). When the animals bay again at 8:25, he switches on the radio. As the station glides into Joe McBride's "Keepin' It Real," wife Brenda beats Eddie to the shower in their large, recently remodeled, faux marble bathroom. She washes her hair with Aussie Real Volume Shampoo, then treats it with Real Volume Conditioner, having colored it a week ago with L'Oréal Preference #9 (Natural Blonde) because, well, she's worth it!

After relinquishing the shower to Eddie and his Get Real Natural lavender shampoo, Brenda blow-dries her hair and adds some Aussie Real Volume Styling

Whip. She then slides on her cotton shirt from Real Clothes over her Hanes Authentic Tagless T-shirt and dons a pair of Ralph Lauren jeans ("Authentic Denim Outfitters"). Done showering, Eddie quickly towel-dries his hair, combs some Just for Men hair color (Natural Real Black) into his increasingly salt-and-pepper beard, and puts on his favorite Faded Glory shirt ("Authentic Style").

Downstairs, Brenda cooks up some scrambled Egg Beaters ("99% real egg whites") with Real Bacon Bits (*"Real* Hormel Bacon Adds *Real* Taste") while Eddie pours a bowl of Post Blueberry Morning cereal ("with Real, Wild Blueberries"). They drink Simply Orange Grove Made orange juice ("made with bits of real orange") and watch CNN Headline News ("Real News. Real Fast.") while the Gloria Jean's coffee ("Authentic Mocha Java") brews. They agree that after the kids are up she'll head to the grocery store while he runs some errands and then starts some early Christmas shopping.

At Giant Eagle, Brenda first visits the wine department for a bottle of Fetzer white and a bottle of Fetzer red, or perhaps a bottle of rosé instead. She also picks up a twelve-pack of Coors ("Real Rocky Mountain Beer") and some Bud Light ("Fresh. Smooth. Real."). She then loads up on fruity cereal: General Mills' Berry Bust Cheerios ("with *REAL* sliced strawberries"), Kellogg's Rice Krispies ("with REAL STRAWBERRIES"), and Post Honey Bunches of Oats ("with REAL BANANAS"). And because the kids love it: Cocoa Puffs Milk 'n Cereal Bars ("The NUTRITION of a bowl of cereal with Real Milk").

Meanwhile, Eddie makes his first stop at OfficeMax to refill the Hewlett-Packard black ink cartridge ("HP RealLife Imaging System") for the home-office computer.

Brenda strolls the aisles, filling her cart: Betty Crocker Au Gratin Potatoes ("with 100% real Idaho Potatoes"), Stove Top stuffing mix ("with Real Chicken Broth"), Pepperidge Farm Goldfish crackers ("Baked with Real Cheese"), Ritz bits sandwiches ("Made with Real Peanut Butter"), Oscar Mayer Braunschweiger ("AUTHENTIC"), Prego Hearty Meat Sauce ("Authentic Italian Sauce"), and some Premio Sweet Italian Sausage ("Real Italian Taste"). And, oh yes, a bottle of Ditka's Real Pork Chop Sauce. Da sauce!

The next stop for Eddie, PETsMART. He grabs some Pounce Cat Treats ("with Real seafood!") and Cat Sip ("Real Milk") as well as some Alpo ("With Real Liver") and Snausages Roverolis ("With Authentic Italian Aroma!!!"), and—why not—a Rubber R-R-Ruffs ("Really R-R-R-Rugged") dog toy. "R-R-R-Rastro will ruv it!"

Kraft (kraftfoods.com: "real help in real time") enjoys considerable share-of-cart today: Kraft Mayo Hot 'n Spicy ("Real Mayonnaise"), Kraft Easy Cheese cheese spread ("Made with Real K-R-A-F-T Cheese"), and Kraft Velveeta Shells & Cheese ("Real VELVEETA Cheese Sauce"). Yum!

A quick jaunt into Jo-Ann Fabrics & Crafts is next for Eddie, as he picks up that can of Modern Options Instant Antiquing Set ("Create an authentic rust finish in just minutes!") for Brenda. He wonders, "What for?"

Meanwhile, Brenda chooses Quaker Toastables ("Made with REAL FRUIT! Real Fruit. Real Oatmeal. Real Flavor.") over the Kellogg's Pop-Tarts Yogurt Blasts ("Made with Real Fruit"—that's it). And here's the Hunt's Snack Pack Pudding ("Real Non-fat Milk Is Our #1 Ingredient"). Impulsively, she also grabs a box of Dr. Phil's Shape Up! Mix & Drink ("Authentic Chocolate Flavor").

Eddie arrives at Target and heads straight to the toy department. For Tommy, the youngest: a Tinkertoy construction set ("Real Wood Pieces! Real Working parts! Realistic barn!") and, after examining both, he decides on The Home Depot 10-Piece Tool Set ("Real Tools for Kids!") over The Home Depot Builders Tool Set ("They Look Like Real Tools!").

Brenda grabs some Giant Eagle Tortilla Chips ("Authentic Restaurant Style") and, for something different, Lays Sensations Lime & Cracked Black Pepper Kettle Cooked Potato Chips ("with authentic spices and seasoning") and General Mills' Fruit Ripples ("crispy baked real apple pieces"). Beverages? Make it Minute Maid Lemonade ("Made with Real Lemons") and Nantucket Nectars Orange Pineapple Mango juice ("Real is better").

For Susan, the middle girl: Barbie Volkswagen New Beetle ("Trunk really opens! Real key chain too!") and My Beautiful Ballerina ("Performs Real Pirouettes!"). And for Eddie Jr.: a Tony Hawk action figure ("Real-Flex") and a Wilson Mini-sized Replica NFL Game Ball ("Replica Authentic NFL Game Ball").

Brenda likes to bake, so into the cart go Baker's Dipping Chocolate ("Real Dark Semi-Sweet Chocolate"), Hershey's Milk Chocolate Chips (more "Real Milk Chocolate"), and Nestlé Milk Chocolate Morsels (yet more "Real Milk Chocolate"). Then, it's either Luigi's Real Italian Ice ("With Real Fruit Juice") or Tropical Fla-Vor-Ice (ditto). She chooses Fla-Vor-Ice—a Fa-Vor-Ite!

Two more stops for Eddie. First Border's—to load up on some new movies. "Which movie? Let's see: Pleasantville *(seen it),* The Truman Show *(seen it twice),* The Game *(seen it three times),* The Real Cancun *(no, no). Ah, here we go:* EdTV." *Then off to Bed Bath & Beyond. "Where is that great popcorn? Ah, here it is!" He picks up a box of Wabash Valley Farm's Real Theater Popcorn.*

Finally at check-out, Brenda grabs a few impulse items for the kids, Lemonhead Candy ("made with Real Lemon Juice") and Pop Rocks ("Real Popping Action!"), plus a couple of magazines: *Budget Travel* ("Vacations for Real People") and *Saveur* ("Savor a World of Authentic Cuisine"). After paying with her debit card, Brenda sets out for home.

Eddie, now hungry and thirsty, eyes a convenience store on the corner. Once inside, he grabs some Old Settler's Beef Jerky ("REAL WESTERN") and then spies a 23.5-oz. can of Arizona Southern Style Sweet Tea ("Real Brewed"). "Keep it real," says the cashier as Eddie heads out the door.

———————

Back to reality. We actually found all this "real" and "authentic" language printed on the packaging of such generally fake stuff.[1] It would give almost anyone pause, but companies use such language for one simple reason: *people buy it.*

Reality: On the Air and Everywhere

Reality is not only in the air, but *on* the air. Since MTV's *Real World* began throwing unknown but exhibitionist strangers together in 1992, reality TV has come to dominate prime-time programming. (Not coincidentally, daytime television has undergone a simultaneous alteration. With *The Jerry Springer Show* replacing *The Phil Donahue Show* in 1991 as the signature syndication of WLWT-TV, a wave of "trash TV" talk shows featuring lowbrow guests soon came to rival soap operas as the dominant genre of daytime programming.)

The most successful of all reality TV programs? Fox's *American Idol*, which drew far more viewers than the Winter Olympics on NBC in 2006. Remember William Hung and his rendition (if that's the right word) of "She Bangs"? Then CNN host Aaron Brown observed, "The more real people there are on TV, airbrushed and Photoshopped, made over, cut, pasted and polished, the less real they seem. Could it be that we are on the verge of forgetting what real really is? Until William Hung came along to remind us."[2]

At the time of this writing Wikipedia lists over three hundred different reality TV shows from around the world across twelve different genres—and at the time of this reading, it's sure to be more.[3] Many of these genres originated from either the United Kingdom (*Pop Idol* begat *American Idol*, *Canadian Idol*, and *Australian Idol*) or the Netherlands (*Nummer 28* begat *Real World*; *Big Brother* begat *Big Brother* and all its brethren). It's a worldwide phenomenon; a quick spin around the globe yields *Born Diva* (Philippines), *Dream Home* (New Zealand), *Get Gorgeous* (India), *Vyvoleni* (Czech Republic), *Estoy por Ti* (Spain), and *FC Zulu* (Denmark).

These fabricated productions gain the "reality" tag by being unscripted, never mind that they are painstakingly cast and edited.[4] Reality TV stars understand their roles. In *Scars of the Spirit: The Struggle Against Inauthenticity*, literary critic Geoffrey Hartman points out, "Of the reality-revel 'Big Brother,' it was remarked by an organizer that the participants, all nonprofessionals, began to 'produce themselves' as soon as they were on stage."[5]

Even the Public Broadcasting Service gets into the act with its *Colonial House* ("Real Life. Real Tough.") and the Ken Burns documentary series, *American Stories*, about such figures as Thomas Jefferson and Mark Twain (not his real name!).[6] PBS—that government-funded, pledge-drive-supported, big-company-sponsored, noncommercial business with all those increasingly lengthy ads—sought to capitalize on the documentary producer's fame with the tagline "History Made Them Famous. Ken Burns Makes Them Real."

Before discarding all this reality-plugging on the air as some sort of fad, consider for a moment how the prevalence of the "real" on the screen mirrors consumer sentiment among viewers. Media critic John Burmeister contends, "The success of these shows suggests an interesting possibility: that the *other* programming on television hasn't been meeting people's desire for the real."[7]

This desire for the real goes beyond TV programming, of course. Different genres of reality TV merely reflect various segments of consumer purchases and corresponding business growth. For example: *Trading Spaces*—home improvement and the rise of Home Depot and Lowe's; *Iron Chef*—cooking schools and culinary tourism; *Blind Date*—match.com, eHarmony, HeartDetectives; *Punked*—YouTube, Punchbaby, Kontraband; *Deal or No Deal*—lotteries and casinos; *Fear Factor*—extreme sports; *Nanny 911*—day care and parenting; *The Biggest Loser*—diet and weight-loss programs; *The Apprentice*—monster.com and other job-search services.

Traditionally, television does not lead, but follows pop-culture trends—and then takes them to their logical watching extremes. In this regard, reality TV reflects today's desire for authenticity in three fundamental ways:

- People increasingly *qualify* reality. During the sixth episode of the inaugural season of ABC's *The Bachelor*, eventual winner Amanda Walsh, one of the remaining two contestants, and Alex Michel, the bachelor, were sharing a hot tub on their final date. In a moment of intimate confession, Amanda yearned, "I can't wait to get back to real reality."[8] The number of permutations of reality seem to increase every year, and now include hyperreality, everyday reality, psycho reality, social reality, individual reality, transcultural reality, and, of course, virtual reality and its retronym physical reality.

- People further wish to *alter* reality. One TV program, *Extreme Makeover*, subjects volunteers to radical cosmetic surgery (nose jobs, face lifts, liposuction, skin reduction, breast augmentation, and the like) for the entertainment of viewers. These physiological alterations of self, however, only call attention to the mainstream change sought in other, seemingly more mundane, dimensions of everyday consumer lives. Sander L.

Gilman, author of *Making the Body Beautiful: A Cultural History of Aesthetic Surgery,* believes "'Extreme Makeover' is just another name for life in the 21st century."[9] According to the American Society for Aesthetic Plastic Surgery (ASAPS), in 2005 nearly 11.5 million cosmetic procedures were performed, an increase of over 400 percent since the organization started tracking the figure in 1997.[10]

- People often purchase their personal or lifestyle transformations from outside experts and enterprises that *commercialize* reality. Advertisements for goods and services don't tout their features and benefits as much as they push the sensations and impressions derived from their use. More companies seek to appeal to the aspirations (of current self) and the idolization (of future self) that underlies and motivates other desires.

Qualifying, altering, and commercializing reality are the means by which companies capitalize on this new consumer desire for authenticity—and making claims of "authentic" and "real" appear to be the primary means of marketing such offerings. By no means are these practices limited to where Brenda and Eddie shop. They permeate almost every other area of modern life.

Real Goods

Wrangler ads boast of being "Real. Comfortable. Jeans." Ads for Kool cigarettes admonish smokers, "Be Authentic." Weber ("Real people. Real stories. Real grills.") publishes a *Real Grilling* cookbook. BellSouth distributes "The *Real* Yellow Pages." New Balance makes "real shoes engineered for real athletes." Panasonic's plasma TV offers "real high-definition." Cars? Nissan, simply: "Authentic."; the H2 Hummer: "Here's a Real One"; Honda's CRV: "It's a vehicle designed for your adventures in reality." Manufacturers clearly see themselves competing in terms of authenticity.

Real Retail

Ritz Camera describes its retail staff as "Real Photo People" offering "*real* digital camera prints" at "*Real* Low Prices, Guaranteed." FUJIFILM offers "real pictures from your digital camera" at Wal-Mart's One-Hour Photo shops. The Sharper Image features "verified customer letters" as "Authentic true stories . . ." in its catalog. Ads for Simon Property Group's Las Vegas Outlet Center promote merchants selling "Real Brands. Real Selection. Real Savings." while encouraging consumers to come in and "GET REAL." In describing the difference between her company's offerings and those of Victoria's Secret, Frederick's of Hollywood's CEO, Linda LoRe, asserts, "We're more real, more sexy-raunchy."[11]

Other retailers—from Anthropologie to Z Gallerie—have taken conscious steps to differentiate themselves via direct appeals to authenticity.

Real Sports

What better place to start than with HBO's *Real Sports with Bryant Gumbel*? Then there is Unreal Sports with G4TechTV, which, after the 2004–2005 National Hockey League season was cancelled due to a management lockout, broadcast an entire season of virtual hockey games, simulated with Electronic Arts' NHL 2005 video game. Equally unreal: World Wrestling Entertainment, which in 2001 launched a school outreach program called "Get R.E.A.L." (Respect, Education, Achievement, Leadership). Linda McMahon, WWE CEO, said at the time, "We want Get R.E.A.L. to be a real-life solution, helping young people understand the importance of staying in school, reading, achieving good grades, and setting goals that will lead them to personal success as many of our Superstars have done."[12] Meanwhile, a new eight-team league for non-staged wrestling straightforwardly calls itself Real Pro Wrestling. The Cleveland Fusion franchise of the National Women's Football Association bills itself as "Real Women. Real Football. Real Fun!" Juniata College in Huntingdon, Pennsylvania, promotes "Real Students Playing Real Football," poking fun at nearby Penn State and its status as a gridiron powerhouse.

Real Education

Elsewhere on campus, Coe College in Cedar Rapids, Iowa, asks students to "Experience College—for Real." Cornell University uses "REAL IMPACT" in ads for its executive MBA program, and its College of Hotel Administration promotes its own executive education programs as "Relevant, Specific, Real." IMD International in Lausanne, Switzerland, refers to its "Real World. Real Learning" approach. Monroe College in the Bronx, New York, introduced its brand-new King Graduate School of Business with "Finally, a real MBA program for real people." The Banff/Canmore Secondary Schools organization in Alberta, Canada, assists college students financially via its "Make It Real" scholarship program, awarded by a panel of five "Make It Real Judges." And the University of Maryland University College promises "Real life. Real lessons." The virtual school for adult students is based in Adelphi; do not mistake it for the real University of Maryland in College Park.

Real Tourism

Elsewhere in Maryland, the state's Office of Tourism runs ads claiming "Even the Fun is Authentic." Ontario's Niagara Parks Commission heralds Niagara

Falls as "The Authentic Falls Experience." Estes Park in Colorado boasts, "Rocky Mountain National Park is as real as it gets." Scottsdale Downtown and the Scottsdale Convention & Visitors Bureau created ChicagoFest with "All of the authenticity. None of the wind." The Shilla hotel in Seoul bids travelers to "Stay at The Shilla. Discover the real Korea." Greenland proclaims itself "Exceptionally Real." Barbados encourages tourists to "experience the authentic Caribbean" while the rival island of Curaçao proclaims it to be "The Real Caribbean: Curaçao. Real. Different." (As you may have noticed by now: Somehow. Periods. Render. Descriptions. More. Real.)

Real Real Estate

Realty One not only registered the mark "Real Living," its corresponding Web site, RealLiving.com, uses the tagline "It's got to be real." Advertisements proclaim: "It's The Real Thing. Real People Making Real Money at Realty One." Meanwhile, Century21 fights fire with fire by registering "Real Estate for the Real World" as its own tagline. Homebuilders tag along. Dunmore Homes in northern California brags about "real people . . . real satisfaction." Home remodeling follows: Sherwin-Williams offers such colored paints as Realist Beige 6078, Real Red 6868, and Really Teal 6489. Masonite offers Fiberglass Wood-Grain Entry Systems (read: doors) featuring "wood-edge construction for the look and machinability of a real wood door." Jeld-Wen's windows provide "Reliability for real life" and similarly, for kitchen and bath, Knape & Vogt offers "Real Solutions For Real Life." Security Innovations offers a home system called Access-Plus ("Real On-Line. Real Security. Real Integration."). And The Club at Spanish Peaks, a luxury development in Big Sky, Montana, attracts new owners with the plea, "Authentic Montana: Unspoiled. Uncrowded. Unpretentious."

Real Restaurants

The establishment that sparked the whole theme restaurant trend now refers to itself as the "Authentic Hard Rock Cafe." Meanwhile, local chapters of the Council of Independent Restaurants of America, such as the one in Ohio that dubs itself Cleveland Originals, promotes patronage with this vertically oriented tagline:

real

restaurants

real

passion.

And a local tavern outside Cleveland, the 5 O'Clock Lounge, bills itself as "A Real Bar for Real People." The Ohio-based chain of Claddagh Irish Pubs goes so far as to say it is "as authentic as the Guinness we pour." An examination of any other city, state, or country yields "real" cuisine at every turn. Where does one go for "Real Cuban Food. Real Cuban Fun."? The Babalu Grill . . . in Baltimore, Maryland! Perhaps the chain of sixty quick-serve restaurants in England, EAT, sums it up best. It is "The Real Food Company."

Real Wine

Seeking to differentiate its offerings, Brenda-and-Eddie-favorite Fetzer Vine-yards of Mendocino County, California, advertises its wines on TV, in print, and on the Web as "Authenticity personified. Authenticity crushed, aged, and bottled. Fetzer. An American Original." Several wine regions in France—including Champagne, Chablis, and Bourgogne—campaign to defend their original, place-based wines from imposters that would use the same name, but not come from the same region. It's worth sharing at length some of the ad copy, this one from the Vignerons et Maisons de Champagne:

> Champagne Not From Champagne? No way! Oh sure, some sparking wines may look and even taste the part, but if it's not from Champagne, it's simply not true Champagne. That's because Champagne isn't merely a type of wine. It's a specific region 90 miles east of Paris with a long history of winemaking expertise . . . If the grapes aren't from this unique region where winemaking is a special art, then the wine really isn't authentic champagne. It does matter where the wine comes from. A Napa wine is from Napa, a Willamette wine is from Willamette and a Red Mountain wine is from Red Mountain, Washington. And if it's not from Champagne, it's simply not true Champagne.

This is no mere whining, but part of an initiative from the European Union to protect scores of region-based names from imitators; for example, Gorgonzola and Prosciutto di Parma. While campaigns in the past for such products surely discussed availability, cost, and quality, the point of contention today focuses squarely on authenticity.

Fakery: Reflecting This Everywhere "Reality"

With all this talk of real comes an increased infusion of the intentionally fake, reflecting the unreal "Reality" all about us. Fake e-mail, for example, ranges from fake lists of 9/11 donations to solicitations for funds to help a certain Nigerian diplomat's family. So many people now question the validity of Internet and all other sources of information that fake news now finds an audience. For a sampling, take in SatireWire.com, BorowitzReport.com, or theonion.com (an offshoot of the original real fake news magazine, *The Onion*), Jon Stewart's *The Daily Show*, British comedian Sacha Baron Cohen's *Da Ali G. Show*, and Saaed Khalifa's *Hurry Up, He's Dead* in Iraq.[13]

Stewart's show has been well received by viewers—many college students report it as their primary source for news.[14] Critics and journalism experts also admire it; it won a Peabody award in 2005. As did *60 Minutes II* that same year for its Abu Ghraib prison story, written and produced by Dan Rather and Mary Mapes, respectively; but both were later forced from CBS News after the discovery that their story on President George W. Bush's National Guard service was based on faked documents. The *New York Times* lumped them together by subtitling its story on the awards show as "Mapes, Rather and Stewart honored for fake news."[15] The once venerable *Times* has had its own problems with fake news, specifically the scandal involving Jayson Blair, who followed in the footsteps of the *New Republic*'s Stephen Glass, the *Washington Post*'s Janet Cooke, and the *Boston Globe*'s Patricia Smith. How much of the news once fit to print is really faked in print?

It's not as if real life didn't supply enough newsworthy material. Witness these ten examples:

- **Fake actors:** Characters such as S1M0NE, the computer-generated cyberactress, or "synthespian," in the movie of the same name, headline a host of computer-generated digital images now inserted into movies and television shows. Tom Hanks' character appearing in historical footage in *Forrest Gump* represents an early version of the phenomenon. As Andrew Niccol, writer, director, and producer of *S1M0NE*, says, "When so many real actors and models have digital work done to them, we are talking about a very gray area of reality . . . It's gotten to the point that our ability to manufacture fraud now exceeds our ability to detect it."[16]

- **Fake phone calls:** The *New York Times* reports that people it dubs "cellphonies" increasingly employ "cellular subterfuge" to avoid contact with others in close physical proximity (from begging panhandlers to talkative neighbors), impress eavesdroppers, check out or ignore members of the opposite sex, elude salespeople, create excuses for leaving meetings early or arriving late, and gain a sense of security when feeling insecure or in danger.[17]

- **Fake law enforcement:** In a Texas case involving fake drugs, Lori Bailey, a spokesperson for the Dallas Police Department, claims "nearly half of the cocaine and nearly a quarter of the methamphetamine that the Dallas police seized last year have turned out to be gypsum from wallboard." At issue in such circumstances, according to one reporter: "Did the informer fake the drug purchase to obtain money from police?"[18]

- **Fake IDs:** Detecting these is also a growing problem for the police. The crooks now have access to high-tech graphics, photography, holograms, and magnetic-encoding software to produce fake driver's licenses that defy detection by the naked eye. ID-scanner providers like E-Seek and Intelli-Check have emerged in the battle to combat these increasingly sophisticated forgeries.[19]

- **Fake sports:** According to the St. Louis-based Fantasy Sports Trade Association, an estimated ten million people now play fantasy football.[20] Add to that Rotisserie baseball competitions and similar fantasy leagues for other fake sporting events, and it's no shock that these fantasy leagues now warrant television coverage. In the near future, fans may be more interested in watching a customized narrowcast of their own fantasy team—a game that never really happens, anywhere—than broadcasts of the official and actual games. After all, NFL.com's fantasy functionality already allows you to track your fake team, moment by moment, in real time.

- **Fake advertising:** Fake ads are becoming more common, particularly in new media. For example, Raleigh-based Oasys Mobile retained the ad firm McKinney & Silver to place fake ads on a Hollywood gossip blog pointing readers to "pherotone" ring tones that promised to attract the opposite sex. ("Experience the ring tone secret I discovered in Denmark that's too hot for mainstream science.") Then it posted a mock wedding video—capturing a groom leaving the altar to hug a male guest after his cell phone (pherotonically?) rang—on YouTube and other such sites, and fake entries even found their way into Wikipedia. A study by Northwestern University found that a lot of people enjoy being fooled, so much so they willingly point friends to the links even after realizing they've been duped.[21]

- **Fake sales:** You may find this hard to believe, but it turns out that some "Going Out of Business" signs on display at certain storefronts actually belong to ongoing concerns looking to attract more tourist traffic.[22] Amazing.

- **Fake music:** Over a thousand tribute bands registered to be listed in tributecity.com's Tribute Band Directory, covering the likes of the Beatles, U2, and Guns 'n' Roses. Music critic David Bernstein notes, "On any given night in most cities, fans are likely to find tribute bands headlining nightclub shows."[23] And, we might add, they appear at respected venues such as the House of Blues. The bands also headline their own music festivals, such as the six-stop Midwest concert series FakeFest.

- **Fake art:** British graffiti artist Banksy has managed to display his fake art alongside acknowledged masterpieces, successfully avoiding detection by security personnel in the Louvre, the Tate Modern, and the Museum of Modern Art, among others.[24] Unlike Banksy, the fine-art establishment considers Englishman John Myatt a real artist. He holds exhibits in London for new paintings that mimic masters like Van Gogh, Picasso, and Giacometti under the rubric of "Genuine Fakes," a term he writes in indelible ink on the back of every painting. One day Myatt says he wants to produce his own original works; "honest painting," he calls it. Until then he has to contend with "an unidentified forger who has been selling fake Myatts."[25]

- **Fake fixtures:** Landlords equip buildings with fake features. The *Wall Street Journal* reported: "A lot of office thermostats are completely fake—meant to dupe you into thinking you've altered the office weather conditions." Somewhere between 2 and 90 percent (how's that for a real estimate?) of heating, ventilation, and air-conditioning (HVAC) systems in office buildings evidently contain some nonworking features, from "fake thermostats" to "fake white noise" and "fake wiring."[26] And allegedly, many "Close Door" elevator buttons are fake. How does one tell?

One constantly sees commentary on modern-day fakery in the popular and business press—including commentary on each other's publications. *Fortune* magazine once ran an ad containing a spoof of *Fast Company* with a fake cover reading "500 Buzzwords We Just Made Up" and highlighting "Authentifactuation" as a key example.[27]

So What's a Business to Do?

This chapter contrasts the seemingly endless bombardment of "authentic" and "real" marketing messages we see and hear with a similarly seemingly endless array of inauthentic and fake activity we actually experience.

Let us be clear why it's important to understand what's going on. First, the existence of these fake phenomena constantly pushes the issue of authenticity to the fore. We read about the fake all the time. We see it all around us. We hear about it. We can't help but touch it as we live our own lives. The presentation of everyday life in real/fake terms is yet another reason why authenticity is becoming the new consumer sensibility—we can't stand the toxic levels of inauthenticity we're forced to breathe.

Second, behind all of the examples cited in this chapter lie business enterprises generating new economic output judged predominantly as valuable or invaluable according to whether consumers find it authentic or inauthentic. An increasingly unreal world may be emerging—but the groceries and toys, TV programs and university educations, residential homes and vacation destinations, musical recordings and sports entertainment all face the concerted challenge of being perceived as authentic.

Third, the prevalence of so much "real" and "fake" language in the packaging and advertising copy touting this economic output proves that companies and their supporting ad agencies discern the emerging sensibility. Such an approach does not surface by mere happenstance; it's pretty clear that if businesses *claim* to be authentic, they must feel consumers are *demanding* authenticity in what they buy. But, as our survey of companies and offerings asserting they are real reveals, far more businesses *claim* to be authentic than actually *come off* as authentic. As folklorist Regina Bendix notes, today "so much has been declared authentic that the scarcity value is evaporating: once tomato sauce carries the label 'authentic,' the designation loses its special significance."[28] It's worse than that—the very act of proclaiming oneself to be real leads almost inexorably to the perception of being fake.

Think of it on a personal level. Suppose someone comes up to you on the street or at some conference, and the first thing out of his mouth is the statement "I just want you to know how very authentic I am." What's your reaction? Well, no matter how earnestly stated (or even felt) that line is, you would seek a way out of the conversation posthaste. Geoffrey Hartman notes, "'Authentic' may be the most inauthentic word around. The authentic person should not have to trumpet identity statements . . ."[29] Neither should businesses trumpet identity statements about their own offerings, because the same thing happens when potential customers encounter advertising or packaging copy that proclaims the authenticity of an offering or the business that offers it—they head the other way. The very act of *saying* some thing is authentic immediately leads consumers to *doubt* said authenticity.

It's no way to render the real. What University of Texas architecture professor Michael Benedikt says of buildings applies to all economic offerings: "The moment one tries to be real, tries to be authentic, and the trying is detected, the bubble bursts and inauthenticity spills out."[30] Therefore, let us establish these three Axioms of Authenticity:

Axiom 1.

If you *are* authentic, then you don't have to *say* you're authentic.

Axiom 2.

If you *say* you're authentic, then you'd better *be* authentic.

Axiom 3.

It's easier to *be* authentic if you don't *say* you're authentic.

So, do you proclaim your offerings, or your business, to be real? Original? Genuine? Sincere? Authentic? If so, you may find your customers calling you fake. Contrived. Disingenuous. Phony. *Inauthentic.*

Really? Really. Read on.

4

Rendering Authenticity

WHAT TO DO

WHERE DO PEOPLE, AND BUSINESS, TURN TO SATISFY THEIR desire for authenticity? One place is to the past. Being forever gone and inalterable, the past represents an ideal form of authentic experience—the *pure*. Of course, just as travel to past times is impossible, such purity is unattainable. Yet people do gain a measure of this pure past through a whole host of here-and-now experiences. Think of such quintessential cultural encounters as downing a pint of beer in an English pub, sipping coffee with a Sacher torte in Vienna, participating in a formal Chinese tea ceremony, eating sushi in Japan, having a sauna in Finland, and taking in a baseball game in the United States. These activities constitute forms of cultural tourism, encounters with the past preserved in rituals. Not just pastimes but *past times*.

For businesses that do not enjoy such status as an idealized cultural ritual, however, you must move beyond any attempt to be pure—to do so would be rather like telling a start-up enterprise to "be old"—and render authenticity through other methods. To do that, you need your own means of understanding the world of business past, present, and future.

An Economic Theory of Everything

The Progression of Economic Value from our previous book *The Experience Economy* provides an economic Theory of Everything (TOE).[1] Our TOE not only describes events in commerce at a macro-economic level but also prescribes actions for businesses at a micro-economic level.[2] As we shall see, this economic TOE provides a unique perspective on rendering authenticity within companies and their economic offerings.

The concept of "economic offering"—what a company sells to a customer—lies at the very core of the Progression of Economic Value, as seen in figure 4-1. While economists generally recognize three distinct economic offerings (commodities, goods, and services) we discern two more, experiences and transformations:

- *Commodities* are extracted from the earth—raised, mined, or harvested as animal, mineral, or vegetable—and then exchanged in the marketplace as raw, fungible offerings

- *Goods* are the tangible things manufactured from commodities

- *Services* are intangible activities delivered on behalf of individual customers

- *Experiences* are memorable events that engage individuals in an inherently personal way

FIGURE 4-1

The progression of economic value

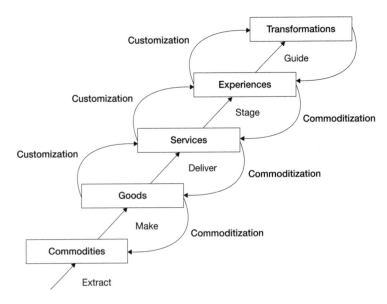

Source: B. Joseph Pine II and James H. Gilmore, *The Experience Economy: Work Is Theatre & Every Business a Stage* (Boston, MA: Harvard Business School Press, 1999), 166.

- *Transformations* are effectual outcomes that guide customers to change some dimension of self

Experiences and transformations have always been around; they're not new economic offerings, just *newly and explicitly identified.* With experiences, customers pay for the time they spend with a company, rather than for the activities the company delivers (as with services), the things it produces (goods), or the stuff it trades (commodities). And with transformations, the customer *is* the product. The customers of a management consulting firm, for example, do not merely want ideas (the commodities of the industry), reports (goods), analyses and advice (services), nor even workshops (experiences); they want to *transform,* to become a better business as a result of purchasing consulting offerings. The same holds true for many consumer establishments—for example, fitness centers, hospitals, educational institutions, wealth management companies. In each case, their customers want to achieve and sustain their aspirations. Such industries proliferate in response to the consumer plea, "Change me!"

So how does this progression—commodities, goods, services, experiences, and transformations—represent an economic TOE? The five forms of economic offerings constitute a simple model explaining the entirety of what can be commodified—bought and sold in commerce. You can classify any commercial offering into one of these five categories.

Furthermore, a set of unifying forces acts to facilitate the progression. The first dynamic is *commoditization,* which, like the force of gravity, is always there, dragging down every offering that isn't already a commodity. In the world of business, goods become commoditized—treated as fungible commodities—when customers no longer care about an item's manufacturer, brand, or features. Instead, customers in essence care about three factors, and three factors only: price, price—and price.

The past several decades have yielded rapid commoditization of goods for two principal reasons: Wal-Mart and the Internet. The former's superior logistics capabilities and buying power greatly reduced the cost of household goods. The latter, by ensuring constant availability and price transparency, compels companies to reduce the cost of their own goods. The rise of the Service Economy exacerbates the trend: increasingly commercialized services cause goods to be commoditized as both consumers and businesses begin to devalue tangible goods in favor of intangible activities. The resulting price pressure causes manufacturers to offer new services to differentiate themselves, which further devalue goods—a vicious cycle.

The same pressure is now exerted on services. First, Wal-Mart increasingly offers such services as food preparation, photo processing, optometry, auto repair, and even banking and healthcare; while the Internet increasingly provides a platform to offer low-cost services such as brokerage, information, and technology. Second, that same vicious cycle of commoditization plays out on this level now that experiences have come to the fore, as both B2C and B2B service providers develop new experiences to differentiate themselves, further devaluing services.

Further, the money consumers save shopping at Wal-Mart or online enable the purchase of other, more highly valued, economic offerings (especially experiences and transformations) that would otherwise not be affordable. Indeed, as economists like to say, all change happens at the margin—and we daresay that at the margin there are families in the United States that can, for example, now send one or more children to college simply because Wal-Mart and the Internet exist.

The other dynamic at play is *customization*, an antidote to commoditization—a means of progressing from one economic offering to the next.[3] Commodities, being fungible, cannot actually be customized, so this dynamic begins with the realization that customizing a good automatically turns it into a service.[4] Consider the three primary economic distinctions between the two. Goods are standardized, but services customized, done *just for a particular customer*. Goods are inventoried after production, but services delivered *on demand*. Goods are tangible, services intangible—but part and parcel of customizing is the *intangible service* of helping customers figure out exactly what they want. Dell, the world's premier mass customizer, does not make personal computers and place them in inventory like most other manufacturers; it is a computer-making service, configuring PCs only in response to actual orders.

Similarly, customizing a service automatically turns it into an experience. A prime example: Cleveland-based Progressive Insurance, which sends its claims adjusters in Immediate Response Vehicles (IRVs) to the accident site itself. Arriving on the scene, the adjuster handles any emergency situation, responds to the claimant's emotional needs, and whenever needed, arranges for a tow truck and replacement vehicle. Then, using a laptop computer, he adjusts the claim right there and then—in the vast majority of the cases handing the policyholder a check on the spot. Progressive turns the pain of an accident—and the avoidance of any claims headaches—into a positive, memorable experience.

Via this same heuristic, customizing an experience automatically turns it into a transformation—for an experience designed to be exactly what an individual person (or business) needs at an exact moment in time, can't help but create what is often called a *life-transforming experience*. If a company customizes one or more experiences so completely in tune with individual needs, the process can't help but transform.

Note how in figure 4-1 the customization and commoditization dynamics stop with transformations. That's because customizing a transformation would mean perfecting human beings—which no longer would be the province of Economic Man.[5] Moreover, transformations can't be commoditized like the other offerings because of the uniqueness inherent in being human.[6] So, there are five and *only* five forms of commercial output—defining everything economic.

Framing the Landscape of Authenticity

Because this Progression of Economic Value—with its five economic offerings and two counteracting dynamics—is an economic Theory of Everything, it frames the possibilities for rendering authenticity. We used it in exploring the landscape of authenticity to discover five genres of perceived authenticity, each corresponding to one of the five economic offerings (while applicable to any and all offerings):

Commodities—*Natural* authenticity

People tend to perceive as authentic that which exists in its natural state in or of the earth, remaining untouched by human hands; not artificial or synthetic.

Growers of organic foods, in forsaking pesticides and fertilizers, appeal to this genre of authenticity. As do numerous soap manufacturers, such as Indigo Wild and the Rocky Mountain Soap Company, which handmake soap in slabs from only natural ingredients (like goat's milk and kiwi seeds), using little packaging and exposing the soap so one can see and touch the bar.

Goods—*Original* authenticity

People tend to perceive as authentic that which possesses originality in design, being the first of its kind, never before seen by human eyes; not a copy or imitation.

Almost everything Apple designs—from the iPod to the Genius Bar in its Apple stores—seeks to appeal to this genre of authenticity. Even its slogan, "Think Different," is originally ungrammatical. Likewise, Blue Man Group appeals to original authenticity, with three blue men doing things on stage no one has ever seen before.

Services—*Exceptional* authenticity

People tend to perceive as authentic that which is done exceptionally well, executed individually and extraordinarily by someone demonstrating human care; not unfeelingly or disingenuously performed.

Any company that encourages its people to genuinely care about customers and respond to their individual needs—think of Nordstrom or Southwest Airlines in industries known for treating customers anonymously and often downright poorly—appeals to exceptional authenticity.

Experiences—*Referential* authenticity

People tend to perceive as authentic that which refers to some other context, drawing inspiration from human history, and tapping into our shared memories and longings; not derivative or trivial.

Those iconic experiences mentioned at the beginning of the chapter—drinking beer in England, the Chinese tea ceremony, and so forth—all exhibit referential authenticity, drawing their inspiration from the rituals of long-standing cultures. Further, whenever you read a review that says a novel or movie is "real" or "authentic" it is because the novelist or director renders their work referentially real, a verisimilitude of real life.

Transformations—*Influential* authenticity

People tend to perceive as authentic that which exerts influence on other entities, calling human beings to a higher goal and providing a foretaste of a better way; not inconsequential or without meaning.

The wave of interest in sustainability in building construction—for homes, offices, and factories—stems from this genre of authenticity, as do fair trade practices and the like. Even Hard Rock Cafe's tagline, "Save the Planet," seeks to render the restaurant venue more real via influential authenticity.

In any offering appealing to authenticity you encounter one or more of these five genres—and occasionally all five. Consider an entity explicitly chartered with preserving the past—the United Nations Educational, Scientific, and Cultural Organization, or UNESCO. In determining which venues it places on its World Heritage List of protected sites, UNESCO issued "Operational Guidelines for the Implementation of the World Heritage Convention"—a set of rules for meeting "the test of authenticity" based on "design, material, setting, workmanship" as well as "use, tradition, and spirit/feeling."[7] The rules follow the five genres of authenticity: "materials" (natural), "design" (original), "workmanship" (exceptional), "setting" (referential), and "spirit/feeling" (influential).

You find the five genres across a wide variety of circumstances. For example, look at the topics addressed in the 2005 Oxford Symposium on Food and

Cookery, as reviewed by the *Financial Times*: the "natural evolution" of European cheeses (natural), "place of origin" of certain dishes (original), "distinctive food" (exceptional), "recreating" dishes (referential), and how "industrialisation caused . . . authentic dishes to disappear" (influential).[8]

The world-renowned timepiece merchant Tourneau once ran full-page ads for its blowout sale, "Watchfest." As "the undisputed authority in the watch industry" (influential), Tourneau touts its sales event as "the biggest thing to happen since Daylight Savings Time" (referential) featuring "the world's largest selection of watches under one roof at one time" (exceptional) including "one-of-a-kind timepieces and new collections never before seen in the United States" (original); and as part of the gala event, one can "enter to win a 10-night trip for two to Australia" (natural). It all adds up to one fine way of rendering authenticity, since you cannot mistake these watches for all the fakes from China.

Interestingly, a place one of us encountered in Chengdu, China—the ten-million-plus-populated capital of the Sichuan province—effectively uses all five genres of authenticity. Jin Li Street exudes authenticity to most anyone who visits. Over four million visitors every year escape the downtown drudgery when they walk through a tower gate and enter a street lined with a tea house, restaurant, hotel, shrine with contemplative gardens, and numerous shops housing artisans who are making and selling their wares on site. Visitors can also experience a ceremonial tea and a Sichuan dinner after they stroll the 350 meters of gardens and shops.

Appealing to natural authenticity, Jin Li's centerpiece is the ancient contemplative gardens, and every material used throughout is traditional, simple, and *natural*—wood, tile, and brick. The native Sichuan artisans gathered from various parts of the province speak directly to *original* authenticity. The street bespeaks *exceptional* authenticity in the uncommon manner everything is done, from construction techniques to ceremonial rituals to personal service. The place even employs *referential* authenticity, for it is not an ancient street—one meaning of Jin Li is "Fantasy Land"—but a former residential area completely rebuilt (except for the original shrine and gardens) and opened in October 2004. One of its proprietors, Xia Jia, remarks, "The ancient Jin Li Street has faithfully restored the style of the ancient town of Western Sichuan."[9] She and her husband undertook this restoration, with financial backing (not to mention artifacts) from the nearby Wuhou Temple Museum, not just to *restore* that ancient style but *preserve* it, not only for tourists to visit but for the artisans to practice their craft and find ready markets—directly appealing to *influential* authenticity. In no way a tourist development, Jin Li Street was created for the inhabitants of Chengdu.[10] If it is now a tourist trap, it's only because it first became a *resident trap*.

Examine any offering you find authentic—commodity, good, service, experience, or transformation—and you will find one or more of these five genres behind your perceptions, whether explicitly or beneath the surface. The categories are admittedly capacious. In finding ways to render your own offerings authentic, it will not suffice to appeal to some generic form of authenticity; rather, employ one or more genres—natural, original, exceptional, referential, or influential—specifically and intentionally. To jumpstart such thinking, let's examine each genre in more detail.

Natural Authenticity: Infuse Elements of Nature

People tend to view as authentic that which is natural—organic ingredients, simple products, unpolished processes, untamed places, and even innate change. When naturally authentic, commodities best remain unprocessed; goods properly exhibit a simple, streamlined plainness; services are straightforward and unassuming; experiences occur without needless embellishment; and transformations happen spontaneously.

Consider this somewhat random assortment of words:

brown   ground   darkened   dirt   burnt   organic   raw
     crude   native   simple   bare   pristine   naked green
  exposed   open   sunlit   sparse   empty   blank ordinary
 island   mountain   clean   rural   khaki   tan   hard   whole
   fluid   airy   attic-like   chocolate   coffee   tobacco flawed
   rough   ragged   coarse   unkempt   crisp calm wild   remote

What images come to mind? What places? Which companies? Which particular offerings? Why? Whatever your particular answers, you can be sure that natural authenticity is at work.

Starbucks poetically describes its Black Apron Exclusives brew of El Salvador Estate Pacamara coffee as follows:

> *The equatorial sunlight*
> *and the rain forest*
> *and the mineral water*
> *and the mist*
> *and the volcanic soil*
> *have made you an exotic cup of coffee*

Think of your favorite or most frequented Starbucks—its earth tones, eclectic music, functional furniture, aromas and tastes. It all represents an appeal to natural authenticity.

Retailers increasingly apply natural authenticity to their design. From large chains—such as Chipotle Mexican Grill restaurants, Bass Pro Shops or Cabela's outfitters, or Smith & Hawken home and garden stores—to any number of local merchants, we see natural elements used to appeal to natural authenticity. Carol Letourneau, proprietor of the hair salon Special Effects in White Bear Lake, Minnesota, remodeled the place a few years ago, taking out the bright lights, the white floor, and the ceiling-high partitions, replacing them with diffused lighting, exposed materials, earth colors, and lowered partitions that greatly increased the level of background noise. Where once people whispered so as not to be overheard, they now talk normally as the ambient noise creates an air of privacy. The hair care products on the shelf: Aveda, naturally, with images of earth, air, fire, and water on all its packaging.

At P.G.C. Hajenius, a cigar shop in Amsterdam, the smell of the raw and lit tobacco for sale permeates the place, with the finest cigars placed on individually cupped wooden display stands. A museum recounting the store's 180-year history graces its second-floor balcony; below, cigar aficionados light up while enjoying a cup of coffee or tea, reading, or conversing with friends. Jan Kees De Nijs, the store's genteel longtime manager, revealed the secret to Hajenius' success today: its management always refused to sell the cigarettes, newspapers, magazines, soft drinks, and lottery tickets on which nearly every other tobacco shop around the globe now depends. Lacking the clutter of such unnatural goods, Hajenius focuses on having the best cigar store experience through its many appeals to natural (not to mention a touch of exceptional) authenticity.

You can also see this approach in the decor and provisions of Anthropologie home and fashion stores, in the setting and treatments of a Canyon Ranch spa, in the entire tenor of L'Occitane en Provence personal body care stores, and in the environs of the Sand Hills golf course in Nebraska. Nebraska's very remoteness contributes to the golf course's natural appeal. One visitor called it "one of the most buzz-worthy courses in the country," noting that the holes spread "so naturally through the remote landscape in Nebraska that it seems more a discovered place than a constructed one."[11] Such appeals to natural authenticity need not start with the ground itself, as at Sand Hills. They can vary from rather mundane enhancements to a current offering, such as unpainted golf tees, to altogether new offerings, such as "crossgolf," where one plays on a fallow field, down an open road, or across an urban landscape.[12]

Tremendous opportunities exist to build big business around natural offerings. Think organic. Organic food represents a $12 billion industry today, and is growing at a rate of over 20 percent per year.[13] Grocery chain Whole Foods lies at the epicenter of this trend, but most grocery stores—even Wal-Mart—now have an organic section, while organic food suppliers no longer consist solely of mom-and-pop farmers, cooperatives, or even such widely distributed brands as Silk Soymilk, Nantucket Nectars, and Honest Tea. This last company exemplifies how to grow a business using natural authenticity. Inspired by the Chinese emperor Shen Nung, who discovered tea in 2730 BC, Honest Tea emphasizes water-and-leaves simplicity. The name of each tea (such as First Nations peppermint and Jakarta Ginger Decaf) tells a story, while primitive art forms (Chinese rubbings, oil paintings, hand sketches, and so forth) adorn the labels. The company formed vendor partnerships with various indigenous peoples and proudly displays the official "USDA Organic" logo atop its bottle caps.

Note that changes in such official standards of authenticity may redefine a business. For example, the loosening of U.S. Department of Agriculture rules in 2005 to allow thirty-eight synthetic ingredients in some organic items set off a firestorm of controversy surrounding just what "organic" means today (and in large part accounts for the rapid growth in the industry as Kraft, General Mills, Dean Foods, and others enter the field).[14] Given this relaxation of standards, businesses must forthrightly state the specific details of their behind-the-scenes operations and candidly share how certain motivations dictate what they will and will not do in their business.

In the food industry, natural authenticity is not limited to organic; heirloom produce makes this appeal, as does "raw-foodism." This nascent movement promotes eating uncooked "living foods," based on the belief that consuming cooked foods leads to illness and lethargy. Witness too the natural wine movement. Going *vin naturel* requires employing wine-making methods (not grape-growing methods—those concern organic farming) that minimize intervention *of any kind* that will affect flavor. Natural wine bars that specialize in such raw vintages have been described as "ragtag" and having "more in common with a college dorm" than a typical wine bar.[15]

Such rawness—a hallmark of natural authenticity—applies in many industries. Everyone knows real leather has blemishes, and that in restoring antiques, one must maintain "the look of wear."[16] The most fashionable T-shirts come off the shelf looking most worn, with crudely drawn images and gruff messages offering a popular alternative to "the bland uniformity of the mass-marketed 'vintage' lines found in every mall."[17] Flaws are all the rage with denim jeans, of course, with some companies such as Prps—whose Web site also exhibits a certain rawness while prominently proclaiming "Authenticity is our first priority"—producing nothing but imperfect pairs. Many jeans buyers now concern themselves not with the quality of material but the "quality of the flaws," with fanatical consumers moving "onto new styles long before actual durability becomes an issue."[18] The International Garment Finish Company processes five thousand pairs of jeans per day—at an average cost of $7 per pair, with some commanding a $50 per pair fee—just to make jeans for such brands as Habitual, Yanuk, Tag, and Taverniti look worn and battered. From basic "denim washing" in an $80,000 Italian-made washing machine filled with pumice stones to create a worn look, lasers and grinders to create holes, brushes dripping potassium permanganate to replicate dirt stains, and staplers making wrinkles (called "whiskers" in the industry), the processing enables the jeans to command hundreds of dollars per pair.[19]

Other companies appeal to natural authenticity by emphasizing a particular raw material. Consider Jamba Juice's countertop growing, cutting, and crushing of wheatgrass to produce shots of "pure liquid sunshine," symbolizing the company's promise to use "wholesome ingredients" and provide "real nutrition."[20] Also consider how companies are integrating wood into otherwise synthetic offerings: Topps embeds pieces of wood from an "authentic game-used bat" inside individual baseball cards; adidas inserts "real hardwood in the heel and forefoot" of its T-Mac 5 model of basketball shoes; and Target provides gift cards of wood.

In contrast, others go bare, and deemphasize materials altogether. Nike's new Nike Free line of running shoes "mimics the feeling of running barefoot on grass."[21] Several motorcycle manufacturers offer "naked bikes" that leave the engine and other parts uncovered by any side panels. Honda's 919 "runs around naked," according to its brochure; Kawasaki's Z1000 is heralded as "the ultimate naked sports bike" and, moreover, "supernaked."[22] Bare Escentuals of San Francisco takes the same tact in the cosmetics industry. Its bareMinerals line offers the "look and feel of beautiful bare skin."

More and more women enjoy the offerings of MaryJanesFarm of Moscow, Idaho. Founder MaryJane Butters proclaims, "I'm going to create the new face of agriculture."[23] Compared to Martha Stewart, MaryJane clearly comes across as more farmhand than homemaker, more country than suburban, and definitely more cultivated than cultured. Butters offers not only organic foodstuffs but also American Rural Made household accessories, subscriptions to *MaryJanesFarm* magazine, and a series of *Farmgirl* books, as well as tours and events at her working farm, a bed and breakfast, and apprenticeships at her Pay Dirt Farm School.

Florida developer St. Joe Company similarly brings a more natural lifestyle to the masses, offering "new ruralism" in some of its residential projects.[24] St. Joe's developed "Rivercamps" communities in areas of Florida with very low population densities, providing rustic homes with instant access to woods and wildlife. Each development includes a resident "camp master" who organizes bird-watching and stargazing for residents. KJW Developers of New Jersey developed an office park in Morris County featuring barnlike buildings and a newly constructed "old mill," marketed to the self-employed as an alternative to working out of a home office in some cookie-cutter development amid the northern New Jersey sprawl (which once was farmland).[25]

These residential and commercial developments foreshadow a significant trend in our living spaces. Journalists often cite William McDonough, former dean of the School of Architecture at the University of Virginia, for introducing "ecological intelligence" into the design and construction of dwellings from skyscrapers to single-family homes. With buildings consuming nearly 40 percent of the energy used in the United States, and the United States consuming a lion's share of the world's energy, "green architecture" has finally started to influence commercial real estate developers. The *Wall Street Journal* called the trend "the most talked-about topic in the architectural universe."[26] So what makes a building green? Use of recycled materials for construction, roofs covered with grass or other vegetation to reduce heat gain, metal floor grates at entrances to minimize flow of particulate matter into the air, air-conditioning systems that capture night air for daytime cooling, water-efficient landscaping, wildlife friendliness (especially to birds), more natural sunlight indoors and less artificial lighting outdoors, and carpets and paints that emit less carbon dioxide and other gases.

Ecotourism exemplifies going green with experiences. Think not only of junkets to Central America and Australia, but also to Sweden, whose largest forest owner, Sveaskog, advertises itself as "opening up its forest and land to organisers of conferences" in eight different wilderness venues specifically designed for green meetings. More and more Europeans are choosing "green burials" in which "no toxic embalming fluids are used" and "the body is buried in a biodegradable casket instead of one laden with copper or lead, which contaminate [sic] groundwater as it breaks down."[27]

Regardless of how you appeal to natural authenticity—figure 4-2 provides a summary of the particular principles exemplified here, and questions to guide

---

FIGURE 4-2

Natural authenticity principles

Stress materiality	What one raw material might serve as a unifying force in rendering authenticity?
Leave it raw	What have others overly produced or perfected that could instead be offered raw or flawed?
Reek rusticity	In what ways could a less sophisticated offering be appealing?
Be bare	What should be stripped down, left naked, or made bare?
Go green	How could you help sustain the natural world?

your inquiry into the applicability of this genre—the results, not the rendering, must be most evident to the customer. Consider your portfolio of economic offerings as a garden and follow the advice of horticulture expert Maureen Gilmer: "It should never look as though it has been pruned."[28] Throughout that unseen pruning, *infuse your offerings with the elements or properties of nature*, without destroying or demeaning. Filthy, damaging, discourteous, disrespectful, and inhumane offerings do little to render natural authenticity.

Original Authenticity: Precede in Time, Depart in Form

People tend to perceive an offering as authentic if it possesses a strong sense of originality. Few people value knock-off, me-too products; they prefer offerings that originate material functions, product features, service benefits, engaging sensations, or life-altering attributes. Businesses that render original authenticity stimulates the buyer's sense of discovery. Customers respond favorably when a previously unknown substance is discovered, a clever invention developed, a better procedure devised, a captivating story told, or a personal insight gleaned.

The foundational rule of originality is espoused in the seminars of creativity guru Mike Vance, former dean of Disney University: Be Original. Do not fear virgin territory, do what no one else has done before. We present examples here—and throughout the book—not for you to copy but to help you be original. *Extract out*, then *apply* underlying concepts to your own business offerings, discovering what practical, new ideas you can generate. Forget "best practices" that yield parity at best. Think *best principles*—examining the intersection of a working principle with your own situation.

Original authenticity encompasses decades-old brands well identified with their categories, such as Cheerios, AT&T, and even Disney, generally recognized as the originator of the theme park industry (even though De Efteling in the Netherlands preceded Disneyland by three years). Goods with a particular design aesthetic, such as the Apple iPod and OXO kitchen utensils, appeal to original authenticity; likewise services that employ unique processes, such as Progressive's claims adjustment system and its concierge Service Centers. So do truly new-to-the-world offerings that flout accepted norms in an industry, including the Geek Squad or anything from the Virgin mind of Richard Branson. Make unfamiliar combinations, like hybrid produce such as rainbow carrots and peacotums, hybrid cars such as Chrysler minivans and the Toyota Prius, or fusion music across its myriad styles.

Think here of Coca-Cola. Its entire brand positioning has centered around being the *real thing* since 1969—a motif the company comes back to time and again in its advertising. With all its color additives, carbonation, and flavor enhancements, the beverage itself cannot appeal to natural authenticity. Rather, Coke proclaims itself—and consumers generally regard it as—authentic be- cause it is the *original* soft drink. Sure, there were other fountain drinks before it, but Coca-Cola invented the entire category as a national phenomenon, and defends its hard-won territory from Pepsi by being originally authentic. Re- member New Coke? It failed not because it tasted worse than the old version; no, it tasted better, sweeter—more like Pepsi—but because it was completely *fake*. It wasn't the *original* real thing.

Being original is more than just introducing something "new." Witness 7 Up. Going to market as the "Uncola" involved nothing new about the formulation of the soda, but called attention to something old but (previously) ignored: its originality as the, well, Uncola.

Of course, many people do not view the Coca-Cola sold in cans or plastic bottles today as the real thing. For many, the *real* real thing only comes in 6½-ounce contoured glass bottles—a design the company commissioned in 1916 (and later patented) precisely to ensure that consumers wouldn't confuse it with imitations.[29] According to the Associated Press, one Linda Taylor of Washington, D.C., drives two thousand miles round trip twice a year to the last place she can get her beloved original glass bottles refilled—the Coca-Cola bottling plant in Winona, Minnesota.[30] For others, particularly those of Mexi- can descent, the *real* real thing only comes in 355-milliliter contoured glass bottles—recycled many, many times over and stamped "HECHO EN MEX- ICO"—with contents sweetened with cane sugar rather than the high-fructose corn syrup Coca-Cola bottlers in the United States switched to in the 1980s to cut costs. An entire underground supply chain satisfies those in the United States with a taste for Mexican Coca-Cola—whose *original* original formula purportedly has a better "mouth feel."[31]

Why must people travel cross-country or buy from bootleggers to get what they see as authentic Coke? Ostensibly because Coca-Cola—whose president of North American operations called this whole issue "an irritation"—doesn't think U.S. consumers would "consider it authentic" and that it also "would un- dermine the myth that the famous soda is identical everywhere."[32] (We should point out that Coke shatters that myth on its own at the company's World of Coke experience by providing multinational tastings.) Or perhaps the com- pany finds itself so strapped by current bottler agreements that it cannot re- spond to the desires that many customers have for what they see as the original more-real-than-the-real-thing original they can procure locally. In either case, Coca-Cola misses the mark on authenticity for many of its customers.

To hit your mark, stress your firsts—most enterprises have start-up stories worth telling. Stating the company's year of origin—as do Deere & Company ("since 1837"), Steinway & Sons ("for over 150 years"), Sherwin-Williams ("founded in 1866"), the Cleveland Browns ("NFL, circa 1946") or Vans (simply, "66")—merely provides a start. Brooks Brothers goes much further than embroidering "Established 1818" on its labels; one particular print ad tells this story: "In 1896, on a trip to England, John Brooks, the founder's grandson, noticed that polo players pinned down the collars of their shirts to keep them from blowing in the wind. The Original button-down shirt was born. The rest is history."

Anniversaries afford special opportunities to celebrate firsts, as Harley-Davidson did on the occasion of its hundredth anniversary. The company staged "The Ride Home," four simultaneous motorcycle trips that began in Portland, Las Vegas, New Orleans, and Washington, D.C., accumulating riders along the way until the four streams of bikes converged in Milwaukee for a three-day celebration in August 2003.

Hard Rock Cafe does a wonderful job of commemorating its origins by stressing not only the month and year but a specific date, June 14, 1971—the day the doors opened at the very first Hard Rock Cafe in London. We happened to be in that city on Hard Rock's thirty-fifth anniversary and witnessed the world's first theme restaurant promoting all its nonalcoholic fare that day at original 1971 prices. Moreover, the original London location celebrates one day every month as "Rita Day" to honor the very first waitress, Rita Gilligan, who still serves dishes "arm style" as she did that very first day. Each of the 128 (and counting) cafes prominently notes its "Opening Date" (see them all at hardrockcafe.com) and features a unique display of rock 'n' roll artifacts. Any retail-oriented company with numerous outlets should note: the process by which a retailer grows its business—namely, adding more outlets—is the very same process that destroys the brand, as sameness—the commoditizing antithesis of originality—creeps in. Ensuring that different outlets have unique characteristics goes a long way toward maintaining a strong sense of authenticity. No matter your business, you should study your firsts to determine which beginnings deserve calling to attention, and figure out how you can commemorate each in original ways.

Reviving a former original affords another way of appealing to original authenticity, but as Mary Lou Quinlan, founder of marketing consultancy Just Ask A Woman, points out, "Brands that *failed* out of existence are different from brands that *faded*."[33] Find the ones that merely faded away from lack of attention, lying dormant in your portfolio past, and rekindle them, as has been done with Ben Sherman, Biba, Blue Nun, Indian Motorcycles, Ovaltine, PF Flyer tennis shoes, and other such resurrected brands. Revived or reinvigorated brands make an appeal to cherished memories with their brand managers acting as a kind of curator of the authentic experiences of bygone days.

As journalist Ruth La Ferla points out, "Consumers, it seems, invest such lines with a credibility and an authenticity that, in their minds, distinguish them from the come-latelys."[34] For many, the demarcation point is this: it's authentic if it's older than you are.

If you don't have any old brands in-house that qualify, consider obtaining the rights to others. Chinese carmaker Nanjing Automobile Group acquired the old MG brand from the MG Rover Group. David E. Davis Jr. of *Automobile* magazine commented, "It wasn't very long ago that nobody believed the Japanese would build plants in the United States; they did, and they blew everyone's pants off."[35] Again, the Japanese did so by mastering quality. Don't be surprised if the Chinese—as exemplified here with Nanjing—do so by skillfully rendering authenticity.

Most appeals to original authenticity depart from the practices evident in present-day offerings by taking some bold new direction in product, process, or practice. Sometimes that involves blending offerings into some original form, such as *mashups* in the music industry. *The Grey Album*, which matched the vocals from rapper Jay-Z's *The Black Album* with the melodies of The Beatles' *The White Album*, represents perhaps the most successful example of the genre, with one million copies downloaded on a single day, February 24, 2004.[36] Such mixing comes fairly easily with digitizable offerings; as *BusinessWeek* reports, "Hordes of volunteer programmers are taking it upon themselves to combine and remix the data and services of unrelated, even competing [Web] sites. The results: entirely new offerings"—known as mashups as well—such as Housing-Maps.com, bookburro.org, DoubleTrust.net, and ProgrammableWeb.com, a mashup directory of over a thousand such hybrids.[37]

Mix-and-mash offerings also exist in the physical realm of goods, such as the BlackBerry, which performs so many different functions while remaining its own thing. Places also provide prime real estate for original mixing-and-mashing. Because the banking industry had become so very commoditized, Mike Frey, president of the Union National Community Bank (UNCB) of Lancaster, Pennsylvania, recognized his company's need to do something unique—to be something unlike every other bank. So he created the Gold Cafe, a real coffeehouse that also houses a real bank, staffed by "financial baristas" trained (by Bellissimo Coffee InfoGroup of Portland, Oregon) to make a great cup of coffee and (by UNCB) to provide full banking services. It so blurs the distinction between coffee shop and bank branch that it is no longer either, yet remains both.

Or consider Maxine Clark's Build-a-Bear Workshops, where children and their families custom-make their own teddy bears and other plush animals. In her own words, these "are special interactive places for families to come together, have fun, and make their own furry friends."[38] The venues mix-and-mash production factory and retail store to become a retail factory, or simply and appropriately enough, a workshop. Interestingly, in her book *The Bear Necessities of Business*, Clark admits to being "a fan of Steak n Shake," especially two of its own mix-and-mash offerings: Sippable Sundaes (milkshakes mixed with ice cream sundaes) and Side-by-Sides (two flavors of milkshakes uncombined in the same glass).[39]

Go visit Gold Cafe for coffee or a loan, build a furry friend at Build-a-Bear Workshop, or sip a sundae at Steak n Shake, and you'll experience truly original offerings. You can also experience work you've never encountered before by booking with VocationVacations, which enables you to "test drive your dream job" (as its Web site puts it). The company offers a wide portfolio of working vacation experiences that mix-and-mash work and pleasure.[40] We call the concept *paying labor*, not unlike the experience of guests at Build-a-Bear Workshop, who pay to make their own teddy bears.

Rather than make unique combinations of well-established activities, sometimes simply going *against* a known, and well-accepted, practice leads to original authenticity. Consider Toy Machine Bloodsucking Skateboard Company, founded by skateboarder and artist Ed Templeton. It employs what one writer calls "the anti-image image, one that hammers away at the absurdity of advertising to a rebel subculture . . . mocking the clichés of the rebel-focused marketing strategies that sell sneakers, sodas and the other trappings of the skater 'lifestyle.'"[41] Unlike the all-too-many, all-too-predictable advertisements of large corporations featuring skateboarding—think of Tony Hawk promoting bagels, Mountain Dew, roller coasters, and various video games—ads for Toy Machine Bloodsucking Skateboard actually hawk skateboards, and in a highly irreverent way.[42]

Such an "anti-" approach can work for less bloodsuckingly in-your-face businesses. Consider various "antimotorcycles" (and one product reviewer's comments on how they radically depart from well-entrenched traditional engineering and design conventions)—the Vectrix electric maxi-scooter ("the main brake is also the throttle"), Honda Big Ruckus ("a two-wheel urban assault vehicle"), and Yamaha Morphous ("long and low to the ground").[43] Whole new industries can emerge from anti-offerings. Take foosball. Since forming in 2002 in Franconville, France, the International Table Soccer Federation has grown to include over forty national federations, each hosting tournaments and promoting sponsor merchandise. Of foosball's growth as an industry, Jim Stevens, owner of Insidefoos.com, a company that webcasts foosball tournaments and sells highlight videos and DVDs of the action, says, "I think some of it is sort of a backlash. It's an antivideo game thing. It's a real sport. It's a real game. You're not pushing buttons playing digital figures. It's real."[44]

FIGURE 4-3

Original authenticity principles

Stress your firsts	What beginnings and anniversaries deserve commemoration?
Revive the past	What brand, advertising, slogan, material, or memory from the past could provide a new source of inspiration?
Look old	What new elements of your offering could look old?
Mix and mash	What could be mixed and mashed into a single new offering?
Anti-up	What move could you make against conventional norms?

When it comes to rendering original authenticity, we recall a television commercial for Mike's Hard Lemonade that stated: "If you're gonna be original, you can count on being copied." This sentiment reveals the highest objective of rendering original authenticity: to let your competitors be seen and known as copiers. Be original to be real. To accomplish that—using any of the five principles provided in figure 4-3—understand this main point about appealing to original authenticity: *present your offerings as preceding in time or departing in form from others of their kind,* without being completely apocryphal or unwarrantedly audacious, as you can't just make up the circumstances. Slapping "New and Improved!" on your offerings furnishes no more the means of rendering them authentic than does proclaiming them to be "Authentic" or "Real."

Exceptional Authenticity: Be Unique or Unusual

In an age of increasing self-service, poor service, and no service, people tend to desire real offerings that businesses execute on an individual-by-individual basis or in some extraordinary way—whether that be in using some unique substance, customizing things, anticipating and responding to problems, arranging for and extending memorable events, or persevering through difficult circumstances. Key to this lies in taking obvious components of an offering and treating them in a nonobvious way, or performing standard practices in uncommon ways. This may mean the use of rare materials, the inclusion of unusual features, responses of an unexpected kind, unpredictable events, and embracing unconventional wisdom.

Ian Schrager conceived a whole new genre of lodging—boutique hotels—when he "used an unconventional approach and outsider mentality that was deeply rooted in the spirit and ethos of the entertainment industry," creating places that serve as an "alternative to the bland, generic, mass-market hotels that populated the landscape."[45] Thus, he took lobbies mass-produced by hotel chains as checkpoints to gather-to-leave, and instead turned them into social places to mingle-and-stay. Granted, Schrager's hotel offerings also appeal to original authenticity, but as they have been increasingly copied, the exceptional character of each Schrager venue stands out as most real.

This character comes through even more clearly now that he has stepped down as chief executive of Morgans Hotel Group, leaving the hotel business to offer residential homes (as he once left the nightclub business to get into hotels). Read this ad copy for his new residential project, 50 Gramercy Park North in New York City: "CITY LIVING REINVENTED by Ian Schrager: One-of-a-kind, show-stopping, Luxury Residences with all the benefits of a five-star, world-class hotel. An unprecedented level of luxury services and amenities simply not available anyplace else." And Schrager had this to say about the idea underneath the residential reality: "I wanted authenticity. The real stuff . . . It's not slick, overdesigned. I wanted to create a one-of-a-kind place. Here you'll find intimacy, authenticity, and personalization—the antithesis of the mass market."[46]

Sandwiching authenticity between intimacy and personalization provides a wonderful picture of how to appeal to the exceptional. It is not just being different, but different in a way that comes across as authentic by exemplifying a certain attitude of accepting nothing but the utmost in excellence and demonstrating that attitude via individual, extraordinary acts. As Schrager says, "the best formula is no formula."[47]

Almost everyone in the higher end of the hospitality industry understands the exceptional authenticity sought by travelers; almost all advertisements tout how hoteliers "genuinely care" about guests' needs. Doubletree Hotels' full-page ads, for example, promised, "Tonight in the lobby: Genuine Interest." Of course, the actual amenities described—"A friendly staff. Comfortable surroundings. Warm cookies . . . being attentive . . . answering questions . . . or simply taking time out for a smile"—would all have to be exceptionally evident to lobby visitors for the hotel to live up to its pledge.[48]

Think of your most recent hotel fiasco—check-in, check-out, or anywhere in between. Now think about a stay at a Ritz-Carlton. It offers *real* service precisely because it's so *exceptional*. With its motto "We Are Ladies and Gentlemen Serving Ladies and Gentlemen," the company goes beyond just doing the right things to doing them in a way that enhances the stay and heightens the experience, including remembering individual names and faces, fulfilling unique preferences, and having employees drop whatever they're doing to help guests in need (never merely pointing them in the right direction, for example, but personally taking them to a queried destination). In fact, the company now teaches other companies how to provide "Legendary Service." If your last hotel fiasco was at a Ritz-Carlton, well, no one's perfect—just exceptional.[49] But should you encounter any problems at one of its hotels, contact the company about the incident and see how they'll strive to make your *next* visit exceptional.

Sharp HealthCare of San Diego took a cue from Ritz-Carlton and other luxury hoteliers when it redesigned its endoscopy unit at its Outpatient Pavilion with the theme "Five Star Experience." After procedures requiring sedation, nurses now deliver cookies or crackers on a silver tray with juice in stemware—which patients occasionally use to toast "Bottoms up!" Thanks to the work of Sonia Rhodes, vice president of customer strategy, all patients get a handwritten thank-you note from someone they encountered during their time there, making everyone feel special, because at Sharp, patients *are* special.

Such an interaction shouldn't come off as artificially friendly—otherwise it can seem forced and presumptuous. Be frank. Candid, plainspoken words—whether in person or on packaging—as well as straightforward and unassuming actions—whether up front or behind-the-scenes—generally render exceptional authenticity more effectively than going through the all-too-typical motions. Even the intentionally snide and obnoxious food servers at places such as Ed Debevic's and Dick's Last Resort come off as real compared with the humdrum help at many casual dining restaurants. So, too, do Amy and Sarah Blessing, owners of men's clothing store Apartment Number 9, located in the hip Bucktown area of Chicago. They practice what they call "the honest crampdown"—unhesitatingly frank opinions about what does and does not look good on each customer. The two mince no words, in a way that one visitor describes as "abruptly charming—adopting the tone of sisters advising an ignorant brother."[50]

Frankness is also called for when making an apology to customers, something the health-care industry in particular has found incredibly effective in limiting liability after an error. Only, however, when "authentically offered," according to Colorado surgeon Michael Woods, who teaches other doctors how to do it right.[51] The recipient of one such apology—from Sharp HealthCare, as it turns out—makes clear the connection to exceptional authenticity: "They honored me as a human being."[52] Southwest Airlines even focuses one executive, Fred Taylor Jr., solely on investigating customer complaints and service issues. He advocates for customers whenever needed, and then personally writes candid—and, this being Southwest, humorous—apologies to every single customer affected.[53]

Southwest also appeals to exceptional authenticity when it forgoes rules for letting workers respond appropriately to any situation. As president Colleen Barrett notes: "We don't always do anything. We believe in individually handling individual situations."[54] Other appeals to exceptional authenticity include:

- Hand-making or craft-producing, as with fine Swiss-made watches, Cuban cigars, or Belgian lace[55]

- Personal training and performance coaching

- Implementing Total Quality Management programs, such as that resulting in Lexus' "Relentless Pursuit of Perfection"

- Designing offerings for a small set of identifiable and close-knit individuals, such as Harley-Davidson's special lines for police officers and firefighters

- Bringing together like-minded individuals around their passions, such as with Regent Seven Seas Cruises' themed enrichment program, Circles of Interest

- Mass customizing, yielding one-of-a-kind, and especially the consumer's own, designs, such as with Andersen windows, Crushpad wine, or Last.fm's broadband radio stations

Recall our definition of authenticity: purchasing on the basis of conforming to *self-image*. When people create their own offerings to meet their individual needs—designing them, shaping them, touching them (even if only virtually), and causing them to come into being on their own behalf—the results automatically come off as authentic, whatever the offering. Whether craft customized (putting together memory scrapbooks at a party or retail store), systematically customized (stuffing your very own bear at Build-a-Bear), or truly mass customized at high volume and low cost (receiving the exact bricks required to construct your dream design from LEGOFactory.com), the output inherently differs from anything standardized or mass produced. It's not the same thing for everybody—it is something specific, exceptional—*just for me*. Such customized offerings resonate as authentic not only because each is unique but because each matches the customer's self-image.

Another practice that resonates with consumers: "pop-up" stores that throw out retail convention and intentionally last for just a short time. Credited as the originator of the concept, retailer Vacant opened its first pop-up store in London in 2001 for only one month.[56] Numerous manufacturers and retailers have since embraced the concept, with great success. Fostering word-of-mouth buzz, pop-ups tend to stay open only as long as knowledge of their existence separates those in the know from the clueless masses. This serves to render them real. Candace Corlett, a partner with WSL Strategic Retail in New York, explains the rationale for the temporary status of the offerings: "It elevates your feelings about the brand, because so many things have become so boring."[57]

Pop-up stores apply the principle of limited editions from manufacturers and bring the approach to services. Similarly, limited-time events bring the same ephemeral appeal to experiences. However "special" such offerings may be, though, does not mean they automatically render exceptional authenticity. Events quickly become boring if the organizer uses the same agenda and footprint year after year. The marketers of Red Bull energy drink understand how to avoid this complacency trap. Starting in 1991, the company has sponsored a human-powered flying machine competition, called Flugtag (German for "flying day"). At these events, local entrants design their own themed flying machines to be launched off a thirty-five-foot high platform into the water below (most can't actually fly; the farthest any machine has ever traveled in the United States is 195 feet). The competitions make for unusually colorful events, to say the least, drawing tens of thousands of spectators.

Not only are the events themselves unusual, the scheduling pattern of the events is equally so. One of us took in the 2004 competition in Cleveland and was thoroughly disappointed not to see the event return the following year (Red Bull only once ever repeated the event in the same city). When in his travels he encountered a Red Bull exhibit at a trade show, he told the staff of his admiration of Flugtag and asked why the event never made a return engagement. After all, over thirty thousand people attended the Cleveland competition. The Red Bull marketing manager responded, "That's not our M.O.; we don't want to become stagnant, and turning locations off, we've found, helps keep the brand real."

Another way to help keep brands real in this fast-paced world is simply to slow down. Slowness allows customers to notice and enjoy the details of your offerings. The Slow Food movement, for example, began in the mid-1980s and formally organized itself in 1989 with headquarters in Bra, Italy. Today, the association maintains offices in Switzerland, Germany, France, the United States, and Japan, and numbers over eighty thousand members in over a hundred countries. According to its Web site the group seeks to protect "the pleasures of the table from the homogenization of modern fast food and life."[58] While certainly making an appeal to the real via natural and even influential authenticity (from a supply-side point of view), for most consumers the real value derived from slowing down comes (on the demand side) from providing an exceptional respite from the daily grind of life.

Since eating represents such a basic need, it's a logical first place to start promoting a Slower life. To this end, Slow Food activists promote gastronomic culture and agricultural diversity, sponsor taste education courses, and strive to protect various "at-risk" foodstuffs. These efforts are decentralized, relying heavily on the appointment of local "convivium leaders" who organize various food and wine tastings, workshops, and other "moments of conviviality." Establishing Slow Cities is next on the agenda. To join, cities must have under fifty thousand residents and agree to such initiatives as establishing specific environmental policies, maintaining traditional infrastructure, embracing particular technologies that encourage slowness while rejecting others that do not, promoting certain foodstuffs and autochthonous sourcing, being hospitable, and building awareness of the overall Slow ethos. A rudimentary online search uncovers a significant network of farms, retail shops, restaurants, and lodging venues, even in cities whose population exceeds fifty thousand.

Slowing down might be a foreign concept to most Americans, and it is this foreignness that renders exceptional authenticity. Anything different from what we're used to—particularly places, the more exotic the better—creates a sense of "other" that comes off as authentic, such as with Chilean beef, Belgian beer, a Singapore Airlines flight, a zorbing experience, or a Buddhist monastery. Japanese clothing chain Uniqlo plays up its foreignness to lure American shoppers tired of The Gap; CEO Nobuo Domae says, "This is the perfect time to take advantage of our Japan-ness."[59] Similarly, L'Occitane en Provence differentiates itself vis-à-vis more established chains like Bath & Body Works. The foreign trumps the familiar when rendering authenticity. The world's largest hot dog chain, Newport Beach–based Wienerschnitzel, certainly conveys foreignness with its name atop the marquees of 350 outlets.

Let us look at foreignness from a European perspective. Europe's largest fast-food chain, Belgium-based Quick, competes with U.S.-based McDonald's and its American-ness. The chain, founded in 1971, did not pick a European-sounding name for its outlets in Belgium, France, Luxembourg, and the Netherlands. Its tagline may be printed in French ("Nous, c'est le goût") or Dutch ("Je gaat voor zijn smaak"), and so might its menu board, packaging, and other printed materials—but not the marquee above the door. For good ol' foreign fast food, it's gotta be: Quick.

To render exceptional authenticity, *shape your offerings around unique tastes or unusual preferences of customers*, without becoming intrusive or inappropriate. If you care too much it becomes bothersome (as when an overly attentive clerk or an ordering system overloads customers with way too much attention and too much choice). Use figure 4-4 to see how you might apply this genre of

FIGURE 4-4

Exceptional authenticity principles

Be direct and frank	Where and how can you interact more directly and frankly with customers?
Focus on uniqueness	How can you respond to the uniqueness of individual customers?
Go slow	What aspect of your business could be accessed in a much slower fashion?
Treat as temporary	What could you "pop up" and then close on a temporary basis?
Be foreign	What foreignness could be emphasized with uninitiated customers?

authenticity to your offerings, but remember: nothing spoils exceptional intention as unexceptional execution.

Referential Authenticity: Reverently Refer to the Real

People tend to consider offerings that honor some previous place, object, person, event, or idea as authentic. In a fully explored planet, saturated with artifacts of human history, one can gain the perception of authenticity by simply referring to that which is natural, original, exceptional, influential—and, yes, referential.[60]

We first recognized this genre of authenticity while watching a weeklong series about Las Vegas on a cable channel. A film crew was conducting man-on-the-street interviews on The Strip. When asked, "Why do you like Vegas?" not just one but *multiple* tourists answered that they enjoyed the place because it was so "real." Wait a second—aren't "authenticity" and "Las Vegas" polar opposites? While many recoil at the thought, nevertheless a number of people do perceive a level of authenticity in that most ersatz of places. In a town where anything goes, what appeals to such consumers? Any number of referents:

- Bellagio (place: Bellagio, Italy, along Lake Como)

- Luxor (place: ancient Egyptian city; and object: pyramid)

- New York New York (place and time: New York City in the 1930s)

- Mirage (object: volcano)

- Wynn (person: Steve Wynn)

All these themed venues are inspired by sources many tourists are unlikely *ever* to encounter personally. In visiting the next-best thing, they find that these places authentically recreate what they could not otherwise experience. Even the Fremont Street Experience in downtown Las Vegas (self-referentially) appeals to referential authenticity (idea and place: history of neon in Las Vegas). As Anna Klingman observes of the entire city in *Brandscapes: Architecture in the Experience Economy*, "The fantasy has acquired authenticity."[61]

Theme *any* place today and you can't help acquiring referential authenticity. In *The Theming of America*, Mark Gottdeiner explains that themes permeate nearly *every* place: "Nature, itself, is not immune from this transformation to motifs. Government regulation and construction redesign have worked over natural wonders, such as Niagara Falls on the New York-Canadian border and the Grand Canyon National Park in Arizona, to heighten the theme of mother nature in an idealized sense."[62] To theme well, you must be not only reverently referential but also compelling and cohesive, harmonizing every aspect of the offering around the inspired theme. Travel writer Katie Kitamura says such "artificially constructed 'foreign' environments" as Japan's Huis Ten Bosch, The Italian Village, and Parque España offer an "idealized distillation of a foreign culture" and "were created with an eye for detail and authenticity," resulting in "faithful reproductions executed with stunning accuracy."[63] Akira Fujiwara of The Italian Village makes the referential imperative for such accuracy clear: "The crowds won't come unless it's real . . . Somebody who has been to Italy can come here and feel like it's the real thing."[64] Many Japanese also opt for American-style weddings and ministers. For some, holding the ceremony in Tokyo Disneyland isn't enough; they go to Walt Disney World. Says one bride, "It's more real here."[65]

Marketers use product placement—or "embedded advertising"—to position their offerings in normal settings on TV shows. Says Brian Bedol, CEO of College Sports Television (CSTV), "In some contexts, certain sponsors bring authenticity."[66] The same is true for movies, in which actual products—versus fake or disguised brand names—enhance the realism, keeping "the authenticity consistent," as communications professor David Natharius puts it, adding as a section header, "Reality Is More Real."[67]

One industry fully recognizes the need to appeal to consumers via referential authenticity and do it well: video and computer games. Designers strive to make their games ever more realistic—with technology fast approaching verisimilitude—putting real-life backgrounds, brands, activities, and events in every release. Many World War II–themed games, such as Activision's *Call of Duty 2* and Ubisoft's *Brothers in Arms: Earned in Blood*, "are going to unusual lengths to add historical authenticity," according to the *Wall Street Journal*. Ubisoft "produced a two-hour documentary for the History Channel that weaves real footage from D-Day with scenes from the game."[68] Will Kassoy, an executive with Activision, says, "Endemic brands in action and sports games lend authenticity . . . We've found the more games represent the real world, the cooler the game is perceived to be."[69] Ex-military officers now serve as consultants during development. One such consultant, who served in Britain's Special Air Service in Desert Storm, explains, "I know what it is like to do it for real. I want to help bring that to life in the game."[70]

Most simulations guide people either to remember or to discover what the real experience would be like. Strat-O-Matic baseball, a statistics-based board game that's been around for almost fifty years, does so in a low-tech way, yet its "realism trumps all . . . Strat-O-Matic enthusiasts echo one another in raving about its simulation of reality."[71] Flightline Flight Simulation Center in Irvine, California, features fuselage housings with separate computers controlling communications, flight control, and graphics for more realistic flight simulation than offered by gaming consoles using joysticks. Said one Flightline customer about his fellow enthusiasts, "They're all looking for real-world camaraderie. You get out, shake hands and brag with each other face to face"; and according to owner Mike Pohl, "Even the most mundane parts, the decisions they make day to day, are just like the fighter pilots."[72] If it doesn't feel and look real, then it won't be perceived as real.

Paying a tribute to past people, times, and events makes present events and times—and the businesses that offer them—come off as more real.[73] Major League Baseball retired Jackie Robinson's uniform number 42 for new players across all teams in 1997; the New York Yankees not only retire the numbers of their most significant (and beloved) players, but honor them with plaques behind the left-field fence. This works across other industries as well. Ads for Gibson Guitars feature Dickey Betts with his 1957 Les Paul Goldtop and Gary Rossington with his Les Paul Standard, paying a double-person tribute to render current guitar models authentic as well. TeleFlora offers a 15"-tall floral arrangement called Monet's Garden Bouquet, featuring, as one ad describes it, "Spring's most fragrant flowers in an elegant art glass vase inspired by the legendary water lily paintings of Claude Monet."

Evoking particular places, Vegas-like, also works. A 1984 fifty-page travel guide, "America! God Shed His Grace On Thee," represents one of the most persuasive pitches for tourism we've ever seen. It features photographs evoking all fifty United States, interspersed with the lyrics of Katharine Lee Bates' famous hymn, yet every single photograph was taken in *Arizona*. The editors of *Arizona Highways* magazine culled from five thousand photographs the 1 percent that best portrayed America's landscape—rendering the beauty of Arizona more real by revering America, the beautiful.

To get into the reverential spirit of referential authenticity, play our bar game inspired by an article one of us saw in the University of Virginia Darden School of Business student newspaper. In "The Death of Rock and Roll?," coauthors Professor Ed Freeman and his son Ben lamented the current state of music and dared readers to name any album recorded in the past twenty years that "belongs in the same breath" as these ten: Led Zeppelin's *Led Zeppelin II*, Allman Brothers' *Live at Fillmore East*, King Curtis' *Live at Fillmore West*, any Jimi Hendrix album, The Beatles' *White Album*, Carole King's *Tapestry*, The Doors' *The Doors*, The Clash's *London Calling*, Bob Marley's *Legends*, and Cheech and Chong's *Big Bambu*.[74]

We began pondering recordings of more recent vintage, first *associating* a new artist to an older one on the Freemans' list, and then *defining* the newer artists as the combination of two previous artists. The result:

Led Zeppelin + Iggy Pop = Red Hot Chili Peppers

Allman Brothers + Paul Simon = Dave Matthews Band

King Curtis + Joni Mitchell = Mary Lee's Corvette

Jimi Hendrix + Tom Jones = Prince

The Beatles + The Beach Boys = Barenaked Ladies

Carol King + Richie Havens = Tracy Chapman

The Doors + Paul McCartney = Nirvana

The Clash + Bootsy Collins = Kid Rock

Bob Marley + Peter Frampton = Lenny Kravitz

Cheech and Chong + Lenny Bruce = Adam Sandler

Try coming up with your own formulas to gain a sense of how offerings can be rendered authentic by referring to other offerings already perceived as real.[75]

If you remember these rock artists from your youth, perhaps this bar game is one of Nostalgic Pursuit. Creating that feeling of nostalgia can appeal to referential authenticity across the entire progression of economic offerings. Heirloom produce, rotary dial phones, full-service gas stations, Renaissance festivals, ballroom dancing—all evoke a past that customers usually perceive as real compared with more modern offerings.

In appealing to referential authenticity, *reverently refer to something already perceived as authentic*, without imitating or trivializing. Theming easily becomes too silly or unbelievable—as in the Grand Canyon Experience in Las Vegas—or too over-the-top or in-your-face (as with most theme restaurants). There are a number of ways to do so, as seen in figure 4-5.

FIGURE 4-5

Referential authenticity principles

Pay personal tribute	What person could you referentially honor?
Evoke a time	What period of or moment in time could serve as a compelling theme?
Pick a place	What particular place could inspire your offerings?
Make it matter	What place, object, person, event, or idea is worth revering?
Be realistic	What simulated experience could be rendered more realistically?

Influential Authenticity: Impart Meaning

The final genre of authenticity stems from a question, conscious or not, people tend to bring to many purchase decisions: How will this change or otherwise influence me, or others, for the better? Those offerings that stand to alter some dimension of self positively, or promote some higher cause, will generally be perceived as more authentic than those that do not. The purchase and use of an offering always involves something beyond its immediate utility, so merely providing objective value does not suffice for many customers. In appealing to influential authenticity, an offering must actually do what it claims to do—while influencing the world for the better.

For example, Eden Alternative, a philosophy and a movement, helps nursing homes transform themselves into elder-centered communities. It focuses on eliminating the loneliness, helplessness, and boredom so endemic in such institutions. Eden Alternative works to change individual nursing homes from within, beginning with staff, then the surroundings, and finally the residents, especially enabling the latter to interact with plants, animals, and children. Dr. William H. Thomas and his wife, Judy, founded the business on the following ten principles.[76]

1. The three plagues of loneliness, helplessness and boredom account for the bulk of suffering among our Elders.

2. An Elder-centered community commits to creating a Human Habitat where life revolves around close and continuing contact with plants, animals and children. It is these relationships that provide the young and old alike with a pathway to a life worth living.

3. Loving companionship is the antidote to loneliness. Elders deserve easy access to human and animal companionship.

4. An Elder-centered community creates opportunity to give as well as receive care. This is the antidote to helplessness.

5. An Elder-centered community imbues daily life with variety and spontaneity by creating an environment in which unexpected and unpredictable interactions and happenings can take place. This is the antidote to boredom.

6. Meaningless activity corrodes the human spirit. The opportunity to do things that we find meaningful is essential to human health.

7. Medical treatment should be the servant of genuine human caring, never its master.

8. An Elder-centered community honors its Elders by de-emphasizing top-down bureaucratic authority, seeking instead to place the maximum possible decision-making authority into the hands of the Elders or into the hands of those closest to them.

9. Creating an Elder-centered community is a never-ending process. Human growth must never be separated from human life.

10. Wise leadership is the lifeblood of any struggle against the three plagues. For it, there can be no substitute.

Any enterprise, *especially* one denoted by the term "institution," would do well to learn from the principles of Eden Alternative.

You can also learn from offerings that focus on consumers' personal aspirations or the betterment of self: commodities such as nutraceuticals and other "functional foods"; goods such as eco-friendly Simple Shoes; services such as Weight Watchers' points program; experiences such as mountain climbing and whitewater rafting; and transformational offerings like GlaxoSmithKline's Committed Quitters program, which helps smokers break the habit.

These aspirations can be as simple as experiencing art for cultural enlightenment. Susan Sontag wrote, "The aim of all commentary on art should be to make works of art—and by analogy, our own experience—more, rather than less, real to us."[77] The same goes for all product design. As art, it lends influential authenticity and embellishes offerings—liquor and perfume bottles, anything made by Japanese cosmetics manufacturer qiora, the cappuccino served at McCafes (it comes with the McDonald's arches etched into the foam).[78]

Offerings such as architecture that are themselves works of art also seem more, not less, real. As Michael Benedikt says, "In our media-saturated times it falls to architecture to have the direct esthetic experience of the real at the center of its concerns."[79] Think of the Frank Gehry–designed Guggenheim Museum Bilbao or Walt Disney Concert Hall in LA, the Sydney Opera House by Jørn Utzon—or even the Bellagio in Las Vegas by Jon Jerde. Jerde's own intention: "Our purpose is to fabricate rich, experiential places that inspire and engage the human spirit."[80] The Bellagio stands apart, even in Las Vegas, because it is filled with art and art experiences: sculptor Dale Chihuly's *Fiori di Como*; the Conservatory & Botanical Gardens; Vegas' first Gallery of Fine Art; the Bellagio Fountain Show; the design of the casino, shopping streets, hallways, rooms; and, finally, the performances of *O* by Cirque du Soleil.

Cirque du Soleil in and of itself appeals to influential authenticity in the way performances show the possibilities of what the human body can do physically, aesthetically, and lyrically. It is an entirely new art form, in fact; founder Guy Laliberté and his troupe combine busking, the circus, and live theatre in never-before-seen ways. Cirque du Soleil therefore also embodies original authenticity, as attested to by such imitators as Cirque Éloize and Le Grande Cirque.

In addition to personal aspirations, connecting with our *collective* aspirations also directly appeals to influential authenticity. Anything hyphenated with the natural term "eco-" or under the rubric of "corporate social responsibility" qualifies. At a local level, Galactic Pizza of Minneapolis calls its food "Pizza with a Conscience" and posts its "Vision of a sustainable and harmonious Earth" on its Web site. It uses only renewable wind energy to power its stores and 100 percent electric vehicles (weather permitting) for delivery.[81] To promote this kind of attitude at other businesses, dotherightthing.com provides "the place where you can learn and share information about how companies impact the world," where anyone can "Share information," "Learn about the activities of companies," and even "Track the 'social performance' of companies."[82]

Many people look to fulfill their aspirations for humanity through tourism. Global Exchange Reality Tours was founded in 1989 on the idea that "travel can be educational, fun, and positively influence international affairs . . . Our tours provide individuals the opportunity to understand issues beyond what is communicated by the mass media and gain a new vantage point from which to view and affect US foreign policy. Travelers are linked with activists and organizations . . . who are working toward positive change."[83] Over twenty thousand "citizen diplomats" have gone on "delegation" trips to five continents. Malia Everette, director of Reality Tours, describes how these tours go beyond most ecotourism and adventure-based travel: "An Amazon tour in Ecuador . . . would include the usual itinerary of jungle hikes and river excursions and interactions with indigenous peoples, but it would also include a toxics tour, looking firsthand at the impact of oil extraction on the Amazon Basin and what it means to live with that impact."[84] Ideally, after returning home travelers would continue to promote what they had seen firsthand.

Southern Cross Experiences, in South Africa, expertly intertwines the personal and collective aspirations in its corporate safaris and culture and heritage tours. Its mission statement: "Through the use of tailor-made travel experiences in Africa we strive to actively promote a deeper understanding of the culture, wildlife, environment and nature conservation in Africa."[85]

This intertwining of personal and collective aspirations also plays in what we call "three-word offerings": free-range chicken, dolphin-safe tuna, shade-grown coffee, pesticide-free fruit, whole-grain bread, low-carb diet, conflict-free diamonds, and the like. Whenever you see such a qualified offering, you can be pretty sure that its creator hopes you perceive it as influentially authentic. Futurist Rolf Jensen notes that eggs from free-range chickens "have conquered over 50 percent of the market" in his native Denmark because "consumers do not want hens to live their lives in small, confining cages; they want hens to have access to earth and sky . . . [C]onsumers are happy to pay an additional 15 to 20 percent for—for the story behind the egg."[86] That story tugs at people's heartstrings and—by getting them to ascend to the proposition behind the product—their purse strings. Such purchases conform to self-image; Michael Brehme, cofounder of Clipper Teas, which offers teas with Fairtrade certification, explains, "What we consume says who we are, not just to others, but to ourselves."[87] We are what we eat and drink.

Although many companies attempt to appeal to influential authenticity by giving to causes, perhaps with some success, working to actually make a difference themselves provides greater appeal. In *Cause Marketing*, consultant Joe Marconi says, "In many circles, the term *social responsibility* has become synonymous with do-gooders—people whose sole aim is not only to contribute but at times just to be recognized for contributing. Real social responsibility has, in fact, been shown to produce benefits that can be measured in both quantitative and qualitative terms . . ."[88] Ethos Water, for example, makes its intentions clear on every label of bottled water: "Helping children get clean water." Unlike other "socially responsible" brands like Newman's Own, The Body Shop, and Ben & Jerry's, Ethos ties its do-good efforts to *specific* initiatives in *particular* places, like water programs in Ethiopia or Bangladesh. Five cents of every two-buck bottle goes to set water projects throughout the less developed world.

Starbucks bought Ethos Water in 2005, the same year it began putting provocative quotes on its cups under the rubric "As I See It." According to spokeswoman Audrey Lincoff, the reflections get people talking: "If you think back to the history of the old coffee houses, before the Internet, these were places to converse. That's part of what the coffee culture has been for a century or more."[89]

One of the quotations comes from Rick Warren, author of *The Purpose Driven Life*: "You were made by God and for God, and until you understand that, life will never make sense." Such a focus on religion provides another means of appealing to influential authenticity, calling us to think about, if not actually seek out, ultimate meaning in our lives. Bishop T. D. Jakes, pastor of The Potter's House in Dallas, stages a series of huge Christian events, including one, MegaFest in Atlanta, that drew over 100,000 people in both 2004 and 2005. Other Christian gatherings have drawn even more, but MegaFest also draws corporate sponsorships, including Coca-Cola, Bank of America, American Airlines, and GlaxoSmithKline. Similarly, Toyota Scion was featured at the three-day Ichthus Christian music festival, and Jones Soda sponsored the Cornerstone Festival, an alternative Christian rock music festival in Bushnell, Illinois. Jones Soda founder Peter Van Stolk explains, "It's not about religion. It's not very difficult for us to look at the event and see that we have an opportunity to talk to so many kids in one space while they're enjoying something they're passionate about."[90] For Van Stolk, that personal passion justifies embracing religious outlets, the places where many people find meaning in this increasingly unreal world.

Dave Norton, founder of insights consultancy Stone Mantel, points out, "Today, participating in meaningful experiences represents the largest unmet need of Americans . . . More precious than economic capital is cultural capital: religion, country, art, family, and education. These are resources that are literally priceless, from which we draw distinctions regarding our purpose in life."[91] Steve Diller, Nathan Shedroff, and Darrel Rhea pick up this same theme in *Making Meaning*: "Worldwide, consumers are increasingly seeking products and services that connect them through meaning, that jive with their sense of how the world is, or should be."[92] The authors provide a list of meanings that people increasingly value, listed alphabetically so as not to imply any order of importance. Reflecting on these meaning-full concepts is quite a good stimulus for thinking about how to appeal to influential authenticity:[93]

Accomplishment: Achieving goals and making something of oneself; a sense of satisfaction that can result from productivity, focus, talent, or status

Beauty: The appreciation of qualities that give pleasure to the senses or spirit

Community: A sense of unity with others around us and a general connection with other human beings

Creation: The sense of having produced something new and original, and in so doing, to have made a lasting contribution

Duty: The willing application of oneself to a responsibility

Enlightenment: Clear understanding through logic or inspiration

Freedom: The sense of living without unwanted constraints

Harmony: The balanced and pleasing relationship of parts to a whole, whether in nature, society, or an individual

Justice: The assurance of equitable and unbiased treatment

Oneness: A sense of unity with everything around us

Redemption: Atonement or deliverance from past failure or decline

Security: Freedom from worry about loss

FIGURE 4-6

Influential authenticity principles

Appeal to personal aspiration	What aspirations of individuals can you help fulfill?
Appeal to collective aspiration	What shared aspirations among customers can you help achieve?
Embrace art	How can you integrate art into your everyday business?
Promote a cause	What greater social cause can you passionately promote, helping to effect its ends?
Give meaning	What meaningful purpose can you infuse into your offerings?

Truth: A commitment to honesty and integrity

Validation: The recognition of oneself as a valued individual worthy of respect

Wonder: Awe in the presence of a creation beyond one's understanding

Such ways of giving meaning is the final of the five principles that we've covered in this section, which are summarized in figure 4-6.

At the highest level, to appeal to influential authenticity, *impart meaning into your offerings and call customers to a higher purpose* without becoming coercive or threatening. Go gently; no one likes to be forced to contribute to disfavored causes—what you deem as worthy must coincide with the aspirations and self-image of your particular customers.

Applying the Five Genres

Creating worth in an increasingly unreal world where people thirst for the authentic is no easy task. First, you must understand what business you are really in, and specifically which of the five economic offerings—commodity, good, service, experience, or transformation—you are selling. Second, apply one or more of the five genres of authenticity—natural, original, exceptional, referential, or influential—to render your offerings in such a way that your customers regard them as authentic. Realize, of course, that just because you try to appeal to one or more particular genres does not guarantee that any or all of your potential customers will view your offerings as real. You must do it well.

Enterprises may focus primarily or even exclusively on just one genre of authenticity as a means to get real. Such opportunities exist within—to give a few examples—space tourism (the next frontier for exploring truly untouched nature), art (the remaining sphere for absolutely original works), mass customization (the sole platform for efficiently serving customers exceptionally), virtual worlds (the digital promise of creating referential life-forms), and health care (influencing one's practices of wellness).

Alternatively, you could examine your offerings to see how you could apply several, perhaps even all, of the five genres of authenticity. That's not always possible, perhaps not even desirable—a clear and forthright focus on one particular genre often best confers competitive advantage. Do recognize, however, that it will be very difficult to be so purely natural as to be perceived as innately wild, so purely original as to be perceived as the one-and-only, so purely exceptional as to be perceived as perfectly executed, so purely referential as to be perceived as reverently begotten, or so purely influential as to be perceived as profoundly meaningful. For most industries and businesses, therefore, an appeal to multiple genres of authenticity must often be made, combining the means of appealing to your particular customers and their desire for authenticity.

Let these questions be your guide:

- Do your past offerings and actions make it difficult to credibly appeal to one or more particular genres of authenticity? Efforts to pursue such genres may be in vain.

- What genre of authenticity viscerally feels like the best course? Explore this option first, and thoroughly.

- Is there a particular place on earth, a certain raw material, or any other connection to the land associated with your business? If so, look to leverage natural authenticity.

- What genre of authenticity intuitively feels like it would provide the least favorable option? Explore it as a counterintuitive means to render original authenticity.

- Write down an exhaustive list of standard practices in your industry. Do any stand out as an opportunity to do something unique as a means of appealing to exceptional authenticity?

- Does a single place, object, person, event, or idea stand out as most significant in the history of your business? If so, richly explore referential authenticity.

- Does some greater purpose lie in the background—or at the core—of your business concern? If so, consider centering appeals to influential authenticity on that purpose.

Finally, you can gain an authenticity advantage when you fully comprehend what the subject truly means within the world of business. It's not enough to embrace our economic Theory of Everything to understand what you offer today and what genres of authenticity to which you can appeal. You also need insight into *how* to apply this understanding. To achieve this, you must contend with the very nature of the philosophical subject of authenticity as it pertains to the economic subject of business. That is where we now turn our attention.

5

ℱake, ℱake, It's All ℱake

WHY OFFERINGS ARE INAUTHENTIC

WHEN WE SPEAK IN THE NETHERLANDS ON THE SHIFT TO THE Experience Economy, someone invariably asks one particular question, to the accompaniment of numerous nodding heads. Well, it's less of a question than an accusation. And it almost always begins with the same two words: "You Americans . . ."

"You Americans," they say, "like your manmade, artificial, fake, *Disneyland* experiences. We Europeans—we like our real, natural, *authentic* experiences." Thus do they raise a real issue, worthy of a considered response.

The Netherlands Versus Disneyland

First, understand that there is no such thing as an inauthentic experience—because experiences happen inside of us; they are our internal reaction to the events unfolding around us. How we react to what happens at a particular venue depends on who we are, what we've experienced before, how we feel at the time, who accompanies us, and so on. No two people ever experience anything alike. This intrinsic characteristic of experiences makes them inherently personal.

Of course, the environment that serves as *stimulus* for the experience may be more or less artificial, more or less natural. Most Americans probably do prefer more artificially generated sensations than Europeans in general and the Dutch in particular, but a large number loathe Disneyland, would not set foot in a Starbucks, and disdain fast food. Some enjoy nothing more than a day at the beach, enjoying a box lunch of organically grown veggies with a bottle of natural spring water. Conversely, many Europeans visit Disneyland Resort Paris annually, McDonald's weekly, or Starbucks daily.[1]

Further, the experiential stimuli at any locale are never purely natural.[2] There is always some manmade element involved, some enterprise out to make a buck. Even if you were to go for a walk in the woods, there's nothing natural about the car that brought you there, the clothes and shoes you'd wear, or the mobile phone service you'd access in the unlikely event you got lost. Then there's the fact that *you* are there in the natural woods at all. Recall the somber words of warning spoken by Bambi's mother in the Disney animated film: "*Man* was in the forest."

This professed desire for only the real, the natural, the authentic is particularly ironic given that *the Netherlands is every bit as manufactured as Disneyland!* There isn't a square meter of land in the country that hasn't been reclaimed from the sea or otherwise moved, modified, and manicured to look as if it'd always been there. As the saying goes, "God created the world, but the Dutch created the Netherlands." Just take a stroll in the woods and you'll find all the trees lined up in perfect rows.

Comparing the Netherlands to Disneyland in this way yields grudging recognition from our Dutch audiences that indeed *both* places are manmade, artificial, and, yes, fake.[3] Landscape architect Jannemarie de Jonge calls the Dutch countryside "EcoDisney." Her fellow countrymen appreciate seeing cows in fields as kind of a "romantic outdoor theatre," she related to us, while also wanting their milk economically produced.[4]

Of course, there are still huge differences in how people view Disneyland versus the Netherlands. If we conducted a survey to rank their relative authenticity, no doubt the country with the artificial parks would overwhelmingly beat the theme park with the artificial countries. Still, in reality, neither is completely natural; both have been manufactured to increase the enjoyment of residents in the one place and tourists in the other.

Venice Versus The Venetian

We do not wish to single out the Dutch. A comparison of The Venetian (the hotel and casino artificially placed in Las Vegas) and Venice (the city artificially maintained above the Adriatic Sea) illustrates the point equally well. Every year more Venetians flee their diminishing islands to live on mainland Italy at higher elevations, dramatically skewing the ratio of residents to tourists, creating what the *New York Times* calls "a kind of high-art Disneyland."[5] Those diehards who do remain increasingly rely on tourism for a living, often wel-coming changes to Venice because they attract more tourists—while repelling yet more residents. Mayor Paolo Costa worries about the continuing exodus: "It would be like you were in Williamsburg."[6] To put his comment in perspec-tive, *Wall Street Journal* architecture critic Ada Louise Huxtable singles out Colonial Williamsburg as "a careful construct . . . where one could learn a lit-tle romanticized history, confuse the real and unreal, and have—then and now—a very nice time." Her main criticism: Colonial Williamsburg lies "frozen in time," restored to an arbitrary date.[7]

But does that not *already* describe Venice? The City of Dreams remains arti-ficially rooted in the past to attract the very tourists who are driving away the residents. Venetians began managing its water levels in the fourteenth century; today, Alberto Scotti, the chief engineer of the Mose Project, the latest attempt to keep Venice above the water line, acknowledges, "Look, there is no natural environment to recover here in Venice anymore. It has been changed by man for hundreds of years."[8] Like both Disneyland and the Netherlands, Venice is completely contrived. Architect David Mayernik concludes his chapter on Venice in *Timeless Cities*: "Whether in politics, ritual or architecture, no city structured her position so theatrically, rigorously, consistently and consciously."[9]

In *Experiencing Architecture*, Steen Eiler Rasmussen further points out that "Venice itself looms like a mirage, a dream city in the ether. And this impres-sion of unreality persists even to the very threshold."[10] And yet—the city clearly transcends this unreality; it is one of the world's most beloved places. As Mary McCarthy puts it in her landmark travel book *Venice Observed*, "But why should it be beautiful at all? Why should Venice, aside from its situation, be a place of enchantment? One appears to be confronted with a paradox. A commercial people who lived solely for gain—how could they create a city of fantasy, lovely as a dream or a fairy-tale? This is the central puzzle of Venice . . ."[11]

Meanwhile, in Las Vegas the rising number of relocations each year steadily *increases* its ratio of residents to tourists. There, across the street from the Mi-rage, sits The Venetian. Its owner, Sheldon Adelson, believes that folks enjoy his place precisely because of its authentic representation of Venice, with its gondoliers singing renditions of Italian songs while "pushing" their gondolas back-and-forth (actually they glide—like a theme park ride—on tracks).[12] While The Venetian was still in development, Adelson told the *Casino Journal*, "We are not going to build a 'faux' Venice. We're going to build what is essen-tially the *real* Venice."[13] W. Easley Hamner, principal at The Venetian's archi-tects, KlingStubbins, explained, "By visiting [T]he Venetian, millions of people who might never have the opportunity of seeing the real Venice can experience at least a portion of its romance and learn of many of its qualities . . . Unlike other destination resorts in the area, the marble is real, the columns and fa-cades three dimensional, and the entire experience unique."[14]

Many tourists do visit both places, and some even prefer the obviously fake Venetian to the seemingly real Venice. Brand strategist Paul Neal tells the story of visiting Venice himself and overhearing two tourists discussing the famous canals. The husband asked his wife, "What do you think?" She replied, "I don't know. It's not as nice as the one in Vegas."[15] Humorist P. J. O'Rourke contrasted the authenticity of the two places by asking, "Is [T]he Venetian 'essentially the real Venice'? For a Venice that's on the wrong continent, in the middle of a dust bowl and was built last year, the Venetian is surprisingly authentic. The Cam-panile, for instance, is fake, but so's the one in really real Venice. The original Campanile, completed in 1173, collapsed in a heap in 1902, and a replica was constructed in its place."[16]

O'Rourke's observation of the obvious does little to persuade most people that Venice itself is as inauthentic as The Venetian, let alone that The Venetian can make any claim to being as authentic as Venice itself. People know the two places differ not just in degree but in kind. But for those who do see The Vene-tian as authentic, it's generally because they see it referentially *honoring* Venice, albeit in that unique Las Vegas way, just as Venice today referentially honors the Venice of the past in its own unique way. Time and again, visitors en-counter features at The Venetian that resonate with those who come to Vegas seeking escape from the humdrum strip malls, service stations, suburban sameness, and exurban detachment so common in everyday life. For them, it all comes off so real. Really? Really.

Nature Versus Nurture

At least nature is really real, right? In the opening of his book *Nature's Keepers*, science writer Stephen Budiansky carefully describes a walk he took outside his home, and then noted:

> [E]verything I saw this morning was a fake. Everything that I might plausibly have passed off as an example of nature raw, pure, and un-tamed was, in truth, nothing but the work of civilized man. The very grasses in my field are aliens, for a start, timothy and bluegrass and red clover brought to America by seventeenth-century English settlers try-ing for a better hay crop. The sheep and horses and cattle that enrich the soil with their dung are alien imports, too. But for their constant graz-ing, and for the annual visit of the haying machines, the open acres that stretch from my window to the copse at the bottom of the hill would in

just a few years' time be choked with brambles and red-cedars. But even that could hardly be counted a natural process; the return of woods to abandoned farm fields is not nature reclaiming her birthright but nature led only farther astray. Red-cedars readily take over abandoned pastures today only because centuries of grazing by livestock has unnaturally suppressed the hardwoods, such as oaks, that would otherwise outcompete the red-cedars; the very abundance of red-cedar today is an artifact of the dietary preferences of imported farm animals.[17]

In other words, *nature is nurtured*. Man has indeed been in the forest. Our every movement, however unintentionally intrusive, alters the landscape, as Gregg Oelofse, environmental policy coordinator for Cape Town, South Africa, notes: "You can't interact with nature without affecting nature. We are affecting things—we just don't know how."[18]

Today we tend to view woodlands, marshes, rainforests, and even oceans as "pristine wilderness," when in reality we've always molded and shaped the environment to fit our perfectly reasonable needs. It's now common, for example, to view the post-1492 march of Western civilization through the Americas as destroying a native civilization of hunter-gatherers and subjugating the natural lands on which Indians lived, but barely disturbed. But this, too, is romantic outdoor theatre. As Luther Standing Bear, born in 1868 and chief of the Oglala Sioux, declared: "We did not think of the great open plains, the beautiful rolling hills, and winding streams with tangled growth, as 'wild.' Only to the white man was nature a 'wilderness' and only to him was the land 'infested' with 'wild' animals and 'savage' people. To us it was tame."[19]

One of the areas tamed by the Indians is Yosemite, widely regarded as one of the most beautiful areas in the United States. It inspired Ansel Adams' celebrated photographs, which had a profound effect on the American imagination. Arizona State University art professor Mark Klett notes: "What we saw in the Adams photographs is: 'This is nature. And it's beautiful because you're not there'"—as straightforward an acknowledgment of the appeal of natural authenticity as you will ever read.[20] "Nature is good. People are bad," a *New York Times* journalist reported; "The problem was that the nature that inspired [Adams] . . . was partly created by people . . . This western Eden may have seemed like the creator's gift to an expanding nation, but it was, inconveniently, the work of the unwelcome Indians."[21] These Indian settlers "were so successful at imposing their will on the landscape that in 1492 Columbus set foot in a hemisphere thoroughly dominated by humankind," according to writer Charles Mann, in an article that argues that all of what we take today as unspoilt "wilderness" is in reality no such thing. How? "A principal tool was fire, used to keep down underbrush and create the open, grassy conditions favorable for game. Rather than domesticating animals for meat, Indians retooled whole ecosystems to grow bumper crops of elk, deer, and bison."[22]

This taming of seemingly primeval nature occurred not just in the Netherlands and North America, but everywhere mankind has settled. According to a rising number of scholars, even that icon of fading nature (and idol of fervent environmentalists), the Amazon rainforest, is artificial—a human artifact and, in the words of one archaeologist, "among the finest works of art on the planet."[23] And as Colin McEwan, Curator of the Department of Ethnography at the British Museum, says, the rainforest "is often characterised as an essentially untouched natural environment in which man's presence is merely incidental. However, the vast reaches of the rainforest have been lived in and shaped by human hands for thousands of years."[24] Even the *terra preta*, or black earth, of the Amazon—richly prized for its "natural" fertility—is an organic artifact of a thousand years of human activity.

As Mann notes, "Native Americans managed the continent as they saw fit. Modern nations must do the same. If they want to return as much of the landscape as possible to its 1491 state, they will have to find it within themselves to create the world's largest garden."[25] The issue is moot: we already have the world's largest garden, and we call it nature. Dean MacCannell, professor of landscape architecture at the University of California, Davis, asserts: "Every nicely motivated effort to preserve nature, primitives and the past, and to represent them authentically contributes to an opposite tendency—the present is made more unified against its past, more in control of nature, less a product of history."[26]

Cultural analyst Margaret King sums it up beautifully: "From the beginning of human history, we have completely reshaped nature to serve our needs and dreams. In doing so, we have transformed the earth into a series of stage-sets for playing out human values in three dimensions. There is hardly a spot on the planet, no matter how seemingly 'natural,' that has not been adapted to better serve the human condition."[27] Her observation fully applies to:

- The nature around us, which *isn't* natural but in fact an artifact of mankind

- The Venetian, which certainly *isn't* Venice but is a stage-set for many who cannot visit the real place

- Venice itself, which *isn't* the natural descendant of an enduring city but rather one that has been artificially maintained for tourists

- Disneyland, which *isn't* a real place after all but a completely fabricated and manicured fantasy environment

- The Netherlands, which *isn't* a natural landmass of abundant resources but rather a wonderfully recreated (and reclaimed) stage-set for Dutch national theatre

It's all fake, fake, fake.[28]

Our Worldview and Welcome to It

Things are not always as they seem. We mold our environs, our talk, our actions, our experiences—the very lives that we lead—so that *everything* comprises a reality we fabricate ourselves—*especially* the economic offerings we create through business. Despite how much people today desire authenticity in a world of paid-for experiences, businesses cannot fabricate authenticity from thin air. Despite claims of "real" and "authentic" in product packaging, nothing from businesses is really authentic. *Everything is artificial, manmade, fake.* And though businesses can appeal to the five genres of authenticity so that customers perceive their offerings as authentic, that view is still a mere perception of reality.

These are bold statements. To see how we came to this worldview requires a brief tour of philosophical thought on authenticity. As a rule, philosophers and social critics discuss authenticity from the viewpoint of the solitary human being. We too must understand the concept from this perspective and then apply that understanding to the world of business. There is, of course, a collection of thought on authentic leadership that follows directly from this focus.[29] In places we necessarily touch on what executives, managers, and workers must do to contend with the new consumer sensibility, yet our focus remains on the larger issue: the authenticity of *economic offerings* themselves and by extension the *businesses* that offer them and the *places* in which they are offered.

In his seminal *Sincerity and Authenticity*, Lionel Trilling observes that authenticity "implies the downward movement through all the cultural superstructures to some place where all movement ends, and begins."[30] It is the alpha and the omega of modern-day man's conception of self, which Trilling recognizes in his discourse as he moves from discussing the "idea of sincerity" to the "ideal of authenticity."[31]

Trilling discusses at length the eighteenth-century philosopher Jean-Jacques Rousseau, who, with his veneration of "the noble savage," was perhaps the first to fully articulate an ideal of authenticity. Trilling observes that, for Rousseau, authenticity consisted in "merely being not inauthentic."[32] Such negation, in fact, drives much of how authenticity has been defined, from Friedrich Nietzsche and Søren Kierkegaard to Jean-Paul Sartre and Albert Camus: "All agree in principle that any positive definition of authenticity would be self-nullifying."[33]

We have distilled three distinct ways in which such philosophers negatively define authenticity:

- **That which is *not* of Man.** Trilling says, "We understand *a priori* that the prescriptions of society pervert human existence and destroy its authenticity."[34] This thrust was the primary contribution of Rousseau, "from whom we learned that what destroys our authenticity is society—our sentiment of being depends upon the opinion of other people."[35] In other words, *qualifying* one's choices by the norms of society (Mankind with a capital M) yields the inauthentic.

- **That which is *not* Mechanical.** Trilling says, "It was the mechanical principle . . . which was felt to be the enemy of being, the source of inauthenticity."[36] In *Inauthentic Culture* Jay Newman calls dehumanization "a central theme of existential philosophy" and states, "As for mechanism, we know how in moments of existential insight we can look at our fellow human beings, and sooner or later at ourselves, and be struck by the degree to which human activities, including creation, promotion, and appropriation of cultural products, have become mechanized routines."[37] In other words, *altering* the natural order with machinery yields the inauthentic.

- **That which is *not* Monetary.** Trilling says, "Money, in short, is the principle of the inauthentic in human existence."[38] Sartre said that his ultimate objective in examining authenticity was to "promote a 'kingdom of ends'" as against modern society with money as its means.[39] Communications theorist Corey Anton, in *Selfhood and Authenticity*, similarly emphasizes this in saying that "Authenticity cannot be bought with either symbolic or monetary capital because money, by its nature, works as a system of exchange and substitution. And substitution . . . is counter to particularity and originality, hallmark characteristics of authenticity."[40] Dean MacCannell puts it simply: "The dividing line between structure genuine and spurious is the *realm of the commercial*."[41] In other words, *commercializing* any activity yields the inauthentic.

Of course, the last two negations follow from the first, as both money and machines are manmade devices, created within and for society.[42]

From this 3M Model of Inauthenticity—Man, Machine, and Money—we can conclude: *Nothing offered by any business is authentic; it's all artificial and utterly fake*, being manmade, mechanical, and monetary.[43] If you *pay* for any thing and thereby enter the realm of the commercial, that thing becomes an offering and therefore cannot be authentic. On the flip side, if you *sell* some thing that is deemed to be a labor of love, then you are regrettably "selling out" to the commercial realm and therefore it becomes indisputably inauthentic.

Fake, fake, fake, it's *all* Fake! We realize many, perhaps most, readers will not like this conclusion, and others won't agree with it. Some may even rebel at it. But all should understand that it is simply the logical conclusion that follows from centuries of philosophical thought on authenticity pointing out how being of Man, of Machine, and of Money makes any one, and any thing not done for or by oneself, inauthentic.

The Authenticity Paradox

Do not despair. Remember what we said at the outset of this chapter: there is no such thing as an inauthentic experience because experiences happen inside us. Therefore, we remain free to judge our experiences with any economic offering as authentic or not. Businesses that offer them therefore can, whether intentionally or by happenstance, gain the perception of authenticity. The best word to describe this process is, once again, *render*. Businesses can render their inauthentic offerings as authentic. Doing so requires embracing this essential paradox: all human enterprise is *ontologically* fake—that is, in its very being it is inauthentic—and yet, output from that enterprise can be *phenomenologically* real—that is, it is perceived as authentic by the individuals who buy it.

This Authenticity Paradox lies at the core of thinking rightly about authenticity in business. Individuals long for authenticity, but struggle with how to gain it. Businesses long to fulfill that need by selling authenticity, but cannot really provide it. Yet consumers do perceive many inherently inauthentic offerings—as they do countries, cities, places, and nature—as undeniably authentic, so enterprises must learn the discipline of rendering their offerings as real.

Recall from chapter 3 how reality TV programs *qualified*, *altered*, and *commercialized* reality—effectively employing the very three factors underlying the 3M Model identified above—to render the patently fake in a way that programmers, viewers, and critics alike all assent to the "reality" label. By staging unusual settings and situations, employing unorthodox camera angles and filming techniques, exploiting behavioral norms, and especially editing footage into compelling drama, such programs render the real. Which is the point: Companies can render some manmade offerings more authentic than others, even though they're *all* fake, fake, fake.

With this paradox now made explicit, we can complete our Axioms of Authenticity. Recall the first three shared at the end of chapter 3:

Axiom 1.

If you *are* authentic, then you don't have to *say* you're authentic.

Axiom 2.

If you *say* you're authentic, then you'd better *be* authentic.

Axiom 3.

It's easier to *be* authentic, if you don't *say* you're authentic.

To those we now add:

Axiom 4.

It's easier to *render* offerings authentic, if you *acknowledge* they're inauthentic.

Axiom 5.

You don't have to *say* your offerings are inauthentic, if you *render* them authentic.

Your business can't claim that either it or its offerings are authentic through marketing or any other means. You must earn the privilege of being deemed authentic only through the act of rendering.

The Culture of Authenticity

So how exactly does something really unreal come to be perceived as real? How do you make that happen not only with intention but as a discipline? It starts with a richer understanding of today's contemporary culture of authenticity. Conservative scholar Dinesh D'Souza discusses authenticity from a fresh perspective in *What's So Great About America*, asserting that authenticity has come to comprise a fundamental aspect of American culture.

D'Souza takes on those critics "who denounce the culture" of America and blame its real problems on "the American system of technological capitalism."[44] He sees authenticity underlying the very notion of the "American dream" as articulated by the founding fathers, dedicating the new nation to economic freedom, political freedom, and freedom of speech and religion. He goes on to point out, "To the American founders' list of freedoms, Rousseau adds a new one: inner freedom . . . Here Rousseau is giving expression to the idea of authenticity, of being true to oneself."[45]

Most importantly, D'Souza challenges fellow conservatives to embrace his icon for this ideal: "the Starbucks guy" working behind the counter with "the Mohawk hair, the earrings, the studs on his forehead and tongue, the tattoos."[46] He imagines that conservatives such as Allan Bloom, Pat Buchanan, Bill Bennett, and Robert Bork would label the fellow a freak, order his arrest, or, at the very least, rail against the ethic beneath his mutilated flesh.

D'Souza shows, not only to them but to businesspeople as well, the importance of authenticity in today's culture: "The Starbucks guy is an idealist, and it would be wrong to trample on that idealism," he explains. "Moreover, his ethic of authenticity is entrenched in his psyche; how realistic would it be to uproot it? A much better approach for conservatives is to acknowledge the legitimacy of the ideal of authenticity, but to make the case that the Starbucks guy has adopted a debased form of it. The Starbucks guy wants to be original, and this is a good thing to be, but it may be pointed out to him that he is not succeeding at this, because every fourth guy at Starbucks looks like him!"[47] That provides a key lesson: authenticity today so permeates everyday morality (and reality)—not just in America but around the developed world—that it is self-defeating for the very reason that it is so very conventional. There is no one so conformist as a nonconformist, as has oft been noted. As D'Souza makes clear, even the Starbucks guy must "realize that his bold stance against the institutions of society—against commerce, against family, against community, against morality—is a bit of a pose. Indeed, it fails by its own standard; it is inauthentic."[48]

There may be readers who, as children of the '60s, identify with the Starbucks guy and on reflection find some discomfort reconciling their bohemian hearts with what they now do for a living themselves—working for, running, or even owning a large, capitalist corporation. We suspect this uneasiness drives the recent interest in working for (or owning) a small, capitalist success story; witness the popularity of such business books as Bo Burlingham's *Small Giants*, Seth Godin's *Small Is the New Big*, and Michael Shuman and Bill McKibbon's *The Small-Mart Revolution*.[59] Many of today's anticorporate activists advise finding altogether different employment, specifically in ventures that lack, minimize, or at least downplay the profit motive in favor of changing the world. It's not an either/or situation, however. We simply advise changing one's view of capitalism.

A Brief Defense of Authentic Capitalism

The new consumer sensibility of authenticity means that every company—from the local to the global, the little to the large, the decidedly nonprofit to the obscenely profitable—must make its way in a world where individuals crave authenticity in what they *buy* just as they crave it across all the choices they make in their private lives. Corey Anton, waxing philosophic, notes: "Authentically dwelling in 'the moment' means choosing in light of the whole of our existence . . . [where] we commemoratively retain the past while resolutely anticipating the future."[50] The choices we make right here and right now, in other words, connect us both with the determined past and the possibilities that lay ahead in the indeterminate future.[51]

Restating in philosophy what economists call the Law of Comparative Advantage, Anton further explains, "I encounter a world whose manifold possibilities are already funded by previous accomplishments."[52] As adumbrated by Adam Smith in *The Wealth of Nations* and codified by David Ricardo in *Principles of Political Economy and Taxation*, this law states that wealth is maximized when nations specialize in what they do best, and then trade with other nations for that which they do best. It is the bedrock of international free trade.[53] The same is true for individuals: wealth is maximized when individuals specialize in what they do best, and then trade with other individuals for what *they* do best. As Anton indicates, it is the bedrock of individual authenticity.

Money is simply the means by which trades may most easily be made. A dollar is a unit of human effort. Someone who elects to buy something instead of generating it on his own—by self-extracting a commodity, self-making a good, self-delivering a service, self-staging an experience, or self-guiding a transformation—is simply choosing to trade the fruits of his own labor for those of another. Money, the very basis of capitalism, therefore enables each individual to dwell authentically in the moment of his choice, in light of his whole intelligence, skills, and preferences, and further to commemoratively retain the past (via purchases) while resolutely anticipating the future (via investments). Rather than bemoan the manmade mechanism of instantiating human effort in the form of currency, any champions of authenticity should *embrace* the spirit and practice of capitalism. As futurist Joel Kotkin concludes, "In a fundamentally capitalistic society, the most important force defending uniqueness and authenticity will be the marketplace itself."[54]

Perceiving and Authenticity

The beauty of marketplaces, of course, lies in their composition—countless unique individuals, all making their own personal decisions that, thanks to Adam Smith's "invisible hand," yield a far better allocation of resources than any other method. The same is true of how authenticity plays out in the marketplace: individuals make their own personal decisions, which apportion perceptions of authenticity throughout the culture.

Indeed, the sole determinant of the authenticity of any economic offering is the individual perceiving the offering. Call it a corollary to the Authenticity Paradox—because our experiences with offerings happen *inside* of us, we become the sole arbiter of what is authentic *for* us. What one person experiences as completely authentic, another may view as completely inauthentic, and a third may be somewhere in between. As Jay Newman says, cultural products rarely exist "in the form of 'black and white.' As authenticity and inauthenticity admit of countless degrees, we find ourselves confronted with innumerable shades of grey."[55]

One such collection of cultural products: country music. In his landmark study *Creating Country Music: Fabricating Authenticity*, Richard Peterson shows how what was deemed authentic in this quintessentially American genre of music changed over time.[56] In each phase, music producers sought out artists who could provide the prototypical style of performance—from the old-timer artistry of Jimmie Rodgers and the hillbilly imagery of the Grand Ole Opry, through the singing cowboys such as Gene Autry, to Hank Williams as the model for everyone thereafter to follow—thus fabricating authenticity for each new generation. Throughout, however, Peterson makes clear that authenticity "does not inhere in the object, person or performance said to be authentic. Rather, authenticity is a claim that is made by or for someone, thing, or performance and either accepted or rejected by relevant others."[57]

"Authenticity," Peterson bluntly states, "is socially constructed."[58] This is not about socially constructed reality, however. The objects we experience are what they are, but we are the ones to ascribe authenticity to the reality we experience.[59] Authenticity, in other words, is *personally determined*.[60] This follows directly from the view that authenticity is that which is not of Man—not imposed by society's views. Jacob Golomb makes this clear when he says, "There is no one exclusive and definitive path to authenticity—to be authentic means to invent one's *own* way and pattern of life."[61] He states point-blank: "We create our authenticity; it is not delivered to us by higher authorities."[62] This holds true whether these authorities be the thrones of CEOs, dominions of chief marketing officers, principalities of brand managers, or the powers of advertising agencies.

Today's focus on authenticity goes too far, however, when people no longer "see themselves as part of a larger order," as Charles Taylor warns in *The Ethics of Authenticity*.[63] Taylor's treatise is rife with references to overcoming self-centeredness and exerting self-responsibility while rising above self-referentiality. As opposed to many existential philosophers, he's careful not to go too far in throwing off society's norms, never reaching the point of "self-determining freedom" represented by Rousseau's noble savage, which "pushed to its limit, doesn't recognize any boundaries, anything given that I *have* to respect in my exercise of self-determining choice."[64]

Former *Reason* editor Virginia Postrel brings authenticity out of the realm of philosophy and into the arena of daily consumer behavior. Explaining "We can decide *for ourselves* what is authentic *for our purposes*," she introduces a useful construct for thinking about personally determined authenticity: "*I like that. I'm like that.*"[65] She uses dreadlocks to make the point. While originally a religious and later subversive symbol, through the passage of time they became "an emblem of reggae music, Afrocentrism, or nonsectarian (as opposed to Rastafarian) spirituality. Over the past decade, the increasing popularity of dreadlocks has eroded even this symbolism."[66] Eventually the style—with all of the concomitant offerings of hair goods and styling services—was adopted by many wishing to proclaim merely that they were artistic, and finally by many who just wished to express a certain degree of nonconformity. At any point in this journey, people can look at the dreadlocks on others and acknowledge to themselves "I like that." Some go further, adopt the style, and declare to others: "I'm like that." Thus the symbol becomes authentic for them, no matter how far removed from its original context, because it conforms to their own self-image and signals their own identity.

This same process plays out in every personal decision and economic purchase people make. The perception of authenticity remains personally determined, not corporately declared. You cannot assume that customers will see authenticity the same way you do. You must reach inside them to match *your offerings* ("I like that") with *their self-image* ("I'm like that").[67]

Such business-rendered authenticity is required precisely because personally determined authenticity extends to every offering, every brand, every business. Ageless marketer David Wolfe tells of a meeting where he "mentioned that *authentic* customer-centric marketing lets customers define a brand." One market researcher was appalled, saying "That's the dumbest thing I ever heard of. You can't let consumers define your brand."[68] Sorry, but brands have always existed *only* in the minds of customers, and never has this been more crucial to understand than when the authenticity of those brands becomes of paramount importance. As Wolfe concludes, "A company may be the *de jure* owner, but customers are the *de facto* owners of the brand."[69]

They are not, however, dictators. They can be influenced. They can be inspired. They can discover authenticity for themselves when you render your offerings in a way that makes that possible. We've already seen how many companies do precisely that through the five genres of authenticity. Our focus in the rest of this book is to provide a way of thinking about authenticity in business that, if followed, will help ensure that whatever methods for rendering authenticity you choose (or invent) will find fertile ground in the minds of your customers.

6

𝒯𝒽𝑒 𝑅𝑒𝒶𝓁/𝐹𝒶𝓀𝑒 𝑅𝑒𝒶𝓁𝒾𝓉𝓎

HOW OFFERINGS BECOME AUTHENTIC

EAL OR UNREAL?" THAT WAS THE OVERARCHING QUESTION posited of the exhibit, "Staging Reality: Photography from the West Collection at SEI" at SEI Investments in Oaks, Pennsylvania. A sign at the entrance described the two trends of the 2002 exhibition: "artist-made models photographed to appear as natural, and straight photographs that give an artificial feeling to settings they represent." Lois Renner's *Fur Metropolis* (1999), for example, looked real but was "a detailed replica of his own studio in Vienna." Conversely, Spessi's *Starmyru* (2000) captured two gasoline pumps in a field in front of a mountain. No road, no tracks, no signs, not even a gas station—seemingly the product of photo-shopping—yet it depicted actual "gas station tanks in native Iceland."[1]

Sid Sachs, Director of the Rosenwald-Wolf Gallery at The University of the Arts, described the SEI collection as "landscapes and interiors where actual locations seem starkly unreal and staged fabrications often seem very real. Thus hyperreality and simulacras blur what is real and what is replicant."[2] In managing perceptions of real and fake, artists "make the viewer question the fabrication of social assumptions, hierarchies, and privilege."[3]

This capability to render the unreal as real and the real as unreal exemplifies the dynamic that characterizes reality in business and commerce. Real or Unreal? Even though some art lovers admire unreal photos over real ones just as some consumers prefer unreal groceries over real ones—and vice versa—the issue matters greatly.

To Be (or Not to Be) Real: That Is the Question

In William Shakespeare's *Hamlet*, Polonius counsels his son Laertes,

This above all,—to thine own self be true;
And it must follow, as the night the day,
Thou canst not then be false to any man.[4]

It is Shakespeare's genius that although Polonius comes off as spouting worn-out platitudes, his advice nonetheless proves to be profound. In it, we find *two* standards of authenticity:

1. Being true to your own self

and

2. Being who you say you are to others.[5]

Authenticity, we believe, flows from these two principles of thought and action. Together, they help us to ascertain the real in an otherwise amorphous landscape. First, the importance of being earnest, consistent, and self-directed centers one on one's perception *of one's self.* Second, being trustworthy, honest, and compassionate focuses one on one's behavior *toward others.*

While one of these may overshadow the other, individuals and companies must contend with both simultaneously.[6] So often today, people distort the first and ignore the second, as habitually found in self-help books, DVDs, and workshops. According to Michael Schrage, their "fundamental message is cruelly specific: *you'd be a much better person if only you were someone else.*"[7]

The Interplay of Real/Fake

In *The Unreal America*, Ada Louise Huxtable acknowledges the unrealness of what surrounds us but notes that "it is increasingly difficult to tell the real fake from the fake fake. All fakes are clearly not equal; there are good fakes and bad fakes. The standard is no longer real versus phony, but the relative merits of the imitation. What makes the good ones better is their improvement upon reality."[8]

Being true to our framework-driven selves, we inexorably see a 2×2 matrix flowing from these words.[9] If there is a *real fake* and a *fake fake*, then there must be a *fake real* and a *real real*. Left with four boxes but no axes to grind, we asked from what dimensions these terms could be derived—and then we hit on it: the two axes must be our two standards of authenticity.

The resulting Real/Fake Matrix (figure 6-1) provides a mental model and a prescription for working out a path toward rendering authenticity with your own offerings. The X-axis describes the self-directed relationship between your company and its own output: is what you offer true to itself and to your company? The Y-axis describes the other-focused relationship between your company and customers: is what you offer what you say it is and not false to any customer? To render authenticity in business, companies must apply these two standards for every commodity, good, service, experience, or transformation offered. Call it the Polonius Test:

1. Is the offering true to itself?

2. Is the offering what it says it is?

The answers constitute four modes of authenticity—Real-real, Real-fake, Fake-real, and Fake-fake—and each represents a means by which customers come to *perceive* various offerings as real or unreal, or as Huxtable might put it, with a diminishing degree of unrealness.

Again, our concern here is not creating sincere leaders or genuine laborers, unless they help render their offerings more authentic; for it is rendering the *output* of an enterprise authentic, and to some extent, rendering the enterprise itself authentic. And yes, we are ascribing human traits ("true to your *own self*" and "what *you* say you are") to inanimate offerings ("true to *itself*" and "what *it* says *it* is"), anthropomorphizing business offerings.[10] Any offering can, nonetheless, be true

FIGURE 6-1

The Real/Fake Matrix

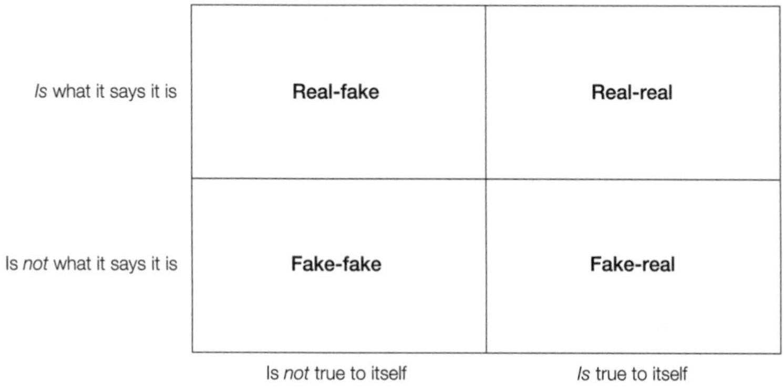

	Is *not* true to itself	Is true to itself
Is what it says it is	Real-fake	Real-real
Is *not* what it says it is	Fake-fake	Fake-real

(or not) to the business that offers it, and that offering can be (or not) what the business says it is.

Many companies fail the Polonius Test because their executives, like Polonius, can't get beyond mere platitudes: "Our vision is to be world-class," "We strive for quality in everything we do," "We give back to the community," "Customers come first," "Our people are our most important asset." Surely customers, shareholders, Wall Street analysts, and especially employees understand how phony these statements sound. Do you? European School of Management professor Hervé Laroche points out that in organizations that demand "*strong* commitment, *deep* motivation, *wide* consensus, *core* values and *unquestioned* loyalty . . . faking becomes the standard mode of operation." Everyone does it, everyone knows it: "[M]iddle managers like high involvement only when it is faked. They themselves will fake it to their bosses, and they expect others—especially their subordinates—to follow suit."[11]

Think about flight attendants blasting through the required preflight announcement, the telephone protocols of inbound call centers and outbound telemarketers, the sales pitches of software consultants, or the advice of financial planners. Even a solitary visit to a Web site is not immune from faked ritual: should you "Skip Intro" when visiting a paying client's or bidding vendor's Web site?

Think too of other offerings from specific companies that you view as altogether authentic and test them against our two standards—being true to itself, and being what it says it is—and you should find alignment. Similarly, test the offerings that you view as thoroughly *in*authentic, and they likely fail both: they are neither true to themselves nor being what they proclaim to be to others.

So much for practices of others. Now, test thyself. Where would you put your own business and your economic offerings on the Real/Fake Matrix? How might you more fully meet the two standards of authenticity?

Pulling a Polonius

Most Elizabethan-trained actors have played the Polonius/Laertes scene as "real advice, fake father."[12] Now flip it: "fake advice, real father." That is what actor Bill Murray did in his portrayal of Polonius in Michael Almereyda's 2000 film adaptation of *Hamlet*. *New York Times* film critic A. O. Scott recognized the significance of Murray's performance: "You can't make Shakespeare up as you go along, but Mr. Murray does just that; he is one of the tiny handful of screen actors who can make Elizabethan stage language sound like natural, human speech. And the result is that the character, and the play, take on a whole new coloration." Scott concludes that Murray's "Polonius knows his language to be inadequate, but it's also the only language he has. He is the biggest phony in the play, but because he is the only person who seems aware of his phoniness, he also becomes the most honest."[13]

That is the first step to rendering *your* offerings more authentic: if you are aware of their phoniness, just say so. They are fake. Go on and admit, "It's all fake." Performer Penn Jillette, the verbal half of the magician duo Penn & Teller, explains, "We tell the audience at the top it's all fake, so there's an underlying moral foundation . . ."[14] By admitting their act is all smoke and mirrors, Penn & Teller render their act more authentic to their audiences.

In our advice to businesspeople, we echo what medieval historian and law professor William Ian Miller observes in *Faking It.* Examining everything from prayers to pick-up lines, Miller takes up the question of self-consciousness, "that unpleasant emotion that interrupts our blithe and unself-conscious 'naturalness,' which, however, may be no more than '*acting* naturally' and not knowing we are." He points out, "The feeling of faking it forces upon us a recognition of a split between something that we flatter ourselves is our 'true' self and the role we are playing."[15]

The task of being real—as a person or a business—would be easier if we were simply unaware of needing to render authenticity; that awareness interrupts our "natural" thought processes and human performances. But we have eaten the apple. We know that all economic offerings are fake, fake, fake. Why do we harp on this point? So that *you*, like Bill Murray's Polonius, become so aware of faking it that you are no longer wary of such fakery; as businesspeople, it is our lot in life. Miller summarizes, "Like it or not, we are stuck faking it."[16]

We are also stuck with customers as the sole arbiters of the Real/Fake status of any offering—since authenticity is personally determined. *Customers alone* decide whether what you sell is (1) true to itself, and (2) what it says it is. Such judgments stem from each individual's self-image and how that image serves to accept, ignore, filter, or translate what you offer and what you say about those offerings. Your company's actions over time, however, greatly influence those determinations.

Assessing the Real/Fake

To see how different companies render themselves authentic in each of the four combinations of the Real/Fake Matrix, let us examine four retail venues within short walking distance of Times Square in New York City—ESPN Zone, Dave & Buster's, the NBA Store, and Niketown. How would you label each venue?

ESPN Zone

The small retail shop near the entrance represents a small portion of the ESPN Zone eating, drinking, and gaming complex. The big draws are the main Studio Grill and the Screening Room with its twenty-eight-foot-long wall of screens and front-row leather seats for MVP Club members. Off to the side, patrons can rent private "skyboxes" for an hourly fee. Throughout are sports artifacts and sports-themed art, the most prominent of which is a large mosaic portrait of Babe Ruth composed of Topps baseball cards of other Yankee greats. Upstairs, the Game Zone transcends the arcade-feel; players use smart cards rather than coins or tokens, throw actual footballs, hit actual pucks, and shoot actual baskets. The "ESPN Hoops Hysteria" basketball station, for example, features regulation-sized backboards and rims and displays one's cumulative free-throw percentage.

More than a sports bar and grill, ESPN Zone is true to itself and is what it says it is—a zone of all things ESPN, the world's foremost all-sports network. This Zone is *so* ESPN, with over 150 video screens showing live events, sports highlights, and other sports entertainment. It seems to us *Real-real*.

Dave & Buster's

Within this sprawling restaurant-cum-carnival are several arcade games, including "Basketball." To play one version, you insert a smart card to get a stream of balls to toss at the hoop, with multiple options for how predictably the rim moves closer to or farther away from you. The ball feels smaller than regulation size, the hoop looks a bit too high, and a successful shot scores only one point. The game resembles basketball but is *not* basketball. It is simply *not* what it says it is.

As an arcade game with a basketball motif, however, it *is* true to itself, fitting in with the rest of the Dave & Buster's pay-per-play experience vending machines. But consider the nature of the venue by examining the "itself" of the entity. Dave & Buster's *what*? Restaurant? Arcade? Carnival? It is all of those and more, and none of those and less. The lack of specificity allows the chain to offer anything and everything where nothing needs to be what it says it is. It offers experiences that we'd call *Fake-real* from classic Skee-ball (Fake-real bowling) to the latest "dance simulator" like Dance Dance Revolution (Fake-real aerobics).

The NBA Store

The signature design element of this store is a 170-foot wood walkway that spirals round (like a basketball going round and round the rim) to the lower level. Alongside a half-court basketball area below are large bins of underinflated basketballs. A sign reads, "Basketballs are for display only. Please do not remove balls from bin." Another sign affixed to the backboard reads, "Absolutely No Dunking Please." The signs seem unnecessary, as racks of merchandise cover the court, making any dribbling or dunking impossible. The *only* hoops game to play is just like the arcade one at Dave & Buster's.

The NBA Store *is* what it says it is, for it is indeed a store, filled with NBA merchandise. In fact, it is *the* NBA store, the league's only freestanding retail outlet, situated near the National Basketball Association's headquarters. But the NBA Store is *not* true to itself. Dunking should be the primary attraction there because it is the primary attraction at NBA games and in NBA marketing: *fan*-tastic, awe-inspiring, "I love this game" slam dunks. The place strikes us as *Real-fake*.

Niketown

Like the NBA Store, Niketown is well designed, intriguingly furnished, and intentionally sensory, but is nonetheless a store. There is no appearance of any town, nor any basketball court, nor any area devoted to athletic activity of any kind. The chain has done nothing to associate it with any New York sports franchises or Nike-sponsored stars who play in New York. (In fact, none of the twelve Niketowns in the United States tries to align with local teams or athletes.) Furthermore, Nike provides nothing to *do* athletically.

The place is *not* what it says it is, a Nike town, and is *not* true to Nike's original internal mantra, "Authentic Athletic Performance," nor to its now-famous external tagline, "Just Do It."[17] Nike does nothing to extend that ethos into its Niketown outlets. It is *Fake-fake*—a Nikestore with absolutely nothing athletic to do.

Taking Real/Fake Action

Given these descriptions, perhaps you are already considering where your business belongs on the Real/Fake Matrix. How can you use it to render greater authenticity? What can you do to manage consumer perceptions of real? The steps below provide your most immediate course of action. After going through each one, we will examine how the process could help ESPN Zone, Dave & Buster's, the NBA Store, and Niketown to render greater authenticity. We will then present broader approaches for you to apply to your own circumstances.

Step 1: Assess Your Current State

Determine what you are as a business and what your offerings are, as well as what you say your business and offerings are. What contributes and detracts from these being true to themselves and being what they say they are? Be honest: Which of the four modes best describe your current state? Be harsh: there are no *purely* Real-real offerings; there is always some dimension of self to which a business is not true, and something said that remains unfulfilled.

Taking this step should increase your awareness of your own inauthenticity and fuel a lively discussion among colleagues. So determine where you lie today on the Real/Fake Matrix: Fake-fake, Fake-real, Real-fake, or Real-real?

Step 2: Accept This State as Your Fate

New businesses can most easily render themselves Real-real because they are starting fresh; consumers have little or no preformed perception of them. For any business entrenched in long-held beliefs and behaviors that doesn't already attain that status, however, any attempt to migrate to Real-real risks being perceived as fully fake on both dimensions.

While in theory the goal for any business might be to offer solely the Real-real, in practice any of the four modes provides a legitimate platform for rendering authenticity. Therefore, embrace your current state. Be your own self—in whatever mode (even the Fake-fake) you have manifested over time—rather than automatically strive to be Real-real. Here's how to leverage each mode as a platform for authenticity rendering:

- If you consider yourself *Fake-fake*, then *celebrate your inauthenticity* and revel in not having to make any claims of being real. Your opportunity lies in deliberately, openly, and cleverly generating fake offerings— proudly, obviously fake offerings—that, like faux furs (or Bill Murray's Polonius), you render real by being *so* honestly Fake-fake.

- If *Fake-real*, then you should *mask your inauthenticity* and create a self-contained offering that obscures the inconsistency between what is said and what is done. Your challenge is to create a compelling and convincing fantasy realm, virtual world, themed environment, or other escapist offering—think of the movies—that downplays its disconnection from reality while simultaneously emphasizing the real value created for customers.

- If *Real-fake*, then you should *acknowledge your inauthenticity,* whether with a wink and a nudge, or a straightforward acknowledgment. Introduce cues that signal to customers your awareness of a particular offering's difference from a true self elsewhere—such as the difference in quality and price between offerings available at a factory outlet and a merchandiser's retail channel.

- If you truly deem yourself *Real-real*, then you should *transcend your in-authenticity*—avoid actions that detract from positive perceptions already gained, and layer on additional components that enhance the perception of authenticity. Be vigilant, because the slightest sign of being fake—think of JetBlue Airways treating customers inhumanely during the Valentine's Day 2007 East Coast snowstorm—becomes magnified and is doubly difficult to undo.

Again, we caution against too hastily deeming your business and your offerings Real-real. Think of it as a corollary to Axiom 3: It is easier to *be* Real-real, if you do not *think* you are Real-real.

Step 3: Overcome the Fake

In this step, focus relentlessly on the dimension for which you must be perceived as authentic. For Fake-real, concentrate on being true to self; for Real-fake, on what it says it is. What causes your offerings to fall short of the appropriate standard? Pinpoint those components of your business and your offerings that create any whiff of inauthenticity and eliminate, alter, or transform them. Review the principles of rendering natural, original, exceptional, referential, and influential authenticity provided in chapter 4. Do any suggest an obvious remedy to currently inauthentic behavior?

You must do all of this, of course, if you strive for Real-real—but also if you revel in Fake-fake. Here, seek out areas where your offerings are overly true to self as well as too overtly what they say they are.

Step 4: Signify the Real

Finally, consider which elements of your business—materials, features, offerings, places, encounters, stories, units, etc.—stand on their own as the *most* of what you want to be, no matter the mode. How could you elevate their significance in how you present yourself to customers? Which Real-real, Fake-real, Real-fake, or Fake-fake elements (as appropriate) could signal, with some management attention and adept design, how you want to present yourself to the world? Think of the utter lack of defect in faux furs, the notice that certain movies are "based on a true story," the signs warning you of quality flaws at factory outlets, and the Customer Bill of Rights promulgated by JetBlue soon after its much-publicized problems. Look to establish such *signature elements*; they go a long way toward rendering authenticity for your overall business and its offerings.

The Foursome Revisited

Let's revisit the four New York City retail venues. First, assume each retailer assesses its current state as we have—ESPN Zone (Real-real), Dave & Buster's (Fake-real), NBA Store (Real-fake), and Niketown (Fake-fake)—and then behaves as if that state were its fate in order to overcome sources of inauthenticity and emphasize signature elements of authenticity. How could each enterprise render greater authenticity?

ESPN Zone

While ESPN Zone could reasonably assess itself as Real-real, it should recognize that its own actions have eroded that standing over time. In its first year of operation, ESPN broadcast half-time reports for ABC's *Monday Night Football* directly from the Screening Room in its inaugural Baltimore venue, charging customers a premium entry fee to watch the game there with Chris Berman and his broadcast team. But ESPN discontinued that distinctive practice after just one season. Also, ESPN Zone once operated actual half-court basketball courts, with referees passing basketballs to shooters. But machines very similar to those at Dave & Buster's have replaced this Real-real activity.

To remain Real-real, ESPN Zone must transcend rival venues and overcome the fake elements it allowed to creep in over the years. It should reinstall basketball courts and offer more nonmechanized sports featured on its channels, such as ping-pong, billiards, and darts. True to its score-streaming self, it should add functionality to its smart cards for tracking—and in-venue scrolling of—individual guest performances. While most individual machines track high scores, each ESPN Zone could track its highest scorer across all machines and perhaps compare them across all venues—just as ESPN monitors scores for the entire sports universe. Such a Real-real capability would provide a signature element to the ESPN Zone offering.

As a truly original offering, ESPN Zone should stress its firsts. An opportunity looms on the horizon to commemorate its beginnings, namely the tenth anniversary of opening its first venue in Baltimore on July 11, 1998. We look forward to seeing what ESPN Zone does to celebrate the occasion and, more importantly, to refresh the experience in Real-real ways. Failure to leverage the milestone in such a way will only exhibit an attitude inclined to erode its perceived authenticity further.

Dave & Buster's

Dave & Buster's successfully carved its niche among the genre of game arcade restaurants, rendering a bar-and-grill feel to a big-box experience. To leverage this Fake-real state, Dave & Buster's must expertly mask its inauthenticity. To date it has managed to achieve this largely through scale—the sheer size of the hangout impresses patrons. As it expands to more locations, taking on the feel of a chain, Dave & Buster's will need to look (and feel) more *local*.

Instead of one sprawling open game pit, Dave & Buster's could create multiple places within the place, each one themed after local franchises, arenas, or activities. This theming would deflect attention from the underlying unreality of its games and onto the fabricated reality of the places-within-the-place that consumers cannot provide themselves when playing their PlayStations or Xboxes at home.

It could introduce mascots (an inherently Fake-real experience element)—not characters like Mickey Mouse or Chuck E. Cheese, but a local "Dave" (someone actually named David) and one "Buster" (which could become anyone's nickname) for each venue. It even could conduct, like *American Idol*, local contests annually (with separate Dave and Buster divisions) to identify a winning pair. However determined, the two would signify the realness of Dave & Buster's.

One of the company's not-true-to-self aspects—thus making for a Fake-real shortcoming—is how it handles prizes. These should be the pinnacle of competition. It could, therefore, open the room up to celebrations and ceremonies, and the prizes themselves should gain signature status. Imagine redeeming points for cash contributions to local charities and not for cheap trinkets. By introducing charitable points redemption as an option, Dave & Buster's could have a significant influence on local communities.

The NBA Store

Accepting its state as Real-fake, the NBA Store must acknowledge its inauthenticity vis-à-vis the NBA itself. It is a store, and so it should behave like a store. It is the NBA Store, and so it should be *the* NBA's store, not just some Dick's Sporting Goods specializing in basketball apparel.

At present, the NBA Store's signature design element—the basketball court at the bottom of the circular walkway—also serves as its primary source of inauthenticity, in that no everyday customers play—are allowed to play—basketball there. Instead, the store should create a Real-fake mechanism whereby *every* guest who so desires gets to dunk the ball (via, say, adjustable rim heights or a trampoline), complete with for-sale video footage of the dunks. Mascots already do this during half-time at NBA games, which points the way to how the court can become authentic at the NBA Store—by being the venue for a *half-time show*, with shorter time-outs celebrated as well.

Daily, halfway through store hours, a showtime extravaganza could commence—bringing down the house lights, swirling spotlights, pumping up the music volume, costuming workers as cheerleaders, introducing dueling team mascots, and inviting select customers to participate in promotional stunts, such as blindfolded shooting. Throughout the day, workers could stage shorter time-out events, with live video of shoppers—like fan cams during game breaks—projected on the store's Jumbotron, and T-shirts or other giveaways shot up the sides of the spiral walkway. (Purists might argue that all these nonbasketball trappings are themselves inauthentic vis-à-vis the game itself. True enough, but the Real-fake NBA long ago embraced this genre of activity! They are now a part of what it is.)

The tagline for the NBA Store reads "One Store. Every Team. Experience it all." The offering will struggle to live up to what it says it is in that tagline through jerseys, shirts, hats, and other merchandise alone. Half-time and time-out experiences would render the place more Real-fake.

Niketown

Nike should admit that its Niketown offerings come off as Fake-fake, but it need not seek Real-real by, for example, turning Niketowns into just-do-it athletic clubs. Rather, it should consider the sources of its present-day inauthenticity: Niketowns are not what they say they are (towns), and they are not true to self (with nothing to "just do"). Using a Fake-fake mind-set, they should *really* not be anything like towns, but over-the-top stores, and revel in shopping as the only activity they offer, perhaps as if shopping were a competitive sport (as it often is in New York City).

Niketowns could entertain shoppers with the complete absence of anything to just do, as a respite from the other shopping that they did that day. Organize it around the simple theme of recovery; after all, every workout should build in respites for recuperation. The Niketown shopping experience would rescue consumers from the tiresome walking and standing associated with shopping and highlight concierge service. Nike could devote a design lounge to NIKEiD, Nike's online program for customizing shoes, so that customers could design their own shoes while relaxing instead of standing at a countertop terminal.

Like ESPN, Nike should stress its firsts—the first manufacturer to use its own retail venues for experiential marketing. Nike's "Just Do It" campaign first ran in 1988; its first Niketown opened in 1990 in Portland. Perhaps no better way exists to mark the twentieth anniversary of each than rendering Niketowns even more Fake-fake than they are already are. They are not yet too inauthentic to be redeemed.

––––––––––

Caution: incremental decisions aimed at increasing availability, lowering costs, or improving quality might erode any earned perception of authenticity or jeopardize any chance of earning a reputation of the real. All companies, not just those examined here, must manage authenticity as a new business discipline in its own right, starting with an honest assessment of its business in terms of Real/Fake—and render from there.

The fours steps above foreshadow four general approaches given below for rendering greater authenticity via each of the modes in the Real/Fake Matrix:

1. **Go Faux:** Celebrate your inauthenticity by boldly embracing your Fake-fakeness;

2. **Create Belief:** Mask your inauthenticity by comprehensively creating an alternate but believable reality;

3. **Reveal the Unreal:** Acknowledge your inauthenticity by emphatically demonstrating where you are not true to self; or

4. **Get Real:** Transcend your inauthenticity by relentlessly pursuing Real-real in all you do.

We explore each of these approaches in depth in the balance of this chapter. The fourth approach remains difficult; it is possible only if you fully understand, embrace, and apply the frameworks in each of the next three chapters.

Go Faux

With authenticity emerging as the new consumer sensibility, "fake" can be a term of derision. Ah, but if we *do* like something that is obviously inauthentic, then it's not fake—it's *faux*. In English, this use of the French word for "false" means we deem the fake desirable and more real. For companies, admitting that offerings are Fake-fake by calling them faux—an action that, you will note, does not violate Axiom 5—helps render them real. Such transparency acknowledges customers' desire for authenticity while simultaneously recognizing—even celebrating—the true nature of the offering, rendering the patently Fake-fake what can be called *fauxthentic*.

Going faux drives many thriving industries today. Consider faux fur more closely. Retailers today sell shearling coats (made from sheep hides, with the sheared side as the inner lining) for thousands of dollars, faux shearling (made from pigskin,with a synthetic fleece lining) for around a hundred dollars, and "faux-faux" shearling (made entirely from polyester) for several hundred dollars.[18] The faux-faux sells for a multiple of the price of the merely faux shearling because it looks more realistic and is more pliable, allowing for more flattering garments than achievable in real hides.

Such faux offerings can vary in degrees of fakeness (and, by implication, degrees of being perceived as real). Even a blatantly fake wristwatch can be *faux-thentic* enough to gain legitimate points of distribution, rather than street vendors or spammers. The "OurVersions" line of wristwatches—often for sale at airport outlets—ranges from brands like Buluga, Courtier, and Moldova—all familiar *sounding*, but all decidedly *not* Bulova, Cartier, and Movado. Displays for each faux brand say what they *are* by explicitly stating what they are *not* (e.g., "Our watches are not manufactured by Cartier, nor are they exact copies. We are not in any way associated with Cartier"). Openly fake, even to buyers thinking that, at that price (one for $12, two for $20), their Courtier could not possibly be a real *Courtier*—let alone a real Cartier.

Businesses make entire classes of offerings transparently fake enough to legitimize them to many, if not most, consumers as *fauxthentic*:

- **Home:** Faux fireplaces, faux furniture, faux plants, faux flowers, faux finishing

- **Beauty:** False eyelashes, fake fingernails, hair coloring and hair extensions, Botox

- **Food:** Artificial sweeteners, faux meat (e.g., soy burgers)

- **Health:** Artificial limbs and organs, heart stents

- **Fun:** Faux news, temporary tattoos

- **Reading:** Tabloid newspapers, "memoirs"

Under what circumstances do people prefer such obviously fake offerings? Generally, when alternatives do a poor job of complying with the three previous business imperatives. First, the *availability* of many Fake-fake offerings exceeds that of Real-real counterparts. Faux grass, for example, succeeds in locales where real grass is difficult to grow. Second, the *cost* of the Fake-fake is usually much lower than the Real-real, particularly when the latter is scarce. Finally, the *quality* of the Fake-fake sometimes surpasses that of the Real-real. Suntanning can be so uneven and time-consuming, for example, that many people use self-tanning lotions and salons for that "perfect" tan every time, including some—such as The Body Shop's Fake it! lotion or the Faux Glow Airbrush Tanning Salon in New York City—that not only acknowledge but positively revel in their Fake-fakeness.

Businesses can render Fake-fake offerings as *fauxthentic* whenever they (1) are true to their Fake-fake selves, and (2) say what they are, never pretending to be anything other than completely inauthentic. And if you can render the patently Fake-fake authentic, surely you can do so with less inauthentic offerings—those deemed Fake-real and Real-fake—as well.

Create Belief

In learning how to render the Fake-real authentic, look to what we consider the iconic exemplar of this mode: Disneyland. Many people decry the place that Walt built and its effects on America's cultural landscape. Ada Louise

Huxtable points to the first area inside the gates—Main Street, U.S.A.—and says "Any architect or historian could do better than these obvious architectural knockoffs. What a missed opportunity!"[19] Historian Daniel Boorstin says guests to the country's first theme park encounter not "originals" but "three-dimensional fascimiles."[20] Intellectual Jean Baudrillard called it "a perfect model of all the entangled orders of simulacra."[21] Architect Michael Sorkin says the place is always "'like' someplace else. The simulation's referent is ever elsewhere; the 'authenticity' of the substitution always depends on the knowledge, however faded, of some absent genuine."[22] And semiotician Umberto Eco calls Disneyland, simply, an "Absolute Fake."[23]

They are all absolutely right; Disneyland is not what it says it is. It is not really Main Street, U.S.A., with shopkeepers who know your family and remember your last visit. It is not really Sleeping Beauty's castle, where if you prick your finger on a spindle, you'll sleep until love's first kiss.[24] It is not really the Magic Kingdom, where only a little pixie dust will have you flying to the second star to the right and straight on 'til morning.

But Disneyland is true to itself and to its originator's vision of "a place for people to find happiness and knowledge."[25] It may not be a capital-M Magic Kingdom, but it is a small-m magical place. Everything inside it—from the nostalgic architecture to the old-fashioned rides, from the mechanically mannered cast members to the meticulously manicured grounds, from the host of physical cues the company harmonizes to the multifarious impressions guests walk away with—everything within it remains true to self. That is what inspired journalist Tom Carson to write, "From whatever angle, *nothing looks fake*. Fabricated, yes—fake, no. Disneyland isn't the mimicry of a thing; it's a thing."[26] Architecture professor Charles Moore calls it "the real heart of Southern California" and goes on to say: "What may come as a surprise is how richly Disneyland offers us insight into many layers of reality. People often use Disneyland as a synonym for the facile, shallow and fake . . . It just doesn't wash: this incredibly energetic collection of environmental experiences offers enough lessons for a whole architectural education in all the things that matter—community and reality, private memory and inhabitation, as well as some technical lessons in propinquity and choreography."[27]

Disneyland is, therefore, Fake-real—certainly not what it says it is, but definitely true to itself. Pointing the way for all other businesses that reside in this mode, it covers over its inauthenticity by creating a *fake reality*.[28] Creating such an offering takes, in poet Samuel Taylor Coleridge's famous phrase, "that willing suspension of disbelief."[29] People put aside what it actually *is*—inauthentic—to believe what it *says* it is. Actually, that is not quite right. In *The Matrix and Philosophy*, Sarah Worth writes:

When we enter into a fictional world, or let the fictional world enter into our imaginations, we do not "willingly suspend our disbelief" . . . [W]e cannot willingly decide to believe or disbelieve anything, any more than we can willingly believe it is snowing outside if all visual or sensory cues tell us otherwise. When engaging with fiction we do not *suspend a critical faculty*, but rather *exercise a creative faculty*. We do not actively suspend disbelief—we *actively create belief*. [30]

Being Fake-real, then, requires fashioning an offering in whose authenticity your customers willingly desire to believe—you must create belief. Experiences specialize in the Fake-real, whether via fantasy realms such as Disneyland, Dave & Buster's, or Kidzania; virtual worlds such as *Second Life* or *World of Warcraft*; themed environments such as The Venetian or Canyon Ranch spas; or any other escape from the real world to other places or times, including movies, plays, and books.

While books provide just such an escape, they are not experiences per se but goods.[31] Commodities similarly may exemplify the Fake-real—the not-actually-pristine wilderness of Yosemite National Park, or so-called Chilean Sea Bass that is really Patagonian Toothfish. There are Fake-real services too, such as personalized customer relationship management (CRM) messages—think of Amazon.com recommendations or Hallmark.com reminders—that do not stem from any real knowledge of you as a person, but provide value through systems that align offerings with what the companies can figure out about your needs. Such transformation offerings as Long Island–based Outward Bound or Muskoka Woods Sports Resort in Ontario create artificial situations—and in the case of places like Equinox Fitness Clubs, artificial environments—in which people can escape from real life to journey down the path of becoming a better person (or team).

Each of these offerings creates value in customers' eyes by shielding the inauthenticity of the environments in which they take place—whether real or fabricated—while simultaneously creating belief in the offering itself and its efficacy. J. R. R. Tolkien, who knew a thing or two about fabricating fictional worlds, called his craft "Enchantment" and outlined how to go about it: "What really happens is that the story-maker proves a successful 'sub-creator.' He makes a Secondary World which your mind can enter. Inside it, what he relates is 'true': It accords with the laws of that world. You therefore believe it, while you are, as it were, inside."[32]

So follow Tolkien in applying these two principles for being Fake-real: (1) never break the circle of belief by pointing out how fake the offering really is, and (2) always maintain the internal self-consistency that allows you to be true to self, lest you be perceived as Fake-fake.

Reveal the Unreal

If Disneyland provides the icon for Fake-real, then its rival for the hearts and pocketbooks of Los Angeles tourists and, moreover, natives—Universal City-Walk—does so for Real-fake.[33]

In the early 1990s, Universal Studios built CityWalk near its studios on a hill overlooking Los Angeles. The venue is an oversized main street for walking, shopping, eating, working, playing, and learning. Its architect, Jon Jerde, calls CityWalk "a collage of the images and characteristics of the City of Los Angeles; it distills the *atmosphere*, the ephemeral quality, of Los Angeles street life, without duplicating any of its iconic architecture," creating "an authentic street quality."[34] While most architectural critics express great reservations about Jerde's work, Huxtable loves how the venue "is being used for its own sake," with "real food" and "a real bookstore" with "real espresso," "real buildings and places," each with "a real purpose."[35] Where Disneyland seeks to hide all things fabricated, CityWalk exposes its fakeness, letting you see past the bright, wondrous fake faces to the real buildings, and past the real buildings to other parts of Universal, and then to the real Los Angeles beyond. It is what it says it is: a great place to walk around and enjoy some of the best of the City, period.

But it is not true to itself. Ed Leibowitz of *Los Angeles Magazine* summarized the general critique of Jerde's designs: "His architecture is a parody of a city, with all the grit and complexity wiped away."[36] It is especially not true to Los Angeles itself, where nobody walks anywhere and the buildings and boulevards alike are impersonal and unremarkable. CityWalk abounds with life-sized, fun-filled, bright facades experienced not from the window of a car on a mission but the up-close vantage point of the sidewalk, going nowhere slowly. Leibowitz calls it "a shopping mall that refuses to be a shopping mall."[37] Everything spills out, over, and around. Jerde says CityWalk is "a great simulacrum of what L.A. should do. This isn't the L.A. we did get, but it's the L.A. we could have gotten—the quintessential, idealized L.A."[38]

Leibowitz echoes Jerde when he points out that "on a Saturday night, City-Walk may be the most vital public space in Los Angeles" and goes on to note:

> People from all across L.A. have gathered here in one great undifferentiated mass, as they rarely do in the city itself. Toddlers are tearing across CityWalk's sidewalk fountain. Salvadoran, Armenian, Korean, black, and white, they squeal as the hidden water jets erupt, soaking their overalls. Hundreds of teenagers who have made CityWalk their hangout are picking each other up and sucking down frozen mochas. Families from Encino to East L.A. are laughing, stuffing their faces, gawking at the bright spires of light. [39]

The obviously fake Universal CityWalk works because it is a Real-fake, showing off its unreality while throwing off all trappings of being true to its locale.[40]

As with all other modes, successful Real-fake offerings run the gamut of economic offerings. They include commodities such as the translucent concrete invented by Hungarian architect Aron Losonczi (is concrete, but does not act like it), goods such as gas-burning fireplaces (is a fireplace, but without real wood logs), services such as Hertz #1 Gold (is your name in lights, but the same basic car as everyone else's), experiences such as CrossGolf (is golf clubs and balls, but not playing on a real course), and transformations such as the become-a-vintner offerings of Crushpad (is your own customized wine, but not your vineyard).

Admittedly, differentiating between the Fake-real and the Real-fake can be confusing. Had we not provided each component above with a description in "is what it says it is, but not true to self" format, most readers would still recognize that these offerings fell short of Real-real, but many would not have known where to place each offering on the Real/Fake Matrix. With Fake-real offerings, perceived authenticity resides on the self-directed axis of Is True to Itself (what we'll often call, for brevity, the "True to Self" axis); therefore, you must focus on how well your offerings maintain *internal consistency* with themselves, where you offer them, and with the nature of your business. With the Real-fake, perceived authenticity resides on the other-focused axis of Is What It Says It Is (or "What It Says"); therefore, you must focus on how well the representation of your offerings maintain *external consistency* with others' direct perceptions of your offerings, your outlets, and your business.

To be Real-fake, never mask your inauthenticity as with the Fake-real; rather, reveal your unreality, whether through façades behind which one exposes the actual buildings as at Universal CityWalk, a central place at which people cannot do what you are known for as with the NBA Store, or signs that inform customers not to look for first-quality goods at a factory outlet.

Get Real

Being Real-real is the hardest of the four modes to achieve, generally taking a few decades, and sometimes many more, of burrowing into the fabric of the culture. We tend to view things as Real-real only if they are older than we are. When we ask people what companies they perceive as Real-real, common answers include Apple, The Body Shop, Coca-Cola, Evian, Harley-Davidson, L'Occitane en Provence, Patagonia, REI, Southwest Airlines, Starbucks, Tiffany, USAA, and Whole Foods. Occasionally a young upstart less than a couple of decades old does make the grade, such as Anthropologie, Honest Tea, Lush, or Restoration Hardware.

Once attained, Real-real is also the easiest mode to fall short of through subsequent activity. Real-real companies are held to high standards—or held up as examples—by patrons, the press, and pundits; the least bit of phoniness on either dimension of the Real/Fake Matrix will not go unnoticed. And phoniness is hard to avoid—there always exists some dimension of self to which a business is not completely true, and some dimension of what a business says about its offerings that it does not completely fulfill. Moreover, being perceived and branded as authentic puts a bull's-eye on your back and fuels suspicion that it might not be so—particularly in people who flaunt their desire for authenticity.

Therefore, think carefully before making this your goal—*especially* if today you deem your business and its offerings as Fake-real, Real-fake, or Fake-fake. If you decide Real-real is truly where you wish to reside, then first identify the sources of inauthenticity that cause your offerings to fall short of either authenticity standard, True to Self and What It Says.

If Fake-real, directly address the need to be what you say you are through actions such as these:

- Change the names of your offering, or even your business, to match what you are as a company.

- Align how you market yourself with what your customers perceive.

- Modify your venues, move your outlets, or change your channels to better fit the nature of your offerings and business.

- Ensure there is no disconnect between what you say about why you are in business—and therefore why customers should buy your offerings—and your real motivations.

- Finally, make sure all the various ways you physically represent your offerings never detract from what they really are. Conduct a top-to-bottom audit to discover all the cues that detract from everything you want to convey.

If Real-fake, then directly address issues of being true to self:

- Modify your offerings until they accurately reflect the very nature of your particular business.

- Ensure that how customers view and use your offerings matches how you view them and their intended use.

- Offer nothing in any way antithetical to the heritage of your company.

- Eliminate offerings (or components thereof) that do not further the purposes of your firm.

- Finally, make sure your company's values come through loud and clear in everything you do, in your offerings, in your marketing, and in the behaviors of your people.

If *Fake-fake* and therefore falling short on both dimensions, obviously you should look to both sets of actions above. Incremental change will not cut it, however. You almost certainly must gain a much better sense of what you are as a company, carry out wholesale changes in your organization to ensure its behaviors match what the company actually is, and make major modifications to your offerings to have any hope of rendering them authentic. And you must start now, because every passing moment, every executed decision, and every developed offering makes it that much harder to attain Real-real.

Finally, *if you honestly deem yourself Real-real today*, you cannot rest. You must even more relentlessly go through each of the actions outlined above and ensure there are no areas where you fall short; there is precious little room for error. To make that easier—not just for this one but all four modes of the Real/Fake Matrix—chapter 7 examines the ten elements of authenticity leading to each of the actions outlined above for Fake-real and Real-fake. These elements will allow you to put a microscope to your business in the search for any inauthenticities that preclude you from attaining your desired mode. Chapter 8 focuses on the What It Says dimension of the Real/Fake Matrix, showing you how to market your offerings in a way that customers will perceive as authentic. And chapter 9 focuses on the True to Self dimension, providing a strategic framework for maintaining your perceived authenticity over time.

7

Deconstructing Authenticity

HOW TO ASSESS YOUR BUSINESS

FTER COLLEGE, ONE OF US WORKED AT IBM FOR OVER A decade. He "bled blue," so much so that his father (himself an IBMer early in his career) once accused him of "being brainwashed," so steeped was he in Big Blue's values, called its "Basic Beliefs":

- Respect for the individual

- Service to the customer

- Pursuit of excellence

Thomas J. Watson Jr., son of the founder of the modern IBM Corporation and CEO of IBM from 1956 to 1971, established these in 1962.[1] He did not *devise* them; he *codified* what he, his father, and every successive CEO considered crucial to IBM's success and core to what IBM already *was*. Watson said at the time, "I believe that if an organization is to meet the challenges of a changing world, it must be prepared to change everything about itself except those beliefs as it moves through corporate life."[2]

While Watson intended IBM's basic beliefs to outlast any change in the information technology industry, he could not anticipate how much the industry would change over the next four decades. IBM's difficulties in maintaining leadership amid change led to the appointment of the first outsider, Louis V. Gerstner Jr., as CEO in 1993. Writing about his time at IBM, Gerstner referred to the durability of the company's values, but also how the errant *interpretation* of the Basic Beliefs had become disconnected from marketplace reality. He felt that the pursuit of excellence had turned into an "obsession with perfection," resulting "in a stultifying culture and a spider's web of checks, approvals, and validation that slowed decision making to a crawl"; service to the customer came to mean "'servicing our machines on the customers' premises,' instead of paying real attention to their changing businesses"; and respect for the individual "helped spawn a culture of entitlement" in which "an IBMer could do pretty much anything he or she wanted . . . with little or no accountability."[3] After turning around the company, Gerstner was succeeded in 2002 by a lifelong IBMer, Samuel J. Palmisano, who revisited the company's values, concluding that its Basic Beliefs had to change:

> An organic system, which is what a company is, needs to adapt. And we think values—that's what we call them today at IBM, but you can call them "beliefs" or "principles" or "precepts" or even "DNA"—are what enable you to do that. They let you change everything, from your products to your strategies to your business model, but remain true to your essence, your basic mission and identity.[4]

One year after taking the helm, Palmisano set out to codify a new body of values that, like the Basic Beliefs, would "be enduring, that would guide the company through economic cycles and geopolitical shifts, that would transcend changes in products, technologies, employees, and leaders."[5]

Palmisano surveyed over a thousand employees for input in structuring a three-day, intranet-based event called ValuesJam. During the Jam, employees submitted over ten thousand comments. Initial critiquing of the exercise itself eventually yielded to a constructive discussion about what was positive and negative about the company's values, its management, and its employees. The process resulted in a revised set of corporate values that Palmisano promulgated in November 2003:

- Trust and personal responsibility in all relationships

- Dedication to every client's success

- Innovation that matters—for our company and for the world[6]

Rather than abandon the Basic Beliefs as a relic, the ValuesJam essentially *brought them into* the present. It placed respect for the individual into the broader context of interpersonal relationships. It focused service to customers on outcomes, not just effort. Pursuit of excellence fueled a quest for innovation. And so the essence of IBM—its very identity—emerged in this re-articulation of the Basic Beliefs.

Only time will tell whether these revised values serve IBM as well as its original Basic Beliefs. Regardless, we applaud IBM's leadership for recognizing that IBM had changed and needed a body of values that better reflected the "essence" to which the company must now "remain true," as Palmisano properly put it, and guide the company into an uncertain future. In effect, he recognized the selfsame IBM would continue to succeed only if it expressed itself differently and relevantly over time.[7]

Further, Palmisano realized what so many CEOs ignore at their peril: "The CEO can't say to them, 'Get in line and follow me.' Or 'I've decided what *your* values are.'"[8] Rather than *devise* and *promote* a set of new values, Palmisano sought to *discover* and *foster* how employees thought about the company's values today and thereby explicitly recognize the shift in IBM's identity over the decades of its existence. He went even further by *saying* what those values were to all 320,000 worldwide employees on the company's intranet in November 2003, to IBM stockholders at the company's annual meeting in April 2004, to customers in sales calls and on its Web site, and to the world at large in, for example, the company's entry in Wikipedia.[9]

Establishing Standards of Authenticity

Every company—whether faced with the scale of industry disruption IBM confronted or simply seeking to contend with authenticity as a consumer sensibility—should seek to understand its own identity, *what it is*. What is the self to which you and your offerings must be true? What is the essence from which all your values flow, and how have your values evolved—for better or worse— over the course of your history? What are the defining characteristics that set you apart from every other company, not just in your industry but in the world? How would you delineate this identity for your enterprise? If you do not know, you cannot possibly hope to remain on the right half of the Real/Fake Matrix by being perceived as True to Self.

Similarly, to remain on the top half of the Matrix by being perceived as real on the dimension of What It Says, you must embrace what exactly you *say* about your business and its offerings, and understand how and whether that matches the reality people encounter. What exactly does your business say about itself? What does it lead others to believe? How does it reveal itself through its words and deeds and how it represents its business and its offerings?

A number of elements define these two standards (True to Self, What It Says) that yield the four modes (Real-real, Fake-real, Real-fake, and Fake-fake) in the Real/Fake Matrix. We offer five factors for each that most directly influence customer perceptions (realize, however, that there may be others uniquely suited to your business). Analyze how well you are doing at being true to the five elements of True to Self and at matching the five elements of What It Says to how customers actually encounter you. All told, the ten elements provide a path to rendering Real-real.

If you choose to accept your fate as Fake-real, focus on how your business should become more fully True to Self. Likewise, if being Real-fake is best for you, focus on What It Says and how well you present your fake self. If you go faux, use the ten elements to identify the inauthentic dimensions of your offerings and business that you should celebrate as Fake-fake, and thereby render *faux*thentic.

State Your Identity

Before you can work at being true to self, you must know the self to which you must be true. While there are myriad dimensions of self, the following five categories should help you determine your business' true identity:

1. **Essence of** *enterprise:* Who you are at your core

2. **Nature of** *offerings:* What you offer others

3. **Effects of** *heritage:* Where and when you came to be who you are today

4. **Sense of** *purpose:* Why you are in business

5. **Body of** *values:* How your identity is manifested

As you read about each of these, think about what your business *is* across all five, thereby arriving at your identity. Afterward, assess how well your business is true to self—how real or fake customers perceive it across each element.

Essence of Enterprise = Entity + Ethos

Consider: *Who* you are at your core—the type of entity, formed via legal charter or other means, as an ongoing concern set apart from others, and the ethos that disposes it to initiate actions in certain directions.

Do you sell to consumers, to businesses, or to both? Are you a conglomerate, corporation, partnership, mom-and-pop shop, sole proprietor, or other entity? Do you operate locally, regionally, domestically, transnationally, or globally? If you have multiple places where customers experience you, do you treat them all more or less uniformly (like The Gap), as unremittingly unique (like Joie de Vivre Hospitality), or somewhere in between (like Starbucks)? Your answers help reveal exactly who you are.

So does your business model.[10] Are you more of a craft (or invention) organization, where you organically figure out everything on the fly? A mass-production outfit producing the same offering repeatedly? A continuous improvement unit striving to get better with every execution? Or do you mass-customize, providing low costs, high quality, *and* individual customization? Of course, any large company will operate across multiple models, perhaps all four. Too often, however, managers apply techniques from one business model to an organization belonging to another, such as forcing continuous improvement techniques like Six Sigma on those trying to invent within Research & Development. It comes off as phony—especially to R&D employees, who know that their processes are (necessarily) not definable and repeatable enough to have such process enhancement methods forced on them.

Ownership and governance also affect who you are. When a publicly traded business goes private through a leveraged buyout, when a company decides to franchise the base business or outsource core operations, or when one acquires or is acquired by another company—all affect the corporate self to some degree, sometimes small but more often great. Sometimes the change is not in degree but in kind, as when one entity is swallowed by another. Netscape, for example, essentially disappeared within AOL. The Geek Squad, on the other hand, remains uniquely itself after its acquisition by Best Buy—something the retail giant very much wanted to preserve—precisely because of the Computer Task Force's ethos.[11]

While we view our primary audience as business enterprises, many readers will belong to other kinds of entities: charitable, governmental, educational, or religious. These four entities do differ *in kind*, not just degree, and therefore readers should carefully reconsider these commercial prescriptions in terms of the essence of the relevant kind of noncommercial enterprises, ensuring in particular that your essence remains true to the raison d'être of your entity discussed in chapter 2.

Consider now the *entity + ethos* of your own enterprise. What changes over time and what endures? Your enterprise has surely shifted over time; all do. But what lies at the core of your entity—your *essence*—to which you must remain unwaveringly true? What remains unique about your ethos, where others in your industry seem uniform? How can you become even more of who you already are? Understanding such uniqueness will help you render authenticity in all your pursuits. Any established enterprise that fails to generate unique offerings, preserve unique heritage, undertake unique purpose, or uphold unique values will wither and die from apathy, the great progenitor of the inauthentic.

Nature of Offerings = Output + Obligations

Consider: *What* you offer others—the category, class, or grade of output generated—and the contractual obligations attached to acquiring such output (especially price).

First acknowledge what business you are in. If you extract commodities, the nature of your offerings will be more raw and unrefined. If you manufacture goods, the offerings will be more processed and packaged. If delivering services, the offerings will be more instantaneous and involved. If staging experiences, they will be more distinct and dramatic. If you guide transformations, the nature of your offerings will require more introspection and intervention.

Your contractual and legal obligations—as buyer or seller—greatly influence this element of True to Self. Commodities differ whether offered FOB origin or FOB destination. Goods differ according to how easy they are to assemble, or whether buyers must purchase another good (e.g., batteries) for the first one to work properly. Services differ in where they occur. Experiences differ in whether the stager carefully scripts and controls guests' every moment or allows guests to self-direct their own time more fluidly. Transformations likewise differ in whether the prime catalyst for change is the elicitor (as with surgery) or the aspirant (as with fitness centers).

Increasingly, the source of one's input affects the nature of one's output. For example, many "pick your own" farms—the kind of "agritainment" venues that offer corn mazes, haunted hayrides, and other fare—often import pumpkins for the fall season and array them as if grown there in a roadside patch. Some farmers freely admit that they cannot meet the demand from their local land, but others falsely claim to have clipped the pumpkins off the vine for reasons of safety and convenience.[12] Honesty should be the seller's minimum obligation—and with the transparency of today's Internet age, dishonest enterprises seldom go undiscovered for very long.

The Internet and various networked mobile devices also influence the nature of one's offerings. Is one's output digitizable? The nature of digital offerings affects how real customers deem them. When does an online publication cease to be a newspaper column and become a fancy blog? Or does the immediacy of blogging, the interconnections between bloggers, and the unedited content and links to related material render blogs more real than highly edited, polished, and produced publications? Does the informality, character, and personableness of Craigslist seem more real than the bland regimented classifieds of any newspaper?

Your offerings should reflect the essence of your enterprise. If you refuse to pander to customers, kowtow to shareholders, or submit to decorum, and instead fashion offerings from a genuine sense of self, then you go a long way to being perceived as authentic. Think of the Grateful Dead, who allowed fans to record every concert and played their own music without bending to critical acclaim or crass commercialism.

New York Times Magazine writer Rob Walker describes certain young product designers as today's "brand underground" whose "real significance . . . may be that no other spectacular subculture has so exuberantly venerated the leveraging of nonmainstream authenticity into entrepreneurial and material success."[13] Richard Branson also fits this mold: "To me, business isn't about wearing suits or pleasing stockholders. It's about being true to yourself, your ideas and focusing on the essentials."[14]

Rocker Mick Fleetwood of Fleetwood Mac is similarly his own bold self. Now a wine aficionado, he produces his own wines for sale. Unlike many celebrities who merely lend their names to the labors of others, Fleetwood involves himself in each of the choices that go into his wines, all blends of particular choice varietals, without regard to cost or quantity. He told us that his sole determinant for what goes into his wine is his own personal taste; each blend "is something special to me. I know what I like and don't worry about what other people think. I do hope they love the experience of drinking it, don't get me wrong, but every wine has to be simple and genuine, a reflection of my style and my journey through life."[15]

Finally, whether you charge a fee or not for your offerings affects their nature. Your output is not an *economic* offering unless customers must pay a price to obtain it. So scrutinize your *output + obligations*. What is for free, and what commands a fee? You are what you charge for.[16] What prohibits you from charging a price for that which saves your customers time and effort? When you get right down to it, you should question any output dispensed without compensation. Either charge for it, or stop doing it.

Effects of Heritage = Origin + History

Consider: *Where* and *when* you came to be who you are today—the place and time in which the enterprise and its offerings originated—with the subsequent history of each in the world, generating the story of who you are today.

Companies, as with people, are the products of nature and nurturing. The circumstances of their inception foundationally shape their identity. How a company comes into being factors into its identity now and in the future. Who were the founders? What kind of individuals were they? What were their backgrounds? Where was the company formed? Why? What was happening at the time locally, nationally, and globally? All these factors help define the heritage of an enterprise and its offerings.

So does everything that happens post-formation. How long before the business consistently generated bottom-line profits? What led to its successfully becoming an ongoing concern? Who joined the company as early employees, and what sort of people came later? What milestone events and heart-wrenching decisions affected it substantively? What fabled stories do employees tell about the company? What rituals have formed over time? All these particulars shape what the enterprise is and does today.

People often use the term "corporate DNA" to describe the basic core of a company.[17] However, the phrase as used describes not merely the "genetics" of a firm's founding (its nature) but in fact the sum total of that company's decisions and activities (its nurture) as well. It describes the company as it exists today—what it is as a result of its heritage, springing from its origin.

Of the five elements, heritage is central to being True to Self—so much so that it forms the basis of the framework in chapter 9, where we focus solely on this dimension of the Real/Fake Matrix. This centrality leads many companies to honor their heritage and make it relevant to customers by creating brand lands, theme worlds, experiential brand centers, brand attractions, and the like—the Guinness Storehouse in Dublin; World of Coca-Cola in Atlanta; the Ford Rouge Factory Tour in Detroit; and Swarovski's Kristallwelten outside its original factory in Wattens, Austria (where you can experience crystal but cannot tour the secret factory).

Each of these places educates customers about the company's history and its current offerings. Self-proclaimed trend scout Christian Mikunda observes, "In the days before the Industrial Revolution the 'making' of products was still immediately accessible for people. They were able to watch the cobbler repairing their shoes and craftspeople making products. This 'presence' created credibility and proximity, and fueled people's demands for buying something new or their desire to use a service. Then the entire production process was locked up in factories . . . [T]his function has now been taken over by those permanent exhibitions arranged at corporate locations."[18]

Most of these places honor the heritage of manufactured goods. Even commodities can garner such adulation; witness heritage-honoring places like the aforementioned Agrodome in Rotorua, New Zealand (a "working-sheep-and-cattle-farm" staging a "real hands-on, live experience of farming" including "a totally recreated, authentic 1950s era shearing shed complete with vintage shaft drive shearing machine"[19]) and the Corn Palace Convention & Visitors Bureau in Mitchell, South Dakota (basically Mitchell's town hall decorated each year with a façade of corn to honor the thousand-year-old history of corn-growing in the region).

A newer breed of cultural heritage centers is also emerging, such as The Tunnels of Moose Jaw in Saskatchewan, and Storyeum in the Gastown section of Vancouver, both designed by Canadian-based Historical XPeriences. Even in this highly security-conscious era, the U.S. federal government provides heritage tours in every significant government building in Washington, D.C. Service provider Nasdaq offers a MarketSite Experience, with the largest permanent LCD display in the world, fronting Times Square.[20] Experience stagers also leverage heritage. The Walt Disney Company honors its founder with "Walt Disney: One Man's Dream" at Disney-MGM Studios. Many sports teams create special places of honor, such as the World of Ajax (in the soccer club's home at the Amsterdam ArenA) and the Packers Hall of Fame (at Lambeau Field in Green Bay, Wisconsin). The National Baseball Hall of Fame and Museum in Cooperstown, New York, the Hockey Hall of Fame in Toronto, and the World Golf Hall of Fame in St. Augustine, Florida, honor both the origin and the history of their respective sports.

So ponder your where and when, your *origin + history*. Which authentic assets from your past deserve celebrating and honoring? What is hidden that you should now highlight? Conversely, which past practices or offerings now seem to downplay—or worse, dishonor—your heritage? Which lowlights from yesteryear should you downplay? Which legacy practices are you continuing solely from inertia? Think richly about the future. Ask yourself: For which future accomplishments do you wish to be remembered? Act on those for sustained heritage.

Sense of Purpose = Intention + Interests

Consider: *Why* you are in business—the intention to which you put the firm, encompassing why the business exists at all beyond merely making a profit, and the interests the enterprise and its employees have in banding together to meet this aim.

The raison d'être of a business—again, its reason for being, including its responsibility to society at large—is to make a profit for the sake of its shareholders and employees, and *thereby* do good. (Not to do good and *hopefully* make a profit, the lack of which does no one good.) But does that really inspire? A company also must have a *purpose*, beyond making a profit, that gives work meaning, defines why the enterprise is more than an accumulation of processes and an aggregation of employees, and points workers toward a common goal. Neil Crofts, founder of Authentic Business in the United Kingdom, believes that "purpose beyond profit" is fundamental to making a business authentic; it "shines through in every aspect of what it does ... In this way, everyone coming into contact with the business will experience the integrity of its purpose—the absolute congruence between what it says it stands for, what it thinks, what it believes, and what it actually does."[21]

Ask yourself about your own congruence: We exist to ... what? Think hard; the real answer to this short but difficult question points to your entity's underlying intention that can enable you to align your employees' interests with those of the company. The late Peter Drucker wrote over fifty years ago in *The Practice of Management*:

> As long as the purpose of the enterprise is seen by the employee as making a profit, he will be convinced of a basic difference between his interests and those of the enterprise. He will also be confirmed in the ancient superstition that production produces a profit, that, in other words, he produces it . . . But if the purpose of the enterprise is to create a customer, then there is harmony instead of conflict. For there can be no job if there is no sale, any more than there can be a sale if there is no job . . .
>
> For this . . . converted profit from something that the worker supplies and the company takes from him, into something that the market supplies and both company and worker need equally. It made workers see that their real stake in the company was identical with the welfare of the company. And it made them see that both required profitability.[22]

Of course, creating a customer is the generic purpose of any enterprise; the question here is the *specific* purpose of *your* enterprise from which customers will be created, interests aligned, decisions made, actions taken, and profits produced.

In the lobby of ServiceMaster's headquarters in Downers Grove, Illinois, stands the company's purpose in the form of four lasting objectives carved into a marble wall with letters almost one foot tall:

To honor God in all we do

To help people develop

To pursue excellence

To grow profitably

In his book *The Soul of the Firm*, C. William Pollard, the company's former chairman and CEO, says, "The first two objectives are end goals. The second two are means goals. As we seek to implement these objectives in the operation of our business, they provide us with a reference point for seeking to do that which is right and avoiding that which is wrong. We are an inclusive environment that accepts the differences among people, yet we have a common standard that provides a unity of purpose."[23] Note how ServiceMaster's objectives distinguish it from any other company.

To differentiate from organizational DNA—which is much more inward-focused—many people, like Pollard, call a company's purpose its "soul." Robert Hall, professor emeritus of Operations Management at Indiana University, states in *The Soul of the Enterprise* that it is "a shared feeling that its objectives are worth sacrifice by those who work in it and by the society it serves."[24] After declaring "Don't get me wrong—I'm in business to make money," Tom Chappell, founder of Tom's of Maine and author of *The Soul of a Business*, says, "But that's not my only goal. I believe that the conventional, sole focus of maximizing gains for shareholders strips away that part of ourselves that needs to thrive. Something in us wants to endure beyond retained earnings, and that something is our soul."[25]

Writing down and promulgating a company's purpose aligns the interests of all who work there with one common intention. We cannot deny that enterprises and employees—not to mention stockholders and managers—have their own parochial interests even when an overarching intention is altruistic. In any large-scale organization, motivating people to ascend to and act on a shared sense of purpose is difficult—as is getting them to read from the same page, jump in the same boat, row in the same direction, and salute the same flag—especially when the organization applies these or any other clichés to its alignment efforts. Such platitudes come from lazy management and thus fail to achieve the organizational cohesion that comes from formulating hard-thought statements of purpose that drive bold strategies and create greater economic value.

Promulgating your purpose means not only solidifying a key element of the self to which you must be true, but codifying what that self is. Therefore, you now also must live up to the stated purpose to be what you say you are to others. Such *expressed statements* are an element of What It Says, so we will discuss such statements later in the chapter, when we address that dimension.

In the meantime, take an honest look at your *intention + interests*. What forms the sense of purpose for your company? What constitutes your enterprise's "soul"? For some it's there from the beginning (in its nature); for others, it must be developed over time (from its nurturing). In either case, a company's purpose flows expressly from its heritage and leads directly to its values. In assessing your purpose, it's important to discern (as Pollard did at Service-Master) what is an end versus what is merely a means. Failure to differentiate between the two makes it impossible to come up with meaningful purpose. How are you making this world a better place? Why is that important to you and your employees? Any interest pursued with wanton disregard for how the world is affected by your actions invites others to see your motives as dishonorable, and your intention as inauthentic.

Body of Values = Beliefs + Behaviors

Consider: *How* your identity is manifested—the principle beliefs through which purpose is imparted, decisions are made, actions are taken, and others (especially customers) perceive the essence of the company through the behaviors of its employees.

Every organization has a body of values that flows from its purpose. It may be explicit (as with IBM's original Basic Beliefs and new corporate values) or implicit—not promulgated, discussed, or perhaps even recognized. In either case, values constitute a good measure (in both senses of the phrase) of what the company *is*, because they influence decisions, affect actions, shape behaviors—and result in profits (or not). Frederick Harmon, former president of the international division of the American Management Association, points out, "In any company, the real source of profit is thousands of individual actions by individual employees. Add value to each of those acts and you add profit. The aim of corporate values is to add that value. In every act. All the time."[26]

Through this element, an enterprise most manifests itself outward to the rest of the world. This body of values, shared by all, forms an integral part of a company's identity, what Terrence Deal and Allan Kennedy label its *corporate culture*, "the fundamental character of . . . [an] organization, the attitude that distinguishes it from all others."[27] In *Organizational Culture and Leadership*, Edgar Schein formally defines culture as "A pattern of shared basic assumptions that the group learned as it solved its problems of external adaptation and internal integration, that has worked well enough to be considered valid and, therefore, to be taught to new members as the correct way to perceive, think, and feel in relation to those problems."[28] He points out that a set of basic underlying assumptions lies below the surface of what people say are their organization's values and "have become so taken for granted that one finds little variation within a cultural unit. In fact, if a basic assumption is strongly held in a group, members will find behavior based on any other premise inconceivable."[29]

Such beliefs can be hard to pinpoint, however, for they often differ, sometimes greatly, from what the organization says it stands for. Harvard Business School professor Chris Argyris calls "the set of beliefs and values people hold about how to manage their lives" *espoused theories of action*, while "the actual rules they use to manage their beliefs" are their *theories-in-use*.[30] While the latter are strongly held, they are rarely, if ever, discussed, remaining below the surface. This also makes them hard to change or to align with espoused values, no matter how good or grand they may be.

Consider Chick-fil-A. Sunday is one of the heaviest sales days in the quick-serve industry, and yet every one of its restaurants is closed the first day of the week. What would possess the company to do such a thing? It flows directly from the beliefs of the company founder, Truett Cathy, to affect the behaviors of everyone in the organization. Called "part of the Chick-fil-A recipe" on the company's Web site, Cathy wanted to ensure that "every Chick-fil-A employee and restaurant operator had an opportunity to worship, spend time with family and friends or just plain rest from the work week. Made sense then, still makes sense now."[31]

People for whom Sunday is just another day may find Chick-fil-A's policy curious, peculiar, quaint, or even stupid. Those for whom Sunday remains something sacred or special, however, are not only more likely to view the company as authentic but also more likely to frequent Chick-fil-A outlets the other six days—precisely because the firm's beliefs and behaviors match their own. Companies whose values conform to their customers' self-image in this way often develop a rabid following, becoming what Alex Wipperfürth calls "hijacked brands" that not only must be true to self, but also must not "stray from the core values and belief systems of their markets . . . staying true to the inherent values of [their] consumers."[32]

One such brand: Starbucks. As Chairman Howard Schultz says in *Pour Your Heart into It*, "Authenticity is what we stand for. It's part of who we are. If we compromise who we are to achieve higher profits, what have we accomplished? Eventually all our customers would figure [it] out . . ."[33] If a company compromises its values for higher profits, customers will most certainly figure it out, and know that it sold out. In February 2007 Schultz himself, however, figured out that the behavior of Starbucks managers and employees was no longer living up to its beliefs. In a memo to CEO Jim Donald widely leaked to the business press, he wrote that management decisions like automating espresso creation and bagging ground coffee in flavor-locked packaging "have lead to the watering down of the Starbucks experience, and, what some might call the commoditization of our brand"; such decisions were "stripping the store of tradition and our heritage," resulting in "stores that no longer have the soul of the past." Schultz pleaded: "Let's get back to the core."[34]

So how about the *beliefs + behaviors* that flow from your core? Does your company have a clear view of what it believes? Are these beliefs more than espoused values—are they actually manifested as values-in-use, ones that actually influence decisions, affect actions, shape behaviors, and result in profits? Some enterprises are all talk. If that describes you, then be frank: What's espoused as a prevailing attitude but exposed as hollow in terms of action? If, on the other hand, you and your colleagues seldom talk about such matters, challenge yourself: What does your enterprise really stand for? What does it stand against? Surely, stated principles not followed through with corresponding behavior yield the inauthentic, but so too does incessant action ungrounded in guiding principles.

What holds for how your identity is manifested—that the actual body of values of the people in the enterprise may differ from what those same people say they are—holds for each of the other elements of True to Self. Your sense of purpose—why you are in business—may be misaligned with what top management says the purpose is (or desires it to be). The effects of your heritage—where and when you came to be who you are today—may vary from what people say about that heritage, the lessons they wish to be learned versus those that have, in fact, been inculcated throughout the organization. The nature of your offerings—what you offer others—may no longer resemble that which you first put into the marketplace and may not match how you talk today about them to customers. Even the essence of your enterprise—who you are at your core—may disagree with who you think you are, and therefore with how you talk about yourself to customers, to employees, to stockholders, and to the world at large.

Identify Your Statements

Before you can work on the second dimension of the Real/Fake Matrix—being what you say you are to others—you must take an inventory of what exactly you say about yourself. While one could again draw up a long list of how companies represent themselves, the following five categories comprise a model for the most important ways a business can talk about its self:

1. **Assigned** *names:* Who you call yourself

2. **Expressed** *statements:* What you articulate you are

3. **Established** *places:* Where and when you're encountered

4. **Declared** *motivations:* Why you say you are in business

5. **Displayed** *appearances:* How you show what you are

These five elements emanate from the five elements for True to Self. Names—explicitly chosen words—epitomize the entity through formal designations; statements directly convey information about the enterprise and its offerings; places attest to an inherited past through a visible present; motivations communicate a company's sense of purpose; and appearances signify values in ways that transcend mere verbal communications.

Of course, more than a mere one-to-one correspondence exists between the elements of What It Says and those of True to Self. Each of these new elements relates to *all* of the previous five:

- Names are assigned to offerings, heritage, purpose, and values—not just the enterprise.

- Statements are made about the enterprise, its heritage, purpose, and values—and not just offerings.

- Places represent not only the heritage of the enterprise, but present its offerings, reveal its purpose, and embody its values.

- Motivations are most intertwined with their corresponding element of purpose, but nonetheless provide the context in which all the others are perceived.

- Appearances manifest all elements of self.

In other words, each of these five What It Says elements manifests a different way to represent the various dimensions of self—entity, offerings, heritage, purpose, or values—each of which you can assign, express, establish, declare, or display in a particular manner.

As a collection, they comprise what the branding community likes to call "identity," often modified by "brand" or "corporate." However, such use confuses *actuality* with *representation*.[35] Corporations, places, and offerings have actual identities (the *selves* to which they must be true to be perceived as authentic), not just articulations of those identities (the *representations* that must accurately reflect those selves to be perceived as authentic). There's an old saw in advertising circles: nothing makes a bad product fail faster than good advertising. There should be a new one in branding circles: nothing makes a real branding effort fail faster than a phony product. Such phoniness results from representations detached from the reality of a company's actual identity.

Contrast Kerrygold and Baileys Original Irish Cream. In an instructive *BusinessWeek* article entitled "The Myth of Authenticity," freelance journalist Alicia Clegg contrasts how these two Irish brands represent themselves. Dairy products producer Kerrygold, Clegg points out, has a "heavy-handed name, hinting cheesily at the crocks of gold from Kerry. The packaging has been updated for some markets; but the website . . . is unashamedly cod 'Irish,' garrulous in style and littered with spurious references to folklore and cultural stereotypes."[36] On the other hand, "So far as the ingredients go, Baileys is what it says: Irish. The production site is Irish, the farms supplying the milk are Irish; the cows . . . are Irish . . . [T]he Celtic motifs on the label surely hint at . . . [an] ancient past . . . [There is] a flowing handwritten signature, R.A. Bailey, underlined with a flourish, as if to scupper any doubts about the author's existence. There is also the name itself—incredibly Irish, without being clichéd."[37] Of course *both* brands are myths, modern-day inventions (Kerrygold was created in the 1960s, Baileys in 1974)—fakes, fakes, fakes. No matter; one renders itself authentic through What It Says, while the other does not.

For this dimension of the Real/Fake Matrix, we address the five key elements that, although not exhaustive, together help to understand the substance of the *other-focused* task of representing your identity in the marketplace. Keep in mind your own business as you read, again without judging how real or fake it is in saying what it is—and just examine *what* it says it is to others and thereby identify your statements.

Assigned Names = Dimensions + Designations

Consider: *Who* you call yourself—the formal designations used to signify various dimensions of your self—especially the names assigned to your company, your brands, and your individual offerings.

As opposed to our personal names, for which we can thank (or blame) our parents, all business names—whether bestowed on a whim or after months of research and study—are chosen specifically to represent one or more dimensions of identity. As the authors of *The Making of a Name* emphasize, "A good name conveys something real and specific about a company, product, or service. [Or any offering.] Meaningful brand names (*Slender* versus *Metrecal*, *DieHard* versus *Delco*, *Budget* versus *Avis*, and *Sprint* versus *MCI*) have an innate memory advantage."[38] As do *Universal CityWalk* versus *Southdale Shopping Center*, *Whole Foods Market* versus *Safeway Stores*, and *ESPN Zone* versus *Applebee's*.

Many meaningful names not only spark memory but readily connote authenticity. Tops on the list are those companies referentially named after their founders, such as Sears, Roebuck and Co., J. C. Penney, Ford Motor Company, E.I. du Pont de Nemours, Kellogg Company, Harley-Davidson, and Levi Strauss & Co. Such appellations refer back to the companies' origin, associating the companies with one or more real, live, breathing people who caused these entities to come into being. Such associations gain strength when companies actively promote their lasting connection to their founders, as do The Walt Disney Company, Hewlett-Packard, Mary Kay, and Carlson Companies, and even more so when they strive to follow the principles laid down and exemplified by their founders, as do Wal-Mart, Deere & Company, Marriott International, and Ogilvy & Mather. As Mark Ritson, professor of marketing at Melbourne Business School, notes, such founders "are the brand and their presence confers an authenticity that no other marketing tool can emulate."[39]

People also tend to perceive companies as authentic when their names place them in particular, well, places. Recall our earlier discussion of such places/names as Champagne and Gorgonzola. Place-based names may come from regions, such as Land O'Lakes and Williams-Sonoma (which is a twofer, combining the name of founder Chuck Williams with the Californian foodies' favorite valley); cities, such as Boise Cascade and Smithfield Foods: or even particular locales within cities, such as Saks Fifth Avenue (New York), State Street Corporation (Boston), and The Savile Row Company (London). Of course, not all companies that *say* they're connected to a particular place really *are*; a quick Google search, for example, found a Savile Row Custom Clothiers of St. Louis, Missouri, and Saville Row Clothiers of Deerfield Beach, Florida. (If you're in the custom clothing business and name yourself after the most famous street in the world for customizing men's clothing—spelled "*Savile Row*"—you had better operate a custom clothing operation—and not just sell suits off the rack—to have any hope of matching what you say you are.)

Names also help render authenticity when they refer back to times when life was simpler, slower-paced, and, seemingly at least, more authentic. Many firms, for example, have "Main Street" in their name for this reason. Such is the case with the Main Street Restaurant Group of Phoenix, the world's largest franchisee of T.G.I. Friday's locations, among other restaurants; "Chain Street Restaurant Group" might more accurately reflect its true self, and such Real-fake acknowledgment of the nature of its business might help overcome the stigma of inauthenticity so often associated with chains.

Others employ words that referentially evoke previous economic eras, including putting "craft" (suggesting Agrarian hands) or "works" (suggesting Industrial labor) in their names, as if every offering were handmade by a skilled craftsman in a workshop or small factory. (Interestingly, Service Economy terms—such as "force" or "center"—have not yet gained the same authentic standing, although in time that may come.) Think of LensCrafters, Image-Crafters, Build-a-Bear Workshop, Bath & Body Works, GameWorks, PhotoWorks, and so forth. This seems to be a tactic to which creative firms in fields like design, advertising, and architecture take a particular liking.

Some firms use names to refer to a heritage, person, or place that simply does not exist. The most famous must be Häagen-Dazs, a company founded by Reuben Mattus in the Bronx, New York, in 1961. Mattus spent his whole life in the ice cream business, single-handedly originating the premium ice cream category with Häagen-Dazs. To give his creation cachet and, according to the brand's Web site, "convey an aura of the old-world traditions and craftsmanship to which he remained dedicated," Mattus gave it a Scandinavian-sounding name.[40] He also reportedly placed maps of Denmark on early cartons.[41] And it worked. (We don't recommend this "try to fool your customers" approach today.)

For new companies, as well as new brands and offerings, choosing a name—not just one that connotes authenticity, but *any* name—has become increasingly difficult. The *Wall Street Journal* has proclaimed that all the real names are gone, as companies increasingly rely on neologisms for corporate names, from Altria to Xilinx, and for brand names, from Acela to Zetia.[42] The resulting perception: fake companies with fake brand names. Of course, acronyms and initialisms also detract from authenticity—after all, they're not real words.

One of the best (or worst, if you prefer) ways to kill authenticity is selling naming rights to the highest bidder, a growing trend with sports stadiums, performance centers, and other venues with edifice-based advertising value.[43]

Any enterprise that does this—a more apt example of selling out in business would be hard to find—automatically prevents people from perceiving the buildings as authentic. The decision says, quite pointedly, that the business cares more about making a quick buck than exemplifying who it is and its own heritage. Hospitals, universities, and other nonprofit institutions should likewise think twice about naming a building, or a wing, or a room after a donor—those intimately associated with the organization and its heritage excepted. The practice puts the issue of money front and center with most visitors, who are highly unlikely to perceive the practice as anything but inauthentic.[44]

How about a real offering with a real name for what its creators want to be perceived as a real place? Consider a new housing development in the Minneapolis-St. Paul suburb of Lakeville. According to *St. Paul Pioneer Press* reporter Bob Shaw, "As a name for a billion-dollar project, 'Brandtjen Farm' had two flaws. One was the word 'Brandtjen.' The other was the word 'farm.'"[45] The development of over two thousand homes on five hundred–plus acres was actually on the site of the original Brandtjen Farm, founded in the 1930s by printing press innovator Henry A. Brandtjen Sr., the son of German immigrants. Developer Rob Wachholz imagined small lots and narrow streets with canopied trees, front porches close to sidewalks, garages in the back, bike trails, and alleyways.[46] He "decreed that authenticity would be the heart of the project" and therefore "was committed to an authentic name."[47] But most of his colleagues and consultants objected; Todd Bolin, head of the agency charged with coming up with the right name, said simply: "You can't live in the past."[48] The right name that would bring the past forward into the present finally emerged: Spirit of Brandtjen Farm.

Businesses should not use authenticity as the sole criterion in choosing company, brand, or offering names, but they should recognize that more than anything else names define *who* you say you are. So reflect on your *dimensions + designations*. Are there any misnomers that do not accurately, appropriately, or adequately convey the essence of your enterprise? Remember: any designation—of your company, your brands, your offerings, employee titles, places, props, promotions, or any other dimension of your enterprise—provides an opportunity to render that thing more authentic.

Expressed Statements = Media + Messages

Consider: *What* you articulate you are—the use of any media—advertising, marketing and sales materials, Web site pages, public statements and filings, and all other communiqués—to send messages about your self.

Most companies express themselves via advertising. What you say in such advertisements still goes a long way to forming opinion about your authenticity, or lack thereof. Companies therefore increasingly focus their advertisements precisely on rendering their offerings as authentic. Mark Wnek, chairman and chief creative officer of the New York office of ad agency Lowe Worldwide, confesses that the old ways of slick advertising "are finished"; rather, "the new big deal is authenticity."[49] Jim Beam's first-ever TV advertisement, released in 2005, tracks the changing look of a rack house and its workers over time as a voice-over declares, "Whoever said change is good knows squat about making bourbon. For 210 years and seven generations, we've stayed true to the original Beam family recipe. Here's to stubbornness."[50] Not wanting to miss a trick, the unit of Fortune Brands employed another time-honored vehicle for expressed statements, the press release, to trumpet, "Jim Beam Bourbon Captures 210 Years of Authenticity in First-Ever National TV Ad Campaign."[51]

Another prime example: Dove's "Campaign for *Real* Beauty," featuring real, full-bodied women under taglines such as "Real women have real curves," challenged stereotypes about beauty (e.g., only the thin, only blondes, or only the young are beautiful).[52] Unilever even put the picture of a beautiful ninety-six-year-old woman named Irene on a giant electronic billboard in Times Square. Unilever public relations told us that "total media impressions" surpassed 650 million by the end of year 2005. Note in particular how Unilever never said *Dove* was "real," only that the featured women were real.

Many companies aim their advertising not just at potential customers but also at employees, to ensure that they "walk the talk" and thereby be what the company says it is in all their interactions with customers. Mars' Masterfoods USA unit dedicated a significant share of a $200 million ad campaign for its Pedigree dog food to ensuring that employees understood what the brand was all about, and even used non-marketing employees to develop the internal program. As vice president of marketing Chris Jones said, employees "would see through" an artificial program: "This is true and it's genuine."[53]

Beware of using advertising to appeal directly to authenticity, because what is said may not correspond to what is, or more accurately, to what customers *perceive* the reality to be. That's why many companies that appeal to authenticity so often use other means of stating what they are. For example, Starbucks rarely advertises to promote its offerings but rather its *self*. Why? Clearly, and precisely, to proclaim its authenticity—without saying so explicitly. Each ad has the same sparse format: a provocative question or statement in all capital letters at the top—including "Owned and operated by human beings." and "What makes coffee good?"—with about a quarter page of text, a pointer to a Web site for learning more, and the company's Siren logo superimposed over a building at the bottom.[54]

Starbucks also makes extensive use of another medium of expressed statements: brochures, placards, handouts, and other printed materials. You will find a plethora of pamphlets in every outlet. One is the ubiquitous customer satisfaction survey ("How are we doing?"); some are primarily functional ("Make It Your Drink: A Guide to Starbucks Beverages" or "Starbucks Careers: Create Escape"); many are strictly marketing ("The World of Undiscovered Beverages," "Apply for the Starbucks Card Duetto Visa," or "Experience Starbucks at Home: A Guide to Our World of Coffees"); but many focus squarely on authenticity in one way or another ("Commitment to Origins," "Living Our Values," "Starbucks and Fair Trade," and "Poems from the Coffee Lands"). All provide evidence of exactly what the company is and what it stands for.[55]

Web sites, whether a company's primary site or special-purpose platforms, have become effectively mandatory for businesses of all sizes, and many, like Starbucks, use them to express what they are, often explicitly; a Google search yields over 350,000 Web sites with all three of the exact phrases "who we are," "what we do," and "how we do it." It can also be done with panache; go to experience creator Jack Morton Worldwide's Web site and encounter "this really long sentence that explains who we are" preceding a really long sentence that explains who they are.[56]

You'll find similar formulations in annual reports and other public statements.[57] Take, for example, communication services group WPP's *Annual Report and Accounts 2004* statement. Before you get to the detailed financial data—the ostensible reason for the report in the first place—one first encounters sections on "Who we are," "Why we exist," "How we're doing," "What we think," "Who runs WPP," "How we behave," and "How we're rewarded."

In addition to annual reports and other legally required documentation, many businesses voluntarily publish reports on corporate social responsibility (CSR). Such reports have become de rigueur, in no small part because political activists clamor for companies to address responsibilities they feel are owed to others besides shareholders, but also because consumers (and investors) tend to see CSR as an authentic response to the issues facing the world. But paying lip service to the issues is dangerous. If some company publishes a CSR report simply because everyone else does, or to get activists off its tail (and on to someone else's), then the company and its offerings will be perceived as what they are: phony.

To avoid that perception companies increasingly rely on various forms of *authentication*—verification that some thing is what it says it is. Since 1935 France has bestowed its Appellation d'Origine Contrôlée (AOC) designation on foodstuffs that meet certain criteria for origin, sourcing, and production methods. The American Heart Association displays a red-and-white "heart-check mark" on foods that meet its health guidelines. PepsiCo places its own "SmartSpot" symbol on offerings it deems healthier. In another such example of authentication specifically authenticating authenticity, if you will, Whole Foods affixes its own seal designating "Authentic Food Artisan" to goods offered by "small, family-run enterprises passionate about handcrafting the finest foods in small batches using traditional methods," such as Big Tree Farms Handcrafted Balinese Sea Salt.[58] Authenticating marks are also getting more sensory—GetHuman created an "earcon," or auditory icon, to indicate the company you called follows its standards, and—more surreal—an outfit called 100% Verified Celebs authenticates that a MySpace profile that purports to be from a celebrity actually is.

Corporate autobiographies provide one more popular way companies express their selves, in what literary critic Geoffrey Hartman calls "a kind of self-authentication." As he goes on to relate, "The struggle of the individual against inauthenticity leads to a distinct increase in autobiographical reflection . . . It presumes a convergence, even coincidence, of first-person narrator and the self being portrayed."[59] In the past, business autobiographies seemed primarily about the person; but this new form of autobiography—including William Pollard's *The Soul of the Firm*, Tom Chappell's *The Soul of a Business*, and Howard Schultz's *Pour Your Heart into It*—represents the confluence of first-person founder with founded company.[60] Some business leaders already use new media to represent self-as-executive-as-company: for example, Jonathan Schwartz, president and CEO of Sun Microsystems, maintains a blog at blogs.sun.com /jonathan.

Consider your own use of *media + messages*. What statements are you articulating about your company, your offerings, your customers, your employees, and your suppliers? How is your choice of media (which, you'll remember from Marshall McLuhan, massages the message in particular directions[61]) enhancing or detracting from the perceived authenticity of those statements? Recognize that any message running counter to what's actually experienced by customers will tend to brand you as inauthentic.

Established Places = Venues + Events

Consider: *Where* and when you're encountered—the indigenous character of your venues—geographical regions and territories (city, state/province, country) as well as particular locales and sites within each—that distinguish you from others, and the events that originate (as sources), traverse (through channels), and exhibit (at outlets) your self in physical and virtual domains.

The growing number of companies identifying with their locale shows the importance of place to authenticity, as we saw with assigned names. One such company in the personal body care business: L'Occitane en Provence, whose name emphasizes its origins—Provence, the southeastern region of France and Occitan, the local language still spoken there (also known as Provençal). CEO Reinold Geiger claims that "'authenticity, sensuality, respect' are the differentiating concepts of the brand."[62] Exemplifying that, workers in its retail outlets make a point to emphasize where the company's goods come from, how they came about, the methods by which they are produced today, and—as L'Occitane's tagline attests—that it is all "A True Story." Olivier Baussan, who founded the company in the mid-1960s with a makeshift still on the back of an old Citroën 2CV and recently returned as a public ambassador, says, "My role is to transmit stories."[63] Further connecting its name to its place of origin and, not incidentally, also to its heritage, the company's Web site proclaims, "With its roots in Provence, L'Occitane shares the colors, scents and traditions of the south of France with the world."[64]

Emphasizing *roots*, with the sense of being extended into the earth at a particular place, lies at the core of such place-based companies. David Boyle of London's New Economics Foundation rightly identifies "rooted" as one of nine strands of what he calls the New Realism, where "Real means rooted . . . Sometimes that means rooted in tradition . . . [b]ut more often it means rooted locally, with a place of origin—rather than the merely manufactured, that appears to come from deep in the countryside but doesn't. Often it doesn't matter where that somewhere is . . . what matters is that it is somewhere specific, made by someone specific."[65] Hence the rise of farmers markets, of restaurants serving locally grown produce and grocery stores selling it, of the French word *terroir* being applied to more than just wine—and the decline of so many chains, in terms of perceived authenticity if not also in operations. It's easier for a small local company to accentuate its locale than for a large national, or especially multinational one. Big companies all too often seem to be from nowhere while chains become perceived as the same everywhere.

To avoid that fate, turn generic space into specific place. As Fred Kent, founder of Project for Public Spaces, says: "What we're hearing more and more is the need for authenticity. The real thing. People want places where they're comfortable, where they feel like they can connect with other people."[66] Richard Florida points out that members of the "creative class" avoid areas that some denigrate as "generica": "An authentic place also offers unique and original experiences. Thus a place full of chain stores, chain restaurants and nightclubs is not authentic: Not only do these venues look pretty much the same everywhere, they offer the same experience you could have anywhere."[67] Florida concludes that how authentic people perceive a place to be—whether a community, building, office, or outlet—depends on two factors: the look and feel of the surroundings, and what actually happens there. In our words, establishing place requires both venue and event.[68]

Hence the rise of "Lifestyle Centers" such as Country Club Plaza in Kansas City (the original of the genre); Crocker Park and Legacy Village outside of Cleveland; Mayfaire Town Center in Wilmington, North Carolina; CityPlace in West Palm Beach, Florida; or The Grove in Los Angeles. Such places remain open-air, where leisurely walking becomes a significant part of the experience.[69] The Grove, for example, appears to rise organically from the adjacent 1930s-era Farmers' Market. Developed by Rick J. Caruso, founder and CEO of Caruso Affiliated, the venue encompasses a trolley barn at one end, the commissioned statue "The Spirit of Los Angeles" near the other, and a wide pedestrian boulevard with antique lights, trees, benches, and distinctive storefronts in between. The Grove mixes in local businesses—such as Bodega Chocolates, Surf City Squeeze, and the Amadeus Spa—with unique (but multistore) companies such as Anthropologie, Quicksilver Boardriders Club, and L'Occitane—plus a few chain stores including the Gap, Barnes & Noble, and Crate and Barrel. Here, however, even these national outfits changed their own retail designs to fit in to this unique locale.[70]

HOK Sport Venue Event of Kansas City, Missouri, architects stadiums, convention centers, and other places of public assembly that fit in their environment so well they practically exude perceived authenticity.[71] HOK Sport cemented its reputation with Oriole Park at Camden Yards, the first baseball stadium to successfully combine a traditional urban ballpark design, firmly rooted in its city setting, with modern game-experience amenities. Most all of the facilities HOK designed since—from Jacobs Field in Cleveland to the St. Louis Cardinals' new stadium, literally built around the old Busch Stadium in 2006, and even minor-league installations such as Durham Ballpark in North Carolina, Harbor Park in Norfolk, Virginia, and The Baseball Grounds in Jacksonville, Florida—directly appeal to authenticity through how they bring in elements of the great ballparks of the past and integrate them into the specific locale in which each stadium is situated.[72] Joe Spear, founding senior principal, told us, "That so many people view our work as authentic is no accident; for each new project we purposefully look at the traditions of the sporting event that will fill the park, the heritage of the team that will play its home games there, and the history where the venue will be situated and use all of it as the primary ingredients to bring forth in our design."[73]

Even if you don't establish your own places, the choice of outlets or channels that sell your offerings say something about yourself. While few companies explicitly manage their perceived authenticity as much or as well as Starbucks, one can't help but wonder why management chose to partner with United Airlines to "Proudly Brew Starbucks Coffee" onboard.[74] It is a risky strategy to put the manifestation of your identity into the hands of an airline, or any other established place where poor experiences are endemic.

As with the heritage element of True to Self, established places is the third of five elements because it is central to What It Says, and will therefore form the basis of the framework in chapter 8, where we focus solely on this second dimension of the Real/Fake Matrix. For now, do survey every—yes every—*venue + event* in your corporate landscape. What venues lack staged events—daily, weekly, monthly, quarterly, annually, once-in-a-lifetime—to render them more authentic places? What events are making do with inadequate venues? Most particularly: where and when do you run the risk of having your names and statements being perceived as inauthentic? Wherever and whenever that is, focus on establishing effectively rendered places.

Declared Motivations = Ideals + Incentives

Consider: *Why* you say you are in business—the public ideals for which you claim to be in business, beyond merely (and rightfully) wanting to make a buck as well as the incentives (both internal and external) that exist to encourage those ideals.

Of all of the elements comprising What It Says, declared motivations seems most intrinsically intertwined with its corresponding element for True to Self, sense of purpose. That's because both spring from the hardest of questions: Why? In any endeavor it's difficult enough just to *understand* our own motivations—so often do we rationalize post hoc what we already decided emotionally—much less codify them in a cogent, compelling fashion.

One form of declared motivation is, we believe, a direct consequence of executives struggling with the company self and what to say about it, who aim it primarily at enlightening and inspiring employees and only secondarily (and often not at all) at informing or influencing outsiders. These are formal statements—credos, manifestos, declarations, and other such proclamations—that document a company's purpose, set forth its ideals, and provide incentives to employees to live up to those ideals.

One of the oldest is the famous Johnson & Johnson credo, written on one page by its longtime leader General Robert Wood Johnson in 1943.[75] It has served J&J admirably over the past sixty-plus years, most notably during the Tylenol scares of 1982 and 1986. Luxury hotelier Ritz-Carlton also has a well-known Credo consisting of only three easily memorized sentences, beginning with the company's purpose, "The Ritz-Carlton Hotel is a place where the genuine care and comfort of our guests is our highest mission."[76] Hotel managers take employees through the Credo or the basic principles derived from it *every single day*.

Something akin to that happens for every single mission undertaken in the United States Army. The former President of the Army War College, Major General Robert Ivany (retired), here describes *commander's intent*, the mechanism the Army uses to motivate soldiers to fulfill battle missions:

> Realizing that fast-moving operations demanded initiative by subordinates, commanders began writing a concise statement explaining the overarching purpose for each operation. Written in his own words and no longer than a short paragraph, the commander provided a "feel" for what he wanted to accomplish . . .
>
> In the absence of specific orders, each subordinate leader was expected to act in accord with the overall purpose or "commander's intent" of the operation. Initiative was encouraged; waiting for orders was not. Soon, "Commander's Intent" statements were required in every order. They became readily accepted as clear, concise statements of what a team must do to succeed with respect to the opposition.[77]

Such declarations have proven critical to Army success, since on-the-ground situations change at a moment's notice, and no amount of specific, detailed guidance can cover all possible circumstances. Any business with a high degree of frontline interaction between employees and customers (who also change at a moment's notice) could similarly create "manager's intent" statements that explain the *why* of the company's mission—its overarching purpose—while giving employees maximum freedom of action to handle the *how* of any particular situation that comes up.

To handle the needs of more long-term transformational change projects, experience design firm Starizon, of Keystone, Colorado, creates a manifesto or declaration for every client as an integrated part of its methodology. These declarations were inspired by James Collins and Jerry Porras' discussion in *Built to Last* of "vivid descriptions" as a way of making goals "tangible in people's minds" though a "vibrant, engaging, and specific description."[78] Starizon helps client teams uncover the operational theme and strategic intention of the experience they want to create—its sense of purpose—but never without discussion and often with dissension. It brings everyone's words and ideas together into a united manifesto that is read aloud to the group. This fuses everyone's individual thoughts into one common purpose, with a structure that inspires and words that vividly describe the intention and stir the emotions. It is not unusual to see tears in the eyes of client participants as they see their work crystallize. As Gary Adamson, Starizon's chief experience officer, related to us, "There's no more powerful way of saying what you are about than through a manifesto. And there is no more powerful way of fulfilling your intention than by making every operating decision pass the standards set out in the manifesto. Its purpose, after all, is to 'make manifest.'"[79]

Starizon's manifestos are meant for *internal* inspiration and operational guidance; declaring motivations *externally* is fraught with peril. Promulgating your purpose publicly makes it all too easy for others to see if your behaviors and actions really match what you say the motivations behind them are. Think of Google and its well-known and high-minded motto "Don't be evil." The company struggles to apply it to increasingly complex situations—where "struggling," whether resulting in success or failure, signifies something better than "paying lip service."[80] It lost one struggle with the Chinese government, however, when the Communist Party objected to people being able to find detailed results to such queries as "human rights" and "things that are democratic." Former hedge fund manager and now technology writer Andy Kessler spoke for many when he responded to the decision, saying "poof" went Google's "cool" and likening it to the dictionary definition of "sellout."[81]

In Unilever's Campaign for *Real* Beauty, Dove's special-purpose Web site declares that it "aims to change the status quo and offer in its place a broader, healthier, more democratic view of beauty. A view of beauty that all women can own and enjoy everyday."[82] To accomplish this ideal, Dove undertook seven distinct initiatives, including the establishment of the Dove Self-Esteem Fund and the Program in Aesthetics and Well-Being at Harvard University, to go beyond merely *saying* that it is for "real beauty" to really *doing* something about it.

But is that all it is doing? It does not discredit the company's motives in the least to point out the obvious: it's also creating incentives for consumers to buy more beauty products. Marketing consultant Mary Lou Quinlan succinctly provides both perspectives: "As a woman, I feel good about [the Dove ads], but as a marketer, I still have to know, Where's the money?"[83]

The same is true for a series of Target ads celebrating various cultural events and charities that declared, right next to Target's bright red target logo, "Giving over $2 million every week. Making a real difference every day." The ads' taglines included "Real stories. Real tradition. Real spirit." and "Real generosity. Real kindness. Real hope." One during the 2005 Christmas season said "Real spirit of the season," and encouraged readers to visit Target.com/salvationarmy to purchase items from Target and then donate them (or cash) to The Salvation

Army. At least here we know where the money is: within all those charitable purchases Target is encouraging (which the company kindly informs donors are tax deductible). Moreover, this was the year after Target's much-publicized banishment of Salvation Army bell ringers from every one of its stores, providing yet another not-fully-altruistic motive.[84]

What happens when we, as businesses or individuals, trumpet our charity? What happens when we *tell* others how much we're giving to the unfortunate (whether for extraordinary events as with Hurricane Katrina or just in the normal course of charitable giving), even if to encourage them to give as well? It ceases to be pure charity.[85] The rationale that Jamie Foxx related at an NAACP event as to why he went to New Orleans to help victims of the hurricane applies not only to celebrities but all too often to companies in the public eye as well: "The reason you have to do this is you have to let them know that you're real."[86]

Again, let us be very clear: it does no disservice to the real help businesses (and individuals) provide at such times, nor to their virtuous ideals, to point out that other motives lurk in the background, and occasionally rise to the fore.[87] But such actions run the risk of being branded as phony when customers perceive either marketing or authenticity-rendering motivations alongside the altruistic. It might be wiser, in terms of rendering authenticity, to not publicize your charitable donations—the transparency of today's Internet Age practically ensures you will be found out anyway!

Consider now the *ideals + incentives* for your own overarching purpose. What *do* you declare about why you are in business internally and externally? What are the ideals you uphold publicly, and the incentives you furnish to ensure everyone is held accountable to those ideals? The proper answers to these questions go a long way to being perceived as authentic. Being half-hearted (ideals without incentives) or fool-hearted (incentives without ideals) provide two surefire paths to the inauthentic.

Displayed Appearances = Representations + Perceptions

Consider: *How* you show what you are—attributes of self communicated beyond text alone, including your logo, symbols, colors, packaging, and other such representations depicting your enterprise and its offerings—to induce a specific set of perceptions from others about your self.

This final element of What It Says comprises the purview of graphic designers, who provide physical cues that create the all-important "first impression" for offerings—and, of course, encourage potential customers to buy them. They should recall the lessons of chapter 3: do *not* slap "real" or "authentic" all over the packaging, but rather *render* such representations to be *perceived* as authentic. Kraft Foods'

Post cereal unit recently changed the packaging of Post Selects Blueberry Morning, for example, to eliminate all such references, instead saying only "Inspired by the taste of home-baked blueberry almond muffins" with images of such muffins next to a bowl of cereal. By no longer screaming "REAL," Kraft renders it more so.

H. J. Heinz Company redesigned its logo and labeling in 2006 specifically to connote authenticity. Rob Wallace, founder of Wallace Church Associates, calls Heinz one of a handful of "icon brands" that "evolve over time . . . but always stay true to their essence." His team designed new labels that effectively "married late 19th century conventions with early 21st century sensibilities."[88] These labels retain the instantly recognizable Heinz "keystone" shape and lettering, but place it in a context where authenticity can be instantly perceived, with "1869," the date of the company's founding, front and center, and whatever natural commodity from which the product was made—tomatoes for ketchup, pickles for relish, and a cornucopia of vegetables for vinegar—on the outside.

Displayed appearances can be *the* crucial element of determining authenticity, particularly for places. Consider Tombstone, Arizona, "The Town Too Tough to Die." It's in danger of losing its National Historic Landmark status because of "fake façades, anachronistic colors and bogus dates painted on newer buildings."[89] A local bed-and-breakfast owner decries, "It's becoming like a Hollywood set instead of an authentic historic Western town,"[90] and State Historic Preservation Officer James Garrison "urged residents to watch out for square nails—the only kind of nail available in the town until 1890. If you find a square nail, make sure that whatever it's holding stays on. That's the original authentic fabric of Tombstone."[91]

Such places, as well as all experience stagers, should focus particularly on the displayed appearance that Dean MacCannell calls "markers." He points out in *The Tourist*, "The first contact a sightseer has with a sight is not the sight itself but with some representation thereof."[92] Whether a road sign that says "Scenic overlook next exit," transparent signage on a Barnes & Noble window, a three-dimensional logo extending from the awning at a Starbucks, a building in the shape of an icon such as the Longaberger Company's home office in Newark, Ohio (which looks just like a giant version of one of its handwoven baskets)—each of these markers signifies a place worth experiencing.

Anything can be a marker. MacCannell treats the term expansively, covering "any information about a sight, including that found in travel books, museum guides, stories told by persons who have visited it, art history texts and lectures, 'dissertations' and so forth."[93] Much of MacCannell's work also ties in with what he calls "the problem of authenticity."[94] Because of this, we extend the term "sight" to *any* economic offering and adapt "marker" further to mean *any* representation by which people can judge that offering's authenticity or lack thereof. This, indeed, is the same sense in which people refer to trademarks, service marks, brand marks, and the like.[95]

One representation that so fully marks identity that it must not be ignored: Web sites. Many people first learn of offerings from such virtual places, which must therefore match what people actually encounter in those offerings—not only in its expressed statements, but in its displayed appearances, its overall look and feel, as well. Contrast www.baileys.com with www.kerrygold.com and see which renders its brand more authentic to you. Go to www.whatmakescoffeegood.com to see how Starbucks connects how it makes coffee with its values. Check out how L'Occitane imparts its philosophy and discover one of its True Stories at www.loccitane.com. And then go to your own Web site and see how authentically it represents your company and its offerings.

Finally, consider anew all of the *representations + perceptions* inherent in your displayed appearances. What depictions have you designed to represent your enterprise, its offerings, and the places in which they are offered? How do current and potential customers then perceive the sum total of these representations? The entire goal of rendering authenticity is to get people to perceive your offerings as real. Because authenticity is personally determined, this perception will come (or not) more from your displayed appearances than from any other element. People may not think much about your names, they may ignore your statements, they may disregard your places, and they may not even consider your motivations—but they will take in your representations and hold you accountable to their personal perceptions of them.

That is not to lessen the importance of the other four elements of What It Says. Your declared motivations—why you say you are in business—are out there, and if your actions clash or diverge, that will become common knowledge. Your established places—where and when you're encountered—always provide the context in which representations are made and perceptions formed, and therefore frame all assessments of real or unreal. Your expressed statements—what you articulate you are—leave no room for interpretation; they are what they are, so you must be what they say you are. And your assigned names—who you call yourself—are such an integral part of identity that poor choices may trump all other aspects while good selections will make the rest of What It Says that much easier. But it is your displayed appearances—how you show what you are—where it all comes together in the minds of individual customers.

Being True to What You Say You Are

In their book *Marketing Aesthetics*, Bernd Schmitt and Alex Simonson distinguish between "expressions" and "impressions":

Customers do not have direct access to an organization's or brand's culture, missions, strategies, values, to the "private self" of the organization or brand—its expressions. This public face is projected through multiple identity elements with various aesthetic styles and themes. It is usually never seen in its totality, but the various perceptions are integrated into overall customer impressions of the organization or its brands.[96]

The impressions formed by individual customers determine how well you have rendered authenticity.[97] Schmitt and Simonson point out that these often conflict with one's expressions, calling such mismatches "projection gaps."[98] That is simply an academic term for being phony, a perception people will have whenever companies do not represent what they really are.

Perhaps there's no greater arena for *how* you show what you are than in the interactions customers have with your workers. In *The Experience Economy* we proclaimed that work *is* theatre, that every time workers are in front of customers they are acting.[99] Whether they know it or not, whether they do it well or not, they are acting and must act in a way that engages the audience, the guests of the experience. Not surprisingly, when we talk (i.e., work) about authenticity in front of our own audiences, someone often brings up acting and how phony it is. That view, however, involves a misconception of acting.

Acting *can* be real. Sometimes, many times, perhaps even most of the time in business, however, it's not. Play-acting, as opposed to real acting, occurs when work becomes merely theatrical rather than really theatre, overly dramatic rather than overtly drama.

Consider the World Famous Pike Place Fish Market in Seattle. This fishmonger puts fish and other seafood on ice in an open-air market with such flair that scores of buyers, patrons, and spectators regularly surround the tables. Employees go through a number of street theatre routines each day as the crowd slowly turns over, but the signature moment happens only when someone makes a purchase. The worker shouts out the order—such as "One salmon flying away to Minnesota!"—with all his colleagues repeating in unison—"One salmon flying away to Minnesota!!!"—as that worker picks up the salmon and *throws* it, often fifteen feet or more, across the counter to another worker who catches it with a flourish, wraps it up, and completes the transaction.

The Pike Place Fish Market was immortalized in the training video *Fish!* from ChartHouse Learning Corporation. The video goes through four principles of acting at work:

- **Play:** Recognizing that it's about being on stage and thereby bringing fun to the process; work shouldn't be drudgery

- **Make Their Day:** Customers are the audience of the performance, and one must focus on them and their needs

- **Be There:** A standard acting technique, "be there in the moment," is about forgetting all else and focusing on the moment, being with this person

- **Choose Your Attitude:** Acting is fundamentally about making choices, choosing what parts of ourselves to portray at this moment in time[100]

We all act differently in different contexts and with different people—with our children or our spouse, our parents or our siblings, friends or strangers, colleagues or customers, underlings or managers, and so forth. These portrayals of self simply reflect the choices we make, consciously or unconsciously, about what parts of ourselves to reveal at those moments with those individuals.

When such portrayals become part of an economic offering, they, too, become fake, fake, fake. But while acting in work is necessarily inauthentic, it also can be *rendered* authentic. To be perceived as acting authentically in business, therefore, exemplify the same two dimensions introduced in the last chapter and expanded on in this one: the self-directed task of being true to self and other-focused task of being what you say you are to others. The workers at Pike Place really are fishmongers who put in an honest (but fun) day's work for a day's wages, and in their roles remain true to their individual selves. The same holds true with the Special Agents, Double Agents, and Counter Intelligence Units at the Geek Squad. The company makes sure to hire real geeks (it even has the tests to prove it) so it can *typecast* them as real Geeks. Southwest Airlines, which always features its own employees (never professional actors) in its commercials, looks for gregarious hires so its typecast flight attendants and gate agents have no problem acting the part in front of fliers.

Most companies, however, do not direct workers to act. Interactions may still come off well, as the workers are what they say they are—receptionists, retail clerks, call center representatives, and so forth. But because so often they're not given the proper tools—a theme to fulfill, roles to characterize, time to rehearse, a stage on which to perform—they have no corporate self to which to be true, and therefore will readily be perceived as phony.

The secret of acting at work appears in the old Shaker motto: "Be what you seem to be, and seem to be what you really are."[101] It applies not only to acting at work—and to living at all times—but to any economic offering. Especially if you desire to be perceived as Real-real, *be true to what you say you are.* That means first understanding both your true business self and what you say that self is via the ten elements we provide in this chapter.

FIGURE 7-1

Ten elemental equations

Is True to Self	Is What It Says It Is
Essence of enterprise = Entity + Ethos	Assigned names = Dimensions + Designations
Nature of offerings = Output + Obligations	Expressed statements = Media + Messages
Effects of heritage = Origin + History	Established places = Venues + Events
Sense of purpose = Intention + Interests	Declared motivations = Ideals + Incentives
Body of values = Beliefs + Behaviors	Displayed appearances = Representations + Perceptions

So now is the time to examine your own business across each of the ten elements, which we compile in figure 7-1 with the complete equations for you to ponder. As Socrates so simply put it: Know thyself. Once you have that grasp of self that comes with Socratic scrutiny, then seek to eliminate those parts of your business and of your offerings that do not match, while bolstering those parts that fit. The next two chapters—each focusing on one dimension of the Real/Fake Matrix—will show you new ways of seeing how to do so.

8

From Marketing to Placemaking

BEING WHAT YOU SAY YOU ARE

WHY DID THE AMERICAN ADVERTISING FEDERATION LAUNCH the campaign "Advertising. The way great brands get to be great brands." in 2001? Because advertising no longer works as well as it once did.[1] Companies in consumer and business markets now pay more and more to reach fewer and fewer households and executive decision makers.

Advertisements appear *everywhere*—we see ads online, on movie screens, on sports uniforms, on the sides of vehicles, on mobile phones, ads nauseum. London-based agency Cunning even pays people, primarily college students, to wear its clients' temporary tattoo-ads and logos on their foreheads.

In an initiative dubbed "Fake Tourist," Sony Ericsson employed actors, called "leaners," to promote its picture-taking cell phones by frequenting tourist traps (e.g., the Empire State Building in New York, the Space Needle in Seattle) and asking tourists to take their pictures. The company also hired models to demonstrate video caller ID and interactive games at nightclubs.[2] For its clients, DVC Experiential Marketing paid "commuters" to read new magazines aboard rush-hour trains; it also paid doormen to display "packages" from catalog merchants in their lobbies, as if tenants had not picked them up yet.[3] Rob Walker, the Consumed columnist for *The New York Times Magazine*, noted that agencies "have concluded that the most powerful forum for consumer seduction is not TV ads or billboards but rather the conversations we have in our everyday lives."[4]

The authors of *Buzz* distinguish between spontaneously generated buzz and *buzz marketing*, which "is the scripted use of *action* to generate buzz. It is deliberate. One of the factors that sets buzz marketing apart from other forms of marketing is the illusion, the invisibility of the marketer. Authenticity is the key driver!"[5] A key driver, yes, but one that so often pushes consumers away; such activity creates the perception of phoniness because it is not what it says it is.

Consider clothing retailer Gap, Inc. Its advertisements over the past decade, featuring line-dancers and celebrities, have had several effects. First, they put off many current customers who saw images portraying Gap as different from how these individuals saw themselves. Gap no longer conformed to (and thereby confirmed) their own self-images. With each successive ad, the *Wall Street Journal* observed, such consumers grew "tired of [the] trendiness."[6] Second, in-store displays merely paid lip service to the advertisements—actual interactions with sales personnel fell far short of the energy and enthusiasm displayed in the ads.[7] Third, Old Navy stores—also owned by Gap, Inc.—carried essentially the same merchandise at a lower price, and without the overtrendiness. As a former Gap executive told the *New York Times*, "Being cool went to [Gap management's] heads, and they lost their focus. They began putting Old Navys in malls right next to Gaps and undermining their own sales."[8] Finally, all Gap stores—thousands of them—look exactly alike. The process by which Gap grew revenues—adding more outlets while increasing advertising—became the process of killing the brand, as the perception of *sameness* permeated the marketplace. Gap's advertising says "Unique," but the in-store experience falls far short of what it says it is.[9]

That is the fundamental problem with advertising: it's a phoniness-generating machine. Think of the appeal of any hamburger in any advertisement versus the reality encountered in the actual establishment. Or think of any airline, hotel, or even hospital; if you could only check into the ads, you'd have a great experience. When you check into the actual place, however, it so often falls short of what the ads represented. When it comes to the Is What It Says It Is standard of authenticity, the easiest way to be perceived as phony is to *advertise things you are not*. This practice, endemic to the industry, may have worked when advertising could promote the availability of a new offering (even if not as new nor as improved as the ads said), when it could promulgate a cost advantage (even when it was short-lived, or came with a catch), or when it could detail a distinction in quality (even though no one might be able to tell the difference). Today, however, wide availability, low costs, and high quality are merely jacks to open when what consumers want above all is authenticity.

What companies need, therefore, is a new approach to demand creation that actually enables—make that *forces*—a company to *be what it says it is*. To borrow the phrase architect Jon Jerde made famous, that discipline is *placemaking*.[10] Places are what provide the primary means for companies to demonstrate exactly what they are for both current and potential customers. Companies that embrace placemaking understand a fundamental dictum for contending with authenticity: The experience *is* the marketing. In other words, the best way to generate demand for any offering—whether a commodity, good, service, other experience, or even a transformation—is for potential (and current) customers to experience that offering in a place so engaging that they can't help but pay attention, and then pay up as a result by buying that offering. Stop *saying* what your offerings are through advertising and start creating places—permanent or temporary, physical or virtual, fee-based or free—where people can experience what those offerings, as well as your enterprise, *actually* are.

How Placemaking Works

Two of the greatest retail failures of this young century resulted precisely because the companies failed to recognize the need to be what they say they are in the places they created.[11] The Walt Disney Company and Time Warner Inc. are two of the premier experience stagers in the world, with prowess in businesses across theme parks, movies, music, and the Web. Yet each shuttered scores of stores built around their beloved cartoon and other characters; Disney sold off all but one of its Disney Stores and the Warner Bros. Stores are now completely gone from the retail landscape. Perhaps afraid to cannibalize such offerings, however, they did not bring what they were—experience stagers—to bear on the design of their retail venues.

Now consider a competitor in the toy business, American Girl, Inc., maker of the American Girl collection of dolls. When founder and ex-schoolteacher Pleasant Rowland decided to go beyond direct catalog sales, rather than merely opening a store she established an experience venue: the American Girl Place, just down the street from the old Disney Store off Michigan Avenue in Chicago.

Here, mothers and daughters (with not a few grandmothers but rarely a man in sight) spend time together at the Theater at American Girl Place, where for $28 apiece they can take in a seventy-minute staged production, which so far rotates between *American Girls Revue* and *Circle of Friends: An American Girls Musical*. They go to the Café for a "grown-up dining experience," paying an admission fee of $18 for brunch, $20 for lunch, $17 for tea, or $22 for dinner. Girls pose for a $24.95 photo shoot to take home a copy of *American Girl Magazine* with their pictures on the covers. They can even make an appointment to have their dolls' hair styled in The Hair Salon for $10 (a simple ponytail) to $20 (restoring the look of its original styling).

Think about it: Families walk into the American Girl Place and spend hundreds of dollars—without buying a *thing*! Of course, each one heads home with more books, more dolls, more furniture, more clothing, and more accessories as *memorabilia* of their experiences. This Place so engages guests that visits average over four hours—and you know the more time they spend, the more money they spend.

American Girl (purchased by Mattel in 1998) isn't committing the same act of inauthenticity as Disney or Time Warner.[12] While these two were not what they say they are when they took their experience-based characters and sold merchandised versions of them in mere stores, American Girl remains what it says it is by *extending* its collection of high-end dolls into the appropriate experience settings created within the American Girl Place; a second Place opened in 2003 on Fifth Avenue in New York City and the third in 2006 at The Grove in Los Angeles.[13]

Companies should follow American Girl's lead and let customers experience their offerings in settings such as these. Recall the central *established places* element of What It Says in chapter 7, where *venues + events* define the where and when of how customers encounter companies. Such acts of placemaking help people perceive a company as authentic on this dimension of the Real/ Fake Matrix in a way that can effectively replace advertising as the primary means of demand generation.

People have become, after all, relatively immune to messages targeted *at* them. Instead, reach current and potential customers by creating experiences—marketing experiences—that they perceive as authentic because they happen *within* them. As Peter Drucker rightly articulated, "The aim of marketing is to make selling superfluous."[14] To that we add: the aim of placemaking is to make advertising superfluous. Get rid of all those manipulative messages that work decreasingly well and all too often say what you aren't. Instead, provide a place for customers to understand, use, play with, and fundamentally *experience* your offerings in a place and time that *demonstrates* you are what you say you are.

Manufacturers such as American Girl seem to have embraced this new placemaking approach more than retailers, perhaps because they are not wed to existing retail paradigms. Nestlé Purina created Purina Farms outside St. Louis so customers could learn more about taking care of their pets—and about its products—via obedience shows and grooming demonstrations in its Canine Competition Center. Whirlpool established the Insperience Studio in Atlanta, letting customers test its appliances in natural settings. Samsung created The Samsung Experience in the Time Warner Center in Manhattan (where, alas, there is no experience for Warner Bros. Studios) so potential customers could try out its electronic products in a place it could control. Steinway & Sons stages a placemaking experience outside of its own place (although it also has a factory tour in Queens): when you buy a grand piano during promotional periods, it offers to put on a concert *in your own home*. It hires a professional concert pianist to show off your new acquisition to friends and neighbors. The person who originally told us about this, the vice president of a bank in Boston, said two of his friends who attended one such in-home concert bought pianos from Steinway afterward.

Service providers also use placemaking for effective demand creation. ING Direct, the North American arm of the Dutch bank, realized its industry was so commoditized that it decided to generate demand through a unique banking experience in a very different kind of place: a European-style coffeehouse called the ING Direct Café. Trained financial professionals fulfill the role of baristas, engaging guests in conversations about their financial needs and thereby encouraging them to place their money on deposit with ING Direct. Over a cup of coffee. According to a company press release, in 2002 customers opened accounts worth more than $300 million within a year of the opening of its two initial Cafés in the United States (in New York and Philadelphia; the latter was actually open for less than six months).[15] The company has opened several more Cafés in the U.S. since then.

Experience stagers themselves can stage placemaking experiences to generate demand for their core offerings. Casinos in Las Vegas specialize in this, turning their markers on the Strip into experiences in their own right. Steve Wynn first did this with the erupting volcano at the Mirage, then the Pirate Show at Treasure Island (which, as Vegas has turned away from a family-friendly orientation and returned to its roots as the original Sin City, became the risqué "Sirens of TI"), and finally the water show at Bellagio. Passersby would experience one of these markers, and thereby be more likely to walk into the casino behind it. To counter the flow of traffic on the Las Vegas Strip, the older, original casinos downtown—where Las Vegas was born in 1905—formed an association and hired Jerde, who also designed Bellagio, to create a placemaking experience that would draw people to them. The result: the Fremont Street Experience, with the Viva Vision electronic light and sound show that goes off every night on the hour via a vaulted canopy covered with over 12 million LEDs and hundreds of speakers producing 550,000 watts.[16]

Transformation elicitors—those who guide customers to achieve their aspirations—can also employ this approach to demand generation. In healthcare, for example—where people primarily want to be transformed from sick to well—Mark Scott, when he was CEO of Mid-Columbia Medical Center in The Dalles, Oregon, created an engaging healthcare experience to draw people to the hospital. Scott took on the Planetree philosophy of patient-centered care—"Personalize. Humanize. Demystify."—as Mid-Columbia's operational theme.[17]

He made sure every board-level decision was aimed at a more personalized, humanized, or demystified healthcare experience. Thus, patients can access their own medical records; rooms look more like a bed and breakfast; and patients and their families have all the information needed about the disease and care path.

Treating patients as human beings needing real care greatly boosted the hospital's financial results. Mid-Columbia even generated enough wherewithal to build the Celilo Cancer Center—a soothing, stress-relieving environment embracing waterfalls, a labyrinth, full meditative spa, and even a musical thanatologist—where workers guide patients and their family members through the most devastating of healthcare diagnoses. Word of mouth attracted cancer patients from seven states in its first year of operation. According to current CEO Duane Francis, as of early 2007 Celilo had drawn patients from *twenty-eight* states.

These transformation elicitors, experience stagers, service providers, and goods manufacturers understand and employ the placemaking principle that the experience is the marketing. Commodity companies can do the same, such as when the North Dakota Farmers Union created the Agraria restaurant in Georgetown to showcase its members' foodstuffs.

Consider again the World Famous Pike Place Fish Market. Although owner John Yokoyama purchased the company in 1965, it took twenty years before he committed himself, and his company, to becoming "World Famous." This declared motivation led to the creation of the engaging routines the workers use to attract customers. When asked what being world famous meant, Yokoyama explained, "It means really being present with people and relating to them as human beings. You know, stepping outside the usual 'we're-in-business-and-you're-a-customer' way of relating to people and intentionally *being* with them right now, in the present moment, person to person."[18] He gave this advice to would-be copycats:

> People want to copy us . . . to do what we're doing. We keep telling them, "Your success isn't in doing what we do; it's in discovering your own way. Don't do what we do. You just have to be. That means commit yourself to being who you say you are: act like, think like, look like, feel like, speak like . . . be it! You will create your own way by doing what you do. Our secret to success lies in our commitment to *being* who we say we are. *Just be it.* Your challenge is to "just be" who you want to be.[19]

Do copy his advice by *not* copying his methods. Be what *you* say you are by finding your very own original way for customers to experience your offerings in the places you establish.

Flagship Locations

You must treat the places you create as distinct experiences that engage your customers and create memories within them—*not* as mere marketing exercises that all too often diminish the perception of authenticity. Be direct: create a *flagship* location that proclaims exactly who you are to the world. Inside an old factory in the center of Amsterdam, Heineken fashioned the Heineken Experience, creating a place worth the €7.50 admission fee. Automaker Volkswagen placed Autostadt, a destination attraction, outside its factory in Wolfsburg, Germany. Guests pay an admission fee to experience each of the company's eight brands in ways the company, for the first time, can fully control. Despite investing $400 million on the effort, VW is extremely pleased: the number of annual visitors was over two-and-a-half times as much as its initial projection of one million. Why the non-touristy town of Wolfsburg? Because of Volkswagen's heritage—that's where the company was founded, and where the company's original Beetle factory was located.[20]

Even public entities can create or become their own flagship locations. Waynn Pearson, the recently retired city librarian for Cerritos, California, grew tired of hearing that libraries would become obsolete as the Internet matured. So he marshaled town resources to create the new Cerritos Public Library, which he calls "the world's first experience library." It's a bright titanium structure—the first use of titanium on any building in the United States—rising from the middle of town and themed "journey through time." Each area within the library is designed with architectural reference to a different point in time; there's a classic period, a modern period, an art deco period, even a futuristic period. The children's area has a prehistoric motif, with a life-sized replica of a Tyrannosaurus Rex. (Opening and closing rituals also take on this theme, with a clock counting down the final thirty minutes before opening, and a movie clip played at closing time for which exited patrons gather.)

Within six months of its grand opening on March 17, 2002, circulation was two and a half times that of the old library. The place had become the flagship venue for *all* of Cerritos, becoming the de facto town center it never had. On average, 7 percent of the town's population visit the library *every single day*.

Business-to-business, or B2B, companies can also build flagship locations. Case Construction Equipment created the Case Tomahawk Experience Center in the north woods of Wisconsin, its home state, to provide an outdoor arena where prospects can try out its large earth-moving gear in a low-key, relaxed atmosphere. Case has found that the relationships created at Tomahawk dramatically increase its close rates. In Fort Collins, Colorado, engineering firm TST turned its own offices into The Engineerium—its place for codesigning projects with clients in a way unlike any other engineering firm. TST permeates its theme of "plants, water, earth, and stone"—the elements it engineers into real estate developments—throughout the space; each room has its own purpose, name, and appropriate components of the theme. Does it work? Clients have been known to drop by with no appointment or reason—just to spend time in the place.

Executive briefing centers, or EBCs, provide many businesses with a place inside their own offices to turn mundane customer visits into engaging demand-generation experiences. Within these EBCs, B2B companies not only can say what they are through presentations, but also can viscerally demonstrate exactly what they are. During the middle of a presentation at the Johnson Controls Showcase in Milwaukee, for example, the company plunges customers into an inky, cold darkness to simulate a winter outage—or bakes them in an arid heat wave—so they quite literally experience how its technology helps them avoid such trauma. At Nortel Networks' EBC in Research Triangle Park, North Carolina, guests receive smart cards that activate and guide their experience with Nortel technology. Potential customers become immersed in personalized presentations employing the latest in experience technologies (including virtual reality) to demonstrate how the latest in Nortel know-how would apply directly to their businesses.

Whether you sell to consumers or businesses, you should think about how to create such flagship locations that provide a place to be what you are, and thereby show customers that you *are* in fact what you *say* you are. A flagship experience, by definition, must be a singular place, necessarily in or near a locale steeped in that central element of True to Self, the heritage of the firm, and indelibly associated with it: where it was founded, where it is headquartered, or where something significant happened in its history and for which it is widely known.[21]

The Placemaking Portfolio

To entice the greatest number of customers to experience you and your offerings, assemble a *rich portfolio* of harmonized places flowing one from another that yield cross-demand throughout the portfolio, generate new forms of revenue, drive sales of your current offerings, and provide places to be what you say you are. Outdoor retailer Recreational Equipment, Inc. (REI) has proved with its flagship location in its hometown of Seattle—complete with an admission-feed climbing mountain as well as a bicycle track, walking trails, and other experiences—that if you get customers to experience your goods, their likelihood to buy those goods goes up. After this place became the number-one tourist attraction in Seattle, with more than two million visitors per year, the company added a second layer of experiences at other locales, including one in Minnesota surrounded by a cross-country ski trail, and one next to a river in Denver that offered a kayaking experience.[22] REI expands its placemaking portfolio further through its fifty-plus retail environments that, while certainly recognized as "stores" by the buying public, do not feel like a chain, thanks to their distinct architecture, ambience, educational classes, and site-specific clinics.

The Viking Range Corporation creates a more varied portfolio, beginning with its own resort hotel. The Alluvian, in Viking's headquarters town of Greenwood, Mississippi, is a place to stay for those attending the Viking Cooking School. The company further established a network of Viking Culinary Arts centers throughout North America and (via acquisition) Viking Home Chef studios in the San Francisco Bay area; it also hosts a series of "World of Flavor" culinary tours, taking paying customers to such cuisine-rich destinations as the Mississippi Delta, Central Mexico, Spain, Italy, India, and Vietnam.

Vans Inc., the forty-year-old manufacturer of athletic shoes particularly popular with skateboarders, grinders, and other extreme sports enthusiasts, developed a different kind of experience portfolio. While fashion retailers always carried its shoes, Vans created its own retail environments—the strength of its brand voiding potential channel conflict for its now 170-plus locales—providing a distinctive shopping experience that continues to exemplify what it is as a company. The company hit its experience stride in 1998 with the Vans Skatepark in The Block at Orange, a mall in southern California, and a second locale in Orlando. There, kids pay $12 to $15 ($5 to $7 for those who pay a $25 membership fee) for two-hour skateboarding sessions in, around, and above ramps, jumps, and combi pools.

The Skateparks, however, do not operate as Vans' flagship. Appropriately for a company whose customers zoom around on skateboards, Vans produces a *mobile* flagship: the Vans Warped Tour, which goes to twenty-plus cities every year. More than an alternative rock concert for alternative athletes, this new genre of experience combines a music festival with skateboarding spectacle. Filling out its portfolio even further, the company created Vans Triple Crown sporting events to give its customers a nationally televised experience as its own show (not a nationally televised commercial interrupting some other company's show). It also stages Skateboard and Snowboard Camps for aspiring enthusiasts at its Skateparks and other venues. Thus, for a generation of skateboarders and other Vans fans, the company not only is what it says it is in each of these venues, but it fully represents who its customers are and provides places for *them* to be who they are.

Therein lies the power of placemaking. By rejecting traditional marketing to instead establish places to be what they say they are, companies fulfill the second, What It Says, dimension of the Real/Fake Matrix. Your own *placemaking portfolio* for creating marketing experiences may not require you to pursue every option everywhere, but as shown in figure 8-1, you should investigate and then invest in how best to take advantage of all five levels of physical experiences.

At the top sits the flagship location. Below it lie four more classes of placemaking: experience hubs, major venues, derivative presence, and world wide markets.

Experience Hubs

When asked why he robbed banks, Willie Sutton famously replied, "Because that's where the money is." In the same way, companies head to experience hubs because that's where the people are. A number of places—entire cities, discrete districts, or particular locales—attract myriad consumers, whether for their natural surroundings, historical sites, shopping possibilities, or other engaging experiences. Las Vegas, Orlando, Times Square, and Chicago's Magnificent Mile in the United States, as well as Amsterdam, London, Sydney, Tokyo, Hong Kong, and Shanghai—to name a few—around the world, have become hotbeds of retail tourism.

Two up-and-coming experience hubs worth mentioning: Dubai and Kansas City. Dubai, with its gleaming new hotels and tourist attractions, is becoming increasingly well known and visited, though it has yet to hit the ten-million-visitors-per-year mark where we would enshrine it as an experience hub. But Kansas City? Kansas? Well, thanks to a unique financing mechanism

FIGURE 8-1

The placemaking portfolio

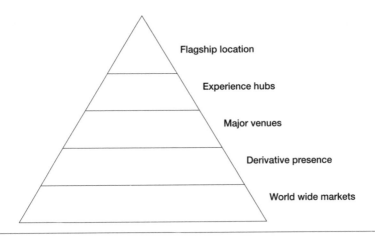

fully developed by Rick Worner of Oppenheimer & Co., called STAR Bonds, the Village West Development northwest of the city is home to, among other experiences, a lifestyle center called the Legends, Cabela's and Nebraska Furniture Mart, T-Rex Café and Dave & Buster's, Great Wolf Lodge, the Kansas Speedway, and the T-Bones' minor league baseball stadium. Plans for yet greater growth are already in the offing.

At least two shopping malls, in and of themselves, represent experience hubs: Minnesota's Mall of America, which draws over forty million visitors every year (more than Walt Disney World, the Grand Canyon, and Graceland combined, as mall management likes to say), and its precursor, the West Edmonton Mall. And we'd add one airport to the list: Schiphol, outside of Amsterdam, which fulfills its theme of "Airport City" by bringing inside almost everything you could want to experience in a city, including extensive See Buy Fly shops, numerous restaurants and bars, the Holland Casino, a branch of the Rijksmuseum, and other places to rest, perchance to dream.

Depending on your business, though, a different hub network may make sense. If you are in the cooking field, you might consider San Francisco or Napa Valley, New York, Paris (skip London), Tuscany, and so forth. If in the automobile industry, check out Detroit, Indianapolis, Daytona Beach, Stuttgart, and maybe the Bonneville Salt Flats, especially if serving B2B customers, not consumers. If you want to sell to college kids, head to Florida during spring break, or to Cancun, Galveston, Lake Powell, Las Vegas, or any number of destinations that attract students for their fling.

Placemaking at experience hubs generally becomes more focused (and less comprehensive) than flagship locations; some companies, however, make them every bit as experiential, from REI's outdoorsy experiences in its Minnesota and Denver hubs, to the hip venues of Morgan Hotels (founded by Ian Schrager) in the hip hubs of New York, Los Angeles, South Beach, London, and San Francisco—a strategic choice for those seeking hotbeds of fashion and nightlife—with every hotel offering a unique experience.

Major Venues

Here lies the "heart" of most companies' placemaking portfolios, where they put their primary outlets that reach the most people right where they live. Situate major venues wherever a large enough population creates sufficient demand, such as:

- Across large cities near great open spaces, as with REI

- Out in hunting and fishing territory, as with competitors Bass Pro Shops and Cabela's

- In stylish locations drawing an artsy clientele, as with Apple Stores or Nokia showrooms[23]

or

- Within any decent shopping mall, as with Bose Corporation's experiential venues, complete with science-of-sound activities, living room and kitchen demonstration spaces, and theater show (where salespeople reveal that the tremendously rich music emanating from huge speaker panels in fact come from teeny, tiny, but never tinny Bose speakers)

Online travel agency Expedia established physical places at two different major venues for the travel industry: airports and hotels. Its Expedia Cafés in such airports as San Jose, Los Angeles, and Kansas City provide a place for travelers to grab a bite and hop online before catching a flight. Through its Expedia!Fun centers in over fifty major hotels (in vacation destinations like Maui and Orlando) existing customers can schedule activities and book various local attractions (as a concierge service), and prospects can become familiar with its travel services face to face. Says Jamie McDonald, vice president of destination services, "Our hope is, if it's your first experience with the Expedia brand, maybe you come back to the site and we'll see some sort of boomerang effect."[24]

Major venues should echo the higher-level experiences (where they exist) and confirm their significance without competing with them. In this way, such locations drive demand for customers to experience the entire placemaking portfolio. Case Construction Equipment, for example, conducts equipment "rodeos" complete with prizes for the best at each event at its B2B dealerships to let customers operate the equipment in a fun environment, giving customers a daylong taste of what its multiday Tomahawk flagship experience is like.

Derivative Presence

The fourth level involves having a presence inside some other venue or event, a place within the place deriving value both from the surrounding environment as well as distilling the essence of flagship, hub, or major venue in a more accessible way. Automakers specialize at this level: General Motors provides the Test Track at EPCOT, Audi supplies actors with high-end cars to drive to the Oscars, and Toyota displays Tundra pickups and offers test drives at hundreds of 84 Lumber stores. Says Jim Farley, head of marketing for Toyota, "We can have the most beautiful advertising but that's not going to change people's minds. The only way you can do that is in person."[25]

Throughout the year, Procter & Gamble's Charmin unit goes to state and county fairs, fiestas, festivals, and other such events to stage the Charmin Potty Palooza. Fitted inside a semi trailer, each "Ultimate Charminized Bathroom" stages the best portable potty experience you'll ever hope to find, with hard-wood floors, a sink with running water, mirror, and a constantly cleaned toilet complete with Charmin Ultra bath tissue. So successful were these places at, um, exposing consumers to its toilet paper—sales went up 14 percent among visitors[26]—that Charmin bounced from these derivative presences to create the Charmin NYC Restrooms at experience hub Times Square throughout the 2006 Christmas season, to huge acclaim and media exposure. Charmin's experience agency Gigunda Group says that the place yielded "over 464,600,000 media impressions, exposure in every major newspaper (domestic and world-wide) . . . and multiple airings on every major TV network."[27] Why advertise when the press (and business book authors) will pick up on your place and tell millions of potential customers about it and your offering?

While for travel companies airports and hotels may comprise major venues, for others they qualify as derivative-presence places. These can be great venues for demand generation, precisely because so many people are "trapped" inside, looking for something to experience. At numerous airports you can encounter Bose demonstrating its wares with kiosks, newspaper and magazine outlets from Fox News and bars from Fox Sports, Budweiser Brewhouse restaurants, Heineken Bars, and, on a slightly higher end of the scale, winery-established bars, such as the Yadkin Valley Wine Bar at Charlotte Douglas International Airport and La Bodega Winery's tasting room at Dallas/Fort Worth International. Starwood Hotels is intent on turning its own properties into premier places for other companies to let guests experience their wares (something that it learned from selling its own Westin Heavenly Beds), including:

- Westin Workout fitness centers, "powered by Reebok"

- Yahoo! Link @ Sheraton Wi-Fi lounges

- A suite at the St. Regis New York designed by Milan-based fashion house Bottega Veneta

and

- Still under discussion, uniforms designed by Levi Strauss for Starwood's new aloft Hotels brand—the first to be opened in 2008

La Ciudad de los Niños in Mexico City provides a terrific showroom for numerous companies. Situated as a sixty-eight-thousand-square-foot anchor in the suburban Santa Fe shopping mall, Kids City engages up to thirty-six hundred kids across two shifts a day. Its theme is "play adult roles," as kids get to be whom they want to be, playing such roles as doctor, construction worker, fireman, stage actor, beautician, newscaster, and archeologist (there are seventy possible roles in total). The admission fee is 160 pesos, or $15, and as you might expect in a city run by kids, parents pay little more than half-price, and grandparents less than that. With the admission fee comes a set amount of the place's own currency—pesitos—that kids can use to buy and make meals and for other activities, such as driving cars or climbing mountains. A kid who runs out of pesitos simply volunteers to work to earn more! Kids City even sends its visitors a monthly bank statement, showing the number of pesitos on account—which of course encourages repeat visits.

While it exists to put big smiles on kids' faces, Kids City finds its success in serving as a premier derivative presence platform for other companies. Unilever's Pond's brand sponsors the beauty shop; Cemex, the Mexican cement giant, the construction site; the F-1 race track is sponsored jointly by Bridgestone and Quaker State; the research lab by 3M, and so forth. Each sponsor helps Kids City create an appropriate experience that puts kids on center stage, provides money for ongoing maintenance and support—and gains tremendous value when customers, potential customers, and future customers play with its offerings in this playful place. Creating its own portfolio, the company has expanded beyond Mexico City under the name Kidzania with places in or soon to be in Tokyo, Jakarta, Lisbon, Dubai, and Monterrey, Mexico.

World Wide Markets

Rounding out the five physical levels in the placemaking portfolio, the world wide markets level comprises every feasible place where customers might encounter a company's offerings. Proceed with caution: ubiquity begets uniformity. Relying too much, or solely, on this level can kill perceived authenticity—as seen with the Gap, as well as virtually all other chains, whether retailers, restaurants, hotels, service stations, or any other such generic outfit. Burt's Bees, the manufacturer of natural personal care goods, has been moving from its heritage of selling at craft fairs into major retail channels. In response to a question about the risk of alienating core customers, CEO John Replogle told *BusinessWeek*, "The authenticity of the brand shines through regardless of whether we're in 10,000 or 20,000 or even 30,000 stores."[28] Perhaps, but for most companies this requires carefully managing perceived authenticity.

Few companies do that as consistently, or as well, as Starbucks. While it still has its original (quite small) location in Seattle's Pike Place Market, the company has no flagship location per se nor any other that provides an exceptional experience above and beyond its day-to-day coffee- and chai-drinking venues. The company does have more than thirteen thousand outlets around the world—and a vision of reaching forty thousand before achieving caffeine-imbibing capacity—and is therefore truly looking for global ubiquity.[29] That's why many people no longer view Starbucks as authentic. Howard Schultz directly addressed this issue in his February 2007 memo, saying outlets now "reflect a chain of stores versus the warm feeling of a neighborhood store."[30]

That the company largely managed to hang on to that feeling for so long was through a deliberate emphasis on design. Wright Massey, now the head of Brand Architecture in Orlando, created a, well, brand architecture for Starbucks by modularizing all of the design elements that go into an outlet—cups, merchandise, collateral materials, store graphics, lighting, fixtures, furniture, and so forth—so that (1) the company could place outlets in virtually any kind of space (rather than requiring the same knockoff footprint every time) and (2) no place looked exactly like another.[31] Even two locations on adjacent blocks in big cities have distinct looks and different feels; people can gravitate toward the one that best conforms to their own self-image.[32] The company must keep innovating in this regard as new competitors are constantly entering this world wide market. The National Federation of Coffee Growers of Columbia—a set of commodity traders seeking to gain more power in the value chain—has opened Juan Valdez Cafés and Italian coffee manufacturer Illy its licensed Espressamente coffee bars around the world, not to mention service providers McDonald's and Dunkin' Donuts, which have upgraded their coffee, as well as other genres of cafés—such as Cereality in the breakfast cereal arena and Ethel's Chocolate Lounge from Mars—appealing to whole new dimensions of self-image.

For any manufacturer, reaching world wide markets involves not only experience places per se but also the experience of *using* its physical goods by its customers, wherever they reside; Apple iPods (themselves becoming ubiquitous) are a prime example.[33] In services, Verizon's V CAST enables mobile experiences, such as streaming video of sports highlights, entertainment clips, and music. For any service provider, this level may mean turning every customer interaction into an experience—even when the circumstances are unfortunate—such as when Progressive Insurance adjusts claims on the spot of accidents, or when the Geek Squad fixes a computer problem in the "found space" of a customer's home or office. Fully understanding the principle that the experience is the marketing, Chief Geek Robert Stephens tells us his goal is to make the encounter so engaging that customers can't wait until their computers break down! And one of Progressive's policyholders related to us, "I didn't used to be a customer of Progressive's until I got hit by someone who was!" She felt, "If I ever have another accident, that's how I want to be treated." This reaction occurs often enough that the company's claims adjusters carry application forms to sign up, on request, *other* people on the scene.[34]

Examine all five levels of the placemaking portfolio to determine which ones would be right for you, and what kind of place you could create. Ask yourself questions such as:

- What eye-catching, one-of-a-kind flagship experience could we create that would proclaim what we are as a company? Where should it be placed based on our heritage?

- What experience hub(s) would make the most sense for us? What attention-getting places—whether temporary or permanent—would draw people in to experience us amidst all the other experience options they have?

- What geographic markets should be treated as major venues for place-making experiences? What experiences could we stage within these places that would be cost-effective across numerous locations?

- What other places would be an authentic fit for our company to partner with, providing value to them while simultaneously gaining access to the people coming to their experiences? What sort of focused experience would be appropriate for this derivative presence?

- How could we reach our current and potential customers in *any* place they're prepared to experience us—even their own places? How can we make every personal interaction we have world wide with customers—whether over the phone, in person, or using our goods—an engaging experience that demonstrates that we genuinely care for them and their needs?

These five levels comprise a hierarchy of *physical* placemaking experiences. Once you have developed a portfolio strategy based on them, however, your work is only half done.

Virtual Placemaking Experiences

Companies should not limit placemaking to the physical, but also look to create *virtual* places. Most companies will render greater authenticity when they integrate the physical and the virtual. REI effectively integrates its Web site, REI.com, into its retail channel with in-store PCs feeding people directly to their Web site, while online presentations (and an order-pickup service) feed people to the company's stores. American Girl leverages its face-to-face interactions at its Places—plus a new Boutique and Bistro format coming out in 2007 in Dallas and Atlanta—to create demand for its remote relationships via its Web site and catalog. Nortel uses its in-person sales meetings to create personalized Web sites based on the technological interactions the person has at its flagship venue (neatly recorded on the individual smart cards). And shoe-maker Vans streams video from its Skateparks so that kids can view what's going on electronically, and therefore think about joining the action.

Vans exemplifies what Peter Chernack, head of Metavision Corporation in Sun Valley, California, advocates as one way of integrating the virtual with the physical: using the Web as a "pre-show" for the live experience. The term, borrowed from Disney's use of its queuing areas to set up the "back story" of its rides, means creating anticipation for the experience ahead. Disney uses its own Web site to enable prospective visitors to view all of its attractions before arriving at one of its theme parks. They can create customized maps of the attractions they most want to experience, which Disney prints and mails as keepsakes.

Use the World Wide Web also for a dramatic "post-show" experience, moving from the physical to the virtual to extend the dramatic structure of the experience online.[35] Disney embraces this principle with its PhotoPass service, which enables family members to arrive home from one of its theme parks, go to a Web site to view professional pictures taken of them by cast members, upload digital photos they took themselves, and then arrange selected photos into a sequence that revisits the drama of the park visit. Disney will then print out a professional PhotoBook or burn a customized PhotoMovie DVD and send it to the family, greatly extending the experience and encouraging repeat visits.

From these and other examples, we have distilled five levels (see figure 8-2) for staging virtual placemaking experiences that fulfill the What It Says standard. These precisely mirror the five levels in the physical half of the hierarchy.

Flagship Site

A flagship site is the singular place (you know: www.yourcompanyname .com) on the Web where people go to find out what you are as a company and what you say about yourself. Unfortunately, too many companies treat their Web sites as pure brochure-ware—sticking to the perfunctory "who we are," "what we do," and "how we do it" outline—rather than as an experience venue worth visiting. Perhaps the best examples of flagship online experiences are those sites that are virtual places unto themselves, such as gaming site www .MaMaMedia.com. Retailer Gallery Furniture of Houston, Texas, takes a different tack, with a slew of in-store mobile cameras that visitors to the Web site control. At wgsn.com, B2B company Worth Global Style Network has become the place to be online in the fashion industry. It employs webcams to stream live video, as well as archive footage, of fashion shows in Milan, Paris, London, and New York. For additional visual intelligence, it hires photographers and videographers to canvas storefronts of clothiers in those same cities, plus some three hundred restaurants and nightclubs throughout the world that WGSN feels the trendsetters in fashion most likely frequent.

Adobe's Flash product has become the standard for many Web-based animation experiences. We're not talking about the all-too-usual "Skip Intros"

FIGURE 8-2

The placemaking portfolio in full

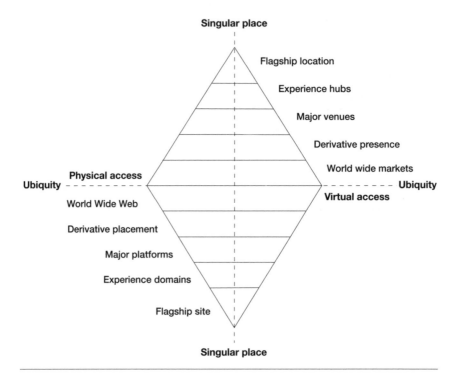

(an invitation that visitors more often than not accept!). Rather, we mean the ways Flash enables new genres of online experiences that demonstrate what the company and its offerings really are to its constituents. General Motors, for example, has for years included on its main Web site a Flash-enabled version of its GM Experience Live that tours from motor show to motor show around the world; now anyone can learn about its current lineup and forthcoming concept cars. The Broadmoor hotel in Colorado Springs lets consumers design their own hotel stay on its flagship Web site via a one-screen Flash session, dramatically changing an experience usually fraught with too many "what-ifs." Finally, Adobe "eats its own cooking" on its own flagship site by providing a Flash-enabled educational experience regarding its own capabilities for corporate clients, centered on the theme of "Experience Matters."[36]

In concert with generating demand, flagship sites (more so than any other level, real or virtual) must proclaim what you are to your current and potential customers. At Façonnable's Web site, designed by Seattle-based ZAAZ, the apparel maker allows guests to puzzle over a timeline of the company's history, enabling it to both honor its fifty-year-old heritage while exhibiting exactly who it is today. On the front page of its own flagship site, ZAAZ proclaims an appropriate point of view about rendering authenticity online: "Your Web site's not about you. It is you."

Experience Domains

Just as people increasingly congregate in and around experience hubs in the physical world, the online space consists of a growing number of experience domains where people spend large, increasing amounts of time. Good old portals such as America Online, Yahoo!, and MSN (the Microsoft Network) provide one class of such domains, furnishing unique virtual placemaking opportunities. Because of the masses who surf via these portals, it often pays to have relationships with them to feature your offerings. At AOL you can click immediately to send greeting cards with American Greetings, try out Netflix, or listen to XM Radio. Yahoo!'s home page leads you directly to innumerable movie trailers, video snippets of TV shows, or domains within the domain coordinated with various partners, including Procter & Gamble, which created a "gathering place" for women called Capessa in Yahoo!'s health section. At MSN, most of the prime homepage spots go to support Microsoft's own offerings (one exception: American Greetings again), although various companies provide or sponsor content on the site, including games featuring such Nickelodeon characters as SpongeBob SquarePants, Dora the Explorer, and Jimmy Neutron.

A second class of experience domains are social-networking sites like YouTube, MySpace, Facebook, hi5, South Korea's MapleStory, and China's QQ, as well as social bookmarking or news sites like Del.icio.us, Digg, and reddit.[37] You'll find, for example, a branded channel from the National Basketball Association available on YouTube, a CIA recruiting presence on Facebook, and independent music labels all over MySpace (through a deal with the Merlin Licensing Agency), which has also introduced a "channel" focused on the 2008 presidential race called Impact.

One final class: virtual worlds like Electronic Arts' *The Sims Online*, Makena Technologies' *There.com*, Linden Lab's *Second Life*, Beijing-based *HiPiHi World*, and Saluke's *Habbo Hotel* (based in Finland but operating separately in over twenty-five countries). As economist Edward Castronova makes clear in *Synthetic Worlds*, more people are spending more of their daily lives online as avatars in what he calls "ubiquitous gaming."[38] Companies already use such virtual places to provide virtual goods, services, and experiences to people while they transform themselves into online avatars, including virtual Pepsi machines in *The Sims Online*, virtual Levi's jeans in *There.com*, and the Target Red Sky

Lounge in the U.S. version of *Habbo Hotel*. The number of offerings inside of *Second Life* are legion: an American Apparel store, a prototype version of Starwood's aloft Hotel, ABN Amro's virtual bank branch, Stagecoach Island from Wells Fargo to teach kids how to handle money, Motorati Island to promote Pontiac cars via concerts and other experiences, a Scion dealership that actually sells virtual cars, and IBM Land, which it uses for client meetings, internal conferences, training sessions, and "business process rehearsals" for clients to try out IBM consulting and technology solutions before they implement.[39]

Admittedly, virtual placemaking continues to evolve. Make sure your efforts enable your company to *be* in a virtual world what you *say* you are in the physical world. (Note that online brochureware represents just the reverse: companies *saying* virtually what they *are* in the physical world.) As Patrice Varni, Levi's director of digital business, told *Business 2.0*, "If the way I dress is part of how I define myself in the real world, and I make style choices and brand choices based on that, it's a logical transition to do those same things in this virtual world."[40] Linden Labs counts at least sixty-five companies that operate inside *Second Life* on behalf of business customers.[41] Many of these are interactive marketing agencies using their own virtual world offices as a showcase for potential clients and a recruiting tool for prospective employees.[42] As the head of one such agency, Reuben Steiger of Millions of Us, says, *Second Life* is "perfect for creating experiences around a brand," because it is "not about 'trapping people' but about captivating and stimulating them."[43]

As with physical experience hubs, there are also subject-specific experience domains, including the women's lifestyle portal iVillage.com, big-city focused HeyLetsGo.com, and book-loving Shelfari. Neopets provides an experience domain for kids the world over, with over 30 million members creating over 100 million virtual pets.[44] "Neopians" spend an average of over six hours on the site every month—largely because if members don't visit, their virtual pets "die"— making it the second "stickiest" site on the Internet, according to comScore Media Metrix.[45] The games kids play that also enhance the site's stickiness are all branded experiences, such as *Pepperidge Farms Goldfish Sandwich Snackers*, *Lucky Charms: Shooting Stars!*, and *McDonald's: Meal Hunt*.

Major Platforms

Companies now find experience domains effective enough to create their own, such as when Wells Fargo moved Stagecoach Island to its own Web site. Other such company-specific virtual worlds include MTV's Virtual Laguna Beach, Mattel's BarbieGirls world, and Webkinz World, where every stuffed animal physically made by Ontario-based Ganz Corporation has its virtual counterpart. KLM Royal Dutch Airlines created a series of social networking sites, such as Club China, Club Africa, and Club Golf, to connect frequent fliers with like interests. Companies like Cisco's Five Across and Ning, founded by Netscape cocreator Marc Andreessen, provide tools for anyone to create a personal social networking site; similarly, IBM's Lotus Connections helps companies create virtual worlds for work colleagues or business customers.

When companies create distinct web domains using resources like these, outside the normal parameters of their own corporate Web sites and outside portals, they effectively create a major platform—a Web site with its own URL separate from the flagship—to call their own. To promote its Raw Tea brand, Smirnoff lets you experience what preppy hip-hop would strangely be like at teapartay.com. Microsoft created clearification.com, featuring the low-key humor of comedian Demetri Martin, to emphasize the clarity Windows Vista can bring to your computer. You can design a caricature of yourself as an M&M candy at BecomeAnMM.com, or see how work is aging you at Career-Builder.com's Age-O-Matic.com. During Christmas season 2006, OfficeMax created not one but *twenty* different sites where office workers could idle away the hours by turning themselves into elves, arm-wrestle reindeer, guess the contents of gifts—even contribute to the "faux charity" of their choice.

Movie studios excel here, creating for nearly every new film a specific platform for online trailers, games, behind-the-scenes videos, and other digital experiences to increase the chances of having a hit on their hands.[46] New Line Cinema all but brought moviegoers into the filming and production process while making *The Lord of the Rings* movies. A full two-and-a-half years before the first of the three premieres, Gordon Paddison, head of interactive marketing at the Time Warner unit, worked directly with director Peter Jackson to launch www.lordoftherings.net, providing stories about the casting, plotlines, film locations, and ongoing production as well as interviews, stills, trailers, screensavers, wallpaper, and customized cursors. In April 2000 a record 1.7 million people downloaded the *LOTR: The Fellowship of the Ring* trailer in its first twenty-four hours—eighteen months before the film opened.[47] Total hits prior to opening day numbered over one *billion*.[48]

Of course, as one movie critic notes, "Today, a movie's run in the [U.S.] theaters is really a marketing campaign for the movie-affiliated products to come. While box office gets the ink, the real profits come from DVDs, videogames, ancillary merchandising, global box office and video-on-demand."[49] Think of it this way: lordoftherings.net was a demand-generation platform for *The Lord of the Rings* movies, which were in turn marketing experiences for the *LOTR* DVDs and ancillary merchandise. All of this generated demand for the shooting locales and sets in New Zealand, which is why Prime Minister Helen Clark of New Zealand named Pete Hodgson to the cabinet-level position of Minister for *Lord of the Rings* in 2001. His placemaking mission: turning the physical production sites into major tourist venues, with the country itself becoming a flagship location for the movies' fans.[50] By 2003, tourism had replaced agriculture as New Zealand's top source of foreign money.[51]

The United States Army produced one of the most innovative—as well as successful—examples of virtual placemaking with its platform site AmericasArmy .com. There, you can participate in the game *America's Army: Operations* where the military service counteracts the countless solo "shoot 'em up" games out there to demonstrate what being in the Army is really like. Visitors first play a single-user game—boot camp at a virtual Fort Benning—before they can interact with others who similarly passed their initial test. Together, they then go out on realistic maneuvers as part of a multiuser game; the objective requires the teamwork for which the real Army is not only famous, but demands for the survival of each soldier and for the accomplishment of its military objectives. Within nine months of its debut on July 4, 2002, over 1.3 million people had registered for the game, with around a half-million playing each weekend.[52] Many of these graduated to follow-on games, *Special Forces* and *Coalition*, as well as gaining insights from real soldiers in *America's Army Real Heroes*. According to a ticker on the platform's home page, over 8 million people registered by early 2007.

Integrating the physical and the virtual, the Army also stages real-world events where civilians and soldiers compete for prizes. In 2007 the Army took a traveling version of its online game, *Virtual Army Experience,* to thirty-five venues around the U.S.[53] The upshot: the Army invites those who do especially well at these virtual games to enlist. According to the director of the program, Colonel Casey Wardynski, 20 percent of those matriculating at West Point in 2005 had played *America's Army,* along with 20 to 40 percent of enlisted soldiers recruited that year.[54]

Derivative Placement

At the fourth virtual level in the placemaking portfolio companies create sites within other companies' Web sites. Perhaps the best example of such digital experiences is the untold number of Web sites where Amazon places components of its own offerings. Sometimes a link points to specific Amazon Web pages, but at other times Amazon.com's book covers, listings, reviews, and ordering and shipping information are viewable right on other sites, with just the actual ordering process clicking over to Amazon.com itself. While experience domains provide similar effects, here the goal should be to identify sites less prominent (and generally less expensive) than full-fledged domains that are also more relevant to the specific interests of the customers you hope to attract.

While not all digital games use the Internet or PC as the experience medium of choice, they do provide yet another route to accessing consumers through derivative placement. The simulated basketball players in Take-Two Interactive's *NBA 2K6* game for Playstation or Xbox, for example, wear the same Nike shoes they do on the floors of NBA games in order "to deliver a new level of authentic basketball experience."[55] The game also integrates a way to customize the game players' own shoes that "mirrors the real-world customization capabilities accessible at the Nike iD [sic] site."[56]

Similarly, players can drive a Ducati Supersport motorcycle in Atari's *Test Drive Unlimited*, tag walls with Montana Gold spray paint in the company's *Getting Up: Contents Under Pressure*, learn about Sony Ericsson phones in Ubisoft's *Tom Clancy's Splinter Cell Pandora Tomorrow*, change oil at Castrol Syntec quick-lube shops in Electronic Arts' *Need for Speed*, and use Visa's fraud-protection service to solve a crime in Ubisoft's *CSI: 3 Dimensions of Murder*.[57] G. Jon Raj, head of emerging-media platforms at Visa, says this technology is more than "just a billboard in a virtual world"; it's an experience that enables consumers to "really engage with the message."[58]

World Wide Web

Finally, matching the physical ubiquity of being available in world wide markets is the virtual ubiquity of being available on every Web site having anything at all to do with the company's offerings. Adolph Coors Brewing Company is, for example, having its Silver Bullet train symbol race across numerous Web sites frequented by its target market of 21- to 34-year-old males—sports, entertainment, and the like—at precisely 4:53 p.m. every afternoon, encouraging them to "Catch the 4:53 to Happy Hour."[59]

And not only did New Line Cinema engineer its own major platform for *LOTR*, as discussed above, it carefully coordinated knowledge- and experience-sharing with myriad fan sites to continually engage prospective moviegoers. A virtual frenzy among fans ensued, as site after site cropped up in anticipation of the movie. (Searching for the specific string of words "lord of the rings" at Google.com results in a mind-boggling 29 million Web pages.)

As with the physical, examine these five virtual levels of the placemaking portfolio to determine which would suit you best, and which you could create. Ask yourself:

- What entertainment, instruction, activities, or environment can we offer at our flagship that go beyond merely providing information to staging an engaging experience? How do we not only say what we are here but *be* what we are?

- Among portals, social networking sites, and virtual worlds, which would be the most appropriate experience domain for people to hang out with our company online? What offerings would provide virtual-world value for potential real-world customers?

- What offerings, categories, messages, or elements of our company could stand alone as a major platform online? How can we connect that platform to our flagship site or real-world places to generate demand?

- What derivative placements at other Web sites would in turn provide the ideal online places for us? What mini-experiences could we create on others' sites to enhance the value of those sites to our partners, as well as reflect an aura of authenticity on to our company?

- What are all the World Wide Web sites—at least by category if not by URL—related to our offerings, our customers, our company, its industry, and the issues we face? How can you connect or link them together into some sort of network that drives people to all the other places (more under our control) we have for experiencing what we are—and purchasing our offerings?

Together with your answers to the first set of questions, you now can begin mapping your own portfolio of placemaking experiences that, harmonized together, will let you be what you say you are with current and potential customers.

Mapping Out Your Placemaking Portfolio

Creating an effective placemaking portfolio to operate requires sound strategic thought. Every company should examine its own situation and determine which levels to occupy and how to integrate every marketing experience into a single set of places that generates demand up and down the portfolio while all the while rendering your offerings, and your business, authentic.

Not every business needs places at every level. Apple, for example, eschews a flagship location, situating its stores solely at major venues around the world, achieving a whopping $4,032 per square foot—an order of magnitude greater than the national retail average.[60] The placemaking framework here serves as a tool to richly explore possibilities for your business. We can offer a few words of advice, however. First, force yourself to conceptualize as many placemaking ideas across as many levels as possible. Second, whenever you introduce a new genre of place, leverage the opening itself as an authenticity-rendering occasion. Consider, for example, how the Geek Squad opened Geek Squad City in Hillview, Kentucky, in October 2006 as an around-the-clock remote repair facility. Since few will actually visit the place, the Geek Squad filmed the grand opening and then posted the video on experience domain Google Video![61]

If each new place proves successful in rendering authenticity, you may find yourself occupying more, not fewer, levels. LEGO System A/S of Billund, Denmark, now has places established at every one of the ten levels, resulting in a portfolio of placemaking experiences to drive demand for LEGO bricks and kits in the hearts (as well as on the floors) of seemingly every kid on the planet. Growing from ad hoc visits to its factory by admiring families, the company's original, flagship LEGOLAND Billund theme park opened in 1968, attracting more than a million visitors every year. More recently, the company moved to experience hubs; LEGOLAND Windsor opened outside of London in 1996, LEGOLAND California outside of Los Angeles in 1999, and LEGOLAND Deutschland outside of Munich in 2002. These introduce youngsters to its brand, create emotional attachments to the brand, and drive demand for its building bricks. Within six months of LEGOLAND California's opening, sales of the company's toys rose over 15 percent throughout southern California.

The company also created several LEGO Imagination Centers at other experience hubs, the Mall of America and Downtown Disney in Orlando, that expose kids to its toys in an interactive, playful atmosphere. It placed Mindstorm experiences in science and industry museums, major venues for attracting youngsters, parents, and teachers. These places increase demand for LEGO toys sold at retail outlets around the world, some of which (such as at the flagship Toys "R" Us store in Times Square, the FAO Schwartz on Fifth Avenue, and even the NBA Store also on Fifth Avenue) have a derivative presence themed by the company itself.

LEGO mirrors this physical portfolio with a virtual one. First, it uses the Internet to reach consumers at children's sites, toy retailers, and search engines across the World Wide Web, tying them together through the International LEGO Users Group Network (LUGNET), which, while independent, enjoys full company support. It has derivative placements inside of *Star Wars* games, as well as on sites like StarWars.com, HarryPotter.com, and brickfilms.com (an independent platform site specifically for stop-action animation films made with LEGO bricks and figures). The company offers its own major platforms for distinct product lines, such as legoland.com for its theme parks and the ongoing storyline at bionicle.com, the characters of which inhabit the tropical island of Mata Nui, where every month guests learn more about this virtual world and its characters through a new episode, a new reason to visit.

The company introduced a new platform site in 2005, the aforementioned legofactory.com, where visitors can create their own virtual LEGO designs and then have the company ship out exactly the bricks needed to complete them. LEGO further employs the power of experience domains MSN (where LEGO supplies content for its kids' pages, such as the *LEGO Builder Bots* and *LEGO: Chic Boutique* games) and AOL (keyword: bionicle). In 2006 it created a theater in *Second Life* to show off its Mindstorm robots. In 2008 it plans to release its own experience domain, a massively multiplayer online game where all the avatars are made from its building bricks.

Finally, LEGO stages its own unique, immersive experiences at flagship site LEGO.com, including story contests, consumer-created movie events, and imaginary worlds to be explored (and that grow monthly)—offerings that it further uses to connect together all the places it manages across all ten levels. The overall goal of LEGO's placemaking portfolio: enhancing children's creativity and imagination by stimulating them to make their own designs from LEGO elements.

Of course, a complete portfolio of placemaking experiences is no panacea. The LEGO company has had to cope with the issues of kids growing up faster every year. Because of the difficulty in competing with video games and other such attention-diverting activities, it sold off its LEGOLAND theme parks to the Blackstone Group in 2005. These experiences were making money, but the core *manufacturing* part of LEGO wasn't consistently turning a profit, and required a different investment model that excluded theme parks. LEGO has an agreement with Blackstone for the parks to continue as premier placemaking experiences in LEGO's portfolio, a portfolio without which LEGO might cease to exist.

Calculating the Value of Placemaking Experiences

Companies that stage placemaking experiences create physical or virtual places to be what they say they are, while simultaneously avoiding the pitfalls of traditional marketing. Indeed, this is the *best* way of generating demand for any offering in our increasingly fragmented world where individuals' desire for authenticity in their dealings with companies is also increasing.

It's *demonstrably* better than advertising. Consider the normal way of measuring the efficacy of advertising: how many people a campaign reaches and their recall rate, divided by the costs of the campaign. In other words:

$$\text{Efficacy of traditional advertising} = \frac{\#\,\text{People} \times \text{Recall}}{\text{Cost}}$$

Of course, because consumers live with almost constant ad bombardment and growing time-constraints, recall rates have fallen through the floor, and so the efficacy of advertising ain't what it used to be.[62]

Now consider the specific benefits of staging demand-generation experiences. Granted, many more people can still be reached with a large-scale advertising campaign than will visit a physical place or surf a virtual one. But people who do experience such places spend not just the few seconds required of an ad, but devote minutes, scores of minutes, and even *hours* immersed in the experience. And they aren't passively watching—or worse, flipping channels, getting a drink, reading a magazine (and probably ignoring its ads, too), talking, fast-forwarding, or TiVo-ing—but generally giving their *full attention*, or close to it, by actively engaging with the place. Moreover, people find far greater *intensity* in an experience, which results in much greater *memorability* of the company's messages, and therefore more word-of-mouth. This leads directly to the desired effect: greater sales—in a way that allows you to be what you say you are in a place you create and control.

So think of it as follows:

$$\text{Efficacy of placemaking experience} = \frac{\text{\# People} \times \text{Time} \times \text{Attention} \times \text{Intensity} \times \text{Memorability}}{\text{Cost}}$$

Traditional marketing such as advertising can, again, reach more people—but every other factor *greatly* favors staging experiences, and augers for shifting dollars away from big ad campaigns to a portfolio of placemaking experiences.

We admit the last couple of these factors are hard to measure—as was the case with establishing new metrics in early quality management and continues to be the case with most marketing methods. Better metrics (and metrics-measuring services) will emerge over time, especially since you generally can at least count the people who encounter you in this way. That's why some just measure the first two factors. Gigunda Group, for example, found rather precisely that the Charmin NYC Restrooms experience engaged 428,328 people for an average of 22 minutes.[63] Think of it as over 150,000 *experience hours* for one location, open for less than six weeks. The twenty OfficeMax platform experiences generated over 26 million visits during their five-week run—that's close to 4 million office hours spent interacting with the company.[64] Americas-Army.com director Colonel Wardynski uses the metric "cost per person hour," estimating in 2005 that the $2.5 million the Army puts into the program each year results in "a cost per person hour of 10 cents, versus $5 to $8 for TV."[65]

You can at least use a back-of-the-envelope calculation on the rest of the measures to figure out whether placemaking experiences make sense for you. Suppose you shifted a few million dollars of your advertising budget to create a place in, say, an experience hub like Times Square, Michigan Avenue, the Las Vegas Strip, or Orlando—places that get upward of tens of millions of visitors per year—or even the Mall of America, with its 40 million–plus annual visitors. You can even calculate the value of the nontrivial benefits of media exposure as well as the millions of impressions for passersby who see your new place-as-billboard without going in.

Of those millions, how many *would* venture in? For how long might they typically *stay*? How much of their *attention*, on average, would they give the place? How *intense* a direct experience of your offerings could you stage? How long would they *remember* it?

Now make the same calculations for an equivalent amount of money spent on your next (or last) advertising campaign, where time is fleeting, attention lagging, intensity variable, and memorability a crap shoot. Which do you think would be a better use of those funds? If the answer is experiences, you really should stop all advertising and shift that money to where it will have the greatest bang for your buck—in staging demand-generation experiences as part of a placemaking portfolio. Remember, such experiences engender emotional connections with which no traditional marketing messages can hope to compete. Many experience stagers do very little advertising or even manage to forgo it completely. The Pleasant Company, Starbucks, the World Famous Pike Place Fish Market, Vans, Recreational Equipment, Inc., and others choose to let their experiences serve as the primary means of acquiring new customers, energizing old ones, and rendering their offerings as real. As Starbucks' Howard Schultz explained, "Mass advertising can help build brands, but authenticity is what makes them last."[66] And experiencing offerings in compelling places is what builds authenticity.

Okay, "stop all advertising" goes too far. There are good reasons for mass advertising, particularly when you must reach tens of millions of people in a fairly short amount of time, such as when turning around common misperceptions, revitalizing stale brands, or launching new offerings—including, we hasten to note, placemaking experiences themselves. Witness the rather effective ads supporting Best Buy's nationwide rollout of its Geek Squad experience across its retail locations. If you still fear going fully into placemaking experiences until they prove their efficacy, then start by putting, say, 20 percent of your traditional advertising and PR budgets into developing and executing placemaking experiences and see what you can make happen.

Further, use your creative *as your R&D*. Don't view your internal marketing talent or your external agencies as resources solely to waste on mere marketing campaigns, but as the very designers of the experiences that drive demand for your offerings. The same folks back in the lab designing your physical goods or in the field developing your new service offerings likely lack the necessary background or skills to design and script, much less construct and cast, an experience.

Think of some of the highly imaginative but increasingly ineffective advertisements of the past few years. What if you unleashed all that creativity on conceiving, designing, and bringing to market revenue-generating—and profit-enhancing—experience places? Such skills should be used to establish ongoing experiences, not mere temporary campaigns. Instead of just creating those wonderful youth-dancing commercials for Gap, for example, what if it contracted its ad agency to conceive, design, and rollout—in other words, innovate!—a compelling dance club where kids pay to gyrate in their jeans? What physical or virtual experiences could your in-house or agency talent unleash?

Designate a Chief Experience Officer

Thinking back to Disney and Time Warner—perhaps the two foremost experience stagers in the entire world—you might now worry that, after all, if they couldn't get it right, then what hope is there for your company? To ensure your success, do something those companies have yet to do: name a Chief Experience Officer. To eliminate any potential confusion, shorten it to CXO, for Chief *Xperience* Officer.

The CXO should be responsible and accountable for developing, launching, and managing the rich portfolio of placemaking experiences you create in order to generate new sources of both revenue and profits in a world where authenticity is becoming the new consumer sensibility. The CXO should have primary responsibility for ensuring that what customers experience in these places matches what you are as a company, so they perceive your offerings and your company as authentic on the What It Says axis of the Real/Fake Matrix.

In creating a CXO position, don't just name your senior marketing executive to the role and call it good. Traditional marketing activities to build brands and create demand must continue apace and, yes, themselves become more experiential over time.[67] Let your marketing organization continue to do what it does as best it can, while you find the right talent to lead your team of experience creators and authenticity renderers.

Remember, the opportunity for new revenue growth within any company lies not only in driving sales of existing offerings, but in creating new place-based experience offerings for which customers prove willing to pay. That is precisely the role of the CXO, a position every company that wants to be what it says it is should have.

Charge Admission

One of the key responsibilities of CXOs—and something that should differentiate it from all the responsibilities of CMOs—is ensuring that the placemaking experiences under their purview are worth an admission fee. Without a doubt the most controversy we encountered over our last book, *The Experience Economy*, centered on our insistence that experience stagers of all stripes—not just those that use them purely to generate demand, but retailers, restaurateurs, hoteliers, and even B2B suppliers—should charge admission for the experiences they stage. But we mean it. Such a step is the logical consequence of recognizing experiences as a distinct economic offering.

Charging admission means that the place exists as an offering in and of itself. It's not the representation of a thing, like an ad; it's a thing in its own right. It's not *just* marketing; it's an actual offering rendered all the more real by its explicit fees. Further, it is only when you *charge* admission that you will be forced to design an experience that's *worth* an admission fee. And if it's worth an admission fee, guests have no problem *paying* that fee.

Realize also that the admission fee serves as its own marker, signaling a place as worth experiencing. If you don't charge for it, customers won't value it. That's why REI went from originally not charging its members to climb its mountains to charging $5 (and increasing the nonmember fee from $5 to $15), and hitting guests' credit cards whenever they make a reservation. Before that, too many people simply didn't show up for their appointed time, precisely because they didn't value the free experience highly enough.

Still, we do admit this is not yet prudent for all companies in all situations—but the exceptions are shrinking fast. If you don't charge admission, budgets will eventually get squeezed. So understand exactly how admission fees affect the return on investment equation that already is the bane of most CMOs' existence (and will be for CXOs if they fail to heed our warning here).

On its face, return on investment for any marketing endeavor is a fairly simple calculation:

$$ROI = \frac{Incremental\ revenue}{Cost}$$

While it's hard enough measuring the incremental revenue a traditional marketing campaign yields—we'll spare you the old saws[68]—you certainly know its cost. So let's focus on the denominator here. When you stage a placemaking experience, its cost is not the only below-the-line factor, for charging an admission fee generates revenue in and of itself.

So the return on investment for placemaking experiences becomes:

$$\text{ROI} = \frac{\text{Incremental revenue}}{\text{Cost} - \text{Admission fees}}$$

Thus, admission fees reduce the denominator of the equation and can therefore make ROI go up dramatically. If you create an unquestionably compelling experience truly worth an admission fee, you actually can *recoup* your costs, and perhaps even make a profit. Although the company will not divulge figures, it seems that most of the experiences at each American Girl Place pay for themselves, if not for the entire venue. As do, we believe, REI with its mountain (which is at least partially paid for by suppliers), Vans with its Skateparks, and—we know, thanks to their sale to Blackstone—LEGO with its theme park experiences. ING Direct, of course, charges for the coffee (and biscotti) in its Cafés, which while technically not an admission fee, the practice certainly sets a price barrier for customers to value the worthiness of each place, and recoup their costs.

With a great placemaking experience—so compelling that your customers gladly pay you to sell to them—you can drive the denominator in the ROI equation down to zero, and thereby have *infinite ROI* on all the incremental revenue you generate. Imagine going in to the CEO or CFO during your next budget cycle and demonstrating how you will achieve infinite ROI on your next demand-generation activity—not by marketing, but by creating places for staging authenticity-rendering experiences.

It's not fantasy; it's reality. Companies are doing just this today by thinking imaginatively about engaging their current and potential customers and designing creatively around admission-feed experiences in ways that no advertisement can do. They have stopped fretting about the declining efficacy of ads, turned their back on how ads tend to make them perceived as fake, and pursued a whole new medium: the placemaking experience, where they can demonstrate exactly what they are, and thereby be perceived as real.

9

From Strategy to Decision Making

BEING TRUE TO SELF

ORAH JONES SKYROCKETED ON THE MUSIC SCENE IN 2002. Her debut album, "Come Away With Me," sold over six million copies worldwide and won in each of the eight Grammy award categories for which it was nominated.[1] While her music found particular appeal among older jazz enthusiasts, many questioned whether Ms. Jones' music was *real* jazz or not. Hers was the first time the famed Blue Note record label (now owned by the larger-scale and more pop-oriented Virgin Records) strayed from its roots in straight-ahead jazz, and some traditionalists accused the label of not being true to itself (or true to the genre) by releasing "Come Away With Me."

Hot on the heels of the album's tremendous success, Jones' eager producers took the then twenty-three-year-old sensation back into the studio to record an album of pure pop (some would say "fluff")—hoping to attract listeners of her own age. Once recorded, however, both the artist and her producers realized that the project should be killed. Releasing such an album would have contradicted who Ms. Jones was and would not honor her style, her audience, or her newfound success.[2] While it certainly would have made money—a lot of money—it would have been the wrong follow-up album at the wrong time and place in her career, and severely lessened the perceived authenticity of Norah Jones and her music. Rather, her motto became, "I'm just going to be myself."[3]

By not going forward with the project Ms. Jones greatly enhanced the likelihood of a longer-lasting and successful career, and of maximizing the money earned over its course.[4] Not until 2004 did she release her second album, "Feels Like Home," one that remained true to herself. How can you tell? Consider another Norah Jones album released the same year, an "artist's choice" CD sold exclusively at Starbucks, for which Jones selected fourteen artists and songs that reflected "music that mattered to her." She explains her selections in the liner notes: "I never listen to music and think, 'Oh I should play like that.' I think the more you listen to stuff, maybe it comes out like language—it comes out eventually in what you do, but I just listen to it because I love it."[5] An extension of that sentiment—*playing* music she loves—reflects who she really is and the real appeal of her music recordings.

Had Ms. Jones come away from the studio with an album she did not love, she might have lost and never recovered her core audience. They would have seen her as *selling out*—once viewed as real but now deemed fake.

Understanding Physical Reality: Minkowski Space

The key to rendering any commercial offering authentic lies in "making it" without selling out. That requires having a keen understanding of your opportunities and pitfalls at any moment in time—particularly the limits to your company's strategic possibilities imposed by the imperative to be true to self. To help you grasp how to meet the True to Self standard of authenticity, we glean some insight from the field of physics.[6]

Understanding what possibilities lie open to a particle of matter based on its history and current position in space-time will enable you to see more clearly what *strategic possibilities* lie open to your business based on your *heritage* and current *positioning*. The particular portrayal of space-time shown in figure 9-1, known as Minkowski Space, was devised by Russian-born mathematician and physicist Hermann Minkowski to express his student Albert Einstein's general theory of relativity.[7]

Here we see a representation of a particle (which, as you will soon see, stands in for your business). The vertical Y-axis depicts the particle's position in time and, for ease of representation, the horizontal X-axis depicts the three dimensions of space (length, width, height) collapsed into one. Where the particle happens to be right now is shown with the vertical dashed line to "Here" on the Space axis, with the horizontal dashed line to "Now" on the Time axis showing when it happens to be. Its past positions are marked as a squiggly line; this is where the particle previously moved around in space since it came into existence in time. Notice that the particle can move only upward; to move downward would mean going back in time, a physical impossibility.

FIGURE 9-1

Minkowski Space

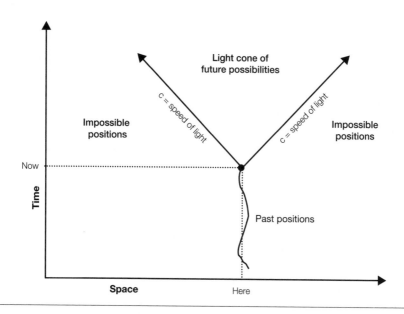

The particle also cannot move to *any* position outside of the two upward-angling arrows (or vectors); to do so would mean exceeding the speed of light, which Einstein also showed to be physically impossible. Therefore the particle *can only move to points between the two arrows*, an area known as its "light cone" (which is the shape it would be if you could see all three dimensions of space).

For any random piece of matter represented, the most likely place for it to move in the future would be pretty much straight up from where it is right now. That simply means it is sitting still as time passes, or as inertia moves it along. Somewhat less likely would be positions just to the left or the right of center, with commensurately decreasing probabilities closer to the edges of the light cone. To reach these places near the limits of physical impossibility the particle would have to travel faster and faster, with little or no change in direction.

Figure 9-2 shows how *any* movement eliminates future possibilities in space-time. Once the particle moves—and in space-time, even sitting absolutely still in space constitutes movement, because time always marches on, moving the particle upward—its light cone shifts upward in the direction of the movement from the old "there-and-then" to a new "here-and-now." Moreover, movement never creates new opportunities for where to be in the future; rather, it constantly *winnows down* future possibilities until the only possible place for the particle to be is exactly where it is.

FIGURE 9-2

Movement in Minkowski Space

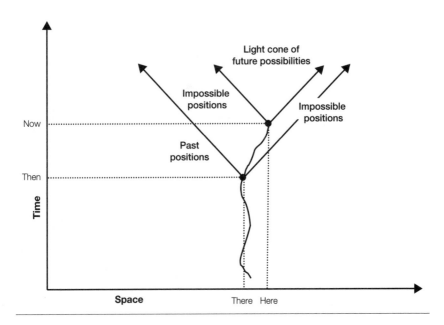

Facing Business Reality: Here-and-Now Space

With that basic understanding of Minkowski Space, let's move from representation of physical to business reality. As shown in figure 9-3, your business resides at a particular point in space-time, what we call Here-and-Now Space. The squiggly tail represents your history, beginning with your company's origin—your heritage, in other words—leading up to what you are today—your identity. Your *execution zone* resides above you, delineating the limits to your strategic possibilities. The preponderance of competitive options lies outside of this zone, as is the case with the entire cosmos outside of a particle's light cone in Minkowski Space. These competitive positionings are strategic impossibilities in Here-and-Now Space—you simply cannot reach these points and remain true to self. They lie outside of the lines of *perfect execution* that bound your execution zone. When we say "perfect" we mean exactly what the word denotes: *perfect*—no strategic zigging or zagging, no bad decisions, no false representations, no capacity underutilizations or capability failures, no dithering, dallying, or doubting, and absolutely, positively no mistakes, missteps, or mishaps.

No one, however, is perfect. In fact, it takes rather disciplined performance merely to move very far afield strategically from where your current strategy

FIGURE 9-3

Here-and-Now Space

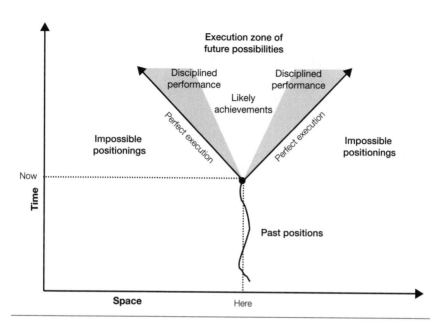

would take you anyway, straight up in time from where you are now. But that doesn't keep companies from trying. Executives often lay out strategies that prove not just difficult but, given the company's heritage and current circumstances, actually impossible. They point their people to goals they cannot possibly attain, and adopt strategic positionings that their customers cannot hope to appreciate or even comprehend.

Such behavior is not true to self. Gunning for a strategic positioning that is not achievable, pushing your people to do the impossible, and forcing your customers to view a completely "new you" means that you, as a company, are aiming outside of the realms of possibility for what you are today, which in turn was created by your past positions in Here-and-Now Space. It is denying yourself and where you have been; it is inauthentic, and that's how it will be perceived. Worst, it means forgoing those possibilities that are both profitable *and* perceived as authentic. It inexorably leads to disaffected employees bemoaning the "flavor of the month" in management tactics, stockholders decrying misdirected strategies, and customers wondering what happened to the company they thought they knew.

Further, just as with a particle in space-time, any movement by a business in Here-and-Now Space eliminates particular possibilities, while making others ever more likely. And remember: you can't help but move forward in time, eliminating some potential positionings while making others more likely, as figure 9-4 makes clear. *Every decision* you as a company make automatically narrows your possibilities, until the only possible place for your business to be is exactly where it is. Even making no strategic decisions forecloses many possibilities on the periphery of one's execution zone—as strategic inertia takes hold, you constantly move through time to a new here-and-now. And pursuing ersatz opportunities in flavor-of-the-month style simply bounces the company back and forth in a random walk through Here-and-Now Space, wasting valuable time that you could have spent in pursuing new, exciting, and profitable trajectories that would let it remain true to self.

While physics inspired this framework, it is not mere metaphor. In fact, the physics flow directly from philosophical thought on authenticity. In *Sources of the Self*, 2007 Templeton Prize recipient Charles Taylor says, "In order to have a sense of who we are, we have to have a notion of how we have become, and of where we are going."[8] He sees identity as an "[o]rientation in moral space" that is "similar to orientation in physical space"; and further, that it consists of "the direction our lives were moving in or could move in," concerning "not only where we *are*, but where we're *going*." Why? Because "we are always also changing and *becoming*."[9]

FIGURE 9-4

Moving from There-and-Then to Here-and-Now

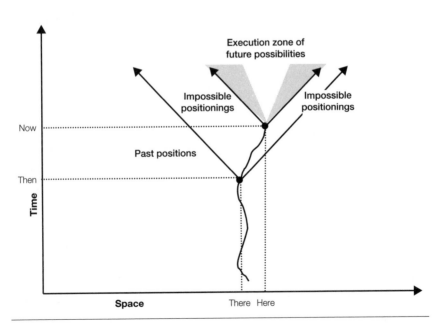

This strain of thought finds perhaps its highest expression (and definitely its least accessible language) in the late German philosopher Martin Heidegger's *Being and Time*. He calls the self *Dasein*, which in German literally means "being there." Heidegger specifically relates *Dasein* to space and time, calling it "Being in the world" (a succinct description of both a particle in Minkowski Space and a company in Here-and-Now Space), writing, "With regard to that space which it has . . . taken in, the 'here' of its current . . . situation never signifies a position in space, but signifies rather the leeway of the range . . . which has been opened up for it in directionality." [10] In other words, *Dasein* exists at a particular position in space, with a certain amount of leeway—but not total freedom—opened up ahead of it in time, the nature of which depends on its current place and direction in the world.

While Corey Anton's book *Selfhood and Authenticity* is a philosophical tome rivaling Heidegger in terms of accessibility, it provides unparalleled perspective on the physical reality now being addressed here. When we "gather into a whole our future and past," as Anton concludes, "we authentically dwell in 'the moment,' meaning that we choose in light of the whole of our existence, and . . . commemoratively retain the past while resolutely anticipating the future." [11] Every company ready to face its real situation in the competitive world must do as much, choosing its path forward in the light of the whole of its existence.

Operating in Here-and-Now Space

To see how this choosing works in practice, consider The Walt Disney Company—not Disneyland or Walt Disney World, not the experiences it stages in theme parks but doesn't in stores, not the influence it has on perceptions of reality among little kids or people from the Netherlands. No, consider The Walt Disney Company as a company in Here-and-Now Space.

A global experience powerhouse formed in the imaginative mind and skillful hands of its eponymous founder, Disney originated to provide fun family experiences for kids of all ages. It started as the maker of sweet, entertaining cartoons, shifted into family films and TV shows, and later created theme parks dedicated to bringing families together with shared experiences. These movements in Here-and-Now Space became the formative events for The Walt Disney Company, solidifying its heritage and identity.

While Disneyland was quite a stretch (creatively and financially) for what was at the time a pure entertainment company, it proved well within the company's execution zone. [12] Drawing directly from his (and the company's) heritage, Walt Disney created it to be a three-dimensional cartoon in which the audience was immersed. [13] He rejected outsourcing management of the place to other companies when his executives pointed out that the company's staff had no experience running an amusement park. First of all, Disney told them, "[T]his is not an amusement park"; it was a *theme* park. Second, while it was a stretch, "[W]e can run Disneyland as well as anyone. All you need are people who are eager, energetic, friendly, and willing to learn. They'll make mistakes, but we can learn from their mistakes."[14] It wasn't so close to the edges of the company's execution zone, in other words, that everything had to go perfectly. It had room—and especially time—to figure it out as it went along.

After Uncle Walt died, the company fell on hard times and lost sight of what it was all about. It undertook a great revival under Michael Eisner, who realized the Disney-created characters lay at the core of the company's identity and set out to better leverage Mickey Mouse and his companions while creating wholly new family-oriented characters, such as Ariel, the Little Mermaid, and Simba, the Lion King. The company even made strategic acquisitions (such as the rights to Winnie the Pooh) and strategic alliances (such as with computer-animated filmmaker Pixar with its Woody the Cowboy and Buzz Lightyear characters) that fit solidly within its execution zone.

However, the company lost its way again as the thirst for still further growth caused it to move far outside its tradition of family-oriented, character-driven experiences. In particular, rather than producing and distributing Disney fare for whatever TV channels could best present it to kids and their adoring parents, in 1995 it acquired its own distribution arm, Capital Cities/ABC. ABC? This was the network that, from *Charlie's Angels* to *Desperate Housewives*, had become affectionately known as the "T&A Network."[15] Even further afield, two years earlier The Walt Disney Company bought the Miramax movie studio, a very edgy producer known for films rated R and even NC-17, such as *The Advocate* and *Priest*. NC-17 of course means No Children under 17 allowed under any circumstances, while R-rated means "Restricted" to youngsters having parental permission. In other words, in chasing the big bucks, Disney sold out—effectively banning the very audiences at the heart of its heritage.

Another Disney studio, Caravan Pictures, hired a convicted child molester to direct one of its films, to a howl of protest. Various family-oriented groups have time and again called for boycotts of Disney offerings, not just for decisions such as these but for what they perceive as an anti-Christian bias and pro-homosexual agenda. Such groups, and many individuals, view Disney as turning its back on its heritage in the here-and-now. And financial performance suffered, as the strategy simply didn't work. Bottom line: many parents no longer trust the offerings of The Walt Disney Company; it's no longer the authentic stager of family experiences, as it is no longer true to self.

You might ask: do we really mean to say that the struggles of The Walt Disney Company can be traced at least partially to its development of R-rated movies and other risqué businesses? (What prudes!) It would be far easier to sidestep the matter so as not to be seen as narrow-minded. But, yes, that is precisely what we are saying. Had management understood that such strategic moves would place the company outside of its execution zone—beyond where it could operate and still be perceived as authentic—it could have made different decisions that would have enabled it to grow while preserving its authenticity. With a proper understanding of Here-and-Now Space, for example, Disney could have:

- Purchased Nickelodeon, the highest-rated daytime channel in the United States, rather than, say, Miramax. The company waited until 1983, four years after Nickelodeon premiered, to launch The Disney Channel and has yet to catch up.

- Created the world's first *theme store* for kids, with experiences worthy of admission fees, rather than wait for American Girl to do it. It could also have outbid Mattel for American Girl back in 1999.

- Applied yesteryear's resolve to relentlessly learn from its mistakes and re-fine new offerings until each succeeds (such as it did with Euro Disney Resort and numerous rides within its parks) to Club Disney (freestanding play centers, now gone) and DisneyQuest (urban theme parks, now down to one in Orlando).[16]

- Sold off ABC to focus on the true jewel in the Cap Cities crown, sports-suffused and family-friendly ESPN.[17] Not only was it firmly ensconced on cable, where it could more readily create economic value amid the increasing fragmentation of advertising-sponsored TV, but ESPN had already launched into its own three-dimensional placemaking, the X-Games, and would soon expand into ESPN Zones and ESPN Skateparks.

If the board or shareholders would not have stood for keeping ESPN while selling ABC, Disney had another strategic choice: it could have treated it as a merger of equals and kept the name "Capital Cities" for the corporate entity, applying "Disney" only to that part of the empire that truly flowed from the man Walt Disney and for which it could properly represent with that heritage-conjuring name. It may seem overly simplistic, but as we saw in chapter 7, designating who you are via naming provides a powerful means of rendering authenticity—or, when done poorly, inauthenticity. The smaller business unit known as Disney would have then been seen as an entity unto itself, unmistakably within its execution zone, while the larger company, Cap Cities, would have been free to pursue family-unfriendly offerings without tainting the offerings that bore the Disney name.

Of course, properly understanding any company's Here-and-Now Space doesn't mean you are stuck with strategies inside your execution zone. Unlike with a physical particle in Minkowski Space, we're not talking physical impossibility here but *philosophical* impossibility. But if you try to operate outside your execution zone there is much less likelihood that the resultant offerings— and the overall company—will be perceived as authentic. Such is the case with The Walt Disney Company today. Because of the decisions it has made in the past couple of decades—and not taking such actions as we outlined above— Disney is no longer perceived as authentic by a large segment of its customer base, and may never fully recover its solid positioning in the hearts and minds of America's families.[18]

Today, CEO Robert Iger ought to make this his foremost goal as he remakes the company. The *Financial Times* credits Iger with rediscovering "a fondness for the sort of innovation so beloved by its founder" and refocusing movies away from Miramax and Touchstone and on to the Disney brand.[19] According to other observers he has "re-imagined Disney.com";[20] rethought Disney's world wide placemaking portfolio;[21] and restored the Mickey Mouse Club— while graciously reflecting credit on to Michael Eisner on the one hand and his management team on the other.[22] His boldest move: buying Pixar in early 2006. Disney's animation unit had fallen on such hard times earlier in this decade that the company actually disbanded its hand-drawn animation team in favor of moving up to computer technology. Even then, however, it knew it could not compete with Pixar, which had performed pretty much flawlessly within its own execution zone, producing hit after hit; one investment columnist called it "priced for perfection."[23]

Purchasing Pixar was rightly seen as redirecting the trajectory of Disney animation back to where it would be solidly within the heritage of Walt Disney— particularly in bringing on board the man "heralded as a latter-day Walt Disney."[24] John Lasseter, the chief creative engine at Pixar and now chief creative officer of Disney's animation unit, believes that animation is "the heart, soul, and engine that drives the train called Disney."[25] He has already created a "story trust" to shepherd each film to fruition and is bringing back shorts, an art form present at the genesis of Disney but neglected for fifty years.[26] Animation historian Charles Solomon noted that Lasseter's films "come closer than anyone else's in this country to capturing the magic that the classic Disney films had"; and one animator who now works for Lasseter commented, "Pixar studios is exactly what Disney used to be. Thankfully it will soon be that way again."[27]

We implore you to understand how to operate within your company's Here-and-Now Space so you avoid the same sort of mistakes Disney made, and not have to spend $7.4 billion to recover from them. To that end, we discuss eight principles that, like time, flow directly from the bottom to the top of the Here-and-Now Space model:

1. Study your heritage

2. Ascertain your positioning

3. Locate your trajectory

4. Know your limits

5. Zoom in your zone

6. Scan the periphery

7. Affix the future

8. Execute well

Let these principles guide you in staking out viable, powerful, and compelling competitive positionings while remaining true to yourself.

1. Study Your Heritage

Just as a particle's present and future positions in space-time depend on its past, so too do a company's present and future positionings build on its past. To remain true to yourself, you must study your heritage and thereby define your possibilities by your unique origin and subsequent history.

The same debate we saw in chapter 7 on nature versus nurture in science applies to authenticity as well. Does being authentic mean to be what you are, actualizing your original self (nature), or does it mean creating a new self according to your own, and not society's, dictums (nurture)?[28] Again, the answer is both/and: we are the product of *both* our nature *and* our nurturing. Every company is the product of its *origin + history*.

Sure, the brand new (and fairly recent) can get away with veering away from poor positionings precisely because they have yet to create significant or even discernable heritages. (Before anyone in the United States had ever heard of Nokia it was in the forest products industry.) Its heritage, however, cements a company in history, shared by all, rooting it into a specific place and time. Therefore, for those companies that have been around long enough to implant a firm set of impressions on the minds of their customers and the public, drastic new strategies simply will not work effectively nor authentically. You cannot take actions antithetical to your past on a wholesale basis and think people will view you as authentic. When it comes to the True to Self axis of the Real/Fake Matrix, the easiest way to be perceived as phony is to *repudiate your heritage.*

Even continuing along one's historical vector of competitive movement can yield poor or problematic results if, as with Disney, a company disowns the values that underlie its heritage in some other area of the greater enterprise. A number of firms attempt to skirt this, entering new competitive arenas by purchasing small, entrepreneurial companies or even starting up their own internal ventures and then never stating the source of capital. But beware the transparency trap: the true story will come out and what is hidden today— *particularly* if the venture becomes successful as the company hopes—will become known tomorrow.

The same applies when a small company is swallowed by a large one. Recall Fetzer Vineyards, the small collection of wineries in California mentioned in chapter 3. Its advertising campaign proclaims, "Authenticity personified. Authenticity crushed, aged, and bottled. Fetzer. An American Original." But Fetzer was purchased in 1992 by Louisville, Kentucky–based Brown-Forman Corporation. What happens when the fine wine–drinking public learns that this small collection of wineries in California is really part of the huge, faceless conglomerate behind Jack Daniels whiskey and 100-proof Southern Comfort, among other spirits and wines (and totally unrelated consumer goods, such as Hartmann luggage)?[29] Some won't care; it makes perfect sense to them for a winery to be owned by a liquor company. Others, however—who perhaps purchased the wine thinking they were supporting an original, American, family-owned vineyard (now where would they get that idea?)—may view Fetzer as a fake, as no longer true to self because its sale to a big corporation repudiates, at least in their minds, its family heritage (not to mention not being what it says it is through its advertising, potentially rendering it Fake-fake).

To its credit, Fetzer acknowledges its Brown-Forman subsidiary status on its Web site, fetzer.com. Former president Paul Dolan at one point credited the parent company with giving it "the support to act faster and better on our quality goals."[30] (But wouldn't a small vineyard of handcrafted wines have higher quality than a faceless mass producer? Wouldn't an entrepreneurial company act faster than a large conglomerate?) Of course, it would be even worse if the company actively tried to hide its ownership. But small companies get swallowed all the time; that alone can't squash, we hope, the possibility of rendering authenticity.

What should a company like Fetzer do? First, it could adhere to the first Axiom of Authenticity by not *saying* it's authentic; the commercials would do an ever better job were they not to proclaim "Authenticity" all over the place. It could further create a vineyard tour, as part of its placemaking portfolio, that goes beyond standard wine-tasting fare to demonstrate fully that it lives up in the fields to the values it proclaims over the air. Further, its Web site could specifically address the ownership issue, briefly discussing the competitive realities of the wine business and how Fetzer combines the best of both worlds—marrying the authentic heritage (and taste) of a decades-old vineyard with the capital, scale, and reach of a large company, all to ensure its original wines get in the hands of you, the waiting customer.[31]

Study your own heritage, seeking to understand your corporate past as well as the effects of its heritage—the central element of True to Self—on the realities of your present competitive positioning. What strategic decisions from the past reverberate now and into the future? How might your heritage point to what you could do—or should not do—in the future? What limitations do your *origin + history* place on what you might say? Which roads less traveled—forgoing the lemming-like paths of most of your competitors—would help your company endure as its own unique self? Which paths not taken should be forever forsaken? Answering such questions helps gain a solid grasp of your past, and provides the only means to demarcate your present, for *you know where you are by discerning where you have already been.*

In trying to remain true to self, you can make no greater blunder than thinking you are over there somewhere when you are really right here, right now—whether due to self-denial, self-delusion, or some other misplaced assessment. To avoid such, we recommend a very practical step more and more companies (such as Levi Strauss & Co., Ford Motor Company, and Nike, to name a few) have taken: Hire a historian to research your origin and analyze your corporate history. Then give them a direct line to top management to declare whenever some move repudiates your heritage so you can alter or eliminate the decision. As corporate historian Phyllis Barr of Corporate Culture Marketing in New York told us, "A company is the result of the who, what, where, when, and why of its history. Studying that past enables companies to prepare for their future."[32]

2. Ascertain Your Positioning

More than your past influences the nature of your present positioning. Surveying your immediate environment—the circumstances surrounding your business here and now—provides an important context for devising a compelling, much less achievable, strategic direction for your enterprise.

Remarkably, too many managers fail to comprehend what is happening—right here, right now—in their industry and to their business. You need look back no further than the dot-com crash to witness how fatal can be the failure in misjudging current positioning; thousands of companies (and multiplied investors) did not recognize how they—along with other Internet "businesses"—had no real sources and few prospects of revenue with which to gain a financial return. Undoubtedly, the World Wide Web back then (as now) represents a new platform for innovative business models (from eBay to *EverQuest*) and novel mediated offerings (from Amazon to Zafu). But from the outset, the most successful companies found ways to explicitly charge for output. How did so many miss this? They simply mistook their strategic positioning by misconstruing the immediate environment.[33]

Start-ups in particular have no excuse for any inaccurate reads of their present positioning; yet some still miss the mark. A distorted view of the present easily creates misguided forays into the future. Even when management mistakes are not fatal, they may permanently diminish what the enterprise might become by making impossible particular (and particularly profitable) future realities. Start-ups have the singular luxury of picking where and when to start; pick an unsuitable Here based on a flawed view of Now and certain destinations will immediately be shut out.

Consider the Segway Personal Transporter (PT), the proclaimed-to-be-revolutionary/proved-to-be-disappointing device. The apparatus is simple and wonderful: tilt sensors detect a rider's center of gravity to get the vehicle to move; riders simply think "forward" or "back" and off they go. Inventor Dean Kamen founded DEKA Research & Development Corporation in 1982 and made a name (and a fortune) for himself by inventing several breakthrough medical technologies, including a miniaturized dialysis machine, a portable insulin pump, and the iBot, a wheelchair capable of climbing stairs. This last device employed the gyroscopic stabilization technology that gave birth to a development project Kamen code-named "Ginger" (to iBot's "Fred" codename) and rabidly curious media dubbed "IT." What ensued between initial concept to eventual commercialization provides a rich lesson in how to incorrectly ascertain a strategic positioning.

Kamen miscalculated in this respect. First, rather than license the invention, he launched his own company, Segway, to manufacture, market, and distribute the PT, something ill-suited to his personal temperament as an inventor.[34] Second, he hosted an executive retreat at which he allowed such luminaries as Amazon's Jeff Bezos and Apple's Steve Jobs to ride an early model; their enthusiasm served only to reinforce Kamen's belief in the world-changing power of his invention.[35] Third, he allowed journalist Steve Kemper inside the new company to witness the development process in preparation for writing a book about Kamen and his new device. Unfortunately, the manuscript proposal inadvertently leaked out, causing the Segway story to escalate, greatly changing the company's environment, and particularly its expectations.[36] Fourth, Kamen viewed the landscape for the PT almost exclusively in technological terms and as a result missed a number of contextual factors, such as a growing societal concern over obesity. Finally, this technology focus led to moving forward with a value proposition based purely on the functional utility of the new *good* rather than the *experience* of using the good. Said Gary Bridge, vice president of marketing for Segway, "We don't play, we ride" as he pointed out that "the last thing we want is to be seen as the snowboard."[37]

How many of the missteps might have been averted had Kamen remained true to form and licensed his invention to another firm, one more skilled in manufacturing and marketing consumer durables? How much hype might have been avoided had Bezos, Jobs, and others not been given glimpses at the gadget? Speculation aside, we know for sure that had access not been granted to a writer until after a successful product launch, the proposal that surfaced on now-defunct Inside.com—claiming that Ginger "represents the first generation of a new mode of transportation that will compete with and possibly replace automobiles"[38]—would never have triggered the frenzy of speculation that far surpassed the reality of execution.[39]

When the Segway finally debuted, the media and the public immediately saw it not as a revolution in personal transportation but as a glorified scooter, "designed as an alternative to walking, not driving."[40] As a futuristic device, the PT evoked the sort of "super-pedestrian emotions that can arise on airport moving walkways."[41] Critics emerged almost immediately, including futurist Paul Saffo, who deemed the device "too expensive, too heavy, and too recharge-dependent to enter the consumer mainstream."[42] The use of the Segway would also mean rewriting municipal laws on sidewalk usage.[43] Instead, cities soon began to ban the device from walkways—not only for safety reasons, but because if the PT were adopted by the masses it threatened to make an already overweight nation even more so.[44] While the device has seen limited success in such applications as warehouse traversing and law enforcement, most people today encounter it only as a toy leased out for events—in other words, as the very experience Kamen and Bridge didn't want it to become.

Now let's see the difference between Segway and a second company, named after another new-to-the-world personal transportation device: Zorb. A zorb is basically a large plastic sphere, or orb, big enough to hold one or two people, and inventor Andrew Aker has never sold a single one. Rather, the zorbs merely serve as props for downhill, half-pipe, and other diverse—and decidedly fun—zorbing *experiences*. Aker told us that the universal reaction to a first zorb experience is pure, childlike laughter. Now imagine Segway's going to market as a prop for various unique experiences. Segway polo, anyone? How about Segway-across-America? Or racing, jousting, ballet-ing, or myriad other such activities that could provide the basis for a real experience business. In March 2005 the company finally started moving in this direction by announcing new models specifically designed for riding experiences, including cross-terrain and golf models, and in August 2006 produced and updated a model geared for "adventure."[45]

Readers need not agree with every detail of our take on Segway. To segue to the application to your own business, the critical point to recognize is that how Segway thought of its positioning in the here-and-now—as a revolutionary manufactured good—greatly influenced the possibilities it could achieve and the success it could have, just as the place-and-time that represents your present strategic positioning forever limits your future possibilities and bounds your success, for *where you are*—or think you are—*affects what you see*. Years ago, one of us worked with a colleague who traveled by air every week of the year, and who once boarded a plane he thought was headed from Cleveland to Houston but was instead bound for Newark. He took the wrong gate as his point of departure—missing all the announcements in the immediate environment warning him to stop, get off, and get to the right Jetway—and ended up at the wrong destination. Don't make the equivalent blunder with your company; ascertain your positioning through a thorough analysis of the world that lies around you—where you really are right now.

3. *Locate Your Trajectory*

Once you fully understand your history and current position, you should determine the direction and speed at which you are moving in Here-and-Now Space. This lets you avoid the opposing vices of meandering around on the one side, and foolishly trying to go places your company has no possibility of reaching; that is, on a trajectory detached from the strategic reality that lies behind, around, and before you.

Many mass producers of processed food wish to take advantage of the trend toward wellness. Some, however, are constitutionally incapable of credibly appealing to consumers on the basis of wellness, because . . . well, because of what they have been producing for decade after decade. Having been in such a business for so long may prohibit going forward with any new wellness-based brand. Some might try, but others may find the proper path forward involves appealing to the desire for healthy living via some other route, perhaps with no-carb lines, genetically engineered nutriceuticals, or leveraging some other non-natural R&D expertise. Strategic positionings such as these could be achievable given current position and trajectory in its Here-and-Now Space, something that a me-too "wellness" positioning never would.

One company that's consistently done well at feeding off its knowledge of where it's at in Here-and-Now Space is Hard Rock Cafe International, founded by Isaac Tigrett and Peter Morton. Many pundits (including us) trace the history of theme restaurants back to the opening of its first venue in London on June 14, 1971.[46] Expansion occurred slowly at first, but accelerated with investment in the business by Mecca Leisure and then with the outright acquisition of the enterprise by the gaming company the Rank Group. The original formula for establishing each unique venue—mixing good grub with rock 'n' roll tunes and artifacts and of course city-specific T-shirts and other memorabilia—proved not only successful but iconic for putting a city on the proverbial experiential map. If a city had a Hard Rock Cafe, many people felt it was a city worth experiencing.

All went smoothly until the late 1990s, when dozens of so-called "eatertainment" restaurants started applying Hard Rock's formula to alternative themes. The banality of Rainforest Café, the bankruptcy of Planet Hollywood, and the banishment of most of the rest provided telltale signs to Hard Rock that it had to distance itself from the very phenomenon it spawned. Management realized that thinking of its business as theme restaurants was sending it in the wrong strategic direction—and that it must reconceptualize its trajectory to be more in tune with its rock 'n' roll roots. It wasn't that the company changed trajectories, but rather it found the proper way of thinking about the trajectory it was on.

As a result, Hard Rock embarked on the multitrack development of new music-related ventures, including Hard Rock Live Events, with sponsored concerts in four different cities; Hard Rock Hotels, complete with music-blaring lounges in ten cities; Hard Rock Casinos in five cities, with numerous music venues at each; and recently the first Hard Rock Bar (in Bristol, England). It also added musical programming to many of its 120-plus cafes in forty countries across six continents—including the establishment of unique venues, such as the nightclub 279 at its second-ever site in Toronto (279 Yonge Street). It renamed menus "Eats," a very roadie-like term. It now offers its internal training program to other companies as a B2B educational offering geared to boomer executives called the School of Hard Rocks: Rock 202. Chief marketing officer Sean Dee explains, "We deliver an authentic experience that rocks. And that's somewhat of an academic statement, but we truly feel we're the only rock 'n' roll brand out there, and we want to deliver a phenomenal guest experience, whether it's in a hotel, casino, resort, or restaurant property."[47] Roll over eater-tainment and dig these rhythm and blues!

It would only be appropriate to locate some rock 'n' roll lyrics to sum up this section on locating your strategic trajectory. Perhaps these "Dancing Nancies" riffs from Dave Matthews Band's *Live at Red Rocks* album express it best:

> *Don't you ever wonder,*
> *Maybe if things had been slightly different*
> *You could be somebody else*
> *Don't you wonder, maybe . . .*
> *If you took a left turn instead of taking a right, You could be somebody different*
> *Don't you ever wonder . . .*
> *Could I have been . . . ?*
> *Could I have been anyone other than me?*

The direction in which your company presently is headed determines not only where you are, but *what* you are, here and now. Are you on the right path, or do you need a course correction? What strategic opportunities open up before you? What if you took a different tack and reconceptualized where you are headed based on a better understanding of your heritage and current positioning? Realize this: *where you head now determines where you soon are, and wherever you are limits where you can go.* So go boldly forward, with no regard for what could have been, only what might still be.

4. Know Your Limits

Being true to what you are as a company also requires determining the boundaries of your execution zone. This lets you winnow down your future possibilities to those that are definable, achievable, and valuable. Existential philosophers use the term "finitude" to describe how people must make hard choices in life because, as Jay Ogilvy of the Global Business Network observes, "In this mortal life you may be able to accomplish almost anything, but you cannot do everything. There isn't time."[48] Reexamine figure 9-3 and recall how your execution zone is delineated first by your origin and history, leading to where you are today in the here-and-now, and then by the lines of perfect execution that limit the possibilities of where you can be in the future while remaining true to self.

You always must be clear about the phony positionings that lie outside of your execution zone, the strategic options that have *already been ruled out* by your past decisions (though you may not yet be aware of it). Perceived as inauthentic by the most casual of observers, they cannot be achieved by your people nor comprehended by your customers. These constituencies may even actively work against them (via internal sabotage or external disparagement). Further, the time wasted on them eliminates other possibilities as time marches on, narrowing one's *useful* strategic options, as illustrated in figure 9-4. For example, in the heady days of Internet hype, companies kept chasing whatever fad venture capitalists were funding at the time—from push media to exchanges to Application Server Providers (ASPs) to B2B commerce, and on and on. Many dot-coms kept changing direction, lurching around in their Here-and-Now Space so much that they never discovered who they really were as a company or what they could really become—may they rest in peace.

One arena where companies need to know their limits is in brand extensions. Too many go too far. Skateboarder Tony Hawk, for example, should have known that a deal to sell clothing at Kohl's instead of Quiksilver would smell like a sellout to many of his fans.[49] Branding firm TippingSprung conducts an annual survey of brand extensions, finding in 2006 that the worst brand extensions, including Cheetos lip balm, Salvador Dalí deodorant stick, Chicken Soup for the Soul pet food, and Diesel Jeans wine, "seemed least to fit with the brand's core values."[50]

These examples aside, it admittedly is not always easy to tell exactly where the limits lie. Consider Porsche, which in 2002 made its foray into sports utility vehicles with the Cayenne. The SUV has been a tremendous success, soon becoming Porsche's top seller in the United States.[51] However, many longtime Porsche enthusiasts vigorously protested the mere announcement of an SUV; they saw it as an inauthentic move. The essence of the Porsche brand is about *sports cars*, not family cars; about high-speed maneuvering, not kids or cargo. The fact that the Cayenne was built at a Volkswagen plant—sharing parts and facilities with the much cheaper VW Touareg as well as Audi's Q7—didn't help. Branding expert Mark Ritson self-effacingly noted, "If Porsche had remained true to its brand, it would have done everything in its power to stop family types like me from buying into it."[52] He pointed out, however, that "Porsche has created a vehicle that is inconsistent with its brand equity, but it has done so for sound financial reasons."[53] The Cayenne is, after all, still a finely engineered vehicle. Does the fact that Porsche sold a lot of them and made a lot of money justify the high degree of perception that the offering was not true to self? Its top brass, who knew the risks, certainly thought so. Nevertheless, some strategic options that Porsche closed off when it took this particular trajectory are now gone forever. Only time will tell how much this perception of inauthenticity affects sales of its bread-and-butter sports cars—or affects *the Cayenne*'s sales, which were down considerably in 2005 and 2006.[54]

You can delineate the edges of your achievable zone—whether near the theoretical limits if you are a fast-moving company, or closer in to where you have always been if you move rather slowly—by delineating the set of actions you *will not do*. These may be behaviors you will not display, offerings you will not undertake, markets you will not pursue, channels you will not employ, businesses you will not establish, competitive arenas you will not enter. Think of cigar store P.G.C. Hajenius refusing ever to sell the cigarettes, newspapers, lottery tickets, and so forth that would have made it like almost every other tobacco shop in the world.

Howard Schultz of Starbucks relates that while he "started out with a long list of . . . things Starbucks would 'never' do, I gradually learned the need for compromise. What I don't do, though, is compromise our core values."[55] It is going against its body of values, as well as any of the other four elements of True to Self, that will brand that company as inauthentic. For Schultz, that came down to four things the company would never do: franchise, put chemicals on its coffee beans, sell beans in plastic bins in supermarkets, and "never, never stop pursuing the perfect cup of coffee by buying the best beans and roasting them to perfection."[56] CEO Jim Donald calls these taboos "invisible guardrails."[57] Marketing SVP Anne Saunders further notes, "If you know where your brand lines really are, you can push them."[58] And if you don't know where your limits are, they will push back right at you whenever you try to go beyond them.

When Robert Stephens founded Minneapolis-based Geek Squad in 1994 he created what he calls a "giant no list," or set of nonnegotiables that would forever delineate where the company would not go and what it would not be, thereby differentiating it from every other computer repair outfit in business. Included in his list of ten nonnegotiables, he related to us, were these items:

- **No copying:** Perhaps the most fundamental of Robert's Rules, directly leading to many of the others. He felt strongly that the Geek Squad had to have (and be) its own unique identity, unlike anything else in the greater computer industry. That mission accomplished, the company now inspires—much to his consternation—numerous companies that have no qualms themselves about copying, such as Geek Rescue, Geek Busters, and Geek on Wheels, as well as many outside the industry, including The Zaud Squad and the Junk Squad in Minnesota, and even the Fall 2007 show *Chuck* on NBC.

- **No minivans:** This led to the "Geekmobile," originally classic antiques but soon new VW Beetles painted black-and-white like squad cars and emblazoned with the orange Geek Squad logo on the side. When entering a new geographic market, Stephens likes to send Special Agents out in pairs. "Seeing one Geekmobile drive by is interesting," he told us, "but two is an event."

- **No polo shirts, no T-shirts, no jeans, no suits:** Thus was born the Geek Squad uniform—the costume for the wonderful theatre each Agent enacts. It consists of white, short-sleeve shirts; black ties (clip-on of course—just in case they caught in the printer); black shoes; black pants with devices hanging off the belts, and perhaps just a little too short, the better to show off the white socks, also part of the costuming.

- **No being even one minute late:** Quite specific, this rule; in fact, "Be specific!" is something Stephens is always saying. Geek Squad Central sets appointments at five minutes to the hour or half-hour—meaning if a customer expects an Agent at, say, 9 a.m., the Geek Squad system sets the time at 8:55 a.m. This further allows Agents to prepare for what they are to do and how they are to perform.

- **No additional policies:** Stephens was inspired here by Nordstrom's legendary one-page Employee Handbook with its single rule to "Use your good judgment in all situations."[59] He believes—and enforces—that every new policy should come with the withdrawal of another (either folded in or completely removed). He also ensures employees know that one of their primary job functions is to "protect or improve the reputation" of the Geek Squad, and so have permission to breach any policy if they feel the company's reputation is at stake. But they must inform management so it can review the policies for possible revision.

Some may say that it's not what you won't do that defines who you are, but what you will do. Stephens does not disagree, but likes to remind people that great companies define *both*. Having your own Don't list, in fact, provides a most useful steppingstone to then developing a Do list. To this day, at the top of his laptop screen Stephens keeps a small reminder, a piece of paper with the words "Say NO" written on it. He related, "It's always much easier to say yes, but saying no requires discipline and knowing who you are. It also forces ideas to prove themselves against the nonnegotiables."

Each of the ten nonnegotiables lets the Geek Squad be true to what it is—by assiduously avoiding what it is not—and enables it to create a unique culture that continues to infiltrate parent Best Buy.[60] No wonder the retailer's CEO, Brad Anderson, says that his "golden rule" is to "remember *who* you are" and thereby "try to be 'a company with a soul.'"[61]

To determine the limits of your own company's execution zone, what should be on *your* Don't list? What behaviors would go against your soul and be antithetical to what you are as a company? (Nike, preventing people from playing basketball at Niketown.) What offerings would repudiate your heritage? (Marriott, perhaps the world's foremost company founded by Mormons, becoming one of the world's largest distribution channels of pornography through its in-room movie offerings.) What branding initiative would be immediately seen, given your history, by your customers as phony? (McDonald's, trying to reposition Ronald McDonald as a youth fitness guru.) Which markets, should you choose to enter them, would cause people to view you as fake? (Volkswagen, for decades maker of the People's Car, entering the high-end luxury market with its ill-fated Phaeton.) What channels of distribution would cause you to partner with some other company that doesn't match your sense of purpose or body of values? (Starbucks, one of the world's premier experience stagers, placing its coffee exclusively on United Airlines, one of the worst offenders in an industry infamous for delivering dreadful service.) What businesses, or business units, should you not establish because it would go against the very essence of your enterprise? (The Walt Disney Company, moving into family-unfriendly fare.) And what new competitive arenas should be forgone because they are outside the limits of your execution zone? (United Airlines again, trying to bring together Westin, Hilton, and Hertz into the "integrated travel services" brand Allegis.)

Do not dream the impossible dream. Rather, discern the widest possible zone within which you may strive and outside of which you refuse to stray. Take this with you: *do something you can, not anything you can't.* Only by knowing your limitations can you maximize your realistic options and find where you should go.

5. Zoom in Your Zone

Just as in the real world of Minkowski Space, where different particles move at different speeds and most go nowhere near the edges of their light cones for the duration of their entire existence, in the business world of Here-and-Now Space different companies move at different speeds—and most similarly go nowhere near the edges of their execution zones. If you have been lumbering along, performing adequately perhaps, but doing nothing special (remaining firmly within the white space of "likely achievements"), then don't expect to accelerate to near-light speed in a short amount of time. Your actually achievable positionings lie well short of the lines of your theoretical limits (the light speed of perfect execution); you will never get close to that level of performance, at least not anytime soon. Your path lies in accomplishing a series of doable goals that successively stretch your capabilities, increase your speed and flexibility, and make strategic positionings at the far edges of your execution zone increasingly likely over time.

Montblanc provides one such example. It turned a hundred years old in 2006. For eighty-five of those years it remained in the "writing instrument" industry, with little deviation across its execution zone. Jan-Patrick Schmitz, president of Montblanc North America, pointed out, "We are a brand which has very serious roots and a very valued history."[62] It therefore needed to move slowly as it shifted away from solely writing instruments to more of a luxury and lifestyle brand. Its first move was into the related desk accessories category in the early 1990s; a few years later it ventured into cuff links, key rings, and money clips—essentially items people carry in their pockets, just like pens. Only after gaining acceptance with these offerings—and a reputation for a certain design aesthetic that made each of its products recognizably part of a single identity—did it move farther toward the edge of its execution zone in 2005 by adding lines of jewelry.[63]

Other companies are highly agile, continually tackling new challenges and making them happen. If yours is such an enterprise, then you can continue to look farther afield for your next strategic positioning. You can operate nearer the edges of your execution zone, the limits of what you can do as a company and still be true to self.

Look at one such company: Dell Inc. The premier mass customizer in the world, Dell executed its business model so well that it took over the personal computer industry in less than a decade and a half of existence from such long-time stalwarts as IBM (the original PC company that finally felt forced to sell the business to China's Lenovo) and Compaq (which sold itself to competitor Hewlett-Packard in 2002, with the combined business finally challenging Dell in the past few years), not to mention a host of also-rans, no-longer-ares, and never-weres.

Dell's business model springs from its heritage. Michael Dell founded the company in his University of Texas dorm room in 1984. He always worked directly with customers—over the phone, live with large businesses, and eventually on the Web. He never built to forecast, in advance of customer order, but rather made personal computers on demand in response to individual customer need. When the business moved out of the dorms and into factories, Dell focused relentlessly on operational efficiency, never putting products into finished-goods inventory and eliminating as much work-in-process inventory as computerly possible. Because of this mass-customizing capability, Dell always had *lower* costs than its mass-producing competitors could manage. The secret to Dell's success is what it calls its "cash conversion cycle"—the time between when it has to pay its suppliers for the components that go into a product and when its customers pay it for that product. It now stands at a *negative*

42 days.[64] In other words, Dell maintains negative working capital, with customers paying it on average *six weeks* before it pays its suppliers.

One of the handful of strategic missteps the company ever made stemmed from an ill-fated foray into retail distribution back in 1991, where for the first time it put finished products into inventory and allowed such stores as Comp-USA and Staples to sell its offerings to their customers.[65] Dell lost money on each computer it sold through this channel, because it had to charge lower (wholesale) prices as well as pay inventory-carrying costs—plus, we suspect, the new channel's inability to represent Dell's offerings as well as Dell itself could. Dell exited the channel in 1994. It discovered that it did not know how to operate in an environment of finished goods inventory, having never in its history produced it before.

After that Dell executed incredibly well, essentially "zooming" in its execution zone, meaning it consistently and forthrightly shifted into new competitive arenas. Taking its vaunted direct-to-the-customer, mass-customization business model and applying it to adjacent but ever-extending products and markets, it first moved into foreign markets where it had no factories—zoom. Then it went beyond desktops to laptops—zoom zoom. Then from personal computers to servers, storage systems, networks switches, printers, even consumer electronics—zoom, zoom, zoom.

With each strategic move, out came the naysayers. Rosendo Parra, who heads up the Americas group, notes, "Every time we went into a new market, people would say, 'Oh, the direct model won't work.' When we first went to Japan [in 1991] we actually listened to what the market said. Our initial implementation wasn't a pure, direct model. And we failed. We actually had to hit the reset button and began to apply the elements of our model."[66]

Today the company even applies those elements to on-demand intangible services, which it brought together under the name of Dell On Call in November 2005, now comprising 10 percent of total revenues.[67] While some may see each one of these new businesses as outside of its personal computer heritage, in reality Dell's execution zone is defined more by the essence of its enterprise—its business model—than by the specific offerings that flow through that model, which therefore reasonably may expand over time. Dell even ventured back into retail in July 2002 via its own manned kiosks in shopping malls, and in 2006 expanding to a few prototype stores, where it could attract new customers, let them experience its wares, and encourage them to use one of the in-store PCs to access Dell.com to place an order. There was still no inventory; customers defined their computer of choice in the store and then and only then would Dell make each one—often in fifteen hours or less—and deliver to each individual customer's office or home.

In another move, Dell began working with Costco in November 2002 to sell PCs through a separate online channel, Costco.com.[68] Again, there was no inventory; sales of PCs would tie into Dell's own system for production and shipment. Dell used the channel to better reach home-based and small offices, to test out different kinds of configurations, and to gather information, both on customers and on retail operations. Three years later, in November 2005, confident both in its relationship with Costco and its understanding of retail, Dell made another foray into finished-goods inventory, placing personal computers on store shelves at discount warehouse club outlets.[69] Its success is unclear—and the company downplayed the effort as temporary, saying it "isn't experimenting with a return to retail-sales outlets."[70] But because Dell has been operating relatively close to its line of perfect execution, it can now contemplate strategic positionings that were always highly unlikely and even failed in the past.

By 2006, however, Dell had unmistakably slowed down in its trajectory. It missed its projected numbers for several quarters beginning in 2005, after slashing prices without seeing the usual gain in volume; its customer service slipped; the SEC began an informal inquiry into its accounting practices; and a problem with spontaneously combusting batteries caused it to recall 4.1 million laptops (the costs of which were shared by battery-maker Sony). *Fortune* reported, "the aircraft carrier Dell can't cruise as fast as the destroyer it once was."[71] Then CEO Kevin Rollins pledged $100 million "to improve the 'customer experience.'"[72] He defended the company vociferously, saying in response to analysts' increasing cry of "the sky is falling" that "you'd think we were not growing or were losing money by what you read. We still have an outrageous track record. Our model still works very well."[73] As troubles mounted and Hewlett-Packard overtook Dell as the number-one personal computer manufacturer worldwide, Rollins resigned in early 2007, which put Michael Dell back in the CEO hot seat. Realizing that his company's competitive space indeed had changed, Dell said, "We had this historical structural advantage . . . and I think we overemphasized the price element and did not emphasize relationship and customization and experience."[74] (True, for what the company most needs, it seems to us, is a placemaking portfolio of demand-generation experiences.)

Time will tell if this course correction—including working with re-sellers[75]—lifts Dell Inc. back to its customary position speeding ahead of all competitors. Perhaps Dell is on its way to becoming one of those lumbering giants that can no longer operate anywhere near light speed. Still, the company made over $55 billion in revenue, and over $2 billion in earnings, in its last fiscal year. Even slowed down, what company wouldn't want its track record of zooming from zero to $50 billion in a scant twenty years?

How can you zoom in your zone? Take everything you've thought about so far regarding your own company in its Here-and-Now Space—its origin and history, its current location and trajectory, the limits of its execution zone—and determine its *most defining characteristic*. Think back to the five elements of True to Self. For some companies like Dell, the *essence of enterprise* best defines it and enables it to enter new markets with one business model. For others such as McDonald's and its fast-food service that make competing on healthy alternatives nigh on impossible, it is the *kinds of offerings*. Others are most definitively characterized by the *effects of heritage*, such as the MGM Grand and other casinos in Las Vegas, which failed as family-friendly attractions in the late 1990s, but are once again zooming in their zones after returning to Vegas' heritage as Sin City (where anything goes, and when it does, it stays there). *Sense of purpose* characterizes companies such as Whole Foods, which therefore can do almost anything in keeping with the soul of the business, in this case bringing natural foodstuffs, organic goods, simple services, and homespun grocery experiences to the masses. Finally, many businesses are best defined by their *body of values*, such as The Body Shop opposing animal testing, supporting community trade, activating self-esteem, defending human rights, and protecting our planet.[76]

Whatever best defines you, follow it into new possibilities for creating value. Exercise some caution: the faster you go, the more quickly you turn options into impossibilities. Speed ahead where and when you are most certain about what you are and what you should do. That doesn't necessarily mean you should go slow when you are uncertain, since sometimes near-reckless speed serves to obsolete old dilemmas. Our advice: *go as fast as you can but as slow as you must*.

6. Scan the Periphery

Dell, with its On Call service operations, now competes against the Geek Squad, which has always done a lot of work on Dell computers, not only because they are so numerous but because in times past the PC maker never really went after that business itself. This new competition was very predictable, however; from their vantage point in Here-and-Now Space, Robert Stephens and his infiltrating agents at Best Buy could see Dell's straight-ahead moves the entire time.

Businesses within a single industry easily foresee new competitive battles like this precisely because they inhabit execution zones in Here-and-Now Space that overlap greatly and trajectories that run fairly parallel. As discussed earlier, it is important to understand these traditional competitors as a means of ascertaining the context of your own current positioning. More difficult is seeing those not-yet-competitors whose execution zones overlap but come from skewed trajectories. Such companies see the same competitive space from completely different angles, from origins far apart, that make a strategic collision highly likely but difficult to detect until it may be too late.[77]

At one point in the not-too-distant past many companies in the information technology and retail industries didn't foresee competing against Microsoft and Wal-Mart, respectively. These then-new companies operated on trajectories skewed to more traditional competition. Now, they have succeeded for so long and grown so big with such encompassing execution zones that there's no longer an excuse. If you sell a commoditized good or service directly to consumers—or one that readily can be commoditized—you know at some point you are going to compete against Wal-Mart. And ditto against Microsoft if you sell anything having to do with personal computer software and many other sectors of IT—particularly if its management views you as a threat. It wants to take over your competitive space before you have a chance to intersect its own space.

To watch for such competitors—while simultaneously seeing if your trajectory empowers you to *become* such a competitor—recall how Hermann Minkowski made Albert Einstein's theory of relativity more easily understood by simplifying its depiction, taking the three dimensions of the universe— time, space, and matter—and placing them in one framework. This model then collapsed the three dimensions of space—length, width, and height— onto one axis. As related together in figure 9-5, Here-and-Now Space similarly simplifies the complete picture of business by collapsing the three dimensions of competitive reality—offerings, capabilities, and customers—onto one axis.[78] Most large companies seem to follow the offerings axis, going where their R&D and incremental improvement activities take them. Other companies

FIGURE 9-5

The three dimensions of the universe, space, and business

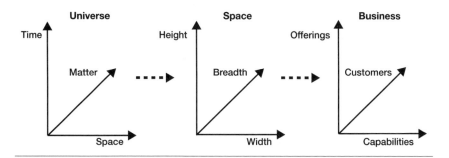

hew closely to the capabilities axis, as we've already seen with Dell Inc., which uses its superior process capabilities for mass customizing to swiftly cross offering boundaries, and as a result continually faces (and, thus far, beats) new competitors focused on offerings. A third potentiality lies in the customers axis, serving a particular set of individual customers so thoroughly and so completely that a company effectively locks them in.[79]

San Antonio–based United Services Automobile Association (USAA) provides a model for moving willfully across the competitive space of other businesses to offer whatever its individual customers need, (almost) no matter where those needs may lead—and therefore also furnishes a warning to those that do not scan their own periphery for such customer-focused competitors. A group of twenty-five Army officers founded the company in 1922 as an association to insure the automobiles of fellow officers, who at the time were considered bad risks by insurance companies. As it grew, USAA took on a mind-set of serving its members—just as its members served their country—reflected in its signature motto, "We know what it means to serve." Beginning in the 1960s, as the company understood that its members required more than automobile insurance, USAA expanded its offerings to serve those members, with these major milestones:[80]

- **1960:** Homeowners insurance through what is now the USAA Property & Casualty Insurance Company, which makes up nearly 14 percent of the company's revenues today

- **1963:** Life insurance through the USAA Life Insurance Company, which since has grown to include health insurance and annuity offerings

- **1970:** Mutual funds through the USAA Investment Management Company, which today offers a wide variety of mutual funds and brokerage services

- **1983:** Consumer goods and travel services through USAA Buying Services (originally created to replace lost or stolen items, but now a major conduit for first-time member purchases)

- **1983:** Checking and savings accounts through the USAA Federal Savings Bank, which today also offers credit cards, cash cards, mortgage loans, and a full range of other banking services

- **1983:** Foreign insurance policies (where the U.S.-based entity was unlicensed) through USAA General Agency Inc.

- **1991:** Survivor assistance through USAA's Survivor Relations Team (started in response to Desert Storm)

- **1997:** Financial consulting services through the Financial Planning Services unit

- **1997:** Financial skills programs for member children and grandchildren, called First Start, College Start, and Self Start

As a result, while USAA stayed essentially with one offering (automobile insurance) for almost four decades, today it provides over 150 insurance products, financial services, consumer goods, travel services, and other offerings—all dedicated to the individual needs of its members as they go through the different stages of their lives. It did expand who comprised that membership (now totaling over six million people), first to the children of members (in 1973) and then to enlisted personnel and noncommissioned officers (in 1996). However, the company knows that expanding beyond the close-knit U.S. military community would not be true to itself. *That* it will not do.

Think about USAA's trajectory through Here-and-Now Space. Originally providing only automobile insurance solely to military officers, it continues to honor its heritage while growing an ever-expanding array of offerings for those family members connected to the U.S. military. It competes with all manner of insurance companies, but also with Wells Fargo in banking, Merrill Lynch in brokerage services, Fannie Mae in mortgages, American Express in both credit cards and travel services, and even with Wal-Mart in consumer goods—not to mention a host of other jewelry, furniture, and clothing retailers. These companies invariably view their competitive spaces based on their traditional industries, while USAA bases its competitive space on its members' needs—to the tune of over $12 billion in 2006 revenue.

So what lies straight up in USAA's execution zone actually *cuts across* the zones of each of the other companies mentioned above—at an angle skewed in a way they may find very hard to detect. USAA scarcely makes the radar screen for most of them—it's not in the consumer goods industry, nor the travel agency industry, nor in credit cards, mortgage loans, brokering, or banking. It resides in the sole "industry" of meeting the needs of individuals in the military community—period—a space inhabited by a single company: USAA.[81]

Not everyone can cut across the competitive space of others as USAA, but for those whose heritage includes serving the needs of a particular customer community, it can provide a clear path to competitive success. What every company must do is *scan the periphery* of its own competitive space to see who is coming from a direction not aligned with its own ways of viewing competition.[82]

Don't get blindsided by competition from the periphery. Markets become disrupted and industries redefined whenever some enterprise enters the execution zone of another, and particularly a collection of staid and comfortable competitors. Bringing a dissimilar heritage that redefines the scene, such an enterprise proceeds along a trajectory that, as it marshals new offerings using unforeseen process capabilities for differently regarded customers, creates a wake of turbulence that causes the old competition to toss to-and-fro in often vain attempts to respond. To avoid such a fate, your company must *move forward but look sideways*. The first actions taken—and the speed taken— influence what you detect in each and every step thereafter.

7. *Affix the Future*

Whether or not your competition comes from the periphery or your traditional industry, you won't surpass your competitors by seeing what they do and trying to do it bigger, better, or faster. In today's environment, having greater availability, lower costs, or higher quality rarely provides the winning strategy.[83] You do it by staking out that one future positioning among all possibilities that *both* meets those past imperatives *and* induces your customers to perceive your offerings and your company as more authentic than competitors. Ogilvy notes, "Authenticity demands fidelity to your past, but also openness to possibilities in the future—not just one possibility (that would be a necessity), but several possibilities. Authenticity is being true to both your [past] . . . and your freedom. It's making choices among possibilities and taking responsibility for your decisions."[84]

Doing this requires formulating your *strategic intention*, not in the sterile analysis of any current or even would-be competitors, but rather in the reality of *your own uniqueness*.[85] This incomparable uniqueness lies in your particular approach to offerings, capabilities, and customers, which find expression in your past and present positionings and current trajectory in Here-and-Now Space.

Positionings that provide the greatest competitive advantage more likely than not lie away from the center of your execution zone. Very few companies have it all figured out, sitting exactly where they should in Here-and-Now Space, content to just let time march on at current direction and speed. (If they think they do, they're probably humming in their hubris rather than zooming in their zone.) Even a company that *is* in exactly the right spot in the here-and-now will not likely find that place to its liking very far down the road as old competition improves, new competition appears from the periphery, and customer demands change over time.

Steve Altmiller, president and CEO of San Juan Regional Medical Center in Farmington, New Mexico, found himself in exactly this position. While San Juan was historically a strong community hospital, by the time Altmiller became CEO in 1999, the present no longer lived up to its past. "[E]verything was out of sync," he said about that time. "We were taking lots of financial hits; our earnings were down, our hospital-sponsored health plan was going bankrupt, unions were trying to organize our nurses, and we were making many operational and management changes that introduced lots of anxiety. It seemed like everything we talked about was negative, one problem after another. My board said we had to find a way to focus on something positive."[86] The something positive involved pulling together a team of top leaders to create a strategy that would define the future state of the hospital. These leaders didn't care about "as is," only "to be": what *should* San Juan Regional Medical Center become? They started calling themselves the Galileo Group, whose goal was "to discover a new and more personally meaningful center of the healthcare universe." The group's explorations resulted in the statement that San Juan Regional should recapture *The Lost Art of Personalized Healthcare*, a declared motivation that would bring its heritage forward well into the future. It knew achieving this strategic intention wouldn't be easy, that it would take many years, and that it would be more than worth the effort.

However, the team's initial attempt at rolling out the first phase of changes, even as many other initiatives were being readied, failed completely. "I realized pretty quickly," Altmiller related, "that while we had done a good job of defining 'the what,' we were doing a bad job of communicating 'the why.'" The team had failed to connect the dots, he said—the dots linking the future vision back into the present reality.

In re-setting themselves to the task, the Galileo Group focused on three key links. The first was gaining employee buy-in, accomplished by immersing San Juan Regional's associates in a story about "Raiders of the Lost Art," which took place in three lands representing medical professionals, the regional community, and patients:

> In the land of Medicus, employees learned how the Baby Boomer generation affects not only the patient population they treat, but also the peers with which they work on a daily basis. In the land of Communia, employees took an in-depth look at the hospital's community satisfaction results and discussed how they could change processes and/or work styles to improve these results in the future. Lastly, in the land of Patiem, employees learned of the exciting new plans built into the Facility Expansion Project, which would provide a unique healing environment for employees as well as all patients and their families.[87]

Physically situated in an abandoned Social Security Building set to look like the lands in the story, nearly 70 percent of San Juan's thirteen hundred employees volunteered to become Raiders and undergo the process, providing nine hundred ideas on how San Juan Regional could indeed recapture the Lost Art of Personalized Healthcare. About half of the suggestions were incorporated into the hospital's plans—further connecting the dots between the major identified links. Moreover, the relationship between employees and management completely changed as the former became intimately involved in the latter's plans, resulting in higher morale, lower turnover, and dramatically increased employee satisfaction scores.

The second link was focusing on the employee first. As Altmiller related, "We can't consistently provide the most personal patient experience until we can consistently provide the most personal, healing, professional experience. If you expect to be successful in individualizing the patient experience you'd better get good at individualizing to the employee." Therefore, a new customized benefit program was put in place with 80 percent of employees signed up, a Child Discovery Center opened with almost 70 percent of its capacity filled by employees' kids, and a completely new healing environment was designed into the facility expansion project that focused as much on employee as patient needs.

The third link consisted of creating the financial wherewithal to make all the envisioned changes. San Juan Regional had gone to its Farmington community three times for tax initiatives and/or bond issues to finance expansion. And three times they'd been voted down. It went to the well one more time—for much more money, nearly three times the total of the previous attempts, reflecting the strength of its strategic intention—but this time it did *zero* politicking:

> The Raiders of the Lost Art story sessions were completed about four months before the gross receipts tax election. Then something amazing happened. Largely without any help from management, employees began to talk to each other, to their families, and to their friends. And their tone was an enthusiastic one; they talked about what the project was and, more importantly, what it meant. They talked about why it was important to patients, families, healthcare professionals, local businesses, even the entire community. In other words, they talked about everything they had learned in—and contributed to—the story.[88]

As a result, on this fourth try the tax initiative passed—with *84 percent* of the vote. San Juan Regional is now constructing the new state-of-the-art facility that will be the physical embodiment of its vision to recapture The Lost Art of Personalized Healthcare.

Figure 9-6 shows how to think about such strategic initiatives from a Here-and-Now Space perspective. The point indicated by there-and-then actually represents the company's *current* positioning, while here-and-now represents the *future* positioning it would like to achieve. To realize that future position-

FIGURE 9-6

Acting as if the future happened

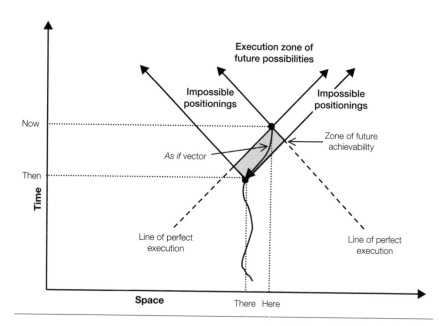

ing, act *as if* that future positioning had already happened, and then work backward to the present, seeing exactly what path must have been followed to achieve the end. Incremental change clearly does not work here; the shift is too great and likelihood too small for positionings near the periphery. Instead, management should view that future here-and-now as a certainty, and then determine what the immediately preceding steps *would have to be* for that certainty to have happened in the future, and then figure out the steps before that, and the steps before that, connecting the dots link-to-link until it constructs the *as if* vector that reaches back in time to the present and back in space to its current place. That's why this vector in figure 9-6 has the arrow heading *back* from the envisioned future into the expectant past. Once management constructs its *as if* vector—exactly as San Juan Regional did in finding the links from its strategic intention back to its present situation—it can then proceed to execute that plan, following the vector from the company's current positioning to that future certainty.

In his work exploring how time, space, and matter impact commerce, business thinker Stan Davis calls this "managing in the *future perfect* tense" where "*the present is the past of the future,* and organization can be used to *push* the strategy toward its realization rather than be *pulled* along by it."[89] Here-and-

Now Space shows that "the present is the past of the future" represents no mere tautology but a profound principle of strategy formulation. You can't divorce where you want to be from where you are now, any more than you can divorce the present from the past and ask for a "do-over." Time connects them all in space.

In San Juan Regional Medical Center's case, the final link to success required an overwhelmingly positive community referendum. The members realized that the story they created to make their strategic intention real to associates must not be a once-and-done exercise. The environment—encompassing medical professionals (Medicus), the regional community (Communia), and patients (Patiem)—was still changing, and it would *always* change, often dramatically. "We learned a whole new way for management and employees to work together to make dramatic new things happen," related Altmiller. "So we have committed to this type of storytelling and feedback to be done every eighteen months. It's just the way we're going to do things from now on."[90] A second story, "The Riddle of the Sphinx," has already been devised, scripted, and produced—with even better internal results than "Raiders of the Lost Art." A third is coming as San Juan Regional begins to zoom in its zone while closing in on its envisioned future.

Do grasp fully the difficulty of achieving strategic positionings that lie near the edges of your execution zone. For the management and employees of San Juan, restoring the Lost Art of Personalized Healthcare was no easy task. Given everything that had happened in the healthcare industry—not to mention in the Farmington community and between management and employees at the hospital—over the preceding few decades, it was difficult to see actually how to achieve such a far-reaching vision. That's why links from that envisioned future back to the present were so crucial. For strategic possibilities to come to fruition, companies should operate as *close* as possible to the line of perfect execution for as *long* as possible. See how in figure 9-6 each movement along or toward this line shifts the strategic intention closer to the center of the execution zone, making it more likely as time goes on—just as each link in San Juan's chain made its strategic intention more and more likely, where each new story effectively lets it operate in ways it now knows how to do.

Reaching points close to the line of perfect execution requires very disciplined execution, which proceeds when every decision and every action of managers and workers align to move the company in the direction of its strategic intention, and the activity of those workers is performed *in order to* effect a movement in that direction. Any wrongheaded decisions, errant moves, or poor performances only steer the strategic intention closer to the edges of the execution zone, making achievement difficult. In other words, in the here-and-now, *everything matters.* You cannot afford anything that detracts from reaching your intention, lest it become a strategic impossibility.

That's because any movement outside the shaded box, what we call here the zone of future achievability, means that the company *eliminates* that future possibility forever. It can no longer be achieved, no matter what happens; that would require *more* than perfect execution, a strategic impossibility akin to exceeding the speed of light.

Peer into your future until you determine where you should go. Envision a future, affix that point as the here-and-now of a declared motivation for all to hear and embrace, and then link from that point back to the present, treating it as a there-and-then position. And this above all: *treat your future not as a destination but as the very origin of the path before you*. Such provides the best means of ensuring you not only have a future but that it will be a prosperous one.

8. Execute Well

Let's list again the principles discussed thus far in this chapter for applying the Here-and-Now Space model:

1. Study your heritage

2. Ascertain your positioning

3. Choose your trajectory

4. Know your limits

5. Zoom in your zone

6. Scan the periphery

7. Affix the future

These principles flow directly from examining the model and its consequences for that particle in space-time—your business. If you apply each of them proficiently, then "all" you have left to do is *execute well*. If we were more into hyperbole we would say "execute flawlessly" or "perform perfect execution," but in reality "execute well" is plenty hard enough as it is, especially since envisioning a future where your strategic intention lies far from the center of your execution zone involves behaviors and activities managers and employees are unused to performing.

Consider British Petroleum—or BP p.l.c. as it is now named. Two years after it bought Amoco and renamed itself in 1998, it launched a series of advertising campaigns to the effect that its initials stood for "Beyond Petroleum." These ads trumpeted BP's investments in solar, wind, and hydrogen energy (and even not-so-green-but-at-least-it's-not-oil natural gas)—all the while continuing and even bolstering its investments in oil extraction in such places as the Arctic Refuge and making relatively minuscule investments in so-called "green energy."[91] The campaign was met with near-universal skepticism; a *Fortune* article on the $174 billion company put it, "If the world's second-largest oil company is beyond petroleum, *Fortune* is beyond words."[92]

By late 2005, however, one commentator could remark, "reality seems to be closing in on perception." Among other successes, BP lowered emissions of greenhouse gases, launched the BP Alternative Energy unit, and saw its Solar unit take 10 percent of the global market and turn a profit for the first time.[93] The company encountered a series of calamities, however. In 2004, an accident at a Texas oil refinery killed two workers—and six months later an explosion killed fifteen at the same refinery. In early 2006, a pipeline in Alaska spilled over 200,000 gallons of oil, while in August the company had to shut down its Prudhoe Bay facilities after discovering extensive corrosion in its pipeline system. Also that year the U.S. Labor Department fined BP $2.4 million for "unsafe operations" at an Ohio refinery; the Justice Department, meanwhile, alleged that traders for the company illegally manipulated the propane market, and then a billion-dollar platform in the Gulf of Mexico didn't hold up during Hurricane Dennis.[94] Once again environmentalists, among many others, questioned the company's motives. Business columnist Joe Nocera put it point-blank: "It'll be a long time before anyone believes anything BP has to say about its environmental sensitivity."[95] Remember how easy being perceived as phony is when you advertise what you are not.

Where does the blame lie? Is BP's strategic intention of going "beyond petroleum," put in place by former chairman Lord John Browne, outside the limits of its execution zone? Is its body of values—or perhaps even its essence of enterprise—at odds with that intention? Or is it simply execution? Craig Smith of the London Business School answers that one: "What we are seeing is not a failure of strategy but of execution."[96] The company itself concurs, making "Executing more effectively" one of four key steps it outlines in its 2006 Annual Report.[97] Even if you affix a future firmly within the limits of what is possible—and we think BP has not yet made its case; it should have waited to proclaim itself Beyond Petroleum until it could at least see that point in its strategic horizon—you still must execute, and execute well.

Contrast BP's experience with that of the company that arguably executes better than any other in the entire world, and has for close to four decades, Toyota. It, too, made a commitment to a future that lay far beyond its line of horizon: to become the world's highest-quality car manufacturer. Few today can remember when Toyota cars were laughed at in the United States as the epitome of "junk"; its first foray into the market, the Toyopet, proved a complete dud in the late 1950s. By applying the lean production tenets of the Toyota Production System, however, Toyota kept improving year after year after year, finally gaining a toehold in the U.S. market in the mid-1960s with the Corona and Corolla.

Still it kept improving. It surpassed Volkswagen as the top import in 1975, while the two oil shocks of that decade caused American consumers to shift to the smaller, more fuel-efficient cars of Toyota and its Japanese brethren. Under pressure from Detroit, by 1984 the American government forced the Japanese to agree to voluntary import quotas, ironically causing further problems for Detroit. Toyota responded by building its first full-production U.S. plant in Georgetown, Kentucky, with the explicit focus of becoming less Japanese and more American.[98] Moreover, according to a *New York Times Magazine* profile, "Its marketing strategists have been trying to establish an aura of American authenticity since the early 1970s."[99] The company succeeded in rendering authenticity with the Prius for the environmental crowd, the Scion line for young, hip adults, and now positioning the Tundra at "true truckers" desiring "truck-driving authenticity."[100]

Still it kept improving. While U.S. automakers said the quotas would give it time to respond to this new competitive threat and improve, they instead raised prices and continued coasting along for years.[101] By the time Detroit pulled its collective head out of the sand to focus on quality improvement, it was too late to keep Toyota from zooming past. In the first quarter of 2007 this Japanese company surpassed Ford Motor Company for second position in the U.S.— and General Motors as the number-one vehicle manufacturer in the world.[102] This directly flowed from its "overarching principle"—its sense of purpose— "to enrich society through the building of cars and trucks" and its core value of continuous process improvement.[103] The phrase "the relentless pursuit of perfection" applies to more than just its Lexus luxury unit. The entire company seeks to execute flawlessly—and immediately correct the process whenever a failure does occur. That is the Toyota Way and has been for decades.

To execute well requires that the organization commit to the course of action defined by its *as if* vector, as was the case with Toyota (*as if* it were the highest quality automaker) and San Juan Regional Medical Center (*as if* it had recaptured the lost art of personalization). Without such a commitment, it is foolish to even try for a strategic positioning very far off-center. In his book *Revival of the Fittest*, Donald Sull discusses the life cycle of commitments every organization undergoes, commitments "to a strategy, a set of processes, resources, values, and relationships with investors, customers, and partners."[104] The first set of commitments he calls "defining commitments" that "form the essential character of the organization going forward."[105] These are the commitments that shape the heritage of the company from its origin through its early history, when you fix each of the five elements of True to Self introduced in chapter 7. Once that happens—once essence of enterprise, kinds of offerings, effects of heritage, sense of purpose, and body of values intertwine to form the roots of the company—then what Sull calls "reinforcing commitments" tend to take over. While managers' defining commitments "tend to constrain their actions" (that is, limit the company's future possibilities exactly as we see in the Here-and-Now Space model), reinforcing commitments "lock an organization into a set trajectory" with little or no change in direction through its execution zone.[106]

When this no longer works and more drastic action is required, it is incredibly difficult to change an organization's reinforcing commitments precisely because they are so good at just that—reinforcing past behavior, actions, and even thought processes. Most companies enter into a phase of what Sull calls "active inertia . . . accelerating activities that succeeded in the past."[107] It's not that managers don't see what's going on, nor are they too lazy, blind, or stupid to respond effectively—even though it often looks like that from the outside. Rather, Sull finds, "When the world changes . . . they respond with more of what worked before . . . [Like] a car stuck in a rut: Managers put the pedal to the metal—and dig the rut deeper."[108]

No, when a company's future strategic positioning lies close to its limits, it needs the last of Sull's life cycle of commitments, "*transforming commitments* that fundamentally realign the organization" with the new trajectory, remaking "an organization's success formula by increasing the cost (or eliminating the possibility) of persisting in the status quo."[109] While these necessarily go against the grain of reinforcing commitments, they don't necessarily countermand defining commitments (which would mean trying to go outside the limits of perfect execution). Rather, they *reinterpret* them for a new environment with a new strategic positioning that cannot be reached without such drastic actions. This is exactly what IBM did under CEO Sam Palmisano; it didn't abandon its commitments to the long-held basic beliefs, but reinterpreted them for a new age—something that was possible only after Lou Gerstner broke the active inertia of an organization having reinforcing commitments to behaviors that no longer worked.

In the previous section we stressed developing an *as if* vector from the future state back to the present circumstances, but you cannot always clearly see the steps needed to get from that future here-and-now to the present there-and-then in figure 9-6. (That was certainly the case with Gerstner, who as IBM's new CEO famously said that "the last thing IBM needs right now is a vision."[110]) Where-and-when this is the case, it is the transforming commitments that guide the way through this trajectory, causing people to make break-through achievements.

Long before Gerstner took the reins, former IBM Fellow Allan Scherr developed a framework for creating breakthrough achievements—programming in major innovations within specific time and cost windows.[111] If people believe—truly believe—they must innovate something particular by a specific date commitment, creating a network of transforming commitments as Sull would say, then you can count on them to figure out how to do so, no matter how unknown the future nor how difficult the task. Scherr's key insight comes from the view that break*throughs* happen because of break*downs*:

> Breakdowns are defined as situations where the circumstances are inconsistent with and fall short of one's committed goals. A breakdown occurs whenever there is a gap between a committed result and the predictable outcome of the current circumstances . . .
>
> A breakdown is a demand for extraordinary action. It causes people to shift attention and see things differently. This perceptual change is often the opening that lets people see opportunities for previously unconsidered actions.[112]

A breakdown occurs when people in an organization maintain their commitments when there exists *no known way of meeting them*. If there is a recognizable, foreseeable execution path from that affixed point in the future to where it is today, then there is no breakdown; the organization can proceed with what it knows how to do. Where-and-when there is no such path *and still* the organization maintains its transforming commitments, a breakdown ensues. The easiest way to resolve it, of course, is by decommitting and thereby relieving the pressure, with the envisioned future quickly slipping outside the limits of the company's execution zone. The hardest way (indeed, the *only* other way other than the proverbial "bluebird of happiness"[113]) is by achieving a breakthrough.

As long as people in the organization cling to their commitments—no matter how bleak their chances of success—then breakthroughs indeed can happen with regularity, as Scherr's work shows. When they do, companies can realize envisioned futures far from center. Such breakthroughs require relentless effort to execute well, as do even those actions of enterprises whose trajectory remains more certain.

In their book *Execution*, Larry Bossidy and Ram Charan see execution as "*a discipline of its own.*"[114] They outline a discerning list of seven essential behaviors that distinguish those leaders being true to themselves, as leaders: know your people and your business; insist on realism; set clear goals and priorities; follow through; reward the doers; expand people's capabilities; and know yourself.[115] While Bossidy and Charan focus on individual leaders while we address the enterprises they lead and the offerings they generate, we all can learn from how the authors end their list of behaviors. Their conclusion points right to the first of our own list of Here-and-Now principles: know yourself by studying your heritage. And thus the last shall be first, as the key to being true to self lies in affixing the future, scanning the periphery, zooming in your zone, knowing your limits, locating your trajectory, ascertaining your positioning, and, once again, studying your heritage. All these you must do, while knowing this: *what you've done is what you are, and what you do is what you become.*

Come away, here and now, and confront your reality.[116] Your future depends on it.

10

Finding Authenticity

THE RIGHT DIRECTION FOR YOU

E ACH YEAR, THE COLOR MARKETING GROUP OF ALEXANDRIA, Virginia, hosts "colorconnects" events for color and design professionals representing ten different industries. Hundreds of designers work in teams across those industries to share non-competitive trend analysis, identify specific design drivers stemming from these trends, and then use those drivers to invent thirty new-to-the-world colors. In 2005, the participants put forth the trend "Contradiction/Juxtaposition" to describe the desire among consumers for "Better than Real" products. The written report stated, "POLAR-IZATION was identified by all industries . . . Our complex world will push us toward living with diametrically opposed values at the same time and place." They identified four drivers, each involving the interplay between two contradictory components: (1) "NATURE OVER TECHNO," (2) "AUTHENTICITY . . . in our quest for real in a sea of confusion," (3) "FEMME TOTALE . . . the duo of sensuality and sexuality together as one expression," and (4) "TOWN-HOUSE TRASH . . . a parody of wealth that not even the über-rich discern . . . and no one can tell real from fake."

This independent analysis demonstrates how at the very heart of the Real/Fake Matrix lies the interplay of contradictory components—the polarity between the *real* and the *fake*. In table 10-1, we combine the Real/Fake Matrix with the five genres of authenticity—essentially colliding them together—to reveal five *genre-based polarities* that describe, even define, the essence of what differentiates Real-real from Fake-fake. By juxtaposing each polarity—rather

TABLE 10-1

The five Real-real/Fake-fake polarities

Genre	◄─────────── Polarity ───────────►			
Natural authenticity	Fake–fake	Artificial ◄──► Natural	Real–real
Original authenticity	Fake–fake	Imitation ◄──► Original	Real–real
Exceptional authenticity	Fake–fake	Disingenuous ◄──► Genuine	Real–real
Referential authenticity	Fake–fake	Fake ◄──► Real	Real–real
Influential authenticity	Fake–fake	Insincere ◄──► Sincere	Real–real

than looking at individual end points—you may discover opportunities for rendering authenticity through new offerings and even new businesses.

Leveraging Real/Fake Polarities

For the polarity between Fake-fake and Real-real for natural authenticity—which we represent as [Artificial ↔ Natural], consider grass lawns. All landscaping is ontologically inauthentic (certainly when compared to unkempt terrain). Natural grass comes off as Real-real, but since planted (or, worse, sodded) and mowed, often fertilized and watered, and even aerated and edged, it's really *fake natural* grass. Long the dominant form of grass lawns, fake natural grass today faces competition from new offerings of artificial grass. *Real artificial* grass. Not the utterly fake artificial *turf*—which first appeared as AstroTurf in 1965 in the Houston Astrodome and, as sports facility magazine *PanStadia* put it, "was actually little more than tufted carpet . . . laid on top of a hard surface."[1] Montreal-based FieldTurf sells a brand of synthetic grass with the "playability" of natural grass, and installations at high school, college, and professional stadiums have risen from a mere handful in 1997 to over twelve hundred today. Its use migrated from sports complexes to other experience venues and even residential properties (primarily across the southern United States), while the Wynn resort in Las Vegas installed over five acres of Orlando-based competitor's SYNLawn on its grounds.[2] This may strike you as rather odd, but juxtaposing "artificial" and something as natural as "grass" makes perfect sense for homes in locales where people find natural grass difficult or costly to grow and maintain. Of course, the emergence of artificial grass as competition gives rise to new natural offerings—from blends of seed mix that require less watering to landscaping methods that eschew green for more earthy and rocky looks.

In *The Real Thing*, Miles Orvell comments: "We have a hunger for something like authenticity, but we are easily satisfied by an ersatz facsimile. And the facsimiles are all around us."[3] Indeed, *real imitations* have long provided Real-real value to consumers, first via mass production (as a means of reducing costs) and today via knockoffs that leverage the [Imitation ↔ Original] polarity.[4] As Randy Cohen, "The Ethicist" for the *New York Times Magazine*, recognizes, "a knockoff apes the appearance of the original but does not present itself as other than what it is. It is not built around fraud," for "drawing on other people's work . . . is how ideas spread through the culture. (Is Eric Clapton a knockoff Robert Johnson? Is that a bad thing? Would absorbing the styles of three or four additional guitar greats make him more virtuous?) Besides, if absolute originality were the summum bonum, how would we get along without network television?"[5] Likewise, why would anyone buy anything sold at IKEA? Or this year's "new models" of cars— *fake originals* that draw so greatly on styling and features of last year's line (and the year before that, and the year before that . . .)?

A *New York Times* article about Pabst Blue Ribbon Beer, entitled "The Marketing of No Marketing," provides a corresponding perspective on the value found in the [Disingenuous ↔ Genuine] polarity of exceptional authenticity. The Pabst brand, once floundering on the edge of extinction, recently gained a following among "the kind of people who detest marketing."[6] Writer Rob Walker contends that marketers at Pabst successfully resisted "all the things marketers do when a product seems to be catching on—a splashy new package design, ads full of glamorously 'edgy' people, etc." Yet Pabst discreetly sponsors myriad placemaking experiences that enhance its perceived authenticity while also providing various in-store (well, in-tavern) marketing and sales support to individual bars and taverns. In the view of loyal Pabst consumers, the brand's "symbolic solidarity with the blue-collar heartland trumps the real thing."[7] The juxtaposed no-marketing marketing continues to help sales of the Blue Ribbon beer. Contrast this *fake genuine* marketing of Pabst with the *real disingenuous* behavior of "local" microbreweries that seek mass distribution to national markets.

For motives that will become clear below, let's turn from the third to the fifth polarity, [Insincere ↔ Sincere]. For this influential authenticity polarity, consider motivational speakers such as Tony Robbins. Undoubtedly, Robbins has a real passion for helping others achieve success (to this end, he recently established a network of certified life coaches); but also fairly apparent is his huge, probably well-deserved, ego. In other words, he's no Mother Teresa, self-lessly caring for others. His is a *fake sincerity*, in which helping others inexorably serves to help him elevate his own status as celebrity helper, and thereby make more money.[8] Similarly, all those appearing on the noncommercial commercials of PBS—Suze Orman on finance, Deepak Chopra on wellness, even Ken Burns on history—mirror Robbins in this regard. Their self-interested self-help helps others as a means to help themselves. The prevalence of such celebrity counselors gives rise to advice in the vein of *real insincerity*. Think of the anticlimactic remarks of Jerry Springer at the conclusion of his TV show, or the irrelevant real-life perspectives offered by cartoon characters on *Beavis & Butthead*, *The Simpsons*, and *South Park*.

We have reserved the polarity for referential authenticity—which is simply and referentially [Real ↔ Fake]—for final treatment for good reason. At a time when authenticity emerges as the new consumer sensibility, it represents the most powerful juxtaposition of seemingly contradictory elements. If you reflect on it, this entire book has been about various facets of the polarity between Real-real and Fake-fake. But here, now, our examination takes a different turn, for using the same constructs as above for the other polarities, we see that this juxtaposition results in outcomes that are either *real fake*—that is, Real-fake—or *fake real*—Fake-real.

Juxtaposing Real and Fake: Think Polarity, Not Purity

While focusing on these five polarities between Real-real and Fake-fake may yield great value, resolving the tension that exists within the other two modes of Real-fake and Fake-real—as seen in each of the examples above—may provide a more powerful platform for forging a juxtaposed identity. To examine such possibilities, view the polarity [Real-real ↔ Fake-fake] as the *defining boundary* separating the modes of Real-fake and Fake-real, as pictured in figure 10-1.

No enterprise remains *perfectly* True to Itself or is always *exactly* What It Says It Is. Any significant deviation from one or the other Real-real ideal soon qualifies the output of an enterprise as either Real-fake or Fake-real, essentially falling off this boundary line to one side or the other, depending on which standard the deviation is most pronounced. Likewise, few if any enterprises so *completely* fail at both standards as to be *wholly* perceived as Fake-fake. Any significant deviation from Fake-fake similarly qualifies the output of an enterprise as either Real-fake or Fake-real, in this case rising up to one side or the other. Recognizing this ontological reality affords an opportunity to acknowl-

FIGURE 10-1

The defining boundary between Real-real and Fake-fake

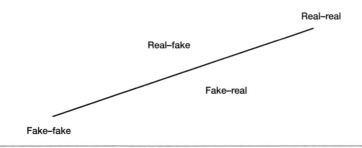

Real–real

Real–fake

Fake–real

Fake–fake

edge the particular natures of your fake self and your fake sayings, and thereby leverage them to render greater phenomenological authenticity. It is the Real-fake or Fake-real modes on either side of the line depicted in figure 10-1 that generally provide a more honest, more transparent, and more authentic positioning and presentation of an offering.

An astute workshop participant once shared with us this perspective on the Geek Squad: "What makes the concept compelling is that these guys are *cool* geeks; it's the juxtaposition that makes them seem so real." The polarized pairing of *geeks* with *cool* provides the very premise for rendering the 24-Hour Computer Support Task Force more real.[9] *Why* do the cool geeks of Geek Squad seem more real than nerdy geeks would? Built into the Geek Squad offering is an acknowledgment of the [Ontological ↔ Phenomenological] reality undergirding the business. It is this transversing of the [Real-real ↔ Fake-fake] boundary line that comes off as so powerfully real to so many consumers. While the Geek Squad is certainly True to Itself *and* also seems so What It Says It Is, the "Special Agent" façade is nevertheless a façade—and thus a fake reality akin to Disneyland, *Second Life*, or The Venetian—deliberately chosen to differentiate the experience from mundane computer support services. It may pain Robert Stephens (and us, his biggest fans) to consider the Geek Squad Fake-real, but that mode best characterizes the cool-geek essence of the enterprise.

None of the company's copycat competitors has yet managed to capture the imagination like the Geek Squad. Much gets lost in translation. (Masking tape on the eyeglasses of Geeks on Call technicians, for example, seems so forced as to render them Fake-fake.) Rather than parody geeks, the best way to compete with the Geek Squad may be to do the opposite, going after Real-fake: *idolize* geeks by creating a whole new genre of hip attire—call it geek-cool—and costume technology specialists accordingly.[10] Then have them tool around not in identical black-and-white Beetles, but Scions individually customized by each specialist. Success may come to the company that exploits the Real-fake possibility of a geek-cool alternative. The greatest potential for rendering authenticity vis-à-vis the Geek Squad lies, we believe, within this polarity:

Real-fake [Geek-cool ↔ Cool-geek] Fake-real

After all, as we've stressed before, *it's incredibly difficult to be Real-real*; such pure authenticity is always very elusive and for some unattainable. Both Real-fake and Fake-real provide much more readily achievable modes of authenticity, and therefore the two approaches discussed in chapter 6 for those modes, *create belief* and *unveil the reveal,* generally provide more worthwhile possibilities than *go faux* or *get real.*

Think polarity, not purity. And if a major competitor has already credibly staked out one mode, as the Geek Squad has done for computer support, pursue the opposite one. Whether you affix a future positioning where your offerings become more Real-fake than Fake-real or more Fake-real than Real-fake, focus like a laser on that end of the polarity.

Aligning Vectors in Here-and-Now Space

Recall how in Minkowski Space a particle's light cone is not a one-dimensional triangle defined by limits on two sides (although that is how it must be represented on flat paper, as in figure 9-1), but in actuality is a three-dimensional cone having length, width, and height. Its limits, therefore, are defined by an infinite set of vectors emanating from that particle's location in space and time. Each vector defines the limit of possible movement and—this is key— has a mirror image, a polar opposite, directly across from it on the other side of the cone that constitutes a diametrically opposed limit of movement in space-time. The actual movement of a particle always aligns with a single vector, heading toward it and away from its polar opposite, coinciding with it only where-and-when the particle moves at the speed of light.[11]

The same is true of this particle's equivalent in the world of business, a company in the Here-and-Now Space of figure 9-3. The execution zone of a company lies within the three-dimensional cone of offerings, capabilities, and customers, whose limits are defined by an infinite set of vectors emanating from that business' location in the here-and-now. Each vector likewise defines the limits of possible movement, and has a polar opposite reflecting diametrically opposed choices across those three dimensions. And as with the particle in Minkowski Space, the actual movement of the business always aligns with a single vector—a single set of choices for offerings, capabilities, and customers—while moving away from its polar opposite, coinciding with any one vector only where-and-when the business moves with perfect execution.

The purity of Real-real and absolute impurity of Fake-fake are two such opposing vectors, of course. But given the difficulty of attaining the pure—think of it as a particularly difficult (and fraught with peril) terrain of the business cosmos—the opposing vectors that interest us here are those representing the Real-fake and the Fake-real, as shown in figure 10-2.

Your business is at the point at the very bottom of this cone representing your execution zone. Your task, as delineated in chapter 9, is to study your heritage in order to ascertain your positioning in the Here-and-Now, locate your current trajectory, know the limits of where you can go, and then affix the future in order to work your way back (in the future perfect sense) to the present, determining what new trajectory, if executed well, enables you to achieve that future positioning.

That affixed positioning is a point somewhere up and inside the cone representing your execution zone in figure 10-2. Expanding on how best to find that point, think of the search for where-and-when it is in terms of the boundaries that define the cone; that is, the set of two opposing vectors that define Real-fake and Fake-real for your business. The promise of rendering greater authenticity

FIGURE 10-2

Opposing vectors of an execution zone

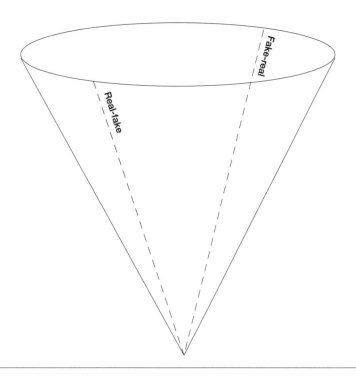

lies in thinking richly about the set of polarities between which your enterprise must act. If you do so, you will find a positioning that takes you from the realization that you *are* fake to a positioning that you *render* real, even if only Real-fake or Fake-real. Moreover, that positioning very well may lead you on a trajectory to rendering your offerings more Real-real over time.

The Five Key Polarities

One particular polarity of perceived authenticity, as seen in table 10-2, typifies how companies render authenticity within each genre. An infinite number of other polarities could define the set of [Real-fake ↔ Fake-real] polarities for an industry or business, any one of which might yield more value *to you* precisely because it lies in more unexplored territory. So after you understand the five we address here and think richly about how they apply to your business, we urge you to envision others that might supply even greater suitability to your particular location and trajectory in Here-and-Now Space.

The Natural Polarity of [Un- ↔ Re-]

The two simple prefixes *Un-* and *Re-* express the key polarity for natural authenticity, as shown in figure 10-3 separated by the [Real ↔ Fake] polarity of [Natural ↔ Artificial].

For an icon of Re-, look no further than The Body Shop. Now owned by L'Oréal, the first store opened in 1976, and from the outset founder Dame Anita Roddick appealed to natural authenticity in positioning the business.

TABLE 10-2

The five Real-fake/Fake-real polarities

Genre	←	Polarity	→
Natural authenticity	Real–fake	Un- ←→ Re-	Fake–real
Original authenticity	Real–fake	Repro ←→ Retro	Fake–real
Exceptional authenticity	Real–fake	Premium ←→ Personal	Fake–real
Referential authenticity	Real–fake	Quasi- ←→ Pseudo-	Fake–real
Influential authenticity	Real–fake	Other ←→ Self	Fake–real

FIGURE 10-3

Polarity of natural authenticity

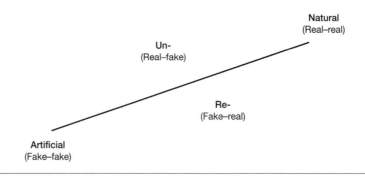

The Body Shop's offerings seemed so much more real than the typical pack-aged goods of corporate giants like Unilever, Procter & Gamble, and Helene Curtis. Underlying The Body Shop's success—it now operates over nineteen hundred stores in forty-seven countries, generating revenues of over €1 billion—can be found in its approach to natural authenticity comprised of an emphasis on all things Re-.

From the beginning, The Body Shop offered a refill service. This fit right into its four-tier approach to managing waste: reduce, reuse, recycle, and (as a last resort), relinquish. Such Re- activities are Fake-real—surely true to self and the values Anita Roddick projects, but just as typically corporate as the en-trenched soap businesses from which it took market share. Moreover, witness the store decor: the dark green walls look so painted; the grasscloth wallpaper fools no one; slickly printed signs overwhelm the place. Plastic bottles off plas-tic shelves go into plastic shopping baskets.

Re-energizing the category, numerous competitors to The Body Shop soon emerged. Notable among these: Lush, which takes exactly the opposite tack from its older competitor. Founder Mark Constantine in fact started the enterprise in 1978 as a supplier to The Body Shop but, stymied in his attempts to introduce a new style of product into the company, eventually went his own way. Today, Lush operates competing retail outlets—over three hundred in thirty-three coun-tries—that carry its own line of soaps, shampoos, and other beauty care items.

Lush exemplifies a Fake-real route to natural authenticity that we call Un-. Nearly everything sold at Lush is unwrapped, un-bottled, and otherwise un-packaged until buyers choose the particular product and exact amount they want, which staff then pack up and place in an un-coated bag. Uncut slabs of soap—as if delivered directly from an artisanal soapmaker—lie on wooden butcher-block tables. The decor is *unfinished*—walls remain exposed and bare, *un*painted and *un*treated. Wood shelving and crates similarly remain *un*-veneered or *un*-anything else that would make them less natural. Concrete floors are *un*carpeted and *un*-tiled. Signs aren't printed on polished stock, but appear handwritten on chalkboards, *un*adorned and *un*fixed. Lush even publishes its catalog in the form of a rough and *un*polished *un*derground newspaper called *Lush Times*.

While both The Body Shop and Lush clearly appeal to natural authenticity, they do so from two completely opposite vectors, the first Real-fake and the second Fake-real. This characterization refuses to be absolute, of course. Elements of Real-fake exist within The Body Shop (especially in its more recently remodeled stores) while Lush maintains some Fake-real features (those apparently "handwritten" chalkboards displaying product names and prices are really printed to look like chalk writing). Nonetheless, the two directly competing retailers—in an industry where applying the precepts of natural authenticity is endemic—overwhelmingly represent two opposing ways of merchandising for today's authenticity-seeking consumers, clearly illustrating the polarity of [Un- ↔ Re-] from which any business can learn.

And they have. You can see the use of Un- in the "un-slick singing" of "un-golden throats" of recording artists like Twista, 50 Cent, Pharrell, Ashanti, and André 3000, all of whom "have learned how to flaunt their imperfections."[12] You also find it in:

- Connoisseur offerings like Grand Marnier's Cuvée du Cent Cinquante-naire—obscure, hard to find, and unpronounceable[13]

- Product categories like Uncola and Unbeer[14]

- No-brand retailers like Japan-based Muji (short for Mujirushi Ryohin, or "no label, quality goods")[15]

- "Attitude-free" boutique hotels like the Beach House Bal Harbour in Surfside, Florida, where owner Jennifer Rubell says "It's all about being real, kind of unpolished, and intensely human."[16]

You can also experience Un- (or not, if you're un-hip) in hard-to-find stores or restaurants without signs or even finished decor, such as underground restaurant Eleven in Amsterdam. Cofounded by Brian Boswijk, Eleven is in the Post CS building behind Central Station, over the river, down the narrow lane, around the security bar, into the unkempt parking lot, through the unpainted door to the condemned building, past the temporary art exhibits, and up the graffiti-filled elevator to the eleventh floor—at least until the building is demolished in the next year or two.

Avant-garde (a phrase connoting Un-) clothing line Comme des Garçons has appeared in a series of "guerilla shops" in the "raw urban spaces" of hip places such as Berlin, Barcelona, Helsinki, and Warsaw. Designer Rei Kawakubo and her husband Adrian Joffe leave the walls undecorated, floors unfinished, and racks un-straightened; the shops do no advertising, don't stay in any one space very long, and don't even change the previous tenant's name outside.[17] And in a *New York Times* piece on "Hot Spots Don't Want Just Anyone to Find Them," Mary Spicuzza discusses bars that reek of Un- because they are "secret"; not tourist traps, they take the opposite tack from trendy nightspots, using the descriptive words "underground," "unfindable," "unlisted," "uncool," and "unseen" across the space of a mere ten column inches.[18]

Colleague William L. Hamilton does her one better—actually, make that ten better. In the article "What Price Authenticity" about how much refurbishment an antique piece can endure before no longer being "original or real," he uses no fewer than fifteen different Re- terms: rebuilt (twice), repainted, reproduced, redefined, refurbishment (of course), restoration (twice again), reconditioned (twice thrice), recalled, revalidated, refinished, recreate, restoring, reconditioning, reproduction, and restored.[19]

One sees Re- throughout the economic landscape: *rediscovering* the usefulness of certain properties of particular commodities; *reproducing* goods and then *replacing* and *replenishing* them on an ongoing basis as a service for existing customers; *refreshing* experiences—in order to *recreate, reenact,* or *relive* memorable events so that a venue doesn't devolve into fake on return visits; *reminding* customers of the means required to achieve the ends to which they aspire, while simultaneously ensuring no *relapsing* transpires.

Are there companies in your industry already applying the polarities of Re- and/or Un-? If not, how might you use them to appeal to natural authenticity? If competitors already stake out those claims, what undiscovered (or rediscovered) vector would take you into rich, if uncharted (or re-charted), competitive space?

The Original Polarity of [Repro ↔ Retro]

The key polarity for original authenticity, as shown in figure 10-4, involves two different ways for enlivening past offerings with an original new spin: *Repro* and *Retro*, often used as prefixes.

Retro designs have difficulty being perceived as Real-real, for while they *are* original, they by definition evoke designs that have come before, which will always be even *more* original. Think of the new Beetle from Volkswagen or the PT Cruiser from Chrysler. Both were successful new models because they tapped into our own recognition of *what an automobile should be*: like the cars of our youth, only sleeker and more stylish.[20]

FIGURE 10-4

Polarity of original authenticity

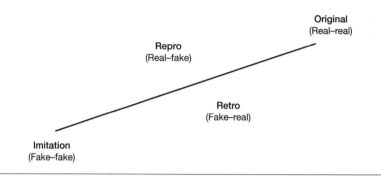

Any number of industries now appeal to original authenticity through Retro, with one of its hallmarks HOK-designed Oriole Park at Camden Yards. The facility is not old but new—while also not new but old—and thus not what it says it is; but it is so very true to baseball, to the Orioles, to Baltimore, and to its specific locale within the city. Retro clothing is all the rage; don't confuse such fashion designs with truly *vintage* offerings, however.[21] That term should rightly be reserved for offerings that truly are old (and original)— hence generally Real-real—not for new offerings designed to look old, and hence merely Fake-real.[22] Numerous apparel companies offer clothing lines that have not been previously owned and worn, yet are labeled "vintage." Despite the original look of such garments, they're not what they say they are.

Nike has now been around long enough to make Retro styles of its own original offerings, such as the Air Jordan, and likes the trend so much that in 2003 it bought Converse, with its line of "Chucks" that hearken back to the original "Chuck Taylor All-Star" basketball shoes of decades ago.[23] Meanwhile, competitor New Balance took note of this Retro move and came out with canvas PF Flyers. Hearst Magazines bought *Seventeen* and relaunched it in a style "bracingly retro and surprisingly demure."[24] And Disney—which sells numerous Retro items of memorabilia reflecting its 80-year history—created a Retro *experience*, the Pop Century Resort outside of Walt Disney World "in which each building is designed to conjure nostalgia for the pop culture of an earlier decade."[25]

With all the attention paid to Retro, the Real-fake alternative has received far less media scrutiny, but made no less impact across myriad industries. We speak here of *Repro*, as in *repro*duction.[26] Such designs look exactly like the originals only on the outside; on the inside, they house completely new mechanisms and technologies. Such old-design/new-production creations show up in watches, rifles, cell phones, computers, and CD players (that look like turntables).[27]

The "Reproduction Movement" is especially big in home furnishings—look at clocks, mailboxes, door knockers, and furniture. Houses themselves can be Repro, such as farm-style homes. The design has been described as "so authentic, it fools people into thinking it's an old homestead farm," when on the inside it is thoroughly modern.[28] Builders increasingly look to whip out "instant patina," using "old logs and antique materials to fashion something that is new but looks old," creating such "authentic recreations" that one buyer says they look "much more real than the real thing."[29] The bible of the movement to create Repro houses? None other than *New Old House*.[30]

Tribute bands are Repro (old songs, new singers). So are all those technologically revived advertisements (with revivified actors) marketers use to hawk new products—such as the Repro Steve McQueen "Bullitt" ad for Ford's Retro Mustang.[31] Flint knappers "who re-create ancient arrowheads, knives and tools using original Stone Age techniques" are Repro craftsmen.[32] There are new Airstream trailers made to look as if they just popped out of the 1950s, but with all new appliances under the varnish and porcelain. The *Harvard Business Review* likes them so much it says Airstream CEO Dicky Riegel "invents the authentic; it's his job."[33] The gas lamps lining old-time streets in such places as San Diego, Palmetto Bluff, South Carolina, Brooklyn, and (of course) The Venetian and Disneyland are invariably reproductions (and often really electric lights, not even attached to a gas line).[34]

The set of rabid fans creating virtual reproductions of now-defunct Disney rides like Mr. Toad's Wild Ride at virtual-toad.com represent Repro experiences.[35] So do all the baseball leagues using 1800s rules and equipment.[36] The golfers at Oakhurst Links in White Sulphur Springs, West Virginia, who must use Nineteenth-century equipment and follow 1884 rules at "America's First Golf Course" also follow this vector.[37] And one finds Repro all over the local arcade; Pac-Man, Tetris, Space Invaders, and other such arcade games stage the original interface via new technology.

Repro automobile shops also proliferate. PGO Automobile in France makes Porsche Roadsters that sell for around $25,000 rather than the $100,000-plus you would shell out for a "well-preserved or well-restored original" (read: vintage).[38] Speedster Motorcars produces a 1939 Lincoln Zephyr; Hot Rods & Horsepower produces a 1932 Ford Roadster; Downs Manufacturing manufactures a 1937 Ford coupe. And of course numerous do-it-yourselfers fabricate similarly Repro automobiles in their own garages, wheels far less expensive than the original vintage automobiles.[39] But wait—why should, say, Ford Motor Company let all these mom-and-popster roadster shops have all the money and the fun? Rather than just employ Repro advertisements, for example, Ford could launch a fee-based Ford Mustang Club, through which members could buy Repro Mustangs—exact reproductions of the outside chassis, starting with the original 1964½ model—but with all the modern technology and safety features inside. Such an offering would provide a viable alternative, perhaps more lasting, than the current wave of Retro designs.[40]

Some new Repro offerings may escape notice, or fail to achieve their full upside potential, as producers mistakenly go to market as Retro or vintage offerings, perhaps because they tend to garner much more media attention than under-the-radar Repro. Witness Elmira Stove Works and its line of Northstar appliances pitched as "50's Retro Refrigerators" in print ads, and as "retro-styled refrigerators, ranges, and range hoods" online. The company's Web site, however, acknowledges that the appliances are in fact "'Nifty-fifty' on the outside; the state-of-the-art features you want on the inside." Repro!

Do you similarly already have a Repro line of offerings but mistakenly call it Retro (or vintage)? Then certainly make it more What It Says. Do you have any categories of offerings that have been around long enough that harkening back to original authenticity through either Retro or Repro makes sense? If so, chances are some competitors already staked out Retro territory; so what nifty old designs could you resurrect and fill with modern technology?

The Exceptional Polarity of [Premium ↔ Personal]

Two words denoting a high level of exceptional care but of distinctly different kinds, *Personal* and *Premium*, define the key polarity for exceptional authenticity, as shown in figure 10-5.

FIGURE 10-5

Polarity of exceptional authenticity

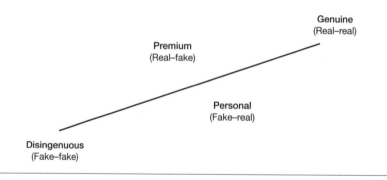

In bygone days merchants knew individual customers personally, by name, as a function of the genuine care and attention inherent to operating a local, family-owned business. With the advent of the distant, professional management of regional, national, global, and—coming soon via space tourism companies—intrasteller chains, such genuine personal interaction no longer occurs, at least not in large companies, while that instigated from on high via procedural rules or information systems can at best provide a reasonable fascimile. The grandfather-like greeter at Wal-Mart, however friendly and welcoming, simply lacks the Real-real appeal of a small-town grocer. Everyone at Wal-Mart, after all, is *told* to smile at any customers within ten feet of them and ask if they need assistance. For big business today, *Personal* does not mean truly knowing all your customers on an individually intimate level.

Even small businesses often find it necessary to implement systems that ensure they come across to customers as small, genuinely caring businesses. John DiJulius, head of John Roberts' Hair Studio & Spa in Cleveland, discovered that endeavors to deliver personal attention have the greatest value when not detected by customers. The subtitle of his book *Secret Service* is most telling: *Hidden Systems That Deliver Unforgettable Customer Service.*[41] At his three salon and spa locations, stylists and massage therapists record the contents of each conversation with customers in a database. Before each customer's next appointment, staff reacquaint themselves with the last conversation—as if actually remembered—in order to make a more real impression.[42]

With any offering denoted Personal, the company sets something *apart* for individual customers. The opposite approach lies in setting something *atop* normal fare in the form of the Real-fake *Premium*, such as offering perks. Airlines have of course offered free first- and business-class upgrades as a Real-fake premium—differing from the Real-real first-class status of every seat on the Signature Service flights of Midwest Airlines or the all-business-class transatlantic flights of upstart Eos Airlines and MAXjet.[43] Even the actual service—no matter how secured—falls far, far short of Real-real on most airlines (the wonderful first-class experiences at Singapore Airlines, Cathay Pacific, and Virgin Atlantic excepted). Sure, you get slightly wider seats with somewhat longer legroom, free drinks, and, in today's cost-conscious times, the occasional meal—while those in coach suffer with peanuts or pretzels (and increasingly not even that). But the flight attendants and ground personnel don't know you personally, treat you specially, greet you genuinely, or serve you sincerely.

VIP rooms offer another means to provide premium value, as many restaurants, nightclubs, and hotels (and increasingly B2B trade shows) can attest. Newer venues often place the VIP happenings within full view of other guests, not in some unknown and secluded back room as might have been done in the past with Real-real VIP areas. Today, the high-roller VIP check-in at most Vegas resorts is clearly visible to low rollers, although real "whales" still get their own backdoor admittance. Increasingly, casinos also provide them with new private, closed-door gaming rooms as well as very private and *tres* premium accommodations such as the opulent hotel-within-the-hotel that is The Mansion at MGM Grand.[44] Even famously egalitarian Club Méditerranée has realized the value in Premium, recently creating resorts-within-the-resorts such as Le Riad at La Palmeraie in Morocco.[45]

Sanderson Hotel in London, famous for its "white bar" that attracts scores of street business from chic patrons, maintains a separate, smaller "guests only" bar, off the same lobby and in full view of the white bar, offering a particular premium that only overnight guests may enjoy. Commenting on a similar scene at the Moroccan-themed nightspot Opia in New York, one critic writes, "from the inside, it resembles a plush opium den; from the outside, it looks like a stage"—one where "privacy has gone public."[46] Public privacy? A juxtaposed polarity that is quintessentially Real-fake.

As are many other appeals to Premium. Premium-grade commodities include filling up at your local gas station with—what else?—premium. Many automobile companies recommend this grade of gasoline for their high-end vehicles, but is it truly necessary—or just another way of calling attention to the Premium nature of certain models? (The way to find out if it's for real: fill 'er up with regular and see if the engine pings or knocks.) Many manufacturers, whether traditionally luxury or ordinary, offer premium versions of their goods, including limited edition prints, leatherbound books, haute couture clothing, signature collection handbags, and specially produced pens. Nokia launched a premium brand, with the veritable name Vertu, of high-end phones costing thousands—some, tens of thousands—of dollars.

Being a polarity of the exceptional genre of authenticity Premium translates into a plethora of service offerings, including all of the airlines, rental car companies, credit card issuers, and others that differentiate their customers into such categories as "silver," "gold," and "platinum." Many service companies provide a further, unpublished stratum of Premium, such as VIP status with airlines (which among other perks means one is always met at the gate by a company representative), or the American Express Black card, sent to those Platinum cardholders whom the company deems worthy. With all the businesses out there making it difficult if not impossible to reach a real, live human being through their 800 numbers, forcing people away from manned counters to kiosks, or otherwise technologically mediating service interactions, many try a new tactic: telling customers self-service is actually *better* service. The sad part? They are usually right. The *Wall Street Journal* reviewed the use of kiosks and other modes of self-service in the travel industry and proclaimed its conclusion right in the headline: "How to Have a Pleasant Trip: Eliminate Human Contact," with the subhead kicker: "1,300 Miles, No Fake Smiles."[47]

It's no wonder, then, that actually talking to someone who actually helps, whether over the phone or face-to-face, has become a highly sought-after level of premium service. Try to get help with your iPod or Mac through the telephone—and we mean it; just go ahead and try!—and it almost invariably leads only to frustration. Go to an Apple Store, however, and encounter a real, live (and exceedingly helpful) Genius at its Genius Bar. Apple's senior vice president for retailing, Ron Johnson, calls these "the soul of the stores" and says they were "inspired by Four Seasons, Ritz-Carlton, and other hotels where service is paramount."[48] Oh—and for $99 a year you can get a ProCare membership that allows you to make appointments up to a week in advance with whichever Genius you prefer. (Such premium premium service borders on the Real-real.)

Plain-old Real-fake experiences that appeal to exceptional authenticity abound in premium access offerings, such as the privileged admittance American Express offers cardholders to events like the Tribeca Film Festival in New York as part of its Experience Rewards program.[49] Others include the private loge boxes in stadiums (echoed at most ESPN Zones) or, better yet, special in-clubhouse, on-field, or between-bench seats available at some venues.[50] Many experiences, from Las Vegas nightclubs to movie theaters to theme parks and museums, offer VIP access (including premier parking, secluded entrances, front-row seats, private tours, and backstage activities)—for a fee. The *Wall Street Journal* says that according to these companies, "what consumers really want now are experiences that used to be off-limits to people like them."[51]

Similarly, certain transformation elicitors offer premium passage and prowess. These include personal trainers volunteering their private cell phone numbers and on-call availability; doctors providing express availability to a limited number of practice members (not just via cell phone but e-mail and—imagine!—house calls); universities creating special programs for select students (usually pre-testing and always charging them extra); and spas, fat farms, and detox centers furnishing secluded areas to keep the hoi polloi away from the high and mighty.

Whatever your economic offering, which is more in tune with your essence of enterprise: Personal or Premium? If Personal, what systems can you put in place to make each one of your customers feel special, offering personalized attention that stands in sharp contrast to the standard routines prevalent in your industry? If Premium, what privileges of membership can you offer, placing customers within categories where members of each tier enjoy exceptions to the rules those below must follow?

The Referential Polarity of [Quasi- ↔ Pseudo-]

As seen in figure 10-6, referential authenticity yields a most interesting prefix polarity: *Pseudo-* and *Quasi-*.

The Fake-real *Pseudo-* burst on the sociological and political scene in 1961 with Daniel Boorstin's book, *The Image*. The social historian coined the term "pseudo-events" to describe the "synthetic novelty" of various news-making activities associated with photography first and then television—press releases, photo opportunities, anniversary celebrations, interviews, and panel discussions—representing human experiences that "are somehow not quite real" in that they are staged solely for the purpose of drawing attention to themselves.[52] The book prefigures not only the staging of 24-hour cable news reports, 7-day celebrity coverage, and 365-day reality TV programming, but also the explosion of *pseudo*nyms—consider Madonna, Prince, and Bono; Oprah and Dr. Phil; Dylan and Dubya, not to mention the nicknames the latter dubs ya' should you become close—as well as pseudo-experts including not only Tony Robbins in motivation but Martha Stewart in homemaking, Chris Matthews in politics, Paul Hewson in philanthropy, and Deepak Chopra in spirituality.[53] (What did these folks actually do before being experts? And how come each appears to have avoided the work of actually *becoming* an expert before being one?)

Various pseudophenomena have crept into business as well, not only in the obvious form of product launches and anniversaries, store openings, contests and promotions, buzz campaigns, and other experiential marketing events staged to support actual offerings, but also pseudo-offerings that require actual marketing. The best of breed may be the $19.95 DVD from the "Counter Counterfeit Commission (CCC)," that "shows you how to detect a fake" MINI

FIGURE 10-6

Polarity of referential authenticity

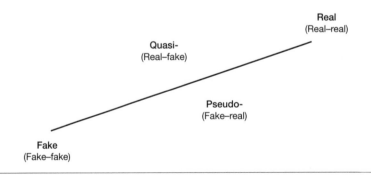

Cooper, "highlights genuine MINI signature traits," outlines the four "CHEP" steps—Cooperation with law enforcement, Hope, Education, and Protection—necessary to "protect yourself from the humiliation of owning a fake," and "features a large overly-dramatized [sic] explosion." The DVD features farcical examples of "counterfeit" MINI Coopers—various SUVs, muscle cars, and old jalopies adorned with racing stripes and oversized MINI logos. Developed by Crispin Porter + Bogusky, BMW's marketing agency, the Fake-real product is bogus, not really what it says it is—pretending to be a self-help DVD, when it's really hawking a car—yet it remains true to the spirit of MINI Cooper production and ownership.

When performed well, as with CCC's DVD, a pseudo-offering serves to render greater referential authenticity through its representation of that which it is really not. Sure, the similarity can be pretentious, denoting some unusual or irreverent relationship to the referent, or perhaps even deceptive—without any actual relationship or association to the referent whatsoever. But as Boorstin points out concerning the coming of "The Image" in which "verisimilitude took on a new meaning,"[54] the appearance of being real is often accepted as real. Such surely helped Fake-real *American Idol* winners Kelly Clarkson and Carrie Underwood go on to win Real-real Grammies.

It's worth a more detailed look at the dozen characteristics that Boorstin identifies with pseudo-events. Being Pseudo-, he says, entails being planned, not spontaneous; planted, in order to be reported or reproduced; ambiguous concerning the underlying reality; and self-fulfilling. Moreover, compared to what Boorstin calls "spontaneous" (read: Real-real) events, the Pseudo- is more dramatic, easier to disseminate, more repeatable, more costly (and therefore more in tune with some particular self-interest), more intelligible, more convenient to witness or behold, more conducive to shaping popular opinion or knowledge, and more likely to spawn other pseudo-events.[55] That icon of Fake-real, Disney, is of course full of such pseudo-events at such pseudo-places as its Port Orleans Resort at Walt Disney World, which, after Hurricane Katrina, appeared to be "bustling with New Orleans-lovers seeking a substitute for the real thing."[56] As one such guest put it, "You can never recreate the real New Orleans because it's all about the people and the history, but I'd say this place definitely gives you a bit of the feeling of the real New Orleans."[57] It may be Pseudo-generated, but it's a real feeling.

Boorstin's list also describes the nature of many other referential offerings put forth by businesses today. Consider Dunkin' Donuts' new "un-Starbucks" store format, which it hopes will help it expand from less than five thousand stores today to over fifteen thousand by 2015.[58] The new design features a heated bakery and espresso machine up at the front counter (not in the back of the house), a wall-to-wall display of doughnuts and other bakery items, a plethora of coffee drinks and other beverages (as well as refrigerated parfaits and fruit), and restrooms moved from down a side hallway to more user-friendly locations. The company's director of concept development, Jimmy FitzGerald, explains its plans this way: "We're going for an industrial bakery look, not a fast-food look."[59] Despite what it says, of course, the new Dunkin' Donuts is not a Real-real industrial bakery; it just *looks* like one. Ah, but the Fake-real appearance does help render greater authenticity. Why? Because the pseudo-offering restores some sense of self. The chain had over time become too *much* like a fast-food joint, and the new look better reminds customers that it actually bakes the donuts on site.

Or consider how many hotel companies open "local" or "street" restaurants that offer no clue that they are actually owned by the hotel chain in which they reside. Paul Keeler, vice president of food and beverage for Hilton, says, "The last thing we want to be known as is a 'hotel restaurant.' We'd rather be thought of as a restaurant that just happens to be in a hotel."[60] Of course, no such pseudo-hotel restaurant just happens without being planned and planted in some unambiguously self-serving way. Most such restaurants provide a separate outdoor entrance so nonguests can visit without having to trek through the lobby.

The Real-fake flip side to such offerings is *Quasi-*. Where Pseudo- merely appears to be a representation (to some referential context) that is not actually the case, Quasi- bears a real resemblance to the referent, just not fully so. While quasi-events are indeed real, the premise underlying each one is not true to itself. Consider the $65,000 "Game Day with John Elway" once sold by home-furnishings merchant Frontgate. Item #17993 in the catalog, it was a "one-time offer to live the 20-yard-line dream" at Invesco Field at Mile High Stadium, home of the Denver Broncos. In addition to lunch with one of the game's greatest quarterbacks, the experience itinerary consisted of touring the stadium with Elway for an opportunity to "tread the turf"; tossing a football back-and-forth, including 15-yard down-and-out throws into the end zone in order to "relive defining moments of sports history" (one can only assume that Elway tells tales of his many comeback heroics); and an autograph session—all before kick-off of a regular-season Broncos game. The Real-fake experience offers exactly what it says it is, and any rabid Broncos fans who would buy the offering must certainly value it tremendously—or they wouldn't fork over the five-figure admission fee.

What makes it Quasi-, however, is that "Game Day with John Elway" is true neither to Frontgate nor John Elway. First of all, what is Frontgate doing selling such an offering amid all the home furniture and lawn-and-garden accessories that make up its stock in trade? If it seeks to sell a premium product à la Nieman Marcus' famous Christmas offerings at exponentially higher price points, would not a day with some home-design guru like *Extreme Home Makeover* host Ty Pennington or *Queer Eye for the Straight Guy*'s Thom Filicia be more fitting? Furthermore, Frontgate is part of Cornerstone Brands, headquartered in Ohio—not exactly friendly turf for Broncos fans who remember Elway's two AFC Championship victories over the Cleveland Browns. Finally, John Elway *never played a single game* at Invesco Field at Mile High. He played his last game in Denver in 1998 at the original Mile High Stadium, three years before Invesco Field opened. One can't exactly "tread the turf" Elway trod or "relive defining moments" that never happened on that field.

Quasi-vegetarianism is "the freshest trend in food today" according to Britta Waller in a column for Delta's *Sky* magazine.[61] Real-fake vegetarians like Waller embrace certain ethical or nutritional reasons for refraining from eating meat, but recognize that a completely meatless diet deprives them of certain savory dishes and delights. They believe "there is more than one way to dine with a clear conscience." Ellen Speare, corporate nutritionist for Wild Oats Markets, says these consumers "don't want to go to these extremes" of avoiding certain foods altogether—and she employs the quasi-terms "humane foods" and "cleaner eating" to position Wild Oats' use of hormone-free, pesticide-free, and antibiotic-free milk, eggs, and meat as healthy supplements to a meat-minimizing diet.

As with all things Real-fake and Fake-real, you can create real value through either Quasi- or Pseudo-. But which one is right for your company? Of all the polarities, this one ties most closely to the corresponding approaches we outlined for the Real/Fake Matrix. If you are a Real-fake, then be sure to reveal the unreal behind your Quasi- positions, letting customers know you know your offerings are not really real so you can more fully be what you say you are. If you are a Fake-real, then be sure to create belief in your Pseudo- offerings so customers don't dismiss them out of hand. With those provisos, do richly explore the vector best aligned with your approach for new landscapes as yet unexplored by the competition.

The Influential Polarity of [Other ↔ Self]

As we complete our tour through the five key polarities arising from the [Real-fake ↔ Fake-real] diagonal of the Real/Fake Matrix, let us briefly revisit the progenitor of the model, Shakespeare's character Polonius. His twofold advice to his son Laertes "to thine own self be true" and "not be false to any man" again laid out the dual standards comprising authenticity, the first self-directed and the second other-focused. It is exactly these two ideas that comprise the key polarity of influential authenticity shown in figure 10-7: *Self* and *Other*.

FIGURE 10-7

Polarity of influential authenticity

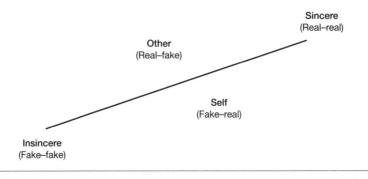

Sincere
(Real–real)

Other
(Real–fake)

Self
(Fake–real)

Insincere
(Fake–fake)

The primary place for seeing the Fake-real Self lies of course in the whole self-help realm of books, analyses, seminars, and coaching (not only from personal improvement "experts" but also business management "gurus"). Self-help sages generally are true to self—but whose self? Today's large-scale motivational conferences or late-night infomercials parade a plethora of self-proclaimed, other-directed self-help experts, reducing the category to wholly self-focused. Nonetheless, people really are helped, even if not all people and those not all the time. The offerings might fall short of being Real-real, but the best of the category do provide people with meaning, if not generally call them to any higher goal than their own "self-actualization."

But contrast that with the Real-real contents of *Self-Help*, the book that originated the term.[62] Written in 1859 by Samuel Smiles, it is a book *about* self-help, not a book *as* self-help. As a social treatise, it positions self-help as the necessary alternative to an unhealthy dependence on the "over-guidance" and "over-government" of the state (which was a pittance 150 years ago compared to what it is now). A Calvinist to the core, Smiles emphasized self-denial, self-reliance, self-respect, and self-control, while wisely warning against the self-indulgence naturally flowing from financial wealth. Self-help meant hard work and industry; it was the desired ethos of the working class versus that of the genteel. Self-help was the means by which an individual bettered society, not the substance of an individual's narcissistic ends. Offering no "how-to" steps to help, Smiles' work truly was self-directed *and* other-focused.

Looking beyond self-help gurus, American Girl also renders influential authenticity by appealing to a better Fake-real Self. Consider first its portfolio of "character dolls"—Addy, Elizabeth, Felicity, Josefina, Kayo, Kirsten, Kit, Molly, Nellie, and Samantha—each from a particular period of American history, each with a "life story" concocted and chronicled in a series of books. The characters are Fake-real, true to American Girl and its values, not actual historical figures. Consider too the ever-expanding set of experiences offered at American Girl Places—theater productions, "grown-up dining" venues, cooking classes, hair salons, photo shoots, and so forth. The mother-daughter (and occasional father-daughter) time spent in such a made-up place is not Real-real parenting, but certainly augments real parenting and enhances each parent-child relationship.

Parents who buy the merchandise and experiences at an American Girl Place must realize this; they know they seek to acquire more than things through these purchases.[63] Some may want to instill a better self-image in their daughters. Others simply may want to prolong girlhood for their girls—"Prolonging girlhood" being the unpublished theme of American Girl and its places.[64] Frankly, some parents may be living vicariously through their children—managing Self by proxy, as it were—and wish they, too, could have had these wonderful girlhood experiences. In any case, even though it may fall short of Real-real rendering (although perhaps not, we realize, in the perception of many!), it provides real value by appealing to Self.

Interestingly, in an age of "extreme makeovers" and women's magazines saturated with ads for products aimed at enhancing physical appearance, American Girl recognizes the parental desire to create greater self-esteem in their daughters; in 2004 it released an "advice and activity" book, *Real Beauty: 101 Ways to Feel Great About YOU*. The opening pages read, "Dear Reader, So what *is* real beauty? . . . It's the knowledge that *you* like yourself, and that *you're true to your own heart*."[65] There is precious little, however, about being other-focused, about how girls should be what they say they are to others—and when there is, it immediately wraps back around to Self. For example, number 98 of the 101 ways to *Feel Great About YOU* asks "Did you ever notice that when you criticize others, you end up feeling bad about yourself? *Insulting others insults your own spirit*. Don't go there!"[66] The parenting assistance is even more Fake-real than the doll characters and American Girl Place productions. It really is inquiring, "What makes *you* feel great about yourself?"[67] It signifies feeling great, not *being* great, and thereby falls short of offering a Real-real focus on a girl's true self. Few concerned and involved parents would not find the *Real Beauty* advice and activities compelling, however.

Despite the value found by many in the influentially Fake-real, nonetheless it falls short of the Real-real. Maybe Samuel Smiles himself is to blame for so much of today's culture devoting itself to the first dimension of authenticity at the expense of the second, to self-perception over other-deportment, to Self rather than Other. As *The Economist* stated in its modern-day review of *Self-Help*, "Like other self-help gurus, Smiles probably affected behaviour less than self-perceptions."[68] We can only wonder how different the genre might have become if the progenitor of the category had opted instead to title his book, *Other-Help*. Then perhaps the world today might have less zen and fewer motorcycle riders, with greater catechization and more Mother Teresas.

Necessarily lacking the real selflessness (i.e., other-focusedness) of such an icon, many companies nonetheless appeal to influential authenticity through the Real-fake Other. All "socially responsible" brands like The Body Shop, Patagonia, or Ben & Jerry's (at least pre-Unilever[69]) purport to make the world a better place with every purchase, as do each of the three-word offerings cited when first we introduced influential authenticity—free-range chicken, dolphin-safe tuna, shade-grown coffee, and the like. (If these were Real-real, then their *business* would be about helping people and places around the world, rather than a mere sideline at least partially done to make more money at their real business.) Indeed, it has become positively de rigueur for any company whose business has anything to do with the environment—whether extracting commodities such as food growers, releasing pollutants into the air such as steel companies, or both, such as gasoline refiners and retailers—to not only reduce any harm it may do (or do other things to at least partially make up for it) but to proclaim it far and wide. For example, in spring 2006 Nucor began running a series of two-page ads directly appealing to Other; one boasted that the steelmaker "is helping to reduce $CO2$ in our atmosphere. (We're like the rainforests of the steel industry.)"

Toronto-based Second Cup—the Starbucks of Canada, although since it actually opened its first café before Starbucks (in 1975; it now has over 350 cafés in the Great White North and a smattering in other places) it might prefer to have that appellation reversed—furnishes a particularly noteworthy illustration. According to one of its brochures, the company not only commits "to providing the 'ultimate coffee experience'" but doing so under a set of "guiding principles" that "enable farmers and mills to invest in their land, their equipment and their people." The brochure—entitled "Solid Grounds: Our Commitment to You" (despite really being more of a commitment to others)—proclaims: "Some of the initiatives Second Cup premiums have funded include the building of schools, improving housing, paying premium wages, establishing health care programs and workers' retirement funds, and building sedimentation ponds to dramatically reduce waste run off into the local water systems." The company further states that "Since 1996, Second Cup has been making a lasting difference in the lives of children in the communities where we purchase our coffees . . . Money raised from Second Cup is directed into essential projects like agricultural training, vaccination, health and sanitation, classroom construction and other school initiatives to help coffee growing communities address their needs and prepare a better future for their children."[70]

Of course, Starbucks—the Second Cup of the South (and increasingly East and West)—similarly appeals to Other in its own work with third-world suppliers and related endeavors. After purchasing the influentially named Ethos Water, it now sells the bottled brand in its thirteen thousand–plus retail venues. Its concept: water for water, as Starbucks funds specific projects around the world to the tune of five cents of every purchase, with a stated goal of raising $10 million by 2010. (That means $200 million in sales.) Ethos Water cofounder Peter Thum says the company is about more than raising money: it "allows people to understand the world water crisis and feel as if they are connected to the solution" and thereby contributes not just to individual projects but to the furtherance of a movement.[71] The other cofounder, Jonathan Greenblatt, adds: "It's about being part of the global community and making a difference and enabling those consumers who want to, quote-unquote, do more."[72]

That telltale "quote-unquote" and its visual representation, the air quote, is the hallmark of the Real-fake side of the polarity. Its polar opposite for Fake-real is, like, "like" (with perhaps its visual representation being a slow twist of one's hair). In both cases, real value can be created for both customers and the businesses that supply them by focusing on a key polarity as the means of appealing to any one of the five genres of authenticity. If influential authenticity makes the right appeal for your business, on which side of the line should you fall—Self or Other? If the former, how can you lead your customers in becoming more true to *themselves*, and more of what *they* say they are? If the latter, how can you lead them to improving the world around them, leaving it a better place thanks to their interactions with you?

Even these appeals fall short of the Real-real, but in an increasingly unreal world it becomes harder and harder to reach that ideal. It becomes necessary, and often sufficient, to stake out the opposite poles defined by the Real-fake and Fake-real no matter what the genre of authenticity to which you appeal.

Finding Your Direction

The five key polarities together furnish a new context for making strategic decisions concerning how to render greater authenticity. They provide a set of opposing vectors that can and should be used to define a differentiating future for your business. Remember that the essence of strategy is differentiation. And then ask yourself, should your offerings:

- Be more Re- or more Un-?

- Go more Retro or more Repro?

- Get more Personal or have more Premium?

- Come across as more Pseudo- or as more Quasi-?

- Cause customers to focus more on Self or more on Other?

Develop a perspective on each question and then use that perspective to take bold new directions in bringing greater natural, original, exceptional, referential, and influential authenticity into your business.

While you could use these five polarities as a tool in designing your offerings and go no further, we recommend you think more broadly about your business and your offerings. Rather than settle on one or more of these five already well-trodden vectors through Here-and-Now Space, identify *your very own* set of opposing vectors, polar pairings based on *your uniqueness*—the combination of your heritage, current positioning, and execution zone in Here-and-Now Space. We offer a three-stage process for getting there.

1. Rally Around the Pole

First, uncover the *dominant polarity* that constitutes the primary opposing vectors (i.e., [Real-real ↔ Fake-fake]) for your enterprise, just as [Artificial ↔ Natural] represents the dominant polarity for natural authenticity, [Imitation ↔ Original] for original authenticity, and so forth. To illustrate this foundational step, consider a trade show that we attended at the Las Vegas Convention Center on behalf of *Exhibitor* magazine. The exhibitors at the Real Deal Expo, jointly sponsored by the American Wholesale Marketers Association (AWMA) and the Snack Food Association (SFA), distribute staples to convenience stores—beverages, food snacks, candy, tobacco, general merchandise, novelties, and so forth. Like so many trade show floors, the Real Deal Expo seemed to offer neither rhyme nor reason as to what was placed where. We struggled with how to even conceptualize what was on display and, after a frustrating hour or so, escaped to a small lounge area to sit, relax, and collect our thoughts.

There a delegate saw our "Press" credentials and struck up a conversation. A few minutes later that delegate, Joseph Buchanon, CEO/president of Leverage eSourcing, shared an insight that helped uncover the essence of the event. He confided, sotto voce, "This is the Vice industry." He meant that it served a channel that relied heavily on alcohol, tobacco, and lottery tickets to make a profit. Ah! Armed with this newfound knowledge, we returned to the trade show floor.

While no beer and alcohol companies were exhibiting, there were plenty of Vice companies represented, from Altadis (makers of fine cigars) to Zig-Zag Cigarettes (yes, the rolling papers company now offers a product with tobacco inside). But alongside all the vice ware, we also saw anew another breed of company that we branded the Nice-nice, such as Hershey's with its large "Candyland" display of candy, logos, and playfully colorful graphics. Then we realized there was Vice disguised as Nice—a boardroom-looking exhibit from Philip Morris in which not a single brand logo could be spotted amid all the information about Corporate Social Responsibility. Nice-vice! And we even saw Nice trying to be Vice—sweet-as-could-be Hooters girls hawking Hooters BBQ Potato Chips. Vice-nice! The Hooters exhibit resided near the folks pushing Indo Shag rolling papers (not necessarily for tobacco, you think?) beneath a picture of Snoop Dogg—without apology, Vice being Vice. Vice-vice! The always-vivacious Chubby Checker promoted his snack foods right down the aisle from the always-hazardous Checkers cigarettes. So it went, on and on— and with each successive aisle and booth serving to confirm a dominant polarity at play: [Vice ↔ Nice].

Identification of this dominant polarity would prove invaluable to show management at AWMA and SFA. How so? Well, if you've talked lately to the executive director of your own industry's trade association or professional society, then you know of the tremendous turbulence afflicting association management. In years past, these once-stable organizations were the sole providers of the annual conferences and trade shows that everyone who was anyone faithfully attended. Now, they confront competition from alternative offerings sponsored by scores of publishers, consultancies, research firms, and industry participants themselves. Further, many companies no longer rely on trade shows as the primary means of engaging customers, opting instead to host private product-launch events, user conferences, mobile marketing tours, and dealer/distribution meetings.

The Real Deal Expo itself faces defection to confectionary-only shows by candy manufacturers tired of (guess what?) exhibiting alongside all the Vice! Denying the reality of the dominant [Vice ↔ Nice] polarity means missing crucial moments where-and-when tough strategic decisions must be made. What you will not acknowledge, you cannot manage. Indeed, the easiest way to make the wrong choice is failing to recognize there is even a choice to be made. Should AWMA and SFA have moved to stage two separate events scheduled six months apart? Should one annual show be maintained, but house two distinct experiences? Or should Vice and Nice be juxtaposed in a more thoughtfully staged way as a means of enhancing the authenticity of the event? In one of these or possibly other ways, the Real Deal Expo needs to deal with the reality of Nice/Vice.

2. Assume the Juxtaposition

Identifying the dominant polarity in your business allows you to render greater authenticity by juxtaposing industry- and even company-specific vectors. Madison Avenue understands the power of juxtaposing such elements into compelling themes. Consider the television commercials that ran in 2005 for DC Shoes featuring James Lipton, the grandiloquent host of the BRAVO cable show *Inside the Actors Studio*, incongruously matched with five rather grungy extreme-sports celebrities. Mark Woolsey, vice president of marketing for the company, said "the contrast with our athletes is brilliant, juxtaposing the world he comes from and the world they come from."[73] Or consider the 2004 Victoria's Secret commercial featuring not only the scantily clad model Adriana Lima but also one Bob Dylan—with the Dylan tune "Love Sick" playing on the soundtrack. The spot juxtaposed not only bras, panties, and high heels with Dylan's gruff voice and beard, but also Dylan's own grungy demeanor with his white-tie attire. (When still an emerging folk hero, Dylan was asked at a 1965 press conference if he would ever "sell out to commercial interests" to which he "reportedly deadpanned, 'Women's undergarments.'"[74])

As the *Wall Street Journal* points out, advertisers today employ untold "counterintuitive songs" to promote their offerings in ads: Credence Clearwater Revival's "Fortunate Son" (about the sons of affluent parents avoiding service in the Vietnam War) for Wrangler jeans; the Buzzcocks' "What Do I Get?" (about angst-filled teenage romance) for Toyota; Donna Summer's "Bad Girl" (about prostitution) for Nabisco's SnackWell cookies; Psychic TV's "Roman P." (about Roman Polanski and Charles Manson) for Volkswagen; and Iggy Pop's "Lust for Life" (about a recovering heroin addict) for Royal Caribbean Cruise Lines.[75] The juxtaposed use of glossy product visuals with such discordant soundtracks certainly cannot be justified on the basis of cost (the advertisers must pay more for the right to use these songs than for commissioned jingles) nor for quality purposes (if anything, based on any traditional view of what constitutes a good spot, the commercials are flawed). They exist because the producers believe the combination of clashing sights and sounds comes off as more real.

Let us look beyond commercial-making for further evidence of the power of such juxtaposing polarization. A. O. Scott, the *New York Times* film critic (whom we cited earlier with regard to his analysis of Bill Murray as Polonius), once wrote a telling piece about his family's annual vacation destination, Deer Isle, Maine. Entitled "Rustic Romance," Scott constructs the essay around the only two FM radio stations to be found on the car radio in the northern New

England town—one playing "the earnest sounds of the latter-day folk revival" and the other "pre–rock 'n' roll American pop"—stations that "would seem to occupy cultural poles."[76] Yet, Scott points out, "the two frequencies are not so much opposite as complementary. They conjure oddly compatible aural landscapes, the one of a vanished, chummy world of 5 o'clock martinis and after-dinner bridge games, the other of an alternative world in which everyone thinks globally and buys organic produce locally."

The two radio stations iconically represent the mix of locals and tourists that coexist as "real Maine"—a place where for tourists, like Scott, "to feel awkward and slightly unwelcome . . . is a very comforting form of discomfort." The juxtaposition of the polar opposites of tourist and local serves to render the place more real. Downtown development councils and regional tourism bureaus take note: instead of spending more marketing dollars in efforts to attract more outsiders to your city or state, perhaps you should invest more in making the place more livable for residents. Or, alternatively, provoke existing residents to explore their own place as a backyard destination.

3. Explore Your Polar Options

Finally, explore as many polarity possibilities as you can imagine. Thinking about the polarity inherent in Un-/Re-, Retro/Repro, Personal/Premium, Pseudo-/Quasi-, and Self/Other is one good way of doing so, but we encourage you to go farther. Much farther. Each of these approaches was derived from the juxtaposed notions of Real-fake and Fake-real, but as we related in introducing the very notion of polarity and show more clearly in figure 10-8, these are but five among an infinite number of potential pairings that could serve to define your execution zone. It is well worth it, therefore, to take the time to generate a robust list of additional polarities that more fully define your unique Here-and-Now Space. In fact, the more Fake-fake you feel, the more polar options you should explore. After you have a dominant polarity and figure out how you might connect two poles into a Real-fake juxtaposition, try naming two more polarities; then four more; then eight more; even sixteen or more. (And if you have a difficult time identifying your dominant polarity, this exploration would help sort that out, too.)

Consider the 2006 Winter Olympics. It suffered from a terrible case of being perceived as fake. Contrived. Disingenuous. Phony. *Inauthentic.* One night while watching the Ice Dancing competition on NBC, one of us asked (not to the other, but to his wife), "Why are we watching this, this fake figure skating?" He turned the channel and caught the concluding celebratory dance of Drew Lachey and Cheryl Burke after they had been crowned champions of ABC's *Dancing with the Stars.* (We weren't the only ones changing channels. Fox's

FIGURE 10-8

Five among an infinite number of polarities

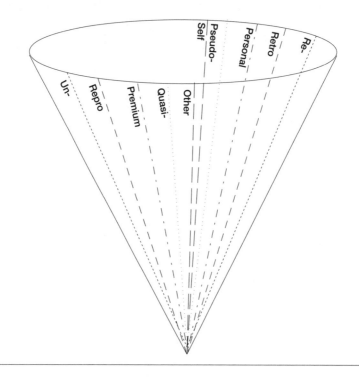

episodes of *American Idol*'s auditions—*auditions*, not even the finals!—routinely drew twice the number of American viewers as NBC's coverage of the Winter Games.) In that moment, the ballroom dancers—the polar pairing of amateur Lachey with professional Burke—struck us as more real than the dancing Olympic skaters. Really? Really.

Consider the fakeness of the Olympic fanfare. Scoring for real figure skating now involves a convoluted scheme that required NBC to immediately offer post-performance commentary of the scoring system itself after every score was posted. The system was mind-numbing—offering less an assessment of how the athletes performed than a safeguard against wayward French judges. In contrast, viewers readily understand the judging for *Dancing with the Stars* and *American Idol*: immediate commentary about the performance from three experts, followed by hard voting tallies of all those who saw the performance and cared enough to pay to phone in. And in Alpine skiing? Bobsled? Luge? Skeleton? Times separating medalists from nonmedalists differed by mere tenths, even hundredths, of a second. In the Men's Giant Slalom, for example, Austria's

Benjamin Raich defeated France's Joel Chanel over two runs, 2:35.00 to 2:35.07—an average of .035 seconds faster per run. The winners of such events seem determined more by the limits of current timekeeping technology than by any differences in skill. How about Olympic hockey? With professionally paid NHL players now dispersed across all the contending teams, a more authentic experience could be had by throwing in a DVD and watching the movie *Miracle*, in which Kurt Russell as coach Herb Brooks leads a bunch of U.S. college players—real amateurs—to win the gold at the 1980 games in Lake Placid.

Note the influence the elements in our 3M Model have on how people perceive these games, like any other offering. Professional athletes now participate in the previously amateur competitions (the Monetary rendering inauthenticity); technology determines who wins many events (Machinery rendering inauthenticity); and set rules arbitrated by judges determine the rest (Man rendering inauthenticity). Even the quintessential Olympic elements—Gold, Silver, and Bronze medals—looked fake here, like music CDs gift-wrapped with big red bows.

So what could be done to render the 2010 Winter games more authentic? First, uncover the dominant polarity of the Olympics—we might suggest [Amateur ↔ Professional] sports. Then, assume some juxtaposition—perhaps [East ↔ West]; after all, it was the global tension between the good ol' U.S. of A. and the evil U.S.S.R. empire that made so many Olympics such compelling drama (at least to us Americans served by NBC). The International Olympic Committee could then identify additional polarities and explore various options for rendering the games more real.

What two sports did we, like many other viewers, find most real in 2006? Speedskating and curling. It suggests a [Fast ↔ Slow] polarity. Consider some other top-of-mind Winter Olympics polarities:

- [Indoor ↔ Outdoor]: Let the NHLers play all Olympic games outdoors, without boards or body checks, à la real "pond hockey"? How natural!

- [Men's ↔ Women's]: How about nations fielding mixed hockey teams— perhaps with alternating male and female lines at two-minute intervals? How original!

- [Speed ↔ Style]: For *every* event; scoring for both, not just one or the other, already helps render various upstart snowboarding events more real. Very exceptional!

- [Individual ↔ Team]: Have both individual and team competitions in figure skating, much like gymnastics in the Summer Games. How referential!

- [Family ↔ Friends]: NBC already inundates us with the backstories of how individuals overcame long odds in their own lives; let's hear more about how they help friends and others. How influential!

We could go on:

- [Televised ↔ Un-televised]

- [Live ↔ Recorded]

- [Old School ↔ New Wave]

and so forth. Even [Pole ↔ Equator] might yield some interesting new ideas for competitions, juxtaposing latitude with longitude; after all, don't people who live in tropical climes play games in the winter too? The International Olympic Committee itself ought to go on and on, lest the 2010 Winter Games in Vancouver become nothing more than a giant commercial for Intrawest's Whistler Blackcomb resort. And so, too, ought you identify imaginative polarities for your business, and see what trajectory they lead you down.

Learning the Discipline of Rendering Authenticity

In chapter 1 we saw how, with the rise of authenticity as the new consumer sensibility, what consumers really want is the real from the genuine, not the fake from the phony, and therefore increasingly make the distinction between the two. In chapter 2 we ascertained the fundamental drivers of this shift in sensibility from the fake to the real, and in chapter 3 found how some companies are responding on the supply side by slapping "authentic" and "real" on everything in their attempts to avoid being slapped with "inauthentic" and "fake" by everyone. We introduced the five genres of authenticity in chapter 4 as a way of seeing how many companies the world over today appeal—and, more pertinently, how you and your company specifically can better appeal— to authenticity to avoid the fate of being called a phony.

Then, in chapter 5, we made the case that when it comes to economic offerings it's all fake, fake, fake—and yet people may perceive them as real, real, real. This philosophical understanding provides a fulcrum to this entire discussion of what it means to compete in a world where authenticity has come to the fore. In chapter 6 we introduced the Real/Fake Matrix, framing the rest of the book in its terms, and provided approaches to each of the four modes it defines. We delineated in chapter 7 the ten key elements of exactly what makes economic offerings—and, by extension, the places in which they are offered and the businesses that offer them—be perceived as real or as fake. Then, finally, in chapters 8 and 9 we took the two axes of the Real/Fake Matrix and showed how companies can be perceived as *Is* What It Says It Is as opposed to Is *Not* What It Says It Is by mapping its Placemaking Portfolio, and *Is* True to Itself rather than Is *Not* True to Itself by navigating through Here-and-Now Space.

Now, here in chapter 10, we have collided the five genres of authenticity with the Real/Fake Matrix to see that each genre self-referentially juxtaposes the real with the fake, feeding back on itself in a way that represents the foundational polarity of [Real-real ↔ Fake-fake] in five distinct forms. While these five versions of the [Real-real ↔ Fake-fake] polarity define a richer set of options with which to think about rendering greater authenticity, their usefulness may be greatest when considering them in light of another [Real ↔ Fake] tension—the one between the ontological and phenomenological at the core of chapter 5. Consider this polarity of [Ontological ↔ Phenomenological] authenticity: it all *is* fake (in being), but it can be *so* real (to me).

You need to find your own way through this polarity to where *your* customers find *your* offerings to be so real to them. Then you will have gained a true understanding of the new discipline of rendering authenticity.

NOTES

Chapter 1

1. Per the *Oxford English Dictionary*, 2nd edition, one definition of *sensibility* is the "[p]ower or faculty of feeling, capacity of sensation and emotion as distinguished from cognition or will." We use it here as the general subject of that feeling—"sensitiveness *to*, keen sense *of* something."

2. David Lewis and Darren Bridger, *The Soul of the New Consumer: Authenticity—What We Buy and Why in the New Economy* (London: Nicholas Brealey Publishing, 2000), 3.

3. Ibid, 14–20.

4. Richard Florida, *The Rise of the Creative Class: And How It's Transforming Work, Leisure, Community, and Everyday Life* (New York: Basic Books, 2002), ix.

5. Ibid.

6. Ibid., 167, 187.

7. *The Authenticity Factor* is the title of Ray's forthcoming book, which he described in a presentation at a *P+@Work* magazine-sponsored conference in the Netherlands, "Health as a Marketing Tool," June 14, 2005.

8. Paul H. Ray, Ph.D., and Sherry Ruth Anderson, Ph.D., *The Cultural Creatives: How 50 Million People Are Changing the World* (New York: Three Rivers Press, 2000), 8.

9. David Boyle, *Authenticity: Brands, Fakes, Spin and the Lust for Real Life* (London: Flamingo, 2003), 43.

10. Rob Dreher, *Crunchy Cons: How Birkenstocked Burkeans, gun-loving organic gardeners, evangelical free-range farmers, hip homeschooling mamas, right-wing nature lovers, and their diverse tribe of countercultural conservatives plan to save America (or at least the Republican Party)* (New York: Crown Forum, 2006). For a shorter take, see the article that inspired the book, "Birkenstocked Burkeans," *National Review Online*, July 12, 2002, www.nationalreview.com /dreher/dreher071202.asp.

11. One who agrees: Harvey Hartman, who writes in *Marketing in the Soul Age: Building Lifestyle Worlds* (Bellevue, WA: The Harman Group, 2001), 4: "We don't think that it's useful to think about them as a particular, well-defined market segment. Hardly anyone lives a consistent lifestyle that is shaped by the attitudes that Ray describes as typical for the Cultural Creative. But almost everybody is influenced and attracted to different parts of the cultural movement that is creating the attitudes that Ray describes. We think that this movement is driven by a deep cultural longing to find a more 'soulful' way of living . . ." At the core of Hartman's model for marketing in the Soul Age is authenticity.

12. Trends consultancy The Future Laboratory "asked 1,000 consumers across the UK to describe their perfect brand characteristics and they came up with the following terms: friendly (44%), authentic (36%), personal (40%), human (30%) and local (30%)." We assert that each of the last three responses—and possibly the first—indicate an implicit thirst for authenticity just as much as the explicit second response. See *Future Laboratory* newsletter, Autumn–Winter 2005, www.thefuturelaboratory.com/newsletters/2005FutureLabAutumnNewsletter.pdf.

13. Regina Bendix, *In Search of Authenticity: The Formation of Folklore Studies* (Madison, WI: The University of Wisconsin Press, 1997), 17.

14. Frederik Balfour, "Fakes!" *BusinessWeek*, February 7, 2005.

15. In an article about marketing *to* Chinese consumers "desperate for . . . a genuine Western experience," *CMO* magazine points out that many Chinese buy "low-priced knock-offs" as a means to afford "premium" services and experiences. See Constantine von Hoffman, "China: More Questions than Answers," *CMO*, January 2006, 19–26. In the piece, Dean Barrett, senior VP of global marketing at McDonald's, offers this Western perspective: "You can't copy a culture, a motivation, or an innovation. Ray Kroc once told me anybody can sell hamburgers, but only McDonald's can sell the experience."

16. Erik Sherman, "Fighting Fakes: It's Not Just Gucci," *Inc.*, February 2005, 45–46. The list of countries and corresponding products appeared in a sidebar entitled "A World of Pirates."

17. Balfour, "Fakes!"

18. Ted C. Fishman, "Manufaketure," *New York Times Magazine*, January 9, 2005, 40–44. Fishman points out the differing quality of forgeries: "If bad imitations are a big problem, good imitations may be a bigger problem." See also

Neil King Jr., "Sisyphus in China: U.S. Lawyer's Antipiracy Task Is Endless," *Wall Street Journal*, July 26, 2005, which discusses the day-to-day struggles to curb counterfeiting.

Chapter 2

1. Robert Ebbin, "Americans' Dining-Out Habits," *Restaurants USA*, November 2000. See also "Fact of the Day" at www.restaurant.org for November 30, 2003. Note that "prepared away from home" includes meals that are bought elsewhere but eaten at home.

2. Alvin Toffler, *The Third Wave* (New York: Bantam Books, 1980).

3. This is addressed more fully in B. Joseph Pine II, "Using Digital Technology for Competitive Advantage as Goods and Services Commoditize," *New Paradigm Learning Corporation*, Big Idea Paper, Information Technology and Competitive Advantage (IT&CA) Program, 2005, 19–25 in particular.

4. Hewlett-Packard's Mobile Bristol Centre provides a technological platform and toolkit for such mass customized experiences. See, for example, Josephine Reid, Erik Geelhoed, Richard Hull, Kirsten Cater, and Ben Clayton, "Parallel Worlds: Immersion in location-based experiences," in *Proceedings of the SIGCHI Conference on Human Factors in Computing Systems*, ACM, April 2005, 1733–1736, available at www.mobilebristol.com/PDF/reid05b.pdf.

5. For two riveting accounts of such travails, see Katie Hafner, "Customer Service: The Hunt for a Human," *New York Times*, December 30, 2004, and David H. Freedman, "Service with a Smile. Really," *Inc.*, October 2005.

6. Bruce Horovitz, "Whatever Happened to Customer Service?" *USA Today*, September 26–28, 2003.

7. David B. Wolfe with Robert E. Snyder, *Ageless Marketing: Strategies for Reaching the Hearts & Minds of the New Customer Majority* (Chicago: Dearborn Trade Publishing, 2003), 29.

8. We called 1-800-555-9129 only to encounter this all-too-typical prerecorded message: "Thank you for calling Geico Direct. All calls may be monitored or recorded for quality purposes. If your automobiles are not presently insured by Geico and you would like to inquire about a new policy, please press 1. Otherwise, please press 2." Pressing 1 yields another recording: "If you or your spouse are active duty, guard, reserve, or retired military, press 2. Otherwise, press 1." Pressing either finally yields a human. But pressing 2 at the first fork in the menu yields four choices. Pressing 3 at this point, "for home or boat insurance," yields five more choices. Then pressing 2, "for new homeowners," triggers a request to key in one's three-digit area code. That then finally yields a human. Asking that human "Does Geico offer insurance where I live?" yields a very human answer: "Where do you live?" (Evidently one's area code is not used to retrieve automated location information, so who knows why it is requested.)

9. That number: 1-800-ALLSTATE. GetHuman.com does list Allstate Road Service as one of those companies where you can go "direct to human."

10. Or that they'll provide what you request. America Online famously wouldn't let people cancel their accounts when they reach "retention consultants" who try to "save" each account; see Randall Stross, "AOL Said, 'If You Leave Me I'll Do Something Crazy,'" *New York Times*, July 2, 2006. Stross gave the example of one Vincent Ferrari of the Bronx who, trying and trying to cancel his account, recorded his priceless five-minute conversation with an AOL representative and placed it on his blog, insignificantthoughts.com/2006/06/13/cancelling-aol/.

11. Robert Johansen and Rob Swigart, *Upsizing the Individual in the Downsized Organization: Managing in the Wake of Reengineering, Globalization, and Overwhelming Technological Change* (Reading, MA: Addison-Wesley Publishing Company, 1994), 105.

12. Gina Piccalo, "Looking for 'Real,'" *Los Angeles Times*, December 6, 2003. She went on to say in the next sentence: "Or a really authentic imitation of it."

13. Mark Slouka, *War of the Worlds: Cyberspace and the High-Tech Assault on Reality* (New York: Basic Books, 1995), 7.

14. Jeffrey F. Rayport and Bernard J. Jaworski argue in *Best Face Forward: Why Companies Must Improve Their Service Interfaces with Customers* (Boston: Harvard Business School Press, 2005) that the use of technology for customer interfaces in and of itself will actually humanize the workplace. On pp. 16–17 they state: "If managed appropriately, the front-office revolution will bring machines into positions that they perform well—and, more important, it will bring people into roles they perform best . . . [W]e believe technology can create more ennobling jobs in frontline positions, resulting in better experiences for customers and greater competitive advantage for companies."

15. Ian Urbina, "Computer Voices Win Customers and Stardom," *International Herald Tribune*, November 26, 2004.

16. Ibid.

17. Neal Gabler, *Life the Movie: How Entertainment Conquered Reality* (New York: Alfred A. Knopf, 1998).

18. Thomas de Zengotita, *Mediated: How the Media Shapes Your World and the Way You Live in It* (New York: Bloomsbury, 2005).

19. See, respectively, Daniel J. Boorstin, *The Image: A Guide to Pseudo-Events in America* (New York: Vintage Books, 1992, originally published by Harper & Row in 1961); Marshall McLuhan, *Understanding Media: The Extensions of Man* (Cambridge, MA: MIT Press, 1994, originally published by McGraw-Hill in 1964) and Marshall McLuhan and Quentin Fiore, *The Medium Is the Massage* (Corte Madera, CA: Gingko Press, 2001, first published by Random House in 1967, the title was supposed to be *The Medium Is the Message*, but McLuhan found the typesetter's error most amusing and kept it); Jean Baudrillard, *Simulacra and Simulation* (Ann Arbor: The University of Michigan

Press, 1994, originally published in French by Éditions Galilée, 1981); Umberto Eco, *Travels in Hyperreality* (San Diego: Harcourt Brace & Company, 1986, originally published by Gruppo Editoriale in 1983); and Neil Postman, *Amusing Ourselves to Death: Public Discourse in the Age of Show Business* (New York: Penguin Books, 1985).

20. Dean MacCannell, in *The Tourist: A New Theory of the Leisure Class* (Berkeley: University of California Press, 1999, first published by Schocken Books in 1976), 107, points out that, in the very act of how he comments on this activity he sees in others, Boorstin finds himself in the same boat with those he decries: "Rather than confront the issues he raises, Boorstin only expresses a long-standing touristic attitude, a pronounced dislike, bordering on hatred, for other tourists, an attitude that turns man against man in a *they are tourists, I am not* equation."

21. Walter Truett Anderson, *Reality Isn't What It Used to Be: Theatrical Politics, Ready-to-Wear Religion, Global Myths, Primitive Chic, and Other Wonders of the Post-modern World* (New York: HarperCollins Publishers, 1990).

22. Jane Flax, "Responsibility Without Grounds," in *Rethinking Knowledge: Reflections Across the Disciplines*, eds. Robert F. Goodman and Walter R. Fisher (Albany, NY: State University of New York Press, 1995), cited in Charlene Spretnak, *The Resurgence of the Real: Body, Nature, and Place in a Hypermodern World* (New York: Routledge, 1999), 65.

23. Sherry Turkle, *Life on the Screen: Identity in the Age of the Internet* (New York: Simon & Schuster, 1995), 164.

24. Quoted in Stephen Totilo, "Do-It-Yourselfers Buy into this Virtual World," *New York Times*, November 11, 2004.

25. Peter Svensson, "Telecommuting to the Twilight Zone," *St. Paul Pioneer Press*, November 7, 2005.

26. Edward Castronova, *Synthetic Worlds: The Business and Culture of Online Games* (Chicago: The University of Chicago Press, 2005), 13.

27. Anderson, *Reality Isn't What It Used to Be*, 268. This of course is the fatal flaw with socially constructed realities and all such "there is no objective truth" worldviews. The fact that SCRs themselves are socially constructed means that there has to be something outside of SCRs, and so not all of the cosmos can be said to be socially constructed. That's just a specific instance of the philosophical fact that saying there is no objective truth makes a claim of objective truth, and therefore is self-defeating. Of course, there are those today who do have different beliefs *about* the rules of logic, but there's no arguing with them.

28. Plato, *The Republic*, Book VII, trans. Benjamin Jowett (Mineola, NY: Dover Publications, 2000), 177–202. For a discussion of Plato's allegory of the cave and authenticity, see Jay Newman, *Inauthentic Culture and Its Philosophical Critics* (Montreal: McGill-Queen's University Press, 1997), particularly chapter 4.

29. www.wsu.edu:8080/~wldciv/world_civ_reader/world_civ_reader_1/plato.html, which appears to be excerpted from Paul Brians, "Plato: The Allegory of the Cave," in *Reading About the World*, vol 1, 3rd ed., ed. Paul Brians et al. (New York: Harcourt Brace Custom Publishing, 1999), 78–81.

30. James W. Carey, *Communications as Culture: Essays on Media and Society* (New York: Routledge, 1992; first published in 1989 by Unwin Hyman), 87. This point was suggested to us by the indirect citation of Carey in Joel Black, *The Reality Effect: Film Culture and the Graphic Imperative* (New York: Routledge, 2002), 15. To put the quote in context (which our use does not), here's a fuller excerpt from Carey: "Reality is, above all, a scarce resource. Like any scarce resource it is there to be struggled over, allocated to various purposes and projects, endowed with given meanings and potentials, spent and conserved, rationalized and distributed. The fundamental form of power is the power to define, allocate and display this resource. Once the blank canvas of the world is portrayed and featured, it is also preempted and restricted. Therefore, the site where artists paint, writers write, speakers speak, filmmakers film, broadcasters broadcast is simultaneously the site of social conflict over the real."

31. "Consumers become original-content creators" is the last entry, for 2005–2007, in a timeline of "authenticity's recent evolution" from Portland, Oregon-based Ziba Design, Inc. The first entry? "1955: Disneyland opens." See Bill Breen, "An Authenticity Timeline," *FastCompany.com*, April 2007, available at www.fastcompany.com/articles /2007/04/who-do-you-love-authenticity-timeline.html.

32. Ann Mukherjee, a vice president of marketing overseeing Doritos within Pepsi's Frito-Lay division, said that part of the appeal of letting consumers design its Super Bowl ads was "the genuineness of letting people express themselves." In Brian Steinberg, "Super Bowl Advertisers Hand Amateurs the Ball," *Wall Street Journal*, January 12, 2007.

33. Lev Grossman, "Power to the People," *Time*, December 25, 2006–January 1, 2007, 53.

34. Quoted in Julie Bosman, "TV and Top Marketers Discuss the State of the Medium," *New York Times*, March 24, 2006.

35. Ken Dychtwald, Ph.D., and Joe Flower, *Age Wave: The Challenges and Opportunities of an Aging America* (New York: Bantam Books, 1990), 13. Just preceding this the authors point out that "To the extent that America has been a leader in world culture, the boom generation has enormously influenced life on the rest of the planet as well."

36. Wolfe and Snyder, *Ageless Marketing*, 17, 85.

37. See "Basic Characteristics of Life Development Stages. Chart of cultural values relative to age stages," The Center for Cultural Studies & Analysis, available at www.culturalanalysis.com/docs/background.html#.

38. Conversation with authors.

39. While nostalgia furnishes merely one component of authenticity, professors Robert Schindler of Rutgers University and Morris Holbrook of Columbia created a "nostalgia-proneness index" and found, as reported by Steven Zeitchik, "Nostalgia Isn't What It Used to Be," *Wall Street Journal*, July 22, 2005, that the index "is a constant and tends not to change over one's life. It well may be that a younger person is more nostalgic than an older one." For the details, see Robert M. Schindler and Morris B. Holbrook, "Nostalgia for Early Experience as a Determinant of Consumer Preferences," *Psychology & Marketing* 20, no 4 (April 2003), 275–302, 288 in particular.

40. The *New York Times* led off its coverage of hotels frequented by rock 'n' roll bands with The Phoenix; see Steven Kurutz, "Rock 'n' Roll Hotels for a New Generation," July 9, 2006.

41. Chip Conley, *The Rebel Rules: Daring to Be Yourself in Business* (New York: Fireside, 2001), 194–195.

42. Christopher Lasch, *The Culture of Narcissism: American Life in an Age of Diminishing Expectations* (New York: Warner Books, 1979), 285–293.

43. Quoted in Ruth La Ferla, "A New Generation Discovers Authenticity's Many Charms," *New York Times*, December 31, 2002.

44. Our source for much of the details on Guinness is Realbeer.com. See also Scott Kirsner, "Guinness Storehouse Is a Way to Get in Touch with a New Generation," *Fast Company*, May 2002, 92–100.

45. Scott Kirsner, "Brand Marketing," *Fast Company*, April 2002, 92.

46. Conversation with authors.

47. Todd Foster, Ronald I. Miller, Ph.D., and Stephanie Planich, Ph.D., "Recent Trends in Shareholder Class Action Litigation," NERA Economic Consulting, January 2007, available at www.nera.com/Publication.asp?p_ID=3028.

48. The text of this speech is available at media.ford.com/article_display.cfm?article_id=6217.

49. Ford Motor Company, section 1 of the Environmental Report, 9, in *1999—Connecting with Society*, available at www.ford.com/en/company/about/corporateCitizenship/connectingWithSociety/default.htm.

50. See en.wikipedia.org/wiki/Ford_Motor_Company.

51. Quoted in Emilia Askari, "Ford CEO Says He's Green," *Detroit Free Press*, October 31, 2001, www.corpwatch.org/article.php?id=1453.

52. Geoffrey Johnson, "'Greenwashing' Leaves a Stain of Distortion," *Los Angeles Times*, August 22, 2004.

53. Daniel F. Becker, quoted in Micheline Maynard, "Ford Plans Shift in Focus Away From Hybrids," *New York Times*, June 30, 2006.

54. Nancy Keates, "Schools Turn Down the Heat on Homework," *Wall Street Journal*, January 19, 2007, citing the results of a study by the University of Michigan.

55. "Homeschooling in the United States: 2003 Statistical Analysis Report," National Center for Education Statistics, Table 1, available at nces.ed.gov/pubs2006/homeschool/TableDisplay.asp?TablePath=TablesHTML/table_1.asp.

56. Tom Wolfe, *I Am Charlotte Simmons* (New York: Farrar, Straus and Giroux, 2004).

57. Michael Bérubé, "How to End Grade Inflation," *New York Times Magazine*, May 2, 2004. See also Ross Gregory Douthat, *Privilege: Harvard and the Education of the Ruling Class* (New York: Hyperion, 2005).

58. Kate Stone Lombardi, "Tour Guides at Universities Master Diplomacy and Deal with Reality," *New York Times*, July 5, 2006.

59. Conversation with authors.

60. Kseniya B., testimonial, www.theu.com/tpr/Brown.

61. Henry Mintzberg, *Managers Not MBAs: A Hard Look at the Soft Practice of Managing and Management Development* (San Francisco: Berrett-Koehler, 2004).

62. See www.impm.org.

63. Warren G. Bennis and James O'Toole, "How Business Schools Lost Their Way," *Harvard Business Review*, May 2005, 98–99.

64. Kathleen Parker, "Watching Politicians Playing Redneck Is Always Embarrassing," *St. Paul Pioneer Press*, December 7, 2006.

65. Crispin Sartwell, "Will the Real Al Gore Please Sit Down?" *Los Angeles Times*, July 10, 2002.

66. Ibid.

67. *Time*, January 12, 2004.

68. See Byron York, "Faux, Maybe; Novel No," *National Review*, April 11, 2005, 26–27.

69. Quoted in an interview on *The Bob Edwards Show*, June 7, 2006, on XM Public Radio channel 133.

70. Paul Starobin, "The Authenticity Sweepstakes," *National Journal*, February 23, 2007.

71. For more on the "New Philanthropists" see "Doing Well and Doing Good," *The Economist*, July 31, 2004, 57–59, and "The Business of Giving," *The Economist*, February 25, 2006, 3–16. For actions foundations are taking to appeal to this new breed, see Peter Elkind, "The Man Who Sold Silicon Valley on Giving," *Fortune*, November 27, 2000, 182–190.

72. Pam Belluck, "Failing to Shed Air of Aloofness, Church Frustrates Even Its Faithful," *New York Times*, August 11, 2002.

73. Terry Mattingly, "Pastors and Their Leaders on Different Sides of the Aisle," *Cleveland Plain Dealer*, February 22, 2003.

74. See Patricia Leigh Brown, "Megachurches as Minitowns," *New York Times*, May 9, 2002, and Haya El Nasser, "Megachurches Clash with Critics Next Door," *USA Today*, September 23, 2002.

75. Matt Young, "Preachers Make Their Points with Multimedia Programs," *Cleveland Plain Dealer*, September 7, 2002.

76. Samuel G. Freedman, *Jew vs. Jew: The Struggle for the Soul of American Jewry* (New York: Simon & Schuster, 2000), 338–339 and 354–357.

77. Pope John Paul II, "I Wish to Reaffirm the Catholic Church's Respect for Islam, for Authentic Islam," September 24, 2001, catholiculture.com/docs/doc_view.cfm?recnum=3974.

78. Ibid. Robert D. Lee, professor of political science at Colorado College, acknowledges in *Overcoming Tradition and Modernity: The Search for Islamic Authenticity* (Boulder, CO: Westview Press, 1997), 2, that "In the minds of many scholars and laymen, both in the Middle East and in the West, cultural authenticity has become synonymous with reaction and fanaticism" while asserting on the next page, "The search for authenticity, while dedicated to the destruction of modern impediments to human fulfillment, is equally committed to a program of reconstruction and refounding. It is a search of new, more robust, more legitimate foundations."

Chapter 3

1. In writing about such phenomena, we constantly have to decide what to put into quote marks and what to leave as plain text. (And in conversation the same issue arises around the use of "air quotes"—raising both hands and scrunching the first two fingers to represent quote marks.) Sometimes, surely, we'll mistakenly use them or not. Call those err quotes.

2. *Newsnight with Aaron Brown*, CNN, February 22, 2004.

3. See en.wikipedia.org/wiki/List_of_reality_television_programs.

4. In an interview with Amy Carlson Gustafson, "Reality of Reality TV," *St. Paul Pioneer Press*, April 15, 2005, Rebecca Epley, a contestant not selected as *America's Next Top Model*, said of the show, "I'm very happy with the way they edited me."

5. Geoffrey Hartman, in *Scars of the Spirit: The Struggle Against Inauthenticity* (New York: Palgrave Macmillan, 2002), 22.

6. Of note: Andrew M. Allison, *The Real Thomas Jefferson: The True Story of America's Philosopher of Freedom*, 2nd edition (Malta, ID: National Center for Constitutional Studies, 1983) and "The Real Mark Twain," *Literary Digest* 17 (September 24, 1898), www.boondocksnet.com/twaintexts/real_mt.html.

7. John Burmesiter, "S1M0NE," *Business Reform*, March–April 2004. Not coincidentally, Christian business magazine *Business Reform*'s tagline is "Real Faith. Real Business. Real Success."

8. ABC, *The Bachelor*, April 25, 2002.

9. Sander L. Gilman, "Plastic Surgery Goes Prime Time," *New York Times*, December 21, 2002.

10. "11.5 Million Cosmetic Procedures in 2005," news release, American Society for Aesthetic Plastic Surgery, February 24, 2006, www.surgery.org/press/news-release.php?iid=429.

11. Tracie Rozhon, "A Lingerie Maker Returns to Its Racier Past," *New York Times*, October 25, 2002.

12. WWE Entertainment, Inc., press release, "WWE Entertainment, Inc. Launches 'Get R.E.A.L.' Educational Campaign," October 2, 2001, corporate.wwe.com/news/2001/2001_10_02.jsp.

13. We owe this one to Michael Luo, "A TV Comedy Turns an Unconventional Weapon on Iraq's High and Mighty: Fake News," *New York Times*, October 24, 2006.

14. See, for example, "ECU Researchers Study Effects of 'Daily Show,'" www.ecu.edu/cs-admin/news/releases /2006/07/07dailyshow.cfm.

15. David Carr, "'60 Minutes II' Wins a Peabody Award," *New York Times*, April 8, 2005. Carr notes that while *The Daily Show* "gleefully engages in the production of fake news," it was the award to *60 Minutes II* that "set tongues wagging."

16. Niccol's remarks, made while "S1M0NE" was still in progress, are quoted in Ruth La Ferla, "Perfect Model: Gorgeous, No Complaints, Made of Pixels," *New York Times*, May 7, 2001. He also claimed that "People are fine with fake now . . . Very soon we will be able to turn on our television sets and not know if the presenter is fake or real, and frankly we won't care."

17. Amy Harmon, "Reach Out and Touch No One," *New York Times*, April 14, 2005.

18. Cited in Ross E. Milloy, "Fake Drugs Force an End To 24 Cases in Dallas," *New York Times*, January 16, 2002.

19. Warren St. John, "In the ID Wars, the Fakes Gain," *New York Times*, March 6, 2005.

20. Richard Sandomir, "Reality of Fantasy Football," *New York Times*, September 13, 2002.

21. Julie Bosman, "Fakin' It," *New York Times*, February 16, 2006.

22. "Bargain-Hunting Shoppers Beware," *Cleveland Plain Dealer*, April 16, 2002.

23. David Bernstein's "Not Quite the Real Thing," *New York Times*, September 30, 2003.

24. Randy Kennedy, "Need Talent to Exhibit in Museums? British Artist and Prankster Says Fake Beard Is Enough," *New York Times*, March 24, 2005. How did he get away with these pranks? Banksy issued this statement to *Wooster Collective*, "A Wooster Exclusive: Banksy Hits New York's Most Famous Museums," www.woostercollective .com/2005/03/a_wooster_exclusive_banksy_hit.html: "This historic occasion has less to do with finally being embraced by the fine art establishment and is more about the judicious use of a fake beard and some high strength glue."

25. Sarah Lyell, "Saturday Profile: After Stint of Crime, Art Forger Sells Genuine Fakes," *New York Times*, March 4, 2006.

26. Jared Sandberg, "Cold, Hot, Cold, Hot: Employees Only Think They Have Control," *Wall Street Journal*, January 15, 2003.

27. Tim Carvell, "Sketchpad," *Fortune*, April 15, 2002. Separately, *Fast Company*'s flagship leadership event is called "realtime."

28. Regina Bendix, *In Search of Authenticity: The Formation of Folklore Studies* (Madison: The University of Wisconsin Press, 1997), 7.

29. Hartman, *Scars of the Spirit*, 5.

30. Michael Benedikt, "Reality and Authenticity in the Experience Economy," *Architectural Record*, November 2001, 86.

Chapter 4

1. For the past thirty years or so physicists have been searching for what they call TOE, or a Theory of Everything, to explain the universe as we know it. They seek a single, unified theory that, for the first time, would bring together Einstein's theory of general relativity (which describes how objects interact in space and time at a macro level) with the theory of quantum mechanics (which describes how particles interact at a subatomic level).

2. B. Joseph Pine II and James H. Gilmore, *The Experience Economy: Work Is Theatre & Every Business a Stage* (Boston: Harvard Business School Press, 1999). Previous versions of the Progression of Economic Value can be found in B. Joseph Pine II and James H. Gilmore, "Welcome to the Experience Economy," *Harvard Business Review*, July/August 1998, 97–105; and James H. Gilmore and B. Joseph Pine II, "Beyond Goods and Services," *Strategy & Leadership* 25, no 3, May–June 1997, 10–18.

3. See B. Joseph Pine II, *Mass Customization: The New Frontier in Business Competition* (Boston: Harvard Business School Press, 1993); James H. Gilmore and B. Joseph Pine II, editors, *Markets of One: Creating Customer-Unique Value through Mass Customization* (Boston: Harvard Business School Press, 2000); and Pine and Gilmore, *The Experience Economy*, chapters 4 and 5. A second antidote to commoditization: re-innovation—bringing to market a demonstrably better version of the original good, essentially going *down* the commoditization arrow and back *up* the arrow signifying commodification—as Michael Schrage makes clear in "The Myth of Commoditization," *MIT Sloan Management Review*, Winter 2007, 10–14.

4. This realization is in fact how we discovered the Progression of Economic Value with its offerings beyond services.

5. For a more complete picture of this, see Pine and Gilmore, *The Experience Economy*, 249 and 205–206.

6. This view is bolstered, at a minimum, by eBay, which (thus far, at least) steadfastly pulls down any auctions for human beings or any derivatives thereof (e.g., organs and body parts).

7. The guidelines can be found at whc.unesco.org/archive/out/guide97.htm. We are indebted to Herb Stovel, Assistant Professor of Heritage Conservation at the School of Canadian Studies at Carleton University, for his analysis of the World Heritage Convention's guidelines, as well as the so-called "Nara Document on Authenticity." See especially his "World Heritage Context" diagram at www.jpf.go.jp/e/culture/news/0412/iimg/pdf/report19.pdf.

8. Nichola Fletcher, "In Search of the Real Meal Deal," *Financial Times*, August 13–14, 2005.

9. We spoke to Xia Jia, who does not speak English, through an interpreter. This sentence in fact comes from a promotional brochure in both Chinese and English sent to us. In it, four key words (impressions, really) are used to describe the place, each again related to a particular genre of authenticity: simplicity (natural); skillfulness (original); uniqueness (exceptional); and exquisiteness (referential). To which we would add a key word she used with us in discussing why she and her husband created the place: preserved (influential). While Jin Li Street is a place that must be experienced to fully appreciate, one can also find the result of such appeals to authenticity in Jack Quian, *Jinli Street: A Road Untouched by Time* (Chengdu, China: Chengdu Times Press, 2006).

10. In 2006 Starbucks opened its first outlet in Chengdu on Jin Li Street. We can fully appreciate why Starbucks would find this the exact place it would want to be, as Jin Li would lend its own authenticity to the new brand. We thought it could only lessen the authenticity of *the place itself*; however, a subsequent visit back to Jin Li surprisingly found the café fully integrated into its surroundings, looking as if it had always been a vital part of the space.

11. John Paul Newport, "Golf Journal: How a Course Goes Cold," *Wall Street Journal*, July 22–23, 2006. The course's Web site, "History & Information," www.sandhillsgolfshop.com/About_SHGC.html, makes it clear that the impression of discovered vs. constructed is no accident: "To people unfamiliar with the project, the questions [sic] persists: 'Why build a golf course in the middle of nowhere?' For those of us who believe some of the best golf courses are discovered, not created, we trust part of the answer is obvious: the natural contours found in our unique valley."

12. Hamburg-based Natural Born Golfers represents one of the leading crossgolf organizations among the dozens springing up around the globe. See www.naturalborngolfers.com/2006/. Two books provide additional perspective: Alex R. Straus, *Guerilla Golf: the Complete Guide to Playing Golf on Mountains, Pastures, City Streets, and Just About Everywhere but the Course* (Emmaus, Pennsylvania: Rodale Books, 2006), and André Tolmé, *I Golfed Across Mongolia: How an Improbable Adventure Helped Me Rediscover the Spirit of Golf (and Life)* (New York: Thunder Mouth Press, 2007). Tolmé laid out a par 11,880 crossgolf "course" across the country of Mongolia and proceeded to shoot 12,170. For more details, go to www.golfmongolia.com.

13. "Countering the Corporate Attack on Organics and Fighting for the Family Farmer," *Organic Consumers Association*, www.organicconsumers.org/organic/index.htm.

14. To gain a sense of how controversial the subject of "organic" has become, see Melanie Warner, "What Is Organic? Powerful Players Want a Say," *New York Times*, November 1, 2005, and M. P. Dunleavey, "What Does 'Organic' Really Mean?" *New York Times*, July 29, 2006. Dunleavey quotes Wal-Mart CEO Lee Scott as saying, "We are particularly excited about organic food, the fastest-growing category in all of food."

15. Alice Feiring, "Bevy of Wine Bars Go au Naturel," *New York Times*, September 25, 2005.

16. Alexandra Wolfe, "Refinishing School," *New York Times*, January 14, 2005.

17. Guy Trebay, "Keeping T-Shirts In the Moment," *New York Times*, July 21, 2005.

18. Rob Walker, "Jeans Engineering," *New York Times Magazine*, August 28, 2005, 15.

19. Joel Stein, "Getting That Vintage Look," *Time's Style & Design*, Summer 2005.

20. Jamba Juice also highlights the significance of this particular material by having on sale at most outlets copies of Steve Meyerowitz's book, *Wheat Grass: Nature's Finest Medicine* (Great Barrington, MA: Sproutman Publications, 1999). Meyerowitz devotes one whole chapter, naturally, to "Real Stories from Real People."

21. The *Wall Street Journal* twice reviewed the shoes within three months, in Stephanie Kang, "Barefoot(ish) in the Park," June 3, 2005, and Robert J. Davis, "The Science of Running Barefoot—in Shoes," September 13, 2005.

22. Norman Mayersohn, "The Trend to 'Naked' Lures Back Ex-Bikers," *New York Times*, February 28, 2003.

23. Quoted in Dana Godyear, "The Simple Life, Inc.," *The New Yorker*, October 11, 2004, 70–77.

24. Abby Goodnough, "In Florida, Big Developer Is Peddling Rural Chic," *New York Times*, August 22, 2005.

25. John Holusha, "Going Modern While Looking Colonial," *New York Times*, September 7, 2005.

26. Alex Frangos, "Greener and Higher," *Wall Street Journal*, January 31, 2005. See too Frangos' piece, "Is It Too Easy Being Green?" *Wall Street Journal*, October 19, 2005, and William McDonough and Michael Braungart, *Cradle to Cradle: Remaking the Way We Make Things* (New York: North Point Press, 2002).

27. John Kuehner, "Alternative Burial Method: Leave Your Body to Nature," *Cleveland Plain Dealer*, May 17, 2002.

28. Maureen Gilmer, "Natural Pruning of Shrubs Makes for a Better Solution," *Cleveland Plain Dealer*, September 25, 2005.

29. See www2.coca-cola.com/ourcompany/historybottling.html.

30. "Woman Travels Far for Coke in Bottles," *St. Paul Pioneer Press*, November 25, 2005.

31. See Chad Terhune, "U.S. Thirst for Mexican Cola Poses Sticky Problem for Coke," *Wall Street Journal*, January 11, 2006.

32. Don Knauss, cited in ibid.

33. Quoted in Rogier Van Bakel, "The Art of Brand Revival," *Business 2.0*, September 2002, 45.

34. Ruth La Ferla, "Hooked on a Feeling," *New York Times*, April 27, 2006.

35. Quoted in Nick Bunkley, "On the Road Again," *New York Times*, July 12, 2006.

36. "Mainstream Mash-Up" in "The 4th Annual Year in Ideas," *New York Times Magazine*, December 12, 2004, 82–83. The mashup tracks circulated online until EMI, which owned the copyright to "The White Album," threatened litigation, further enhancing the perceived authenticity of "The Grey Album."

37. Robert D. Hof, "Mix, Match, and Mutate," *BusinessWeek*, July 25, 2005, 72 and 75.

38. Maxine Clark with Amy Jooyner, *The Bear Necessities of Business: Building a Company with Heart* (Hoboken, NJ: John Wiley & Sons, 2006), 25.

39. Ibid., 26.

40. We commend to all in the tourism industry, as well as to anyone that tours, *Working at Play: A History of Vacations in the United States*, by Cindy S. Aron (New York: Oxford University Press, 1999). See especially chapter 4, "Self-Improvement Vacations," and chapter 7, "Extending Vacations to the Working Class."

41. Rob Walker, "Decked Out," *New York Times Sunday Magazine*, February 6, 2005, 24.

42. If Tony Hawk misses the mark, it's not for a lack of understanding the issues. As Pat Hawk, chief operating officer of Tony Hawk Inc. and sister of the eponymous skateboarder, notes in Stuart Elliott, "Tony Hawk's New Trick: 2 Marketers in 1 Campaign," *The New York Times*, October 23, 2006, the young customers for these products " 'can smell it a mile away' when an endorsement rings false," adding that "The consumers know the difference, what's authentic and what's not authentic."

43. Brian Alexander, "The Roar of the Anti-Hog: Make Room for the Scooter," *New York Times*, October 26, 2005.

44. Associated Press, "A Sport Played by Plastic Men Begins to Find Its Kick Around the World," *New York Times*, February 5, 2007.

45. Ian Schrager, "Reflections," *Hotels*, August 2006, 34J.

46. Quoted in Keith Bellows, "Hotelier as Entertainer: Ian Schrager," *National Geographic Traveler*, September 2006, 10.

47. Schrager, "Reflections."

48. That has not always been the case. Perhaps Doubletree's new focus on being genuinely interested in its guests is the result of the famous—make that infamous—set of PowerPoint slides entitled "Yours Is a Very Bad Hotel," which very tired consultants Shane Atchison of Zaaz, Inc., and Tom Farmer, now of Solid State Information Design (both in Seattle), created after a Doubletree Club hotel refused their guaranteed reservation in the wee hours of November 15, 2001. While only intended for the Doubletree chain itself, and shared with a few friends, the presentation soon made its way around the world, much to the consultants' chagrin and Doubletree's lasting embarrassment. One place to read about the story is at the *Urban Legends* Web site www.snopes.com/business/consumer/badhotel.asp.

49. Since being purchased by Marriott in 1990, the number of Ritz-Carlton properties has quintupled, appearing to lessen its appeal to exceptional authenticity. As Christina Binkley reports in "Room Reservations," *Wall Street Journal*, April 8, 2002, its "growth spurt has also left the Atlanta-based chain noticeably struggling to maintain its service standards while grappling with high expenses. Like Calvin Klein, Pierre Cardin and other luxury purveyors who lost cachet by vastly expanding their franchises, Ritz has slipped from its perch atop the high-end hotel business." As one

person noted in the piece, whose latest hotel fiasco *was* with the company, "I've become a little bit prejudiced against Ritz-Carltons. Some of them are fakes." And even the author of *Andrew Harper's Hideaway Report*—the name is a pseudonym to protect the newsletter author's identity, ensuring that he can publish his impressions of hotels "without fear or favor"—when asked by *Forbes FYI* (in "Checking In, Sir?" Fall 2004, 108) whether "some places go overboard with obsequiousness" replied, "Yes, some of it's fake. At the Ritz-Carlton, for instance, every guest's request is answered with 'My pleasure.' And you think: Well, no, it's not. How can cleaning up my breakfast tray be your pleasure? It's not sincere." It's also no wonder the company has recently dropped its insistence on such phrases for more genuine wordings by its employees; see Peter Sanders, "Takin' Off the Ritz—a Tad," *Wall Street Journal*, June 23, 2006.

50. Jeff Bailey, "Service and Niche Products Win Holiday Sales," *Wall Street Journal*, November 12, 2002.

51. Quoted in Rachel Zimmerman, "Doctors' New Tool To Fight Lawsuits: Saying 'I'm Sorry,'" *The Wall Street Journal*, May 18, 2004.

52. Charles Utley, quoted in ibid.

53. Jeff Bailey, "Airlines Learn to Fly on a Wing and an Apology," *The New York Times*, March 18, 2007.

54. Quoted in Samar Farah, "Staying Power," *CMO Magazine*, October 2005, available at www.cmomagazine.com/read/100105/staying_power.html. Sociologist Arlie Russell Hochschild based her landmark work, *The Managed Heart: Commercialization of Human Feeling* (Berkeley, CA: University of California Press, 1983)—where she coined the term "emotional labor"—on her quite detailed studies of Delta flight attendants. She cites example after example of how they were trained to emote, and in particular to smile, whether or not it was genuine, including techniques for generating that genuineness or at least a reasonable facsimile thereof. We're sure that's talked about in Southwest training, but we suspect there is a difference in kind, not just degree, in how the company hires flight attendants (and others) for gregariousness, trains in the appropriate skills required, and then lets them loose.

55. Which, it turns out, is rarely if ever produced for sale in Belgium, production having moved to India thanks to Belgian missionaries. See Ellen Byron, "In India, Women Work to Preserve a Fading Craft," *Wall Street Journal*, February 14, 2006.

56. Bridgett Finn, "Why Pop-Up Shops Are Hot," *Business 2.0*, December 2004, 34.

57. Contance L. Hays, "Stores That Pop Up and Go Away, on Purpose," *New York Times*, December 7, 2004.

58. See www.slowfood.com.

59. Quoted in Amy Chozick, "Selling 'Japan-ness,'" *Wall Street Journal*, July 14, 2006.

60. In "Consumer Perceptions of Iconicity and Indexicality and Their Influence on Assessments of Authentic Market Offerings," *Journal of Consumer Research*, vol 31, September 2004, 296–312, Kent Grayson and Radan Martinec divide the world of "authentic market offerings" into two different types, with "iconic authenticity" more or less equating to referential authenticity, describing "something whose physical manifestation resembles something that is indexically authentic" (p. 298). Indexically authentic, the second type, describes "something that is thought not to be a copy or an imitation" (p. 297), equating to original authenticity.

61. Anna Klingman, *Brandscapes: Architecture in the Experience Economy* (Cambridge, Massachusetts: The MIT Press, 2007), 197. Chapter 7, "(M) Architecture," 191–237, shows many ways in which Las Vegas appeals to referential authenticity.

62. Mark Gottdeiner, *The Theming of America: Dreams, Visions, and Commercial Space* (Boulder, Colorado: Westview Press, 1997), 3. For a discussion specifically of Niagara Falls and authenticity, see Ernest Sternberg, *The Economy of Icons: How Business Manufactures Meaning* (Westport, CT: Praeger, 1999), chapter 6.

63. Katie Kitamura, "For Curious Japanese, Nibbles of Foreign Cultures," *New York Times*, July 30, 2006.

64. Quoted in ibid.

65. Quoted in Laura M. Holson, "For $38,000, Get the Cake and Mickey, Too," *New York Times*, May 24, 2003.

66. Quoted in Nat Ives, "Television Shows Like 'Nike Training Camp' Widen the Scope of Product Placements," *Wall Street Journal*, October 27, 2003.

67. David Natharius, "When Product Placement Is NOT Product Placement," in *Handbook of Product Placement in the Mass Media: New Strategies in Marketing Theory, Practice, Trends, and Ethics*, ed. Mary-Lou Galician (Binghamton, NY: Best Business Books, 2004), 215.

68. John Jurgensen, "Waging War Over Reality," *Wall Street Journal*, December 2–4, 2005.

69. Karen J. Bannan, "Advertising: Companies Try a New Approach and a Smaller Screen for Product Placements: Video Games," *New York Times*, March 5, 2002. Nielsen Entertainment conducted research on behalf of Activision that showed: "A majority of gamers . . . found relevant advertising enhances the realism of games," in Nick Wingfield, "Videogame Makers Try to Land More Advertising with Research," *Wall Street Journal*, December 5, 2005.

70. Michael Marriott, "Beyond War's Hell, the Bedeviling Details," *New York Times*, October 3, 2002.

71. Lorne Manley, "X-Box Thrives, but the Throwback Endures; Strat-O-Matic Still Lives," *New York Times*, January 13, 2006.

72. Frank Ferrante, who goes by the handle Trapdoor, quoted in Tim Gnatek, "Flights of Imagination," *New York Times*, September 15, 2005.

73. Michael B. Beverland, in "Crafting Brand Authenticity: The Case of Luxury Wines," *Journal of Management Studies*, vol 42, no 5, July 2005, 1003–1029, makes the point that history, culture, and especially place provide the most meaningful referents.

74. Ed Freeman and Ben Freeman, "The Death of Rock and Roll?" *Cold Call Chronicle*, September 4, 2004.

75. Hugh Barker and Yuval Taylor examine authenticity and music—including how performers build on each other—in *Faking It: The Quest for Authenticity in Popular Music* (New York: W. W. Norton & Company, 2007).

76. From "The Eden Alternative—Ten Principles" at www.edenalt.com/region7/EdenWeb/TenPrin.htm. See also William H. Thomas, M.D., *Learning from Hannah: Secrets for a Life Worth Living* (Acton, MA: VanderWyk & Burnham, 1999).

77. Susan Sontag, "Against Interpretation," in *Against Interpretation and Other Essays* (New York: Picador USA, 2001, originally published in 1964), 14.

78. Stan Davis and David McIntosh argue in *The Art of Business: Make All Your Work a Work of Art* (San Francisco: Berrett-Koehler, 2005) that all businesses, in addition to an economic flow, have an "*artistic flow*" that satisfies "customers' desires for beauty, excitement, enjoyment, and meaning" (p. x).

79. Michael Benedikt, *For an Architecture of Reality* (New York: Lumen Books, 1987), 4.

80. Jon Adams Jerde, "Visceral Reality," *The Jerde Partnership International: Visceral Reality* (Milano: l'Arca Edizioni, 1998), 9.

81. "Vision of the Future," www.galacticpizza.com/gpvsnof.html.

82. See dotherightthing.com/index/tutorial.

83. "Reality Tours: Educational, Cultural, Socially Responsible," www.globalexchange.org/tours/index.html.

84. Quoted in Patrick Joseph, "Changing the World While on Reality Trips," *Cleveland Plain Dealer*, February 20, 2005.

85. "Company Profile," Southern Cross Experiences Pty. Ltd, www.southern-cross-exp.com/about_us.htm.

86. Rolf Jensen, *The Dream Society: How the Coming Shift from Information to Imagination Will Transform Your Business* (New York: McGraw-Hill, 1999), 3.

87. Quoted in Nick Edwards, "Tea Turns Over a New Leaf to Lure Coffee Drinkers," *Financial Times*, June 6, 2006.

88. Joe Marconi, *Cause Marketing; Build Your Image and Bottom Line through Socially Responsible Partnerships, Programs, and Events* (Dearborn, MI: Dearborn Trade Publishing, 2002), 10.

89. Quoted in "Starbucks' Cup Quotes Stir Debate," Barista Guru, www.baristaguru.com/ news/?p=45.

90. Quoted in Lorce Stark, "A Spiritual Experience," *Event Marketer*, October 2005, 25.

91. David W. Norton, Ph.D., "Toward Meaningful Brand Experiences," *Design Management Journal* (Winter 2003): 19, 20.

92. Steve Diller, Nathan Shedroff, and Darrel Rhea, *Making Meaning: How Successful Businesses Deliver Meaningful Customer Experiences* (Berkeley, CA: New Riders, 2006), 31.

93. Ibid., 32–36. We cite only the first, definitional, sentence rather than the full paragraph for each item.

Chapter 5

1. *Disneyland Resort Paris*: While its initial difficulties were squarely blamed on a lack of understanding the differences between American and European culture (most famously, the routine serving of wine with meals), since its opening in April 1992, Disneyland Resort Paris has grown steadily to become one of the top tourist attractions in all of Europe.

McDonald's: We've had discussions in Europe with those who decry the very notion of fast food, yet in most European city squares we see indigenous fast food vendors selling their wares more to locals than to tourists. Note too how European revenues for McDonald's now exceed that of the United States; see Matthew Kirdahy, "Update—Europeans Eating Up McDonald's," *Forbes.com*, www.forbes.com/markets/2007/04/20/mcdonalds-earnings-update-markets-equity-cx_mk_0420markets25.html.

Starbucks: The company—whose cafés were inspired by the coffeehouse culture of Italy—opened its first European venue in London in September 1998 and now has hundreds of European locations, primarily in England, but also in at least Scotland, Wales, Switzerland, Greece, Germany, Spain, Austria, and Romania, with more to come.

2. Ever since the Fall, man's relationship with nature has been mediated, with the loincloth being the first manmade invention altering our interaction with the world (Genesis 3:7). Even those few people today who seek to abandon clothing must do so through the manmade invention of the "nudist colony" (not to mention a high fence).

3. This is not a new observation, of course. In a different context, Joel Kotkin, in *The New Geography: How the Digital Revolution Is Reshaping the American Landscape* (New York: Random House, 2000), 61, notes that "On every level—social, technological, economic, artistic—Holland was, as French priest, Pierre Sartre, observed in 1719, '*ce pays tout est nouveau*,' a country where all is new."

4. Conversation with authors.

5. Stephen Holden, "A Portrait of a City Being Admired to Death," *New York Times*, March 16, 2003, a movie review of the documentary "The Venetian Dilemma." The film is highly critical of efforts to foster additional tourism to the city, which codirectors Carole and Richard Rifkind find already overrun by tourists. The ratio of annual tourist visits to residents is now more than 200 to 1, with an estimate of 15 to 18 million tourists a year, according to Elisabetta Povoledo of the *International Herald Tribune* in "Vanishing Venice: A City Swamped by a Sea of Tourists," reprinted in *New York Times*, October 1, 2006. Adds Povoledo, "Should the trend continue, newspapers fretted recently, by 2030 authentic Venetians could disappear here and the historic center could be reduced to a shell subsisting only on tourism." That is not a real city, which is what prompts economist John Kay to favor the approach of "managed tourism," going so far as

to suggest that Disney take over management of Venice—after all, "Venice is already a theme park"—in "The Magic Kingdom Could Save Venice from Destruction," *Financial Times*, June 13, 2006.

6. Frank Bruni, "If Sea Gates Don't Work, Call Canute," *New York Times*, February 26, 2003. We are amazed, as you may be as well, at how often the *Times* discusses Venice, and think the reasons directly relate to the issues raised here.

7. Ada Louise Huxtable, *Unreal America: Architecture and Illusion* (New York: The New Press, 1997), 15, 16. For an architecture critic who found Colonial Williamsburg to be surprisingly authentic after having anticipated the opposite reaction, see Martin Filler, "Williamsburg CONFIDENTIAL," *Departures*, January–February 2005, 79–84.

8. Quoted in Elisabeth Rosenthal, "Venice Turns to Future To Rescue Its Past," *New York Times*, February 22, 2005. The Mose Project, for Modulo Sperimentale Elettromeccanico, consists of over seventy sea gates to control the water levels from the Venice Lagoon into the city's famous network of canals.

9. David Mayernik, *Timeless Cities: An Architect's Reflection on Renaissance Italy* (Boulder, Colorado: Westview Press, 2003), 132.

10. Steen Eiler Rasmussen, *Experiencing Architecture* (Cambridge, MA: The MIT Press, 1995, originally published in 1959), 83.

11. Mary McCarthy, *Venice Observed* (Paris: G. & R. Bernier, 1956), 50.

12. We took a joint gondola ride at The Venetian during our 2001 thinkAbout event held in Las Vegas as the event participants toured The Grand Canal Shoppes. After finishing a rousing aria, our gondolier responded to our applause by saying "Grazie, grazie" followed by a perfect rendition of Elvis' famous line—"Thank you. Thankyouverymuch"—in effect, genuinely winking at Vegas' entertainingly authentic inauthentic self.

13. As related by Joe Bob Briggs, the self-proclaimed "Vegas Guy," on his Web site at www.joebobbriggs.com /vegasguy/vg20011120.html.

14. Quoted in John R. Connolly Jr., "The Merging of the Past, Present and Future," *Inland Architect Magazine*, www.inlandarchitectmag.com/f_ppfuture.html.

15. Cited by Heidi J. Stout, "'Authentic' attractions could aid state tourism," *Business Journal of Portland*, April 18, 2003, www.bizjournals.com/industries/travel/tourism/2003/04/21/portland_story4.html.

16. P. J. O'Rourke, "Venice vs. the Venetian," *Forbes FYI*, March 6, 2000, www.forbes.com/fyi/2000/0306/086 .html. Although he doesn't mention the Campanile, Professor Michael J. Lewis of Williams College provides a great discussion of the issues, negative and, at the end, positive, surrounding replicating structures like this to fulfill "a plaintive longing for authenticity," in "It Depends on How You Define 'Real'," *New York Times*, June 23, 2002.

17. Stephen Budiansky, *Nature's Keepers* (London: Weidenfeld & Nicolson, 1995), 3–4.

18. Quoted in Yaroslav Trofimov, "Angry Surfers Say Cage-Diving Changes Great White's Way," *Wall Street Journal*, September 24, 2005. Oelofse's comments were related to the Shark Alley controversy over cage-diving adventure groups feeding sharks off the coast of Cape Town, and particularly a practice called chumming. It seems the technique may teach sharks to associate humans with food, much to the consternation of local surfers. The two experience-seeking factions war over the issue; regardless: Man is also in the ocean.

19. Luther Standing Bear, *Land of the Spotted Eagle* (Boston: Houghton Mifflin, 1933), xix, cited in Peter Coates, *Nature: Western Attitudes since Ancient Times* (Berkeley, CA: University of California Press, 1998), 10.

20. Quoted in James Gorman, "Yosemite and the Invention of Wilderness," *New York Times*, September 2, 2003. Klett is working to rephotograph some of the same scenes immortalized by Adams, and has discovered that Adams carefully staged many of the images to eliminate signs of man's presence in the park, such as parking lots, buildings, and electrical wires.

21. Ibid. We loved this oxymoronic phrase Gorman used to describe how nature got to the beauty it exhibits today: "engineered virginity."

22. Charles C. Mann, "1491," *Atlantic Monthly*, March, 2002, www.theatlantic.com/issues/2002/03/mann.htm. See also his full-length treatment, *1491: New Revelations of the Americas Before Columbus* (New York: Alfred A. Knopf, 2005).

23. Clark Erickson, cited in Mann, "1491."

24. Colin McEwan, "Unknown Amazon," *History Today*, November 2001, 6–7, available for a fee at www.history-today.com/dm_getArticle.asp?gid=17686. See also Colin McEwan, Christiana Barreto, Eduardo Neves, editors, *Unknown Amazon* (London: British Museum Company, 2001).

25. Mann, "1491."

26. Dean MacCannell, *The Tourist: A New Theory of the Leisure Class* (Berkeley: University of California Press, 1999; first published in 1976), 83.

27. Margaret J. King, "The Power of Place," unpublished research document (Philadelphia: Cultural Studies & Analysis, 2003).

28. "It's all fake" includes cherished national traditions, as made clear by the anthology *The Invention of Tradition*, Eric Hobsbawm and Terence Ranger, editors (Cambridge, England: Cambridge University Press, 1992, first published in 1983). In "Introduction: Inventing Traditions," Hobsbawm states (p. 1–2) that "'Traditions' which appear or claim to be old are often quite recent in origin and sometimes invented . . . However, insofar as there is such reference to a historic past, the peculiarity of 'invented' traditions is that the continuity with it is largely factitious"—that is, made up.

29. See, for example, Robert W. Terry, *Authentic Leadership: Courage in Action* (San Francisco: Jossey-Bass, 1993); Bill George, *Authentic Leadership: Rediscovering the Secrets to Creating Lasting Value* (San Francisco: Jossey-Bass,

2003); Kathy Lubar and Belle Linda Halpern, *Leadership Presence: Dramatic Techniques to Reach Out, Motivate, and Inspire* (New York: Gotham Books, 2004); Robert Goffee and Gareth Jones, *Why Should Anyone Be Led By You? What It Takes to Be an Authentic Leader* (Boston: Harvard Business School Press, 2006); and Mark Albion, *True to Yourself: Leading a Values-Based Business* (San Francisco: Berrett-Koehler, 2006). So why is it no one concerns themselves with authentic workers? Is authentic followership an oxymoron? Not necessarily; Goffee and Jones do have a chapter on the topic. See also Kenneth Cloke and Joan Goldsmith, *The Art of Waking People Up: Cultivating Awareness and Authenticity at Work* (San Francisco: Jossey-Bass, 2003).

30. Lionel Trilling, *Sincerity and Authenticity* (Cambridge, MA: Harvard University Press, 1971), 12.

31. Ibid., 92, 94.

32. Ibid., 94.

33. Jacob Golomb, *In Search of Authenticity: From Kierkegaard to Camus* (London: Routledge, 1995), 7. One exception: Martin Heidegger, as Golomb points out on p. 94: "Unlike previous thinkers who arrived at the notion by examining inauthentic patterns of life, Heidegger starts with a positive definition. Both authenticity and inauthenticity are defined positively . . ." See Martin Heidegger, *Being and Time*, translated by John Macquarrie and Edward Robinson (New York: HarperSanFrancisco, 1962), 67–71 and 219–224, for example.

34. Trilling, *Sincerity and Authenticity*, 138, 143, and 161.

35. Ibid., 93.

36. Ibid., 126–127. On p. 128 Trilling further notes that "in many quarters, whatever can be thought susceptible of analogy to the machine, even a syllogism or a device of dramaturgy, is felt to be inimical to the authenticity of experience and being."

37. Jay Newman, *Inauthentic Culture and Its Philosophical Critics* (Montreal: McGill-Queen's University Press, 1997), 24. In a less philosophical context, market researcher Harvey Hartman echoes this when he says, "one of the hallmarks of the authentic experience is a direct reference—literal or symbolic—to a pre-modern, less industrialized era" in *Marketing in the Soul Age: Building Lifestyle Worlds* (Bellevue, WA: The Harman Group, 2001), 43. And David Lewis and Darren Bridger in *The Soul of the New Consumer: Authenticity—What We Buy and Why in the New Economy* (London: Nicholas Brealey Publishing, 2000), 198, say point blank: "One cannot mass produce authenticity."

38. Trilling, *Sincerity and Authenticity*, 124.

39. Golomb, *In Search of Authenticity*, 128.

40. Corey Anton, *Selfhood and Authenticity* (Albany, NY: State University of New York Press, 2001), 151.

41. MacCannell, *The Tourist*, 155.

42. This point is well made by James Park, *Becoming More Authentic: The Positive Side of Existentialism* (Minneapolis: Existential Books, 1999), who wrote "we must either *create ourselves* or allow ourselves to be *shaped by the cultural forces around us*" (p. 3).

43. Note how in the quote at the front of this book from Michael Crichton's *Timeline* (New York: Alfred A. Knopf, 1999, 400–401 and 436–437) protagonist Robert Doniger asserts that authenticity is "anything . . . not devised and structured to make a profit" (i.e., not Monetary), "anything . . . not controlled by corporations" (i.e., not of Man), and "anything that exists for its own sake, that assumes its own shape" (i.e., not Mechanical). Of course, Doniger then goes on to violate every one of the 3Ms through his vision of creating a corporate money-making machine (his potentially $100 billion company, ITC) by taking modern man where he decidedly does not belong (the past) through what would be the absolute pinnacle of technology (the quantum mechanics of time travel). Of course, *all* companies must defy the 3Ms of inauthenticity to participate in present-day commerce, but in doing so they can render authenticity without irony (only, as we shall see, paradox).

44. Dinesh D'Souza, *What's So Great About America* (Washington, DC: Regnery Publishing, Inc., 2002), 137–138. Note how in this one phrase he so eloquently captures the 3Ms of inauthenticity: the American system = of Man; technological = of Machines; and capitalism = of Money.

45. Ibid., 142.

46. Ibid., 157.

47. Ibid., 156–157.

48. Ibid., 159.

49. Bo Burlingham, *Small Giants: Companies That Choose to Be Great Instead of Big* (New York: Portfolio Hardcover, 2005); Seth Godin, *Small Is the New Big: and 193 Other Riffs, Rants, and Remarkable Business Ideas* (New York: Portfolio Hardcover, 2006); and Michael H. Shuman and Bill McKibbon, *The Small-Mart Revolution: How Local Business Are Beating the Global Competition* (San Francisco: Berrett-Koehler, 2006).

50. Anton, *Selfhood and Authenticity*, 142.

51. This directly relates to the Here-and-Now Space framework we reveal in chapter 9.

52. Anton, *Selfhood and Authenticity*, 131. Earlier on this page Anton declares: "I have become who I am through others."

53. See Adam Smith, *An Inquiry into the Nature and Causes of the Wealth of Nations*, edited by Edwin Cannan (New York: The Modern Library, 1994; originally published in 1776), 521: "But that trade which, without force or constraint, is naturally and regularly carried on between any two places, is always advantageous, though not always equally so, to both." This can also be found online at the Library of Economics and Liberty, www.econlib.org/library /Smith/smWN1.html. See also David Ricardo, *Principles of Political Economy and Taxation* (New York: Prometheus

Books, 1996, originally published in 1821), chapter 7 in particular, which can also be found online at the Library of Economics and Liberty, www.econlib.org/library/Ricardo/ricP2a.html.

54. Kotkin, *The New Geography*, 138.

55. Newman, *Inauthentic Culture and Its Philosophical Critics*, 17. On p. 22 Newman notes that "cultural products" include "goods, services, or experiences."

56. Richard A. Peterson, *Creating Country Music: Fabricating Authenticity* (Chicago: The University of Chicago Press, 1997). For a discussion involving all forms of popular music, see Hugh Barker and Yuval Taylor, *Faking It: The Quest for Authenticity in Popular Music* (New York: W. W. Norton & Company, 2007).

57. Richard A. Peterson, "In Search of Authenticity," *Journal of Management Studies*, vol 42, no 5, July 2005, 1086.

58. Ibid., 1083.

59. Kent Grayson and Radan Martinec make this point for economic offerings in "Consumer Perceptions of Iconicity and Indexicality and Their Influence on Assessments of Authentic Market Offerings," *Journal of Consumer Research*, vol 31, September 2004, 296–312. For how consumers navigate these issues, see also Kent Grayson and David Shulman, "Indexicality and the Verification Function of Irreplaceable Possessions: A Semiotic Analysis," *Journal of Consumer Research*, vol 27, June 2000, 17–30.

60. That is why throughout this book we have been very careful, when talking of offerings or businesses, to use such terms as "seems real," "perceived as authentic," "viewed as real," "rendered authentic," etc. Of course, we do not hesitate to say particular offerings are inauthentic, unreal, fake, etc. Because they are.

61. Golomb, *In Search of Authenticity*, 19. In his conclusion, p. 200, Golomb says "To conclude is to reach an end together, but the authentic posture, as understood by the philosophers of authenticity, forbids me from presuming to conclude for *you* or for *us*. Each individual has to come to her *own* conclusions about authenticity." While we do conclude from reading Golomb and the other philosophical works cited in this chapter that authenticity is personally determined, we do not presume to tell *you* what is authentic *to* you.

62. Ibid., 25. That does not prevent higher authorities from trying; see the Special Issue on Manufactured Authenticity and Creative Voice in Cultural Industries, *Journal of Management Studies*, vol 42, no 5 (July 2005), in particular Richard A. Peterson's "In Search of Authenticity," 1083–1098.

63. Charles Taylor, *The Ethics of Authenticity* (Cambridge, MA: Harvard University Press, 1991), 3.

64. Ibid., 68.

65. Virginia Postrel, *The Substance of Style: How the Rise of Aesthetic Value Is Remaking Commerce, Culture, and Consciousness* (New York: HarperCollins Publishers, 2003), 113.

66. Ibid., 97.

67. Even when their self-image is purely aspirational, bearing little resemblance to who customers really are today. As the always interesting and ever publishing Seth Godin says in his book *All Marketers Are Liars: The Power of Telling Authentic Stories in a Low-Trust World* (New York: Portfolio, 2005), 15–16, "I wasn't being completely truthful with you when I named this book. Marketers aren't liars. They are just storytellers. It's the consumers who are liars. As consumers, we lie to ourselves every day. We lie to ourselves about what we wear, where we live, how we vote and what we do at work. *Successful marketers are just the providers of stories that consumers choose to believe* . . . The only way your story will be believed, the only way people will tell themselves the lie you are depending on and the only way your idea will spread is *if you tell the truth*. And you are telling the truth when you live the story you are telling—when it's *authentic*."

68. David B. Wolfe with Robert E. Snyder, *Ageless Marketing: Strategies for Reaching the Hearts & Minds of the New Customer Majority* (Chicago: Dearborn Trade Publishing, 2003), 55.

69. Ibid.

Chapter 6

1. Quotes are those used to describe the respective pieces of art in "Staging Reality: Photography from the West Collection at SEI," SEI Investments in Oaks, Pennsylvania.

2. Sid Sachs, "Sites Unseen," in "Staging Reality: Photography from the West Collection at SEI," August 2002.

3. Ibid.

4. William Shakespeare, *Hamlet, Prince of Denmark*, Act I, Scene 3, lines 80–82.

5. Jacob Golomb, *In Search of Authenticity: From Kierkegaard to Camus* (London: Routledge, 1995), 204, says, "To be human is to search for one's true self and to yearn for authentic relations with others," while Corey Anton puts it this way: "we are mostly ourselves when we concernfully face others," in *Selfhood and Authenticity* (Albany, NY: State University of New York Press, 2001), 149. We should also point out that, taking after Rousseau, Lionel Trilling, *Sincerity and Authenticity* (Cambridge, MA: Harvard University Press, 1971), would disagree with us. He discusses these same three lines at the beginning of this book, deciding that only the first, self-directed, standard is truly about authenticity, while the second, other-focused, standard is merely about sincerity. With Charles Taylor, *The Ethics of Authenticity* (Cambridge, MA: Harvard University Press, 1991), we believe today's conceptualization of authenticity goes too far in the direction of complete autonomy; both dimensions are integral to a proper view of the concept.

6. The first standard, being true to self, corresponds to definitions 5 ("Real, actual, 'genuine'") and 8 ("Acting of itself, self-originated, automatic") of "authenticity" in the *Oxford English Dictionary*. The second standard, being what you say you are to others, corresponds to definitions 3 ("Entitled to acceptance or belief, as being in accordance with

fact, or as stating fact; reliable, trustworthy, of established credit") and 6 ("Really proceeding from its reputed source or author; of undisputed origin, genuine"). All other *OED* definitions of the term are either obsolete or technical.

7. Michael Schrage, *Shared Minds: The New Technologies of Collaboration* (New York: Random House, 1990), 66.

8. Ada Louise Huxtable, *The Unreal America: Architecture and Illusion* (New York: The New Press, 1997), 75. Astute, longtime readers will remember that in our discussion of esthetic experiences in *The Experience Economy: Work Is Theatre & Every Business a Stage* (Boston: Harvard Business School Press, 1999), 37, we quoted the exact same passage for completely different reasons.

9. See James H. Gilmore and B. Joseph Pine II, "Foreword," in Alex Lowy and Phil Hood, *The Power of the 2x2 Matrix: Using 2x2 Thinking to Solve Business Problems and Make Better Decisions* (San Francisco: Jossey-Bass, 2004), xiii–xv.

10. It is the business, after all, doing the offering and the saying, and businesses are entities akin to persons. In the 1886 case of *Santa Clara County v. Southern Pacific Railroad Company*, the Chief Justice of the Supreme Court, Morrison R. Waite, indicated under the heading "Statements of Fact" that corporations were "persons" according to the Fourteenth Amendment. Other rulings have cited this as precedent even though such statements are not an official part of the decision. *Santa Clara County v. Southern Pacific Railroad Company*, en.wikipedia.org/wiki/Santa_Clara _County_v._Southern_Pacific_Railroad_Company. We know of no such rulings on the personhood of economic offerings.

11. Hervé Laroche, "The Power of Moderation," *MIT Sloan Management Review* 46, no 1 (Fall 2004): 19–20, 21.

12. Imagine Rodney Dangerfield reading *Proverbs* aloud.

13. A. O. Scott, "Murray's Art of Losing," *New York Times*, September 14, 2003.

14. Quoted in Elena Roston, "Penn Ultimate," *Los Angeles New Times*, May 23–29, 2002, 21, cited in Craig Detweiler and Barry Taylor, *A Matrix of Meaning: Finding God in Popular Culture* (Grand Rapids, MI: Baker Academic, 2003), 53.

15. William Ian Miller, *Faking It* (Cambridge: Cambridge University Press, 2003). Miller devotes many pages, 109–115 in particular, to discussing Hamlet and the three lines at play here.

16. Ibid., 233. It is worth quoting the fuller passage in which these words appear in Miller's afterword: "Do not read me as willing to martyr myself for faking it, or as irremediably hostile to the idea of authenticity. But, like it or not, we are stuck with faking it. If we try to avoid it by refusing to don masks or strip our veils we are only playing a role that has a lengthy and complex history, predating the cynics, and ever so susceptible to hypocritical and false forms. Some accommodations with faking it is in order. And though quests for authenticity prompt some raillery from me, not all such quests are silly, and some indeed are necessary or unavoidable."

17. Scott Bedbury, *A New Brand World* (New York: Viking, 2002), 51.

18. Tracie Rozhon, "At Fashion Forward Retailers, Faux-Faux Is the Way to Go," *New York Times*, December 24, 2002.

19. Huxtable, *The Unreal America*, 53. This is in the middle of a chapter entitled "America the Faux" that contrasts Disneyland with Universal CityWalk, the upcoming iconic example for Real-fake.

20. Daniel J. Boorstin, *The Image: A Guide to Pseudo-Events in America* (New York: Vintage Books, 1992, originally published by Harper & Row in 1961), 103.

21. Jean Baudrillard, *Simulacra and Simulation* (Ann Arbor, MI: The University of Michigan Press, 1994; originally published in French by Éditions Galilée, 1981), 12.

22. Michael Sorkin, "See You in Disneyland," in *Variations on a Theme Park: The New American City and the End of Public Space*, ed. Michael Sorkin (New York: Hill and Wang, 1992), 216. Actually, as one nostalgic visitor—journalist Jerry Shriver in "Disneyland memories stay forever young," *USA Today*, March 11, 2005, recalling his first visit to the park in 1963—makes clear, the referent for Disneyland's referential authenticity was the company's own TV shows used to finance the park: "I was swept up in a half-dozen fantasy worlds that I previously had glimpsed only through a box in the living room. Only now they were real."

23. Umberto Eco, *Travels in Hyperreality* (San Diego, CA: Harcourt Brace & Company, 1986; originally published by Gruppo Editoriale in 1983), 40.

24. It's not even modeled after the real Sleeping Beauty Castle, which one of us has visited in Sababurg, Germany, but rather a much larger (and prettier) castle known as Neuschwanstein in Bavaria, outside of Fussen. This was built by King Ludwig II in the late 1800s and is itself really a fake castle, fashioned in the style of centuries earlier and inhabited for only a few months before the king was deposed. The real Sleeping Beauty Castle dates to the early fourteenth century and, after it fell into disuse, reportedly only then became the setting of the original Brothers Grimm fairy tale in the early nineteenth century.

25. From the first written description of Disneyland, cited in Bob Thomas, *Walt Disney: An American Original* (New York: Hyperion, 1976), 246.

26. Tom Carson, "To Disneyland," *Los Angeles Weekly*, 27 March, April 2, 1992, 19.

27. Charles Moore, Peter Becker, and Regula Campbell, *The City Observed: Los Angeles: A Guide to Its Architecture and Landscape* (Santa Monica, CA: Hennessey+Ingalls, 1998; originally published by Vintage Books in 1984), 35.

28. In *Marketing—the Retro Revolution* (London: SAGE Publications, 2001), 146, Stephen Brown, professor of marketing research at the University of Ulster, summarized his chapter study of Disney and other themed places with a good description of the Fake-real done well: "[T]hemed environments in general and retroscapes in particular are

often described as imitations, as simulacra, as parodies, as superficial tissues of ill-chosen quotations, as preposterous monuments to postmodern artifice. *And so they are.* But they are also much more than that, insofar as the environments attempt to capture the cores of the concept concerned. They are epitomizations not imitations, syntheses not simulacra, the pith rather than parodies, the quintessence rather than quotations."

29. Samuel Taylor Coleridge, *Biographia Literaria*, from *The Major Works* (New York: Oxford University Press, 2000; originally published in 1817), 314. In this compendium of thoughts on his literary life and writing Coleridge talked of writing poems where "the incidents and agents were to be, in part at least, supernatural; and the excellence aimed at was to consist in the interesting of the affections by the dramatic truth of such emotions, as would naturally accompany such situations, supposing them real." This would be done "so as to transfer from our inward nature a human interest and a semblance of truth sufficient to procure for these shadows of imagination that willing suspension of disbelief for the moment, which constitutes poetic faith." *The Rime of the Ancient Mariner* was one such poem.

30. Sarah E. Worth, "The Paradox of Real Response to Neo-Fiction," in *The Matrix and Philosophy: Welcome to the Desert of the Real*, ed. William Irwin (Chicago: Open Court, 2002), 184.

31. Economist Stanley Lebergott makes the point, in *Pursuing Happiness: American Consumers in the Twentieth Century* (Princeton, NJ: Princeton University Press, 1993), that all goods are purchased for the experiences they enable.

32. J. R. R. Tolkien, "On Fairy-Stories," in "Tree and Leaf" in *The Tolkien Reader* (New York: Ballantine Books, 1966), 73, 60. As David Boyle points out in *Authenticity: Brands, Fakes, Spin and the Lust for Real Life* (London: Flamingo, 2003), 151, storytelling "is part of this same search for authenticity . . . Robert McKee says that real stories are about making sense of reality, and I think he's right. That might make dour kitchen-sink dramas potentially fake, while the obvious success of *Harry Potter* and *Lord of the Rings* a glorious return to authenticity. That would make fairy stories, if not quite real, then at least true to the basic structures of human life."

33. Disney itself made a foray into Fake-real with its California Adventure theme park, opened up across the street from Disneyland in 2001. Like Universal CityWalk, Disney's California Adventure acknowledges its own fakery, most tellingly with the fake sky backdrop that stands at the end of "Hollywood Boulevard" in the Hollywood Pictures Backlot. It has been a critical and financial disappointment, however, in our opinion largely because, for iconically Fake-real Disney, the place isn't *real Disney*.

34. "Universal CityWalk," *The Jerde Partnership International: Visceral Reality* (Milano: l'Arca Edizioni, 1998), 37.

35. Huxtable, *The Unreal America*, 58.

36. Ed Leibowitz, "Crowd Pleaser," *Los Angeles Magazine*, February 2002, 52.

37. Ibid., 50.

38. Quoted in ibid., 52.

39. Ibid., 50.

40. Pundit and longtime Los Angeles resident Virginia Postrel, in *The Substance of Style: How the Rise of Aesthetic Value Is Remaking Commerce, Culture, and Consciousness* (New York: HarperCollins Publishers, 2003), xiii, sums up her own description of the place by saying, "So much for the assumption that artifice and interaction are contradictory, that the only experience a 'simulacrum' can produce is inauthentic." We're indebted to Postrel's discussion of CityWalk for making the Real-fake nature of CityWalk clear.

Chapter 7

1. Watson did so first in a series of lectures to Columbia University in the spring of 1962, and later that summer in a Management Briefing to all IBM Managers: Thomas J. Watson Jr., Management Briefing Number 2-62, June 14, 1962, in *Thirty Years of Management Briefings* (Armonk, NY: IBM Corporation, 1988), 47, where he listed them as "respect for the individual, giving the very best possible service, and the pursuit of perfection."

2. Thomas J. Watson Jr., *A Business and Its Beliefs: The Ideas That Helped Build IBM* (New York: McGraw-Hill Book Company, Inc., 1963), 5. In this compilation of his Columbia lectures, Watson phrased the basic beliefs as "respect for the individual" (p. 13), "give the best customer service of any company in the world" (p. 29), and "an organization should pursue all tasks with the idea that they can be accomplished in a superior fashion," also stated as "striving for perfection" (p. 34).

3. Louis V. Gerstner Jr., *Who Says Elephants Can't Dance? Inside IBM's Historic Turnaround* (New York: Harper-Collins, 2002), 185–186.

4. "The HBR Interview: Samuel J. Palmisano: Leading Change When Business Is Good," interviewed by Paul Hemp and Thomas A. Stewart, *Harvard Business Review*, December 2004, 62. Palmisano then went on to describe how each of the Basic Beliefs had morphed over the decades into principles that exhibited a culture of arrogance, using words, unsurprisingly, very similar to Gerstner's several years earlier.

5. Ibid., 65.

6. Ibid., 61–63. Note that we changed the order of the new values given here to demonstrate their correspondence to the Basic Beliefs.

7. It is worth noting here an important distinction to be made about the nature of self, one we first encountered in Michael Horton's contribution, "Image and Office," to *Personal Identity in Theological Perspective*, eds. Richard Lints, Michael S. Horton, and Mark R. Talbot (Grand Rapids, MI: Wm. B. Eerdmans Publishing, 2006), 159–177. Horton references "[Paul] Ricouer's distinction between *idem*-identity and *ipse*-identity, the former referring to a permanent and immutable self-sameness (*soi-même*), while the latter . . . is a temporalized self of a given narrative" (p.

197). Palmisano's work here served to preserve IBM's *idem*-identity by recognizing IBM's need to create the next dramatic installment of its *ipse*-identity. Relatedly, see our treatment of [drama = strategy] in B. Joseph Pine II and James H. Gilmore, *The Experience Economy: Work Is Theatre & Every Business a Stage* (Boston: Harvard Business School Press, 1999), 108–110.

8. "The HBR Interview: Samuel J. Palmisano," 63.

9. See en.wikipedia.org/wiki/International_Business_Machines. See also "Chairman's Letter," *Annual Report*, www.ibm.com/annualreport/2003/noflash/cl_p7.shtml and "Management System," www.ibm.com/ibm/responsibility /company/management/. Palmisano's speech to the stockholders is at www.ibm.com/ibm/sjp/04-27-2004.html.

10. The framework behind these four business models is (naturally) a 2x2 matrix, a rather robust one with a long history. An entire book could be written on it—indeed, one has, which we heartily recommend: Bart Victor and Andrew C. Boynton, *Invented Here: Maximizing Your Organization's Internal Growth and Profitability* (Boston: Harvard Business School Press, 1998). For a concise discussion, see B. Joseph Pine II, "You're Only as Agile as Your Customers Think," *Agility and Global Competition*, no 2 (Spring 1998), 24–35, and for a description of its own heritage, see Pine and Gilmore, *The Experience Economy*, endnote 7–24, 221–223.

11. For a snapshot of the success of the Geek Squad post-acquisition, see J. D. Biersdorfer, "Doctors May Not Make House Calls, but These Computer Doctors Will," *New York Times*, November 2, 2005.

12. Julia C. Mead, "Psst! You Pick It, but They Grow It Someplace Else," *New York Times*, October 8, 2005.

13. Rob Walker, "The Brand Underground," *New York Times Magazine*, July 30, 2006, 52.

14. Quoted in an ad for "The new business collection" from Samsonite with the tagline "Life's a journey." Jackson Mahr of London-based branding consultancy Kodimedia makes this point well in "Vespa: viva," *brandchannel.com*, October 31, 2005, brandchannel.com/features_profile.asp?pr_id=256. He points out that "Brands such as Levi's, Harley-Davidson, and Marlboro all have an indisputable authenticity, the strength of which relies on whom it doesn't cater to."

15. Fleetwood wines have won many prizes and awards, as well as wide acclaim. Reviewers Dorothy J. Gaiter and John Brecher named his first vintage, the Mick Fleetwood Private Cellar Cuvée from 1998, its "Best Wine by a Living Musician," in "Intersection of Hollywood and Vines," *Wall Street Journal*, June 16, 2006.

16. See Pine and Gilmore, *The Experience Economy*, 61–68 and 192–194.

17. See, for example, Gary Neilson, Bruce A. Pasternack, and Decio Mendes, "The 7 Types of Organizational DNA," *Strategy + Business*, Summer 2004, which builds on their own "The Four Bases of Organizational DNA," *Strategy + Business*, Winter 2003.

18. Christian Mikunda, *Brand Lands, Hot Spots & Cool Spaces: Welcome to the Third Place and the Total Marketing Experience* (London: Kogan Page, 2004), 37, first published in Germany as *Marketing Spüren: Willkommen am Dritten Ort* (Heidelberg: Redline Wirtschaft bei Ueberreuter, 2002). See also Scott Kirsner, "Are You Experienced?" *Wired* 8.07, July 2000, 188–194.

19. "Agrodome: The Unique NZ Experience!" www.agrodome.co.nz.

20. It does seem that more service providers should create brand lands. Most such companies deliberately hide their call centers, computer centers, and cubicle farms from public view. But why not treat them as heritage centers in addition to operating facilities—and offer tours of service activities? Letting consumers see firsthand the number of transactions processed in a bank, or insurance agency, or telecommunications company—indeed, any service provider—might go a long way toward gaining greater respect as well as rendering greater authenticity when customers interact with such companies.

21. Neil Crofts, *Authentic Business: How to Create and Run Your Perfect Business* (Chichester, U.K.: Capstone Publishing Limited, 2005), 17; "Purpose Beyond Profit" is the section title beginning that chapter on p. 9. See also Rajendra S. Sisodia, David B. Wolfe, and Jagdish N. Sheth, *Firms of Endearment: How World-Class Companies Profit from Passion and Purpose* (Upper Saddle River, NJ: Wharton School Publishing, 2007).

22. Peter F. Drucker, *The Practice of Management* (New York: Harper & Row, 1993; originally published in 1954), 316–317.

23. C. William Pollard, *The Soul of the Firm* (New York: HarperBusiness, 1996), 19.

24. Robert Hall, *The Soul of the Enterprise: Creating a Dynamic Vision for American Manufacturing* (Essex Junction, VT: Omneo, 1993), 26.

25. Tom Chappell, *The Soul of a Business: Managing for Profit and the Common Good* (New York: Bantam, 1993), xv. This book provides an instructive example of a company, and its founder, finding a way to determine and portray its purpose through direct involvement of its employees. It will also prove instructive to see what happens in the next decade or so of the company's history; in 2006 founders Tom and Kate Chappell sold 84 percent of the business to Colgate-Palmolive. They said at the time, in "Colgate Purchasing Tom's of Maine" press release, available at www.toms ofmaine.com/about/press/2006_03_21_Colgate.asp: "We chose Colgate as our partner because they have the global expertise to help take Tom's of Maine to the next level. Just as importantly, we see Colgate as an excellent fit with our own cultural values."

26. Frederick G. Harmon, *Playing For Keeps: How the World's Most Aggressive and Admired Companies Use Core Values to Manage, Energize, and Organize Their People, and Promote, Advance, and Achieve Their Corporate Missions* (New York: John Wiley & Sons, Inc., 1996), 3.

27. Terrence E. Deal and Allan A. Kennedy, *Corporate Cultures: The Rites and Rituals of Corporate Life* (New York: Perseus Books, 2000; originally published in 1982), 23. While the authors quite nicely discuss shared values here, the company examples that immediately follow are all one-line statements (e.g., "Make great ads" for Leo Burnett Advertising

Agency, "Better things through better living through chemistry" for DuPont) that would be better called a common purpose, if not mere tagline.

28. Edgar H. Schein, *Organizational Culture and Leadership*, 2nd edition (San Francisco: Jossey-Bass, 1992), 12. On pp. 8–10 Schein discusses ten major categories of things "shared or held in common" by groups: observed behavioral regularities when people interact; group norms; espoused values; formal philosophy; rules of the game; climate; embedded skills; habits of thinking, mental models, and/or linguistic paradigms; shared meanings; and "root metaphors" or integrating symbols.

29. Ibid., 21–22.

30. Chris Argyris, *Overcoming Organizational Defenses: Facilitating Organizational Learning* (Boston: Allyn and Bacon, 1990), 13. See also Chris Argyris and Donald A. Schön, *Theory in Practice: Increasing Professional Effectiveness* (San Francisco: Jossey-Bass, 1974).

31. See www.chickfila.com/Closed.asp. See also S. Truett Cathy, *Eat Mor Chikin: Inspire More People* (Decatur, GA: Looking Glass Books, 2002), 100 and 192–194 in particular.

32. Alex Wipperfürth, *Brand Hijack: Marketing Without Marketing* (New York: Portfolio, 2005), 39.

33. Howard Schultz and Dori Jones Yang, *Pour Your Heart into It: How Starbucks Built a Company One Cup at a Time* (New York: Hyperion, 1997), 242.

34. Quoted in "Starbucks Chairman Warns of 'The Commoditization of the Starbucks Experience,'" *Starbucks Gossip*, starbucksgossip.typepad.com/_/2007/02/starbucks_chair_2.html.

35. Laurence D. Ackerman recognizes this in *Identity Is Destiny: Leadership and the Roots of Value Creation* (San Francisco: Berrett-Koehler, 2000), x: "In the field of human behavior and psychology, the notion of identity reflects the things that make a person unique—the rich and varied set of traits that fuels differentiation and inspires contribution. Within this field, identity stands as the single most powerful force. In failing to apply this deeper definition of identity to 'corporate beings' as well, we have done business a great disservice; indeed, we have perpetrated a fraud upon ourselves. Without intending to, organizations have violated the true meaning—and thus the value—of identity, leaving its productive potential untapped."

36. Alicia Clegg, "The Myth of Authenticity," *BusinessWeek*, August 12, 2005, www.businessweek.com/innovate/content/aug2005/id20050812_942858.htm.

37. Ibid.

38. Steve Rivkin, Fraser Sutherland, and Jack Trout, *The Making of a Name: The Inside Story of the Brands We Buy* (New York: Oxford University Press, 2004), 67.

39. Mark Ritson, "Show Me the Founder, and I'll Show You the Brand," *Marketing*, August 18, 2004, 17.

40. See "Brand History" at www.haagen-dazs.com/coibrh.do. Other sites state the date of company founding as 1959; we suspect the ice cream was first sold under Mattus's family company in 1959, and then the company created around 1961.

41. See "History of Ice Cream," at www.pastrywiz.com/letseat/icecream.htm, among other online resources.

42. Sharon Begley, "New ABCs of Branding—Product Names Pack Punch One Letter at a Time; StrawBerry Is No BlackBerry," *Wall Street Journal*, August 26, 2002. Her exact, rather colorful, phrase was "winning hybrids of real words become scarcer than a telecom firm with a rising stock price."

43. For an interesting piece on how many fans aren't going along with the names on some stadiums, see Erik Malinowski, "Corporate Branding Strikes Out," *Wired*, January 2006, 34–35. Interestingly, the new Cleveland Stadium sold the rights to each entrance gate, rather than the stadium itself—forgoing some incremental revenue but preserving a greater sense of authenticity. Somehow, saying "I'll meet you at the National City Gate" (rather than, "I'll meet you at Gate A") doesn't seem so objectionable.

44. We recognize that many donors won't give money without getting a named entity in return, but if they fully understood the issues perhaps at least some would assent to giving their money without the quid pro quo.

45. Bob Shaw, "What's in a Name?" *St. Paul Pioneer Press*, February 6, 2005.

46. Bob Shaw, "Different by Design," *St. Paul Pioneer Press*, December 12, 2004, and Shaw, "Revising a Vision," July 31, 2005.

47. The first quote is from Bob Shaw, "Barn Re-Raising," *St. Paul Pioneer Press*, April 10, 2005, and the second from Shaw, "What's in a Name?"

48. Todd Bolin, cited in Shaw, "What's in a Name?" In Shaw's companion piece, "Branding Adds Spirit to Development Pitch," *St. Paul Pioneer Press*, February 6, 2005, Bolin asserts, "I'd say 80 percent of a brand is embodied in a name."

49. Quoted in Brian Steinberg, "Ordinary People Starring in Ads Convey Realistic, Genuine Feel," *Wall Street Journal*, September 5, 2005. Such ads will cycle, of course, since advertisers constantly seek out the new, as Stuart Elliott points out in "For Everyday Products, Ads Using the Everyday Woman," *New York Times*, August 17, 2005: "The waxing and waning of so-called real women in advertising comes as marketers and agencies embrace the idea, then revert to traditional images when they believe it is time for a new direction as consumers lose interest."

50. Stuart Elliott, "After 210 years, Jim Beam Discovers the Power of TV," *New York Times*, September 8, 2005.

51. "Jim Beam Bourbon Captures 210 Years of Authenticity in First-Ever National TV Ad Campaign," Fortune Brands press release available at www.fortunebrands.com/news/ReleaseDetail.cfm?ReleaseID=172549&ReleaseType=Corporate. The ad text provided in this press release differed somewhat from that given in the article from the previous endnote. Having not seen the actual ad, we took the release's text, assuming the company ought to know, while using the article's punctuation for aesthetic reasons.

52. Suzanne Vranica and Brian Steinberg, in "Ads Reach for 'Reality'," *Wall Street Journal*, December 21, 2005, said the ad campaign was the best one of 2005.

53. Quoted in Brian Steinberg, "House Training: Now, Employees Get Brand Boost," *Wall Street Journal*, January 18, 2005.

54. The ads direct readers to www.starbucks.com/aboutus and www.starbucks.com/goodbusiness where they can read, among other things, that Starbucks is proud to be on *Fortune* magazine's list of 100 best companies to work for, its mission statement, and about career opportunities; visitors can also download the company's Corporate Social Responsibility Annual Report. At another directed Web site, www.whatmakescoffeegood.com, visitors learn how coffee gets from farmer to outlet and all about Starbucks' values.

55. Another ad, running in the *New York Times* September 13 and 14, 2005, was about affordable healthcare coverage, with the headline "Wake Up and Smell the Coffee." It proclaimed "We are proud to join with other business leaders in Washington, DC" for "the CNBC DC Summit," encouraging readers to watch live coverage on CNBC.

56. See www.jackmorton.com. The sentence, preceded by the phrase "Take a deep breath . . ." and followed by "And exhale . . . ," is: "As a leading experiential marketing agency, we help the world's best companies build brands, sales and success by creating experiences that engage and transform employee, business and consumer audiences."

57. Paul G. Haschak compiled a list of the official missions, goals, principles, and philosophies as expressed in the corporate statements of over 900 public and private companies in *Corporate Statements: The Official Missions, Goals, Principles and Philosophies of Over 900 Companies* (Jefferson, NC: McFarland & Company, 1998).

58. "Product Information," www.wholefoodsmarket.com/products/afa/index.html.

59. Geoffrey Hartman, *Scars of the Spirit: The Struggle Against Inauthenticity* (New York: Palgrave Macmillan, 2002), 9.

60. A short sampling of others includes Chip Conley, *Rebel Rules: Daring to Be Yourself in Business* (New York: Fireside, 2001); Rich Teerlink and Lee Ozley, *More Than a Motorcycle: The Leadership Journey at Harley-Davidson* (Boston: Harvard Business School Press, 2000); and Paul Dolan, *True to Our Roots: Fermenting a Business Revolution* (Princeton, NJ: Bloomberg Press, 2003).

61. See Marshall McLuhan and Quentin Fiore, *The Medium Is the Massage* (Corte Madera, CA: Gingko Press, 2001, first published by Random House in 1967).

62. Quoted in Emilie Boyer King, "L'Occitane en Provence: Breaking Out," *brandchannel.com*, November 1, 2004, www.brandchannel.com/features_profile.asp?pr_id=204.

63. Quoted in Dorren Carvajal, "Whiffs of Combat Waft over Natural Cosmetics," *New York Times*, August 12, 2006. The early days of Mr. Baussan starting the company can be found in Pierre Magnan, translated from the French by Richard Seaver, *The Essence of Provence: The Story of L'Occitane* (New York: Arcade Publishing, 2001), 32–40 in particular.

64. "Our Philosophy," usa.loccitane.com/our_philosophy/index.asp.

65. David Boyle, *Authenticity: Brands, Fakes, Spin and the Lust for Real Life* (London: Flamingo, 2003), 20–21.

66. Quoted in Elizabeth A. Evitts, "The Art of Placemaking: A Conversation with Fred Kent," *Urbanite*, no 26, August 2006, www.urbanitebaltimore.com/sub.cfm?sectionID=4&articleID=435&IssueID=38.

67. Richard Florida, *The Rise of the Creative Class: And How It's Transforming Work, Leisure, Community and Everyday Life* (New York: Basic Books, 2002), 228. The term "generica" comes from p. 187, where Florida decries the "insidiousness" of the "Experiential World" primarily because "the packaging and selling of experience is often perceived to be—and often is—inauthentic." In reality they are *always* inauthentic and *sometimes* perceived to be authentic.

68. For those who work for cities and other governmental units that wish to create places that attract people and businesses, we recommend Tony Hiss, *The Experience of Place* (New York: Vintage Books, 1990).

69. Some see the rise of lifestyle centers and other such suburban "downtowns" as threatening the life of real downtowns. See, for example, Thaddeus Herrick, "Fake Towns Rise, Offering Urban Life Without the Grit," *Wall Street Journal*, May 31, 2006, and Angelo Carusi, "When 'Authentic' is Fake," *RetailTraffic*, May 2003, 198–202. One person who has a "knee-jerk aversion to malls" as "fake places," architecture critic Philip Nobel, found lifestyle centers, much to his surprise, "unadulterated good news"; see "Good Malls and Bad Cities," *Metropolis*, March 2007, 72–74.

70. In an editorial asking whether lifestyle centers were "Authentic or not?," retail expert Beth Karlin, in "True Blue Myths," *Retail Traffic*, December 2005, 2, concluded that The Grove provided "a sense of place" most welcome "after driving through the vast LA sprawl."

71. For more on the role of architecture in this context, see B. Joseph Pine II, "Architecture in the Experience Economy," *DesignIntelligence*, January 2006, 15–16, and especially Michael Benedikt, *For an Architecture of Reality* (New York: Lumen Books, 1987).

72. Regarding our earlier discussion of naming rights, notice how many of these ballpark names help render them authentic.

73. Conversation with authors.

74. "We Proudly Brew Starbucks Coffee" seems to be a signal from the company not to blame them if something isn't right—after all, it isn't a *real* Starbucks.

75. The original Johnson & Johnson Credo, available at "Our Company," www.jnj.com/our_company/our_credo/, was a pamphlet Robert Johnson wrote for his fellow industrialists in 1935, entitled "Try Reality," in which he laid out the case that in the modern corporation management's priorities should be first to customers, then to employees, third to the community in which the employees reside and work, and finally to stockholders.

76. "Gold Standards," corporate.ritzcarlton.com/en/About/GoldStandards.htm.

77. Robert R. Ivany, "Action-Learning Teams and the Transformation of the U.S. Army," a special contribution to Bruce LaRue, Paul Childs, and Kerry Larson, *Leading Organizations from the Inside Out: Unleashing the Collaborative Genius of Action-Learning Teams* (New York: John Wiley & Sons, 2004), 50–51.

78. James C. Collins and Jerry I. Porras, *Built to Last: Successful Habits of Visionary Companies* (New York: HarperBusiness, 1994), 233. Those familiar with the book will of course realize the authors weren't talking about any old goals here, but Big Hairy Audacious Goals, or BHAGs, which we'll discuss briefly in the next chapter.

79. Conversation with authors.

80. See Josh McHugh, "Google vs. Evil," *Wired*, January 2003, 130–135.

81. Andy Kessler, "Sellout.com," *Wall Street Journal*, January 31, 2006. Kessler relates the little-known story that Jimi Hendrix was another classic definition of sellout from the rock music world, where the term came into vogue: "despite using Gibson guitars on his albums, he signed a deal with Fender Guitars for cash and as many Stratocasters as he needed, as long as he appeared exclusively in concert and photos with Fenders. He took the deal, and with his unlimited supply of Fenders, began smashing them at the end of every concert, for fans who never knew he sold out."

82. "Dove support," www.campaignforrealbeauty.com/supports.asp?id=94&length=short&section=campaign.

83. Quoted in Diann Daniel, "Real Beauty = Real Sales?" *CMO*, 2005; no longer available online.

84. See, for example, the discussion of this (Status: *True.*) on Snopes.com, the *Urban Legend* Web site, available at www.snopes.com/inboxer/charity/sallyann.asp.

85. The same is true for the earlier discussion of donors providing money to nonprofits in exchange for getting their name on the door or building. It lessens both the charity—the donor is gaining value in return—and the perceived authenticity. As Richard Tomkins, columnist on consumer culture, points out in "Sex Will Sell but Sustainability Is the New Self-Satisfaction," *Financial Times*, March 7, 2006: "Perhaps reflecting more cynical times, the idea of charitable giving changed. Once, it meant just that: giving, in a private act of self-denial, to a cause. Now, it is less often a donation and more often a transaction—a two-way process in which the charity benefits but you get something out of it too."

86. "Jamie Foxx Meets with Victims of Katrina," *USA Today*, September 8, 2005, www.usatoday.com/life/people/2005-09-08-foxx-katrina_x.htm?POE=LIFISVA#.

87. This is becoming known as "transactional" or "strategic philanthropy"; see Robert J. Hughes, "Firms Funding Arts Seek a Return," *Wall Street Journal*, February 9, 2007, and Tomkins, "Sex Will Sell but Sustainability Is the New Self-Satisfaction."

88. Rob Wallace, "Tried and True," *The Hub*, March 2006, 8, 9.

89. Mitch Tobin, "Tombstone Tries to Dodge Bullet," *Arizona Daily Star*, September 5, 2005.

90. Quoted in Andrew Pollack, "Wyatt Earp Fought Here, but the Corral Isn't O.K.," *New York Times*, August 8, 2005.

91. Tobin, "Tombstone Tries to Dodge Bullet."

92. Dean MacCannell, *The Tourist: A New Theory of the Leisure Class* (Berkeley, CA: University of California Press, 1999; first published in 1976), 110.

93. Ibid.

94. Ibid., 92.

95. Not to mention experience marks; see B. Joseph Pine II and James H. Gilmore, "Experience Management: EM 'em!" *EM*, November/December 2002, 8.

96. Bernd Schmitt and Alex Simonson, *Marketing Aesthetics: The Strategic Management of Brands, Identity, and Image* (New York: The Free Press, 1997), 49. They attribute the inspiration for relating expressions and impressions to the field of psychology, and in particular to Gustav Ichheiser, *Appearances and Realities: Misunderstandings in Human Relations* (San Francisco: Jossey-Bass, 1970).

97. We use the term "impressions" in the exact same way we did in chapter 3 of *The Experience Economy*, pp. 52–55 in particular. For more on impression management, acting at work, and authenticity, see Brian Moeran, "Tricks of the Trade: The Performance and Interpretation of Authenticity," *Journal of Management Studies* 42, no 5 (July 2005): 901–922, and Kent Grayson and David Shulman, "Impression Management in Services Marketing," in Teresa A. Swartz and Dawn Iacobucci, editors, *Handbook of Services Marketing and Management* (Thousand Oaks, California: Sage Publications, Inc., 2000), 51–67.

98. Schmitt and Simonson, *Marketing Aesthetics*, 72, italics removed.

99. See chapter 6 of *The Experience Economy*; the issue of real versus fake acting is explored on pp. 110–112.

100. *Fish! Catch the Energy. Release the Potential* (Burnsville, MN: ChartHouse International, 1998). These principles are also provided in Stephen C. Lundin, Ph.D., Harry Paul, and John Christensen, *Fish! A Remarkable Way to Boost Morale and Improve Results* (New York: Hyperion, 2000).

101. Related to us by John Stahl-Wert of the Pittsburgh Leadership Foundation.

Chapter 8

1. The Magazine Publishers of America followed suit in 2006 with a $40 million campaign to get more advertisers into magazines; see Stuart Elliott, "Working to Sell Advertisers on Newspapers and Magazines," *New York Times*, February 15, 2006.

2. Suzanne Vranica, "That Guy Showing Off His Hot New Phone May Be a Shill," *Wall Street Journal*, July 31, 2002.

3. Lenore Skenazy, "Shills Are New Form of Covert Marketing," *St. Paul Pioneer Press*, August 13, 2002. In the piece, the editor of *Advertising Age*, Scott Donaton, concludes, "It's impossible to be too cynical about marketing right now."

4. Rob Walker, "The Hidden (in Plain Sight) Persuaders," *New York Times Magazine*, December 5, 2004, 68–75, 104, 130–131.

5. Marian Salzman, Ira Matathia, and Ann O'Reilly, *Buzz: Harness the Power of Influence and Create Demand* (New York: John Wiley & Sons, 2003), viii.

6. Amy Merrick, "Gap's Image Is Wearing Out," *Wall Street Journal*, December 6, 2001.

7. CEO Paul Pressler, since let go, admitted that his focus on costs shortchanged "creating amazing product and compelling store experiences." Quoted in Jonathan Birchall, "Faded Denim Fails to Put Colour Back in Gap Sales," *Financial Times*, April 11, 2006.

8. An anonymous executive quoted in Leslie Kaufman, "Scrambling to Regain Its Cool," *New York Times*, February 24, 2002.

9. So ingrained is advertising at Gap that the company apparently considers it, not its offerings or its stores, to be its heritage. As VP of marketing Kyle Andrew said, in Julie Bloom, "The Boot-Cut Slim-Fit Bell-Bottom Boogie," *New York Times*, July 16, 2006, "For our return to television advertising this fall, we wanted to return to our roots in music and dance to illustrate the energy, attitude and versatility of our new denim collection." No wonder that, after taking over as interim CEO, Robert Fisher said "We've got to have a clear point of view about who we are," quoted in Amy Merrick, "Gap Aims to Unleash Creativity for Revival," *Wall Street Journal*, March 6, 2007.

10. See The Jerde Partnership, "Firm Profile," www.jerde.com/about/, as well as Frances Anderton, "Urban Transformations," in The Jerde Partnership International, *You Are Here* (London: Phaidon Press Limited, 1999), where she writes on p. 21: "Jon Jerde has invented a lexicon of words and phrases to articulate his concepts . . . One of the most embedded terms is 'placemaking,' to describe the making of places rather than buildings." According to *Word Spy*, www.wordspy.com/words/placemaking.asp, the earliest citation of the term was "Lancelot Brown called his work 'placemaking,'" in Ruth Stingo, "Christmas Books: What Capability Did," *The Times* (London), November 30, 1985.

11. Much of the rest of this chapter is based on previously published material appearing in James H. Gilmore and B. Joseph Pine II, "Customer Experience Places: The New Offering Frontier," *Strategy & Leadership*, July/August 2002, 4–11, and James H. Gilmore and B. Joseph Pine II, *The Experience IS the Marketing* (Amazon.com: BrownHerron Publishing, 2002).

12. Eventually Disney tried this approach with its one remaining company-owned store (on Fifth Avenue in New York), renamed the World of Disney Store. It added Cinderella's Princess Court, a $75 admission-feed experience in which girls could be princesses themselves for an hour, but couldn't make a go of even that single in-store experience on prime real estate in Manhattan. It closed down as of January 2, 2006, after a mere fourteen months.

13. Further, rather than create experiences true to their heritage, Disney and Time Warner opened mere stores, doomed almost from the outset. Not only weren't they what they say they are, they also weren't being true to self; the stores were therefore Fake-fake. The American Girl Places, on the other hand, are not a repudiation of the company's doll manufacturing heritage but a natural extension of it, as they provides places where the company immerses consumers in an environment dedicated to the brand both company and customers adore.

14. Peter F. Drucker, *Management: Tasks, Responsibilities, Practices* (New York: Harper Business, 1993), excerpted at www.welchco.com/02/14/01/60/93/01/0101.htm.

15. "ING DIRECT New York Café Marks One Year Anniversary," press release available at home.ingdirect.com /about/press/ing_04302002.html.

16. See en.wikipedia.org/wiki/Fremont_Street_Experience. The original design (it was redone in 2004) used 1.9 million light bulbs and produced "only" 350,000 watts.

17. See Susan Frampton, Laura Gilpin, and Patrick Charmel, eds., *Putting Patients First: Designing and Practicing Patient-Centered Care* (San Francisco: Jossey-Bass, 2003).

18. John Yokoyama and Jim Bergquist, "The World Famous Pike Place Fish Story," *Retailing Issues Letter*, vol 13, no 6 (November 2001), 2.

19. Ibid., 3, with the emphasis exactly as in the original (as always, unless otherwise noted).

20. According to Phil Patton in "Meet the Beetles," *Metropolis*, November 2000, 135, Wolfsburg was originally a planned Nazi worker town that "the locals simply referred to . . . as car city, Autostadt. Wolfsburg was a name borrowed from a nearby castle by British occupation authorities in 1945."

21. As the *Oxford English Dictionary* explains, a *flagship* is "A ship bearing an admiral's flag." (As with the President and the Air Force One designation, should the Admiral change ships, his flag changes with him to the new ship.) Therefore, there should be only one flagship, and its location cannot be just anywhere.

22. REI executives had their own internal argument over the term "flagship," with some saying the place in Seattle was its only flagship, with others saying the term could include the other, experiential, stores like it. They compromised, and now call such places "flagship-class." Cabela's calls its twenty-plus huge experiences "destination stores."

23. Nokia mistakenly calls each of the eighteen places it plans to open around the world (the first opened in Moscow in Spring 2006) "flagships."

24. Bob Tedeschi, "In Pursuit of Face-to-Face Sales and Web Site Traffic, Expedia and Travelocity.Com Open Shops in Tourist Areas," *New York Times*, January 17, 2005.

25. Quoted in Bernard Simon, "Consumers Get to Meet the New Toyota Pick-Up," *Financial Times*, September 15, 2006.

26. Rich Karlgaard, "Pyro Marketing," *Forbes*, April 24, 2006, 31.

27. "Charmin—NYC Restrooms," *Welcome to Gigunda Stories*, www.gigundastories.com/charmin.htm.

28. Quoted in Andrew Park, "Burt's Bees: Up from Craft Fairs," *BusinessWeek*, August 7, 2006, 59.

29. "Starbucks Coffee Company Outlines Core Strategies to Continue Delivering Long-Term Shareholder Value in Sixth Biennial Analyst Conference," investor.starbucks.com/phoenix.zhtml?c=99518&p=irol-newsArticle&ID =912921&highlight=.

30. "Starbucks Chairman Warns of 'The Commoditization of the Starbucks Experience,'" *Starbucks Gossip*, starbucks gossip.typepad.com/_/2007/02/starbucks_chair_2.html.

31. For more on Starbucks' design architecture and how it caters to particular locales, see Janet Adamy, "At Starbucks, Coffee Comes with New Decor," *Wall Street Journal*, November 10, 2006; and especially Arthur Rubinfeld and Collins Hemingway, *Built for Growth: Expanding Your Business Around the Corner or Across the Globe* (Upper Saddle River, NJ: Wharton School Publishing, 2005), 63–77.

32. Rubinfeld, a former executive vice president with Starbucks for whom Massey worked, related in ibid., 73, how the company put two places right across from each other in Vancouver, BC: "One store was in a traditional brick building, the other in a newly erected modern building. Using the new designs, we created two distinctly different visual atmospheres: one that appealed to the general population that frequented the brick building and one that appealed to the hip crowd that frequented the new building to see and be seen."

33. See *The Experience Economy*, 15–20, for more on how to experientialize the us*ing* of goods.

34. Conversation with authors.

35. Brenda Laurel, in *Computers as Theatre* (Reading, MA: Addison-Wesley, 1993), advocates viewing computer interactions as a medium with dramatic structure rather than as a static interface. Read especially her discussion of the anatomy of drama, pp. 81–92, where she discusses Freytag diagrams. From nineteenth-century German performance theorist Gustav Freytag, these diagrams delineate how all experiences should be structured with drama, from the exposition to the inciting incident, through the rising action and crisis, and then to the climax of the experience, followed by the falling action and dénouement. It is the first and last segments—exposition and dénouement—that can be extended to the Web as pre- and post-shows, respectively. While Ms. Laurel's treatment is more detailed and actionable, the original can be found in Elias J. MacEwan, *Freytag's Technique of the Drama: An Exposition of Dramatic Composition and Art by Gustav Freytag* (New York: Benjamin Blom, 1968), an authorized translation from the sixth German edition, particularly pp. 114–140. Other resources for applying drama or otherwise designing engaging virtual experiences include Nathan Shedroff, *Experience Design 1* (Indianapolis, IN: New Riders, 2001); Mark Stephen Meadows, *Pause & Effect: The Art of Interactive Narrative* (Indianapolis, IN: New Riders, 2003); and Janet H. Murray, *Hamlet on the Holodeck: The Future of Narrative in Cyberspace* (New York: The Free Press, 1997).

36. "The Business Impact of Rich Internet Applications," available at www.adobe.com/resources/business/rich _internet_apps/overview/.

37. For a review of authenticity issues surrounding social networking sites, and in particular MySpace as "one huge platform for 'personal product placement'" and Friendster with its "fakester" profiles, see Wade Roush, "Fakesters," *Technology Review*, November–December 2006, 72–74.

38. Edward Castronova, *Synthetic Worlds: The Business and Culture of Online Games* (Chicago: University of Chicago Press, 2005), 91.

39. Sandy Kearney, IBM director of emerging 3D internet and virtual business, quoted in Chris Nuttall, "Virtual Mirror on the Real World," *Financial Times*, December 15, 2006.

40. Quoted in Julian Dibbell, "Meet Your Next Customer," *Business 2.0*, March 2003, 74.

41. David Kirkpatrick, "It's Not a Game," *Fortune*, February 5, 2007, 62.

42. See Emily Steel, "Avatars at the Office," *Wall Street Journal*, November 13, 2006.

43. Quoted in "Living a Second Life," *The Economist*, September 30, 2006; the second quote is not Steiger's, but an unnamed journalist's.

44. As of May 2006: "Frequently Asked Questions," *Neopets*, info.neopets.com/presskit/faqs.html.

45. David Kushner, "The Neopets Addiction," *Wired*, December 2005, 271.

46. Realizing that it has to start all over again with a totally new design once a movie leaves the theaters, according to Kate Kelly, "Fox Atomic Aims to Be Web Crash Pad," *Wall Street Journal*, July 19, 2006, Fox Searchlight studio created a "new Web platform" at foxatomic.com that it hopes "can draw young users . . . on a daily basis with intriguing and fresh content" that "will create a built-in fan base once the label's movies are playing in theaters."

47. "The Hobbit; Or, There and Back Again . . . Already?" *New Zealand Edge*, May 11, 2000, www.nzedge.com /media/archives/archv-arts-lordoftherings.html.

48. Prime Minister Helen Clark, "Some facts about The Lord of the Rings," www.executive.govt.nz/minister /clark/lor/lor.htm.

49. Jesse Eisinger, "Weekend Box Office Isn't the Ticket," *Wall Street Journal*, May 25, 2005.

50. For more on the effect of filming *The Lord of the Rings* on the perceived authenticity of New Zealand, see Deborah Jones and Karen Smith, "Middle-earth Meets New Zealand: Authenticity and Location in the Making of *The Lord of the Rings*," *Journal of Management Studies*, vol 42, no 5, July 2005, 923–934.

51. "From Fantasy Worlds to Food," *The Economist*, November 11, 2006, 73. The piece does note, "Now that the magic has faded, it [New Zealand] has started emphasising [sic] its food and wines in addition to its natural beauty."

52. Thomas Mucha, "Operation Sign 'Em Up," *Fast Company*, April 2003, 44–45. For more on the development of AmericasArmy.com and the Army's portfolio of demand-generation experiences, see the section "Making It Real" in Max Lenderman, *Experience the Message: How Experiential Marketing Is Changing the Brand World* (New York: Carroll & Graf Publishers, 2006), 217–222.

53. "The Virtual Army Experience Launched!" *Total America's Army*, February 14, 2007, www.totalaa.com/forums/showthread.php?t=358.

54. Grace Jean, "Game Branches Out into Real Combat Training," *National Defense*, February 2006, available at www.nationaldefensemagazine.org/issues/2006/feb/games_brance.htm.

55. "2K Sports & Nike Team up for NBA 2K6," *Xbox Solution*, www.xboxsolution.com/2005/09/21/2k-sports-and-nike-team-up-for-nba-2k6/.

56. Ibid.

57. See Erika Brown, "Game On!" *Forbes*, July 24, 2006, 84–86.

58. Quoted in ibid., 86.

59. Stuart Elliott, "Cue the 4:53 Silver Bullet to Happy Hour," *The New York Times*, March 20, 2007.

60. Jerry Useem, "Apple: America's Best Retailer," *Fortune*, March 19, 2007, 108–109.

61. "Geek Squad City Introduction," video.google.com/videoplay?docid=-2105768258195651551.

62. As Maurice Saatchi, executive director of the M&C Saatchi agency, notes in "The Strange Death of Modern Advertising," *Financial Times*, June 22, 2006, "day-after recall scores for television advertisements have collapsed, from 25 per cent in the 1960s to 10 per cent today."

63. "Charmin—NYC Restrooms."

64. From an OfficeMax advertisement in *Wall Street Journal*, January 2, 2007. It included a faux apology "for the recent drop in global productivity," encouraging readers to shop there to regain the time lost.

65. "America's Army game gets new firepower," *GameSpot News*, www.gamespot.com/news/6137060.html.

66. Howard Schultz and Dori Jones Yang, *Pour Your Heart Into It: How Starbucks Built a Company One Cup at a Time* (New York: Hyperion, 1997), 248.

67. While placemaking is not about experience marketing, but *marketing experiences*, we do encourage companies to employ experiential marketing techniques when they must do marketing. On this topic we recommend Lenderman's *Experience the Message* as well as Bernd H. Schmitt, *Experiential Marketing: How to Get Customers to SENSE, FEEL, THINK, ACT, and RELATE to Your Company and Brands* (New York: The Free Press, 1999); Bernd Schmitt and Alex Simonson, *Marketing Aesthetics: The Strategic Management of Brands, Identity, and Image* (New York: The Free Press, 1997); and Ellen O'Sullivan and Kathy J. Spangler, *Experience Marketing: Strategies for the New Millennium* (State College, PA: Venture Publishing, 1998).

68. But we will give you a new old saw. Charlie Rutman, CEO of MPG North America, a unit of giant Havas, says in Brian Steinberg, "They Aren't Queuing Up for the Rides," *Wall Street Journal*, February 28, 2006, that the overarching goal of a new focus on measuring the efficacy of advertising "is to try to find the cause-and-effect relationship between a marketing act and some kind of consumer action." One of the other great things about placemaking experiences is that when you provide a place where customers can not only experience your offerings but buy them right then and right there, the cause-and-effect is pretty obvious.

Chapter 9

1. Jon Pareles entitled his February 24, 2003, story about the Grammy Awards in the *New York Times* "Realism Outshines Glitter in New Pop," concluding, "Honesty is music's new mood for wary times."

2. According to Robert Hilburn, in "A Sweet Mystery," *Los Angeles Times*, January 26, 2003, Ms. Jones had earlier nixed a remix version (engineered with drum machines and the like) of her top single from the album, the very acoustic "Don't Know Why," saying "It was the most absurd thing I've ever heard."

3. Quoted in Jon Pareles, "Norah Jones, Now in Her Own Words," *New York Times*, January 21, 2007.

4. See Terry Teachout, "It Ain't Jazz, Despite the Label," *Wall Street Journal*, July 18, 2002.

5. Norah Jones, *Artist's Choice: Music That Matters to Her* (Hear Music), 2004.

6. We are inspired here by Stan Davis' contention, found on p. 5 of his classic book *Future Perfect* (Reading, MA: Addison-Wesley, 1987): "A basic progression governs the evolution of management in all market economies: fundamental properties of the *universe* are transformed into *scientific* understanding, then developed into new *technologies*, which are applied to create products and services for *business*, which then ultimately define our models of *organization*."

7. The original work can be found in H. Minkowski, "Space and Time," in H. A. Lorentz et al., *The Principle of Relativity: A Collection of Original Memoirs on the Special and General Theory of Relativity* (New York: Dover, 1952),

73–91, cited in scienceworld.wolfram.com/biography/MinkowskiHermann.html. For a more detailed explanation of it in layman's terms, see Paul Davies, *The Edge of Infinity: Where the Universe Came From and How It Will End* (New York: Simon and Schuster, 1981), 45–71.

8. Charles Taylor, *Sources of the Self: The Making of the Modern Identity* (Cambridge, MA: Harvard University Press, 1989), 48.

9. Ibid., 48, 48, 46, and 47, respectively. Philosopher Charles Guignon, in *On Being Authentic* (London: Routledge, 2004), 128–129, echoes this when he says that "the present is experienced not as the one truly existing time, but rather as a point of intersection between future and past, the context of action in which purposes can be realized thanks to what is made accessible from the past. Lived time is linear; it is a forward-directed projection toward what is to come that carries along what has been."

10. See Martin Heidegger, translated by John Macquarrie and Edward Robinson, *Being and Time* (New York: HarperSan Francisco, 1962; first published in German as *Sein und Zeit* in 1927), 428. For an introduction to the concept of "Being in the World," see pp. 24–28 and 65–71. The translators provide the page numbers from the original German addition, apparently for ease of studying the original as well as to share one Index; these passages are 369 and then 5–8 and 41–44.

11. Corey Anton, *Selfhood and Authenticity* (Albany, NY: State University of New York Press, 2001), 130.

12. For the story of the park's creation, see Bob Thomas, *Walt Disney: An American Original* (New York: Hyperion, 1976), 218.

13. This was described to one of us as Walt Disney's own words on a backstage tour of Walt Disney World a number of years ago. We could not find it in print, although "three-dimensional cartoon" is now often used to describe the Toontown area within various Disney theme parks.

14. Thomas, *Walt Disney*, 268.

15. But here in the endnotes we'll proffer "tits and ass." We apologize to those endnote readers whose sensibilities we offend.

16. In both instances, the experiences represented innovative concepts, but were ineptly executed. Visits to both a Club Disney in Southern California and the first DisneyQuest in Chicago found equipment inoperable for long durations of time—the kind of neglect usually associated with cheap arcades at amusement parks, not anyplace run by Disney.

17. The history between ABC and Disney would appear to validate superficially a merger of the two from an authenticity perspective, for the original *Disneyland* show ran on ABC for a number of years. In a 1954 deal crucial to getting Disneyland built in the first place, ABC ended up owning 35 percent of Disneyland. However, Disney bought out the network's interest when their relationship soured in 1960 for $7.5 million (15 times what ABC invested), after which the company started an even longer relationship with NBC, beginning with "Walt Disney's Wonderful World of Color" in 1960. That there-and-then event of leaving ABC behind—with Walt bemoaning the price paid for the network's share of Disneyland, in Thomas, *Walt Disney*, 286, by exclaiming, "What did they do to help build the place?"—should have forever defined future impossibilities, especially since Disney maintained its focus on family-friendly fare while ABC veered off into the prurient. Further, 1995 was no time to move back into the old broadcast medium of over-the-air television, just when the new interactive medium of the Internet—with its entirely fresh set of possibilities for engaging experiences—was about to take off.

18. For much more hard-hitting discussions of Disney as almost the antithesis of family values, see Peter Schweizer and Rochelle Schweizer, *Disney The Mouse Betrayed: Greed, Corruption, and Children at Risk* (Washington, DC: Regnery Publishing, 1998), Perucci Ferraiuolo, *Disney and the Bible: A Scriptural Critique of the Magic Kingdom* (Camp Hill, PA: Horizon Books, 1996), and Henry A. Giroux, *The Mouse That Roared: Disney and the End of Innocence* (Oxford: Rowman & Littlefied, 1999).

19. Matthew Garrahan, "Iger's Bold Steps at Disney Extend His Honeymoon Period," *Financial Times*, October 2, 2006.

20. Ronald Grover, "How Bob Iger Unchained Disney," *BusinessWeek*, February 2, 2007, 79.

21. See Eric Pfanner, "Disney's World Seeks Ubiquity," *International Herald Tribune*, June 13, 2005, and Merissa Marr, "The Magic Kingdom Looks to Hit the Road," *Wall Street Journal*, February 8, 2007.

22. "It was because of Michael that I was able to hit the ground running," and "The story shouldn't be about me. It's about the team." Quoted in Grover, "How Bob Iger Unchained Disney," 74.

23. James B. Stewart, "Common Sense: Investors, Beware: Disney Is Paying Too Much for Pixar," *Wall Street Journal*, February 1, 2006.

24. Laura M. Holson, "He Runs that Mickey Mouse Outfit," *New York Times*, March 4, 2007.

25. John Lasseter as told to Brent Schlender, "Pixar's Magic Man," *Fortune*, May 29, 2006, 142. This was a return to his roots for Lasseter as well: he graduated from the very first Character Animation Program at the California Institute of the Arts that Walt Disney Co. started, working at Disneyland during the summers. He went to work for Disney Studios after graduating in 1979 and soon helped start up its nascent computer animation unit, but was later fired, joining the computer division at Lucasfilm that eventually was bought by Steve Jobs and named Pixar. With his success at Pixar—predicated more on his dedication to the story than to computer animation technology itself—so well thought of was Lasseter within Disney's own animation unit that, as Schlender relates in his introduction to this piece, p. 140: "When Dick Cook, the chairman of Walt Disney Studios, introduces Pixar's John Lasseter, the man who will

soon be their boss, the crowd bursts into cheers and applause that goes on and on . . . 'It was almost like a homecoming,' recalls Cook, who first met Lasseter when the two had summer jobs as ride operators at Disneyland in the late 1970s."

26. Charles Solomon, "For Disney, Something Old (and Short) Is New Again," *New York Times*, December 3, 2006.

27. Both quoted, the animator anonymously, in Joshua Chaffin, "Disney's Prodigal Prince," *Financial Times*, January 28–29, 2006. Neal Gabler wrote in an editorial shortly after the acquisition was announced, "When You Wish Upon a Merger," *New York Times*, February 2, 2006, that "Pixar is the heir to the Disney tradition" that "took animation further into the realm of realism."

28. See, for example, a discussion of these two trains of thought—called biological and artistic models, respectively—within Nietzsche's writings in Golomb, *In Search of Authenticity: From Kierkegaard to Camus* (London: Routledge, 1995), 68–70, plus as related to Camus on p. 191 and Heidegger on p. 120, where Golomb paraphrases the latter's "ontological synthesis" as "Own your Being by creating your self and by appropriating your heritage."

29. www.hoover.com even lists a unit of Brown-Forman as "Brown Forman Fetzer Winery" located in Schaumberg, Illinois, of all places.

30. Seen at "Our History," Fetzer Vineyards, www.fetzer.com/fetzer/wineries/history.aspx. The quote is no longer a part of Fetzer's history page; we assume it was removed after Dolan left the company.

31. For more on how vineyards render authenticity, see Michael B. Beverland, "Crafting Brand Authenticity: The Case of Luxury Wines," *Journal of Management Studies*, vol 142, no 5 (July 2005): 1003–1029.

32. Conversation with authors.

33. We tried to warn them. See B. Joseph Pine II and James H. Gilmore, "Are You Experienced?" in the now itself defunct *Industry Standard*, April 19–26, 1999, 79.

34. See Amy Harmon, "An Inventor Unveils His Mysterious Personal Transportation Device," *New York Times*, December 3, 2001.

35. Harmon, ibid., says Jobs "reportedly said the device could be as significant as the development of the personal computer" while Paul Saffo, in a detailed timeline in "Ginger's Next Trick," *Business 2.0*, February 2002, 24, quotes Bezos as exclaiming, with even greater enthusiasm than usual, "If enough people see the machine, you won't have to persuade them to architect cities around them. It'll just happen."

36. Steve Kemper, *Code Name Ginger: The Story Behind Segway and Dean Kamen's Quest to Invent a New World* (Boston: Harvard Business School Press, 2003).

37. Quoted in Harmon, "An Inventor Unveils His Mysterious Personal Transportation Device."

38. From the book proposal, quoted in "What's IT all about? Answer on Monday," *Cleveland Plain Dealer*, December 1, 2001; John Schwartz, "On the Pavement, a New Contender," *New York Times*, January 23, 2003; and other places. The fact that we share a literary agent with Kemper, Rafe Sagalyn, causes us to demur when it comes to discussing exactly how the proposal became public.

39. The claim might someday prove to be accurate for Kamen, if not for Segway, given further speculation that the inventor is working on an efficient Sterling engine, an emission-free technology first conceived almost two hundred years ago by Scottish minister Robert Sterling but to date never developed cost-efficiently. See Teresa Riordan, "A Publicity Success, the Futuristic Segway Scooter May Be Celebrated for Its Engine," *New York Times*, April 15, 2002; and Stephen Frothingham, "Segway Scooter Inventor Has Sterling Transportation Idea," *Cleveland Plain Dealer*, July 1, 2002.

40. "Personal Transporter," *The Futurist*, July–August 2002, 7.

41. Stuart F. Brown, "'It' Surpasses My Wildest Dreams," *Fortune*, December 24, 2001, 38.

42. Saffo, "Ginger's Next Trick."

43. Sheridan Prasso, "Smoothing the Way for Segway," *BusinessWeek*, April 15, 2002, 10.

44. See Patricia Leigh Brown, "Whose Sidewalk Is It, Anyway?" *New York Times*, January 5, 2003; and Natalie Hopkinson, "Scooting into the Future as Passersby Worry, Wonder," *Cleveland Plain Dealer*, January 19, 2003.

45. See "Segway Inc. Introduces 2005 Product Line with More Power, More Attitude and More Options," *Segway*, www.segway.com/aboutus/press_releases/pr_030105c.html, and "Segway Introduces Next Generation of Personal Transportation," www.segway.com/aboutus/press_releases/pr_081406a.html.

46. Others, including Rocky Aoki, point to Rocky Aoki and his first Benihana in the United States in 1964.

47. Quoted in interview by Constantine von Hoffman, "Heart of Rock 'n' Roll," *CMO Magazine*, June 2005, 18.

48. James Ogilvy, "What Strategists Can Learn from Sartre," *Business + Strategy*, Winter 2003, 7. On that same page Ogilvy further notes that "The word *decision* derives from the Latin for 'cut off.'"

49. Mark Hyman, "How Tony Hawk Stays Aloft," *BusinessWeek*, November 13, 2006, 86.

50. "TippingSprung Fields Third Annual Brand-Extension Survey," *TippingSprung*, www.tippingsprung.com/releases/2006extensionsurvey.html.

51. See en.wikipedia.org/wiki/Porsche_Cayenne.

52. Mark Ritson, "Brand Aberrations Acceptable on Path to Profit," *Marketing*, September 15, 2004, 21.

53. Ibid. For another piece on how "authenticity may be a key factor as to why brands like Burton are shy of moving too far beyond their core audience" see Alycia de Mesa, "Sports Brands Play at Life Style," *brandchannel.com*, October 25, 2004, www.brandchannel.com/features_effect.asp?pf_id=235.

54.	Diana T. Kurylko, "No Cayenne for 2007 Model Year," *Autoweek*, August 21, 2006, www.autoweek.com/apps /pbcs.dll/article?AID=/20060821/FREE/60821003/1041/PROMOBLOG01.

55.	Howard Schultz and Dori Jones Yang, *Pour Your Heart into It: How Starbucks Built a Company One Cup at a Time* (New York: Hyperion, 1997), 165. Interestingly, Schultz uses a quote from IBM's Thomas J. Watson, Jr.'s *A Business and Its Beliefs* as an epigram to begin the chapter on the previous page: "The only sacred cow in an organization should be its basic philosophy of doing business."

56.	Ibid.

57.	Quoted in Jennifer Pellet, "Lessons from Brand Leaders," *Chief Executive*, October/November 2006, 31.

58.	Quoted in Ben Elgin, Michael Arndt, Roger Crockett, Kerry Capell, and Moon Ihlwan, "Protect Your Culture," *BusinessWeek*, August 7, 2006, 56.

59.	Robert Spector and Patrick D. McCarthy, *The Nordstrom Way: The Inside Story of America's #1 Customer Service Company* (New York: John Wiley & Sons, 1995), 16.

60.	The rest of Stephens's rules: No dry voice mail prompts; no more than one transfer; no looking at the competition; no mentioning the competition; no assumptions.

61.	Brad Anderson, "Remember *Who* You Are, Not What," *Business 2.0*, December 2005, 126.

62.	Quoted in Julie Bosman, "Venerable Maker of Pens Turns to Young Designers," *New York Times*, August 7, 2006.

63.	The details in this example are from ibid.

64.	"Form 10-Q" for the quarter ended May 5, 2006, the latest on its Web site, Dell Inc., available at www.dell.com /downloads/global/corporate/sec/10Q07Q1.pdf.

65.	A good source for understanding Dell's strategic moves over the first ten years of its existence is Das Narayandas and V. Kasturi Rangan, "Dell Computer Corporation," Harvard Business School Case no 9-596-058, 1995.

66.	Quoted in Elizabeth Corcoran, "A Bad Spell," *Forbes*, June 19, 2006, 46.

67.	"Commoditise This," *The Economist*, December 2, 2006, 69. For how Dell is applying its factory techniques to call centers, see Louise Lee, "Dell: Facing Up to Past Mistakes," *BusinessWeek*, June 19, 2006, 35–36.

68.	Michael Kanellos, "Dell Selling PCs at Costco," *CNET News.com*, November 3, 2002, news.com.com/Dell +selling+PCs+at+Costco/2100-1001_3-964360.html.

69.	See Michael Singer, "Is Retail Right for Dell?" *CNET News.com*, November 29, 2005, available at news.com .com/Is+retail+right+for+Dell/2100-1003_3-5975652.html.

70.	Bob Sechler, citing Dell spokesman Mike Maher, in "Dell Returns to Retail Shelves with Costco Deal," *Wall Street Journal*, December 1, 2005.

71.	Andy Sewer, "Dell's Midlife Crisis," *Fortune*, November 28, 2005, 152.

72.	Christopher Lawton, "Consumer Demand and Growth in Laptops Leave Dell Behind," *Wall Street Journal*, August 30, 2006.

73.	Quoted in Sewer, "Dell's Midlife Crisis," 148. On the same page Sewer makes the point that "Other companies would kill for Dell's 'disappointing' numbers" and on p. 152, immediately following the phrase we quote in the text, says, "Fact: Between 1995 and 1999, Dell's earnings doubled on average each quarter; in the most recent 20 quarters, earnings on average climbed 43%. That's still amazing, but also dramatically slower."

74.	"This Has Been a Wake-Up Call for Us," interview with David Kirkpatrick, *Fortune*, September 18, 2006, 78. In Damon Darlin, "Dell's Founder Is Rethinking Direct Sales," *New York Times*, April 28, 2007, Michael Dell is quoted as saying in an internal memorandum, "The direct model has been a revolution, but it is not a religion." We trust that in trying finished-goods inventory again, it is because of the capabilities it has gained through the intervening years, and not desperation.

75.	Kevin Allison, "Struggling Dell Widens Focus," *Financial Times*, May 17, 2007.

76.	See www.thebodyshopinternational.com/web/tbsgl/values.jsp. For an opposing view, see Jon Entine, "A Social and Environmental Audit of The Body Shop: Anita Roddick and the Question of Character," July 2003, available via a link at www.jonentine.com/body_shop.htm, and reprinted as Jon Entine, "The Stranger-Than-Truth Story of The Body Shop," in *Killed: Great Journalism Too Hot to Print*, ed. David Walls (New York: Nation Books, 2004), 179–212.

77.	It's useful here to heed the advice of Tony Hiss, an author and investigator into "the emerging science of place," as his bio puts it, who in his introduction to *The Experience of Place* (New York: Vintage Books, 1990), xii–xiii, encourages us to engage all of our senses in an act of "simultaneous perception," through which "the familiar hard-and-fast boundary between ourselves and our surroundings seems softened, expanding our sense of the space occupied by 'here' and the time taken up by 'now,' and uncovering normally ignored patterns of relationships that make us part of larger groups and events."

78.	We discuss various aspects of these three dimensions throughout this book, but for one concise exposition of our view on how managers should really view these three dimensions—as economic offerings, scripted capabilities, and individual customers—see James H. Gilmore and B. Joseph Pine II, "Beyond Goods and Services: Staging experiences and guiding transformations," *Strategy & Leadership*, vol 25, no 3, May–June 1997, 10–18.

79.	For how to do this based on reducing customer sacrifice over time, see B. Joseph Pine II, Don Peppers, and Martha Rogers, "Do You Want to Keep Your Customers Forever?" *Harvard Business Review*, March–April 1995, 103–114; and B. Joseph Pine II and James H. Gilmore, *The Experience Economy: Work Is Theatre & Every Business a Stage* (Boston: Harvard Business School Press, 1999), 81–94.

80. The information given here is from conversations with Paul Berry, USAA public relations, the internally published brochure "A USAA HISTORY: 1922 to 2002," and the "USAA 2001 Report to Members," the member-owned company's equivalent to an annual report. Further details on the history of USAA can be found in Michael R. Vitale, Joyce J. Elam, and John E. P. Morrison, "United Services Automobile Association (USAA)," Harvard Business School Case no 9-188-102, revised September 23, 1993; more information on how it customizes to individual members based on life events can be found in James H. Gilmore and B. Joseph Pine II, eds., *Markets of One: Creating Customer-Unique Value Through Mass Customization* (Boston: Harvard Business School Press, 2000), 73–75, 158, and 161.

81. Other insurance companies certainly will recognize that USAA resides in its industry, but still they have little hope for significant inroads into this community, for 99 percent of active duty military officers are members, and after a decade of opening its membership to enlisted personnel, over 35 percent of them have also signed up. Even among the adult children of members, almost 50 percent of those remain with USAA after they leave home.

82. See also George S. Day and Paul J. H. Schoemaker, "Scan the Periphery," *Harvard Business Review*, November 2005, 135. As a great companion to Here-and-Now Space, Day and Schoemaker ask a series of questions to guide a company's scanning resources, organized by past, present, and future. They also provide a diagnostic tool they call a "strategic eye exam . . . for evaluating and sharpening companies' peripheral vision" (pp. 135–136). They go into depth on the subject and this tool in *Peripheral Vision: Seven Steps to Seeing Business Opportunities Sooner* (Boston: Harvard Business School Press: 2006).

83. In a book review of Robert Goffee and Gareth Jones, *Why Should Anyone Be Led by You? What It Takes to Be an Authentic Leader* (Boston: Harvard Business School Press, 2006), Morgan Witzel, in "A Rewarding Read If You Want to Lead," *Financial Times*, January 23, 2006, writes, "Nor does the book fully reconcile the tension between authenticity and adaptability. To be told on the one hand to be yourself, and on the other constantly to adapt your behavior and attitudes to the environment sets up a paradox that few people are equipped to handle." That same paradox exists for businesses, with the Here-and-Now Space model showing how it can be resolved by delineating the limits to the amount of adaptability that can be achieved while remaining true to self.

84. Ogilvy, "What Strategists Can Learn from Sartre," 10. The term replaced by "[past]" for ease of reading here was in the original "thrownness," a concept introduced by Heidigger in *Being and Time* to describe how each person has a history that "throws" it into the present in a particular place, not just anywhere. *Geworfenheit* in the original German, it is your past instantiated in the present, which in turns limits where you can be in the future.

85. For more on strategic intention and its distinction from strategic intent, see Pine and Gilmore, *The Experience Economy*, 202–203. For more on strategy and authenticity, see Jeanne Liedtka, "Is Your Strategy a Duck?" *Journal of Business Strategy*, vol 27, no 5, 2006, 30–37.

86. All Altmiller quotes, as well as the background of this example, can be found in Gary Adamson et al., "Once Upon A Time . . .," in *What Managers Say, What Employees Hear*, ed. Regina Fazio Maruca (Westport, CT: Greenwood Publishing Group, 2006), 89–103.

87. Quoted in ibid., 93.

88. Quoted in ibid., 93–94.

89. Davis, *Future Perfect*, 8 and 26, respectively.

90. Quoted in Adamson et al., "Once Upon A Time . . .," 96.

91. Let us be very clear here: we think there is absolutely nothing immoral about selling SUVs that are demonstrably safer than alternatives or drilling for oil in places like the Arctic Refuge when that commodity ends up in offerings that make people healthier, wealthier, and wiser. Both offerings are fundamental to advanced economies that, through their growth and size, can yield better standards of living, better health, and even reduced pollution. What we object to is saying one thing and doing another.

92. Cait Murphy, "Is BP Beyond Petroleum? Hardly," *Fortune*, September 30, 2002.

93. Joel Makower, "BP Alternative Energy: It's a Start," *WorldChanging*, www.worldchanging.com/archives /003795.html.

94. These and other events are detailed in John R. Wilke, Ann Davis, and Chip Cummins, "BP Woes Deepen With New Probe," *Wall Street Journal*, August 29, 2006; Joe Nocera, "Green Logo, but BP Is Old Oil," *New York Times*, August 12, 2006; and "BP's Checkered Past," an exhibit to Alan Cowell, "BP's Chief Quits Over Revelations About Private Life," *New York Times*, May 2, 2007.

95. Nocera, "Green Logo, but BP Is Old Oil."

96. Craig Smith, "BP's Failure of Execution, Not Strategy," *Financial Times*, August 9, 2006.

97. *BP Annual Review 2006*, BP p.l.c., 1.

98. See "Why Toyota Is Afraid of Being Number One," *BusinessWeek*, March 5, 2007, available at www.businessweek.com/magazine/content/07_10/b4024071.htm.

99. Jon Gertner, "From 0 to 60 to World Domination," *New York Times Magazine*, February 18, 2007, 58.

100. Ibid.

101. See Micheline Maynard, "Toyota Drove to the Bank in a Ford," *New York Times*, August 6, 2006.

102. Martin Fackler, "Toyota Set to Lift Crown from GM," *International Herald Tribune*, December 22, 2006.

103. Gertner, "From 0 to 60 to World Domination," 38.

104. Donald N. Sull, *Revival of the Fittest: Why Good Companies Go Bad and How Great Managers Remake Them* (Boston: Harvard Business School Press, 2003), 8.

105. Ibid.

106. Ibid., 8, 21.

107. Ibid., 24.

108. Ibid., 24–25.

109. Ibid., 8 and 68, respectively.

110. See Louis V. Gerstner Jr., *Who Says Elephants Can't Dance? Inside IBM's Historic Turnaround* (New York: HarperCollins, 2002), 68–72.

111. Allan L. Scherr, "Managing for Breakthroughs in Productivity," *Human Resource Management* 28, no 3 (Fall 1989), 403–424. In Scherr's work at IBM involving more than twenty large-scale engineering and programming projects undertaken with this model, productivity increased almost three times on average, with equivalent quality and markedly higher morale.

112. Ibid.

113. Ibid. Scherr's model uses this term in allowing for situations in which "circumstances might spontaneously shift and resolve the breakdown."

114. Larry Bossidy and Ram Charan, *Execution: The Discipline of Gettting Things Done* (New York: Crown Business, 2002), 7.

115. Ibid., 57–84. In addressing the "Know yourself" behavior, Bossidy and Charan identify "four core qualities that make up emotional fortitude" (p. 81): Authenticity, Self-Awareness, Self-Mastery, and Humility—a well-executed list, although we can't help but wonder if knowing the work of William Ian Miller in *Faking It* might lead to a different spin on self-awareness and richer appreciation for the difficulty in knowing yourself.

116. As Bossidy and Charan do in their follow-on book, *Confronting Reality: Doing What Matters to Get Things Right* (New York: Crown Business, 2004).

Chapter 10

1. "Artificial Roots," *PanStadia*, August 2004.

2. Sandra Eckstein, "Fake Grass Is Taking Root on Residential Lawns," *Cleveland Plain Dealer*, June 9, 2005.

3. Miles Orvell, *The Real Thing: Imitation and Authenticity in American Culture, 1880–1940* (Chapel Hill: University of North Carolina Press, 1989), xxiii.

4. For more on authenticity and original copies—and copied originals—see Walter Benjamin, "The Work of Art in the Age of Mechanical Reproduction," in *Illuminations* (New York: Schocken Books, 1968; originally published in German in 1955), 217–251.

5. Randy Cohen, "Acceptable Knockoffs," *New York Times Magazine*, May 22, 2005, 24.

6. Rob Walker, "The Marketing of No Marketing," *New York Times Magazine*, June 22, 2003, 42–45.

7. Ibid.

8. Granted, the same may have eventually happened to Mother Teresa, but she did not thrust it on herself.

9. For more on the rise of *cool* and authenticity, see Clive Nancarrow, Pamela Nancarrow, and Julie Page, "An Analysis of the Concept of *Cool* and Its Marketing Implications," *Journal of Consumer Behaviour*, vol 1, no 4, 311–322.

10. Maggie Overfelt, in "Geek Unique? Suddenly every computer service has a sense of humor," *Forbes Small Business*, July–August 2002, describes the Geek Squad's "battle cry" as "Idolize the geek" and that of Geeks on Call as "Spoof the geek." The piece is also worth reading for Robert Stephen's own take on the copycat franchises.

11. Mathematically, the actual movement is *reflected* on a particular vector on the light cone of the particle under consideration. (You can visualize the actual vector by imagining a light source directly above the particle's original location in Minkowski Space—we say "imagining" because in actuality such a source would be in the particle's future—and wherever the particle moves, its shadow from that light source would fall on a specific point on the light cone. Drawing the line that goes between that shadow point and the original spot in space-time would be the vector.) The reflection would merge with that vector when the particle travels at the speed of light, and if the particle changes direction in even the slightest amount it shifts to a new reflected vector.

12. Kelefa Sanneh, "The Sweet Sounds of Really Bad Singing," *New York Times*, January 18, 2004.

13. Julie Bosman, "A Toast to a Liqueur (If You Can Say It)," *New York Times*, November 13, 2005. A Grand Marnier spokesman offered this pronunciation: "CuVAY doo san sin-khan-ten-air." Seems like there ought to be at least one more accented syllable in there somewhere.

14. Andrew Adam Newman, "If the Children Can Drink Uncola, What About Unbeer?" *New York Times*, September 19, 2005.

15. Ian Wylie, "Top Designers. No Brands," *Fast Company*, June 2005, 31.

16. Quoted in Bonnie Schwartz, "Luxury Gets Real," *Fast Company*, January 2001, 68.

17. Cathy Horyn, "A Store Made for Right Now: You Shop Until It's Dropped," *New York Times*, February 17, 2004. See too Amanda Fortini, "The Anti-Concept Concept Store," *New York Times Magazine*, December 12, 2004, 54.

18. Mary Spicuzza, "Don't Look for a Sign," *New York Times*, August 7, 2004.

19. William L. Hamilton, "What Price Authenticity?" *New York Times*, June 16, 2005.

20. For more on retro, see Stephen Brown, Robert V. Kozinets, and John F. Sherry Jr., "Teaching Old Brands New Tricks: Retro Branding and the Revival of Brand Meaning," *Journal of Marketing*, vol 67, July 2003, 19–33—where the

authors suggest *antimony*, or brand paradox, as one of four key themes for retromarketing; and Stephen Brown, *Marketing— The Retro Revolution* (London: SAGE Publications, 2001).

21. Kathy Sena, in "Retro Fashions Comfort the Young," *USA Today*, June 2, 2003, attributes this advice to her friend Roberta: "If you participated in it the first time around, you're too old the second time." See also Tracie Rozhon and Ruth La Ferla, "Trying On the Familiar, and Liking It," *New York Times*, August 15, 2003.

22. There are also *replica* offerings—exact reproductions of the original.

23. See Justin Pope, "Nike to Acquire Converse," *St. Paul Pioneer Press*, July 10, 2003; and Stephanie Kang, "Nike Takes Chuck Taylors from Antifashion to Fashionista," *Wall Street Journal*, June 23, 2006, which says that "Converse is set to launch 'All Star Revolution,' a shoe inspired by the Chuck Taylor look but stuffed with the kind of cushioning and technology that is standard for performance shoes"—Repro, in other words.

24. David Carr, "Reinventing *Seventeen* with a View to Middle America," *New York Times*, November 24, 2003.

25. Brad Wieners, "Disney's New Nostalgia Trip," *Business 2.0*, December 2003, 36.

26. Brown, in *Marketing—The Retro Revolution*, 6, views Repro as "probably the most common variant of retromarketing" while we view Repro and Retro as antinomic. We further reserve Repro for what he calls "*Repro Nova* . . . combining the old with the new, usually in the form of old-style styling with hi-tech technology." His other two categories are "*Repro*," which "pertains to reproducing the old pretty much as it was" and "*Repro de Luxe*, . . . second helpings of the past, insofar as it revives or reproduces something that traded on nostalgia to start with. Neo-nostalgia, in other words."

27. See, for example, Juliet Chung, "A Digital Generation's Analog Chic," *New York Times*, September 9, 2004. She quotes then-fifteen-year-old Andrew Fader as saying "The idea is to get the aesthetics of older technology and mix it with the functionality of new technology"—a better definition of Repro we could not hope to find (even though Chung mistakenly calls it "retro" and "vintage").

28. Molly Millett, "American Icon," *St. Paul Pioneer Press*, September 25, 2004.

29. Respectively, Penelope Green, "The New Old House," *New York Times*, August 10, 2006 (the term "instant patina" occurs in a caption to one of the photographs accompanying the article); Jim Carlton, "Frontier Nostalgia," *Wall Street Journal*, August 14, 2002; and Karen Mandelbaum, quoted in June Fletcher, "This Old House Isn't," *Wall Street Journal*, July 30, 2004.

30. Which is from the publishers of the vintage home bible: *Old Home Journal*.

31. See Jeremy Peters and Danny Hakim, "Is That Steve McQueen in the Cornfield? Yes, Brought Back by Ford," *New York Times*, October 15, 2004.

32. Gautam Naik, "Arrowhead Case: Knapping Hits a Spot for Flint-Stone Fans," *Wall Street Journal*, October 6, 2005.

33. Gardiner Morse, "Conversation: Innovating a Classic at Airstream," *Harvard Business Review*, October 2003, 18–20. See also Chris Dixon, "Time Travel, in a Trailer," *New York Times*, December 26, 2003.

34. Eve M. Kahn, "Light to Soften the Suburbs," *New York Times*, December 23, 2004.

35. See Pamela LiCalzi O'Connell, "A Wild Ride," *New York Times*, December 18, 2003.

36. See David Cay Johnston, "Got Game? Got Old Game?" *New York Times*, July 11, 2003; "Base Ball Like It Ought to Be, and Like It Was," *The New York Times*, August 25, 2006; and Stephen Barbara, "Ball Six: Base Ball à la Bouton," *The Wall Street Journal*, September 23–24, 2006. Note that while this is called "vintage base ball" (never "baseball"), "repro base ball" would be the more precise term. Truly vintage experiences remain impossible outside of time-travel tales like Michael Crichton's *Timeline*, although some businesses do create Repro places to sell vintage items, such as Tokyo's Ichome Shotengai, or District 1 Shopping Area, filled with products from the 1950s and 60s. According to Howard W. French (who mistakenly calls this "retro") in "Hot New Marketing Concept: Mall as Marketing Lane," *New York Times*, January 7, 2003, such places are endemic to Japan where "there has been a real nostalgia boom" and "campy, ersatz re-creations of other worlds" abound.

37. See "Welcome to Oakhurst Links" at www.oakhurstlinks.com/oakhurst_story/index.asp.

38. David Pearson, "Tiny Car Maker in France Retools Classic Porsche," *Wall Street Journal*, March 25, 2003.

39. Some are also doing Resto—restorations—and "rat rods," cars "at the far extreme of authenticity" that are "shorn of finesse, polish or chrome—loud, full of attitude and irresistible to the T-shirt-and-sideburns set," according to Iver Peterson, "The Newest Hot Rods: Retro, Resto and Rat," *New York Times*, December 3, 2004.

40. Retro automobiles tend to have brisk sales for a year or two, but then taper off. See, for example, Earle Eldridge, "Once-Hot Retro Cars Chill," *USA Today*, May 1, 2003, and John Turrettini, "Out with the Old!," *Forbes*, May 26, 2003, 54.

41. John R. DiJulius III, *Secret Service: Hidden Systems that Deliver Unforgettable Customer Service* (New York: AMACOM, 2003).

42. We call this transparent customization, where something is customized unbeknownst to an individual customer, coming off as standard. We discovered a correspondence between the Real/Fake Matrix and our four types of customization framework in *The Experience Economy*, 86–94, where we differentiate between product (what it is) and representation (what one says about it), although with the X and Y axes transposed. The four customization quadrants seem to relate directly to the four Real/Fake modes, where collaborative is Real-real customization, adaptive Fake-fake (after all, the company actually does nothing to customize such offerings for individual customers), cosmetic Real-fake, and, as with this secret service example, transparent Fake-real. The older framework in no way inspired the newer one; we only noticed the correspondence ourselves in the writing of this book. And it became deeper

in the writing. In the four types of customization framework, we originally labeled the no-change/no-change quadrant simply "Mass Production," only later realizing the value to be gained in adaptive customization. Here, we belatedly realized that companies can create value in the Fake-fake, if only they render it faux.

43. Scott McCartney, "Start-up Airlines Fly Only Business Class," *Wall Street Journal*, September 20, 2005.

44. Per changes in Nevada law in 2001, it is no longer mandatory that all gambling be done in public; see Stephanie Paterik, "Whale-Hunting in Vegas," *Wall Street Journal*, August 15, 2002.

45. Doreen Carvajal, "Within Its Walls, Club Med Opens a First-Class Preserve," *New York Times*, September 5, 2006.

46. Jennifer Tung, "Where V.I.P.'s Flaunt It," *New York Times*, March 31, 2002.

47. Kortney Stringer, "How to Have a Pleasant Trip: Eliminate Human Contact," *Wall Street Journal*, October 31, 2002.

48. Katie Hafner, "They're Off to See the Wizards," *New York Times*, January 27, 2005.

49. In Ron Lieber, "Do Yoga with Gwyneth on Friday," *Wall Street Journal*, May 27, 2004, Gordon Smith, president of American Express' consumer card-services group, says, "We realized that very busy people needed us to help them make their lives easier and gain access to things that they couldn't gain by themselves or would require considerable effort."

50. See Michael McCarthy, "Front-Row Tickets Take Back Seat to Once-In-Lifetime Experiences," *USA Today*, March 1, 2006.

51. Paula Szuchman, "Well, Aren't You Special," *Wall Street Journal*, May 14, 2004. The journalist indicates that "the approach can fall short of a true insider experience." She quotes one person who constantly turns down such invitations, hotel developer Jeff Klein: "If you have to pay to be a VIP you're not a VIP in my book. You're just insecure."

52. Daniel J. Boorstin, *The Image: A Guide to Pseudo-Events in America* (New York: Vintage Books, 1992), 9, 11. The original book was published by Atheneum in 1961 as *The Image, or What Happened to the American Dream*. The Vintage edition includes Boorstin's forward to it as the 25th Anniversary Edition, the publication of which he amusingly cites as further "evidence of how hard it is for any of us to escape the passion for pseudo-events that has accelerated, and still accelerates into the foreseeable future."

One example with a memorable phrase: sports columnist William C. Rhoden, in "Its Savior Is Kobe; Its Muse, the Dunk," *New York Times*, February 20, 2006, writing that "The N.B.A. All-Star Game is one of the most fascinating non-event events in sports."

53. Don't recognize Paul David Hewson? Google him.

54. Boorstin, 13.

55. Ibid., 11–12 and 39–40.

56. Corey Kilgannon, "Not the Real New Orleans, but It Will Have to Do," *New York Times*, January 13, 2006.

57. Jack Jacobs, quoted in ibid.

58. Julie Bosman, "This Joe's for You?" *New York Times*, June 8, 2006.

59. Christopher Montgomery, "New Look for Dunkin' Donuts," *Cleveland Plain Dealer*, February 23, 2006.

60. Stephanie Paterik, "Don't Tell, but Hilton Runs this Joint," *Wall Street Journal*, July 3, 2002.

61. Britta Waller, "Quasi-Vegetarianism," *Sky*, November 2002, 75.

62. Samuel Smiles, *Self-Help; With Illustrations of Character, Conduct and Perseverance* (Oxford: Oxford University Press, 2002; originally published in 1859).

63. As written on the small kitchen magnet young Rebecca Pine gave her father the year before her first trip to the American Girl Place in Chicago, "The best things in life are not things."

64. The company did launch a short-lived "Save Girlhood" ad campaign on December 26, 2005, accompanied by the major platform Web site www.savegirlhood.com. It now states that "Although this promotion has ended, the concept of saving girlhood remains at the heart of everything American Girl stands for. And to help you continue encouraging girls to follow their own 'inner star,' check out American Girl's array of ideas, books, and products that teach, challenge, and inspire." It then links to AG's flagship Web site. The campaign was the first in the company's history—it had always let its experience be the marketing—and appeared to be a direct response to complaints and a boycott from the pro-life movement after the company funded the pro-choice group Girls Inc. via "I Can" bracelet sales. See "American Girl Tries to Restore Image Tarnished by Pro-Life Boycott," Pro-Life Action League, www.prolifeaction.org/home/2005/agvictory.htm, and Heather Cabot, "Doll Maker Embarks on 'Save Girlhood' Campaign," ABC News, December 14, 2005, available at abcnews.go.com/Business/story?id=1403610&business=true.

65. Therese Kauchak, *Real Beauty: 101 Ways to Feel Great About YOU* (Middleton, WI: Pleasant Company Publications, 2004), 3. This was soon followed by Elizabeth Chobanian, *Real Spirit: Fun Ideas for Refreshing, Relaxing, and Staying Strong* (Middleton, WI: Pleasant Company Publications, 2005), and Carol Yoshizumi, *Real Fitness: 101 Games and Activities to Get Girls Going* (Middleton, WI: Pleasant Company Publications, 2006).

66. Kauchak, *Real Beauty*, 115.

67. Ibid., 120.

68. "On the Origin of Self-Help," *The Economist*, April 24, 2004.

69. In David Bastone, "Right Reality: Does a Corporate Acquisition Spell the Death of a Social Venture?," *The Wag: The Weekly E-Newsletter of Worthwhile Gain*, February 9, 2005, www.organicconsumers.org/organic/corptrading

20905.cfm, cofounder Ben Cohen laments, "Although there are some wonderful people with a social conscience inside Unilever, most of what was the soul of Ben & Jerry's has been lost."

70. The Second Cup Ltd., "Solid Grounds: Our Commitment to You." (2003).

71. Quoted in Rob Walker, "Big Gulp," *New York Times Magazine*, February 26, 2006, 16.

72. Ibid. In the December 7, 2003, entry "Rant on socially responsible branding" on her blog *What's Your Brand Mantra?* available at brand.blogs.com/mantra/2003/12/brand_honesty.html, Jennifer Rice rightly concludes that "A donation does not a socially responsible brand make."

73. Stuart Elliott, "Bravo's James Lipton to the Extreme, Dude," *New York Times*, July 27, 2005.

74. "For Dylan, the Times Are Really a-Changin'," *St. Paul Pioneer Press*, April 3, 2004.

75. Tom Vanderbilt, "That Selling Sound," *Wall Street Journal*, July 12, 2002.

76. A. O. Scott, "Rustic Romance," *New York Times Magazine*, August 11, 2002, 17–18. Scott also addresses Deer Isle within the context that "destinations are judged not just by natural beauty, proximity to beaches and hiking trails or historical interest, but also by the more elusive criterion of authenticity." He also shares his "disdain [for] the lower coast, with its outlet stores and tourist kitsch" but notes that "a friend with a place farther up the coast, near Machias, invited me for a visit, 'if you want to see what the real Maine is like.'"

ACKNOWLEDGMENTS

This book has been a long time in the making. The subject deserved much study, especially given how elusive an understanding of the topic of authenticity in business proved to be. We found the more we came to understand, the more we understood how little we really understood.

Progress would not have been possible without the initial encouragement of our agent, Rafe Sagalyn, who steered us away from a sequel to *The Experience Economy*. Our most capable, caring, and sometimes cantankerous editor, Kirsten Sandberg, went beyond the call of duty, challenged us from start to finish, and rolled up her sleeves at crunch time to, well, help us finish. Jen Waring helped marshal us through the final steps of manuscript preparation and production at Harvard Business School Press. We're blessed to have such literary support. We also thank all at the Sagalyn Agency and Harvard Business School Press who have helped behind the scenes.

We thank our business partners, Doug Parker and Scott Lash, for so skillfully managing our business at Strategic Horizons LLP and affording us time to devote to researching and writing this tome. A number of clients and partners have provided forums to explore the subject of authenticity with their businesses and industries as a platform for investigation. We wish to specifically thank Carlson Companies (Marilyn Carlson Nelson, Curtis Nelson, Jim Schroer, Rick Clevette, and a cast of thousands), the Association for Christian Retail (Bill Anderson), Color Marketing Group (Nancy Burns and Kathleen Conroy), Design Futures Council (Jim Cramer), Design Management Institute (Earl Powell, now retired), the European Centre for the Experience Economy (Albert Boswijk and Thomas Thijssen), Exhibitor Magazine Group (Lee Knight and Dee Silfies), Hospitality Design (Michelle Finn), HSMAI Nederland (Hans Poortvliet), INJOY (John Maxwell and John Shinabarger), Iowa State's College of Family and Consumer Sciences (Ann Marie Fiore and company), the Lapland Centre of Expertise for the Experience Industry (Sanna Tarssanen and all the rest), The Leadership Forum (John Horton, now with CollierBrown & Co.), LEGO System (Mark Hanson), MarketResponse (Willem Brethouwer), Marriott International (Mike Jannini), MGM Mirage (Felix

Rappaport), MVP Collaborative (Dan Sundt), New England Museum Association (Kate Viens), Oppenheimer & Company (Rick Worner), Penn State Executive Programs (Gini Tucker), Post Properties (Lori Addicks, Dave Stockert, and Tom Wilkes), SEI Investments (the whole Wealth Network team), Starizon (Gary and Leigh Adamson, plus the whole experience guide team), Steak n Shake Company (Peter Dunn and Doug Williard), TED (Chris Anderson), VHA Oklahoma/Arkansas (Bill Gwartney), VODW Marketing (Roger Peverelli), The Walt Disney Company (Scott Hudgins and Linda Warren, among others), and Yamamoto Moss Mackenzie (Shelly Regan, Miranda Moss, and Hideki Yamamoto).

Aware of our efforts to develop this book, several individuals have provided an invaluable service by reviewing portions of the manuscript, being a sounding board on particular issues, and/or routinely calling attention to relevant articles or exemplars bearing on the subject. These include Gregory Beck of Architecture + Experience Design, Mark Dehner of Land as Art, Mike Dover of New Paradigm Learning Corporation, Steve Dragoo of Service Solutions Consulting, Pat Esgate of Esgate & Associates, Stan Hustad of PTM Group, Jeff Kallay of TargetX, Kim Korn of Business Architecture, Melissa Lenk of Cargill, Jeanne Liedtke, Marian Moore, and Phil Pfeifer of the Darden School of Business, Kathleen Macdonald of Macdonald Group, Nic Mepham of Pohjolan Mylly, Dave Norton of Stone Mantel, Sonia Rhodes of Sharp HealthCare, Bob Rogers of BRC Imagination Arts, Dave Travis of Leadership Network, Doug Wilson, formerly of Boston Scientific, and David B. Wolfe of Wolfe Resources Group.

We also thank participants in our annual thinkAbout events, where we have discussed matters of authenticity time and again. We especially wish to thank those who participated in thinkAbout in 2003 in New York, as that event served as the origin for us in introducing the subject of authenticity in a systematically sweeping way. We appreciate their longsuffering and patience in seeing the discussions there-and-then turn into this book here-and-now. We also thank the participants of thinkAbout 2006 in Baltimore for their thorough discussion of a number of issues during Open Space time—especially on what the title of the book should be. Particular thanks go to the (unfortunately unknown) person who suggested "Fauxthenticity," a term we have used inside the book.

We have also learned from every one of our Experience Stager of the Year (EXPY) award winners, many of which we only later discovered exemplified principles not only of experience staging but of rendering authenticity: American Girl Place (1999), Geek Squad (2000), Joie de Vivre Hospitality (2001), LEGO (2002), the Cerritos Public Library (2003), ChartHouse Learning Corporation (2004), HOK Sport Venue Event (2005), and Cereality (2006). There are some other companies (most with individuals very helpful to us) who heavily influenced our thoughts on authenticity by being such robust exemplars: Build-a-Bear Workshops (Maxine Clark), Cirque du Soleil (Daniel Lamarre), The Grove (Linda Berman), ING Direct, Jerde Partnership (Jon Jerde, who popularized the term "placemaking"), Jin Li Street in Chengdu, China (Xia Jia), La Ciudad de Los Niños (Xavier Lopez and, formerly, Ruben Cors), L'Occitane en Provence, Lush, MaryJanesFarm, Oriole Park at Camden Yards, P.G.C. Hajenius in Amsterdam (Jan Kees De Nijs), Pike Place Fish Company, Recreational Equipment, Inc. (Jim Anderson), Ritz-Carlton, San Juan Regional Medical Center (Steve Altmiller), *Second Life*, Southwest Airlines, Starbucks (Anne Saunders), USAA (Paul Berry), Vans, and Whole Foods.

We are indebted to a number of fellow authors, most notably Lionel Trilling, Charles Taylor, Corey Anton, Jay Newman, Jacob Golomb, Charles Guignon, Ada Louise Huxtable, Dean MacCannell, Michael Benedikt, Dinesh D'Souza, Virginia Postrel, William Ian Miller, Tracy Metz, Richard (Pete) Peterson, Charles Mann, and Stephen Budiansky. We could name many others, of course, but these individuals outside the world of business most shaped our own philosophical take on the subject.

Our families deserve our utmost appreciation. Writing a book, any book, takes its toll on the home front. We thank our wives Beth Gilmore and Julie Pine, and children Evan and Anna Gilmore, Becca and Lizzie Pine, for their understanding and support as we headed all too often to the home office to labor on the project. Again, thank you.

Finally, we wish to thank our parents. Jim cannot adequately convey how great the influence his mother and father, the late E. Jean Gilmore and Haydn Lewis Gilmore, have had in forming his self-image. (Thanks, Dad, for training up a child in the way he should go.) Bud Pine, Joe's father, has provided well-appreciated feedback on Joe's thoughts and writings his entire adult life, a life that would not be the same without the support and encouragement of his mother, Marilou, and his late stepfather, Norm Burnett.

INDEX

acting
  as if, 211
  real, 99, 144–145
Adamson, Gary, 140
Adelson, Sheldon, 83
Adobe Flash, 163–164
advertising
  articulating what you are, 132–134
  claims of "real" in advertisements, 36–37
  faked reality examples, 41, 147–148
  fundamental problem with, 148
  imperative that a company is what it says it is
    (*see* placemaking)
  value compared with placemaking experiences,
    172–177
Ageless Marketing (Wolfe), 14
Agrodome, 12
Aker, Andrew, 194
Altmiller, Steve, 208–212
Amazon, 110, 168, 192
American Girl Place
  cross-generational appeal, 23
  influential authenticity, 240–241
  versus inviting friends over, 11
  placemaking and, 149–150, 162
  return on investment of, 177
American Idol, 34, 105, 237, 248
American Wholesale Marketers Association
  (AWMA), 244
Amtrak, 16
Andersen Windows, 65
Anderson, Brad, 199
Anderson, Walter Truett, 17
Anthropologie, 37, 53, 112, 137
Anton, Corey, 88, 91–92, 185
AOL, 119, 165
Apartment Number 9 (store), 64
Appellation d'Origine Contrôlée, 134
appearances, displayed, 128–129, 141–143
Apple, 49, 57, 112, 130, 158, 161, 170, 235
Ardill, Ralph, 23

Argyris, Chris, 126
Army, U.S., 139, 168, 173
artificial
  Amazon rainforest, 86
  Disney, 9
  grass, 220
  Venice versus the Venetian, 82–83
authentication, 135
authenticity
  absence of (*see* inauthenticity)
  assessing your business's (*see* standards of
    authenticity, establishing)
  Axioms of, 43–44, 89–90, 103, 107, 191
  consumer sensibilities and, 5–6
  consumers' search for (*see* demand for au-
    thenticity)
  culture of, 90–91
  genres of (*see* genres of perceived authenticity)
  importance of place, 136
  manifestation in a segment of consumers, 3–5
  need for authentic offerings, 7
  philosophy of, 87–89, 184–185
  prevalence of counterfeiting, 7–8
  rendering (*see* rendering authenticity)
  what authenticity is not, 88
*Authenticity: Brands, Fakes, Spin and the Lust for
  Real Life* (Boyle), 4
authenticity paradox, 89–90
automotive industry, 215
Axioms of Authenticity, 43–44, 89–90, 103, 107,
  191

baby boomers, 20–22
Bailey, Lori, 40
Baileys Original Irish Cream, 129
Banksy, 42
Baudrillard, Jean, 17, 31, 109
Baussan, Olivier, 136
Bedol, Brian, 69
Being and Time (Heidegger), 185

beliefs + behaviors, 125–127
Bellagio, 73
Bendix, Regina, 5, 43
Benedikt, Michael, 43, 73
Bennis, Warren G., 25
Bezos, Jeff, 192–193
Berstein, David, 41
Blue Man Group, 49
Blackstone, 177
Body Shop, The, 204, 226–228
Bolin, Todd, 132
Bono. *See* Paul Hewson
Boorstin, Daniel, 17, 109, 236, 237
Bossidy, Larry, 217
Boswijk, Brian, 228
boutique hotels, 62–63. *See also* tourism
Boyle, David, 4, 136
BP p.l.c., 213–214
Brandscapes (Klingman), 68
Branson, Richard, 121
Brehme, Michael, 75
Bridger, Darren, 3
British Petroleum. *See* BP p.l.c.
Brown, Aaron, 34
Brown-Forman Corporation, 190
Buchanon, Joseph, 244
Buckingham, Jane Rinzler, 22
Budiansky, Stephen, 84
Buffett, Warren, 27
Build-a-Bear Workshop, 6, 13, 60–61
Built to Last (Collins and Porras), 139
Burj Al Arab (hotel), 12
Burmeister, John, 34
Burt's Bees, 160
Butters, MaryJane, 55
buzz marketing, 148

cafepress.com, 13
capitalism, authentic, 91–92
Carey, James, 18
Carson, Tom, 109
Caruso, Rick J., 137
Case Tomahawk Experience Center, 153
Castronova, Edward, 17, 165
Cathy, Truett, 126
Cause Marketing (Marconi), 75
Celilo Cancer Center, 152
Cerritos Public Library, 153
Champagne, 39, 130
Chappell, Tom, 125, 135
Charan, Ram, 217
charge admission, 176–177

Charmin (P&G), 158–159, 173
Chernack, Peter, 163
Chick-fil-A, 126
Chief Experience Officer, 175–176
Chihuly, Dale, 73
China, 7, 8, 60
Chuck E. Cheese's, 10, 105
Cirque du Soleil, 73
CityWalk, 111–112
Clark, Maxine, 60
Clegg, Alicia, 129
Clinton, Hillary, 26
Coca-Cola, 22, 57–58, 75, 112, 122
Coe College, 37
Cohen, Randy, 221
Collins, James, 139
Color Marketing Group, 219
Comme des Garçons, 229
commercialization and authenticity, 88
commodities
    as economic offering, 46
    placemaking experiences and, 152
    seen as natural authenticity, 49
commoditization, 13, 47–49, 127
Conley, Chip, 21
Constantine, Mark, 227
Corlett, Candace, 65
corporate culture, 126
corporate scandals, 23–24
Costa, Paolo, 83
Council of Independent Restaurants of America,
    38
counterfeiting, 7–8
country music, 93
Coverings Expo, 20
create belief (fake-real), 107, 108–110, 224
Creating Country Music (Peterson), 93
Crofts, Neil, 123
Crunchy Cons (Dreher), 4
Crushpad, 65, 112
culture
    of authenticity, 90–91
    corporate, 126
Culture of Narcissism (Lasch), 21–22
customization
    authenticity rendered through, 12–13
    exceptional authenticity and, 62, 65, 77–78
    as dynamic of Progression of Economic Value,
        48–49

Daily Show, The, 40
Dave & Buster's, 10, 100, 104–105

Dave Matthews Band, 11, 71, 196
Davis, Stan, 211
Deal, Terrence, 126
Dean, Howard, 26
De Efteling, 57
Dee, Sean, 195
Deep Ocean Adventures, 12
DEKA Research & Development Corporation, 192
de Jonge, Jannemarie, 82
Del.icio.us, 165
Dell Inc., 48, 201–204, 206
Dell, Michael, 201–204
demand for authenticity
    automation of services, 13–15
    authenticity rendered through customization, 12–13
    consumer frustration with technology, 13–15
    educational institutions and, 24–26
    emergence of experiences, 10–12
    extending authentic experiences, 22–23
    failure of institutions, 23–28
    GenXers and authenticity, 22
    international flavor of experience-based commerce, 11–12
    key drivers of, 9–10
    nonprofit organizations and, 27
    politicians and, 26–27
    prevalence of postmodernism, 16–18
    range of paid-for experiences, 10–11
    religious organizations and, 27–28
    rendering commerce less commercial, 1–13
    rendering generations more cross-genera-tional, 22–23
    rendering institutions more effective, 28–30
    rendering society more social, 18–20
    rendering technology more human, 15–16
    rise of baby boomers, 20–22
    social institutions and, 23–24, 29–30
    social networking and reality, 16–18
derivative placement, 168–169, 170
derivative presence, 158–160, 162
Digg, 165
DiJulius, John, 233
Diller, Steve, 76
    dimensions
        of business, 205–206, 224
        of space, 180–181, 205–206, 224
        of the universe, 205–206
    dimensions + designations, 130–132
Disney, Walt, 185–186
Disneyland, 57, 81–82, 83, 86, 108–109, 223. See also Walt Disney Company

Disney's Animal Kingdom, 9
Disney's Magic Kingdom, 9, 13, 109
Disneyland Resort Paris, 82, 187
Dogg, Snoop, 27
Dolan, Paul, 190
Donald, Jim, 127, 198
Dove soap, 133, 140
Dreher, Rob, 4
Drucker, Peter, 124, 150
D'Souza, Dinesh, 90–91
Dubai, 12, 156
Dunkin' Donuts', 237–238
Dutch, 81–82, 87
Dychtwald, Ken, 20
Dylan, Bob, 236

Eats, 195
eBay, 16, 27, 192,
Eco, Umberto, 17, 109
ecological intelligence, 56
economic offerings, 46–49. See also offerings, nature of
ecotourism, 56
Eden Alternative, 72–73
educational institutions and authenticity, 24–26
efficacy of placemaking experiences versus advertising, 172–175
Einstein, Albert 180, 205
Eisner, Michael, 186
elements of Is True to Itself on Real/Fake Matrix
    body of values, 118, 125–127, 128–129, 204, 216
    categories related to, 118
    effects of heritage, 118, 121–123, 128–129, 204, 216
    essence of enterprise, 118–119, 128–129, 204, 216
    nature of offerings, 118, 119–121, 128–129, 204, 216
    sense of purpose, 118, 123–125, 128–129, 204, 216
elements of Is What It Says It Is on Real/Fake Matrix
    assigned names, 128–129, 130–132
    categories related to, 128–129
    declared motivations, 128–129, 138–141
    displayed appearances, 128–129, 141–143
    established places, 128–129, 135–138, 150
    expressed statements, 128–129, 132–135
Eleven (restaurant), 228
English, Paul, 14

enterprise, essence of, 118–119, 128–129, 204, 216
entity + ethos, 118–119
ESPN Zone, 10, 100, 104
established places, 128–129, 135–138, 150
Ethics of Authenticity, The (Taylor), 93
Ethos Water, 75, 243
Everette, Malia, 74
EverQuest, 11
exceptional authenticity
  be direct and frank, 67
  be foreign, 62
  customized offerings, 65
  embracing of slowness, 66–67
  examples of, 64–65
  focus on uniqueness, 64–65
  go slow, 66–67
  hospitality industry and, 62–64
  limited-time events, 65–66
  polarity of Premium/Personal, 232–235
  principles of, 67–68
  services seen as, 49–50
  treat as temporary, 65–66
Execution (Bossidy and Charan), 217
execution zone, 182–184, 200–204, 212, 224–226.
    See also Here-and-Now Space model
experience domains, 165–166, 170
Experience Economy, The 144, 176
Experience Economy
  appeal of real, 3–6
  authenticity rendered through customization,
    12–13
  baby boomers and authenticity, 20–21
  experience/authenticity relationship, 1–2, 3
  GenXers and authenticity, 22
  international flavor of, 11–12
  range of paid-for experiences, 10–12
  service/quality relationship, 2–3
experience hubs, 156–157, 162
experiences
  as economic offering, 46–47
  placemaking experiences and, 151–152 (*see
    also* placemaking)
  seen as referential authenticity, 50
Experiencing Architecture (Rasmussen), 83
Extreme Makeover, 35–36

Facebook, 19, 165
Fake-fake, 97, 101, 102, 103, 106, 107–108, 110,
    114, 118, 190, 219–222, 223, 225, 247, 251
Fake-real, 97, 100, 102, 103, 104–105, 108–110,
    112, 113, 114, 118, 222, 223, 224–225,
    227–228, 230, 236, 237–238, 239–240 247

Faking It (Miller), 99
fantasy in fiction, 110
fantasy sports, 11, 41
Farley, Jim, 158
faux offerings, 107–108
faux news, 26, 40,108, 236
*faux*thentic, 107–108, 118
Feltzer Vineyards, 32, 190
Fish! (video), 144
FitzGerald, Jimmy, 238
flagship locations, 153–154, 162
flagship site, 163–165, 169–170
Fleetwood, Mick, 121
Flightline Flight Simulation Center, 69
Florida, Richard, 4–5, 136–137
Ford, William Clay, 23–24
Ford Motor Company, 2, 23–24, 215
Ford Rouge Factory Tour, 122
Foxx, Jamie, 141
Francis, Duane, 152
Freedman, Samuel, 28
Freeman, Ed and Ben, 70
Frey, Mike, 60
Frontgate (furniture store), 238–239
Fujiwara, Akira, 69

Gabler, Neal, 17
Galatic Pizza, 74
Ganz Corporation, 166
Gap, Inc., 148, 160, 175
Garrison, James, 142
Geek Squad
  acting authentically and, 145
  after acquisition, 119
  fake-real mode, 223–224
  original authenticity and, 57
  placemaking and, 161, 171, 174
  technology and, 16
  understanding of its limits, 198–199
Gehry, Frank, 73
Geiger, Reinold, 136
genres of perceived authenticity
  applying the genres, 77–79
  correspondence with economic offerings,
    49–50, 52
  exceptional (*see* exceptional authenticity)
  genres examples, 50–52
  key polarities and, 226–243
  influential (*see* influential authenticity)
  natural (*see* natural authenticity)
  original (*see* original authenticity)
  referential (*see* referential authenticity)

GenXers, 22
Gerstner, Louis V., Jr., 115–116, 216
GetHuman.com, 14, 15–16
get real (real-real), 107, 112–114, 224
Gilmer, Maureen, 57
Global Exchange Reality Tours, 74
Gold Cafe, 60–61
go faux (fake-fake), 107–108, 224
Golomb, Jacob, 93
goods
    as economic offering, 46
    commoditization of, 47–48
    seen as original authenticity, 49
    placemaking experiences and, 150–152
Google, 140
Gore, Al, 26
Gottdeiner, Mark, 68
grass and authenticity, 220–221
Green Life, 24
Greenpeace, 24
Greenblatt, Jonathan, 243
Grove, The, 137
Guinness, 22–23, 122

Häagen-Dazs, 131
Habbo Hotel, 165–166
Hall, Robert, 124–125
Hamilton, William L., 229
Hamner, W. Easley, 83
Hard Rock Cafe, 12, 38, 59, 195–196
Harley-Davidson, 59
Harmon, Frederick, 126
Harrah's
    Total Gold program, 13
Hartman, Geoffrey, 34, 43, 135
Haus der Musik, 12
Heidegger, Martin, 185
heirloom produce, 54
Here-and-Now Space model
    affix the future principle, 208–213, 218, 225
    analyze the future, 213
    ascertain your positioning principle, 191–194, 213, 218, 225
    breakthroughs and breakdowns, 217
    business competition and, 204–208
    company limits and, 196–200
    company/product heritage importance, 189–191
    cycle of commitments in an organization, 215–217
    difficulty of working near the edges of your execution zone, 212

essential behaviors for leaders, 217–218
execute well principle, 213–218
execution zone success, 200–204
know your limits principle, 196–200, 213, 225
locate your trajectory principle, 194–196, 213, 218, 225
polarities within, 224–226, 247–248
positioning assessment, 191–194
scan the periphery principle, 204–208, 213, 218
strategic intentions basis, 208–213
study your heritage principle, 189–191, 196, 213, 218, 225
trajectory assessment, 194–196
vectors alignment, 224–226
zoom in your zone principle, 200–204, 213, 218
heritage
    defining commitments and, 215–216
    Dell Inc.'s, 201–202
    effects of, 118, 121–123, 128–129, 204, 216
    flagship locations and, 153–154, 162
    Here-and-Now Space and, 180, 182–183
    principle of Here-and-Now Space, 189–191, 196, 213, 218, 225
    repudiation of, 190, 199–200
    San Juan Regional Medical Center's, 209
    trajectory in Here-and-Now Space and, 208
    USAA's, 207
    Walt Disney Company's, The, 185–186, 187, 188
Hewson, Paul, 236
HeyLetsGo.com, 166
Hi5, 165
HiPiHi World, 165
H.J. Heinz Company, 142
HOK Venue Event, 137, 230
homeschooling, 24
Honest Tea, 54, 112
Honda, 55
hospitality industry and authenticity, 62–64. See also tourism
Huis ten Bosch, 12
Hung, William, 34
Huxtable, Ada Louise, 83, 96, 108–109, 111
hyperreality, 17, 31, 35, 95

IBM, 115–117, 216
IBM Land, 166
ICEHOTEL, 12
ideals + incentives, 138–141

identity
  brand or business, 129
  personal, 17, 20, 21, 43, 94 (*see also* self-image)
Iger, Robert, 188
Image, The (Boorstin), 236
Inauthentic Culture (Newman), 88
Indigo Wild, 49
inauthenticity
  authentic capitalism, 91–92
  "authentic" consumer goods examples, 31–34
  authenticity paradox, 89–90
  Axioms of Authenticity, 43–44, 90, 191
  business's need to come off as authentic, 42–43
  claims of "real" in advertisements, 36–37
  culture of authenticity, 90–91
  fundamental lack of authenticity from
    businesses, 87–89
  individual determination of authenticity,
    92–94
  inherently personal nature of authenticity, 81
  lack of truly pristine nature, 84–87
  manufactured reality of the Netherlands and
    Disneyland, 81–82
  rendering an offering authentic (*see* Real/Fake
    Matrix)
  "real" in tourism, 37–39
  supply of faked reality, 40–42
  TV programs examples, 34–36
  unreality of Venice versus the Venetian, 82–84
  what authenticity is not, 88
infinite ROI, 177
Incredible Adventures, 12
influential authenticity
  appeal to collective aspirations, 74–76
  appeal to personal aspirations, 73–74
  embrace art, 73–74
  focus on bettering the world, 72–73
  give meaning, 76–77
  polarity of Other/Self, 239–243
  principles of, 77
  promote a cause, 75
  three-word offerings and, 74–75
  transformations seen as, 50
ING Direct Cafe, 6, 151, 177
intellectual property rights, 8
intention + interests, 123–125
Internet
  commoditization of goods and services, 47–48
  postmodernism and, 17–18
iPod, 19, 57
Is What It Says It Is standard of authenticity. *See*
    What It Says standard of authenticity
Italian Village, The, 11

Ivany, Robert, 139
iVillage.com, 166

Jack Morton Worldwide, 134
Jamba Juice, 55
Japan, 8
Jay-Z, 12, 60
Jensen, Rolf, 74–75
Jerde, Jon, 73, 111, 149
Jew vs. Jew (Freedman), 28
Jillette, Penn, 99
Jim Beam, 133
Jin Li Street, 51
Joffe, Adrian, 229
Johansen, Robert, 15
Johnson, Geoffrey, 24
Johnson, Ron, 235
Johnson & Johnson, 138
Johnson Controls Showcase, 154
Joie de Vivre Hospitality, 21
Jones, Chris, 133
Jones, Norah, 179–180
Jones Soda, 19, 75
juxtaposition, 219–222, 246–247

Kallay, Jeff, 25
Kamen, Dean, 192–193
Kassoy, Will, 69
Kawakubo, Rei, 229
Kawasaki, 55
Kay, Jane Holtz, 24
Keeler, Paul, 238
Kennedy, Allan, 126
Kent, Fred, 136
Kerry, John, 26
Kerrygold, 129
Kessler, Andy, 140
Kids City (La Ciudad de los Niños), 12, 159–160
Kidzania, 12, 160
King, Margaret, 20, 86
Kitamura, Katie, 69
Klett, Mark, 85
Klingman, Anna, 68
knockoffs, 221
KLM Royal Dutch Airlines, 166
Kotkin, Joel, 92
Kraft Foods, 142

La Ciudad de los Niños (Kids City), 12, 159–160
La Ferla, Ruth, 60

landsend.com, 13
Laroche, Hervé, 98
Lasch, Christopher, 21
Lasseter, John, 188
Las Vegas, 68, 71, 73, 83–84, 151, 156, 157, 174, 204
Last.fm, 13, 65
LEGOFactory.com, 65
LEGO Systems, 65, 171–172, 177
Leibowitz, Ed, 111
Lewis, David, 3
Life: The Movie (Gabler), 17
Life on the Screen (Turkle), 17
Lifestyle Centers, 137
Lincoff, Audrey, 75
Linden Lab, 17
L'Occitane en Provence, 136
Lord of the Rings (movie), 167–168
Losonczi, Aron, 112
Lush, 227–228

MacCannell, Dean, 86, 88, 142
major platforms, 166–168, 170
major venues, 157–158, 162
Making Meaning (Diller, Shedroff, Rhea), 76
Making of a Name, The, 130
Mall of America, 157, 174
Managers Not MBAs (Mintzberg), 25
Mann, Charles, 85
MapleStory, 165
Marconi, Joe, 75
markers, 142–143
marketing
    buzz, 148
    diminishing authenticity via, 147–149, 153, 155–156, 172, 177
    experience is the marketing (principle), 150, 152, 161
    experiences, 150, 156, 167, 170
    placemaking versus, 148–149
Marketing Aesthetics (Schmitt and Simonson), 143–144
Mars' Masterfoods, 133
MaryJanesFarm, 55
mass customization, 48, 65, 77–78, 201–202, 206.
    See also customization
Massey, Wright, 161
Matrix and Philosophy, The (Worth), 109–110
Mattel, 150
Mattel's BarbieGirls world, 166
Mattus, Reuben, 131
Mayernik, David, 83

McCarthy, Mary, 83
McDonald, Jamie, 158
McDonough, William, 56
McEwan, Colin, 86
McLuhan, Marshall, 17, 135
McMahon, Linda, 37
media + messages, 132–134
Mediated (Zengotita), 17
miadidas.com, 13
Microsoft, 165, 167, 205
Mid-Columbia Medical Center, 151–152
MiGs over Moscow, 12
Mikunda, Christian, 122
Miller, William Ian, 99
mini.com, 13
Minkowski, Hermann, 180, 205
Minkowski Space, 180–182, 185, 188, 200, 224
Mintzberg, Henry, 25
Montblanc, 201
Moore, Charles, 109
Morton, Peter, 195
motivations, declared, 128–129, 138–141
MSN, 165
MTV's Virtual Laguna Beach, 166
Murray, Bill, 98–99, 102
Myatt, John, 42
Mydays, 12
MySpace, 19, 135, 165

narcithropy, 27
names, assigned, 128–129, 130–132
Natharius, David, 69
natural authenticity
    applied in retail design, 53
    be bare, 55
    commodities seen as, 49
    ecotourism, 56
    go green, 56
    natural lifestyle marketing by developers, 55–56
    in organic foods, 53–54
    leave it raw, 54–55
    polarity of Un-/Re-, 226–229
    principles of, 56
    qualities of, 52
    rawness purposely put in products, 54–55
    reek rusticity, 55–56
    stress materiality, 55
nature versus nurture
    of companies, 121–123
    of the earth, 84–86
    of self, 189

Nature's Keepers (Budiansky), 84–85
NBA Store, 100–101, 105–106
Neal, Paul, 84
Neopets, 165
the Netherlands, 57, 81–82, 83, 86, 87
Newman, Jay, 88, 93
new ruralism, 55
New Zealand, 12, 167–168
Nike, 19, 55, 101, 106, 169, 230
　　Converse, 19, 230
NIKEiD.com, 13, 169
Niketown, 101, 106
Nokia, 158, 189, 234
nonprofit organizations and authenticity,
　　27
Nortel, 154, 162
Norton, Dave, 76
nurture. *See* nature versus nurture

Obama, Barack, 26
O'Boyle, Jamie, 20
Oelofse, Gregg, 85
offerings
　　economic, 46–49
　　nature of, 118, 119–121, 128–129, 204, 216
　　three-word, 74–75
OfficeMax, 167
Oglivy, Jay, 196, 208
Oppenheimer & Co., 157
organic foods and natural authenticity,
　　53–54
Organizational Culture and Leadership (Schein),
　　126
origin + history, 121–123
original authenticity
　　anti-up, 61
　　be original, 57
　　goods seen as, 49
　　look old, 58
　　mix-and-mash, 60–61
　　perception of originality and, 57–59
　　polarity of Repro/Retro, 229–239
　　principles of, 62
　　revive the past, 59–60
　　stress your firsts, 58–59
Oriole Park at Camden Yards, 137, 230
O'Rourke, P. J., 84
Orvell, Miles, 221
Other/Self polarity, 239–243
O'Toole, James, 25
OurVersions watches, 107–108
output + obligations, 119–121

Pabst Blue Ribbon Beer, 221
Palmisano, Samuel J., 116–117, 216
Parker, Kathleen, 26
Parque España, 12
Parra, Rosendo, 202
Pearson, Waynn, 153
Peterson, Richard, 93
P.G.C. Hajenius, 53, 198
Piccalo, Gina, 15
Pike Place Fish Company, 6, 144–145, 152
Pixar, 188
place-based companies, 136–137
placemaking
　　authenticity gained by creating experiences,
　　　149–151
　　calculating the value of experiences, 172–175
　　Chief Experience Officer position, 175
　　demand creation by service providers,
　　　151–152
　　described, 149, 164
　　portfolio for physical experiences (*see* place-
　　　making using physical experiences)
　　portfolio for virtual experiences (*see* place-
　　　making using virtual experiences)
　　portfolio creation, 170–172
　　return on investment and, 176–177
placemaking using physical experiences
　　company examples, 154–155
　　derivative presence, 158–160, 162
　　determining where your business is, 161–162
　　experience hubs, 156–157, 162
　　flagship location, 153–154, 162
　　major venues, 157–158, 162
　　world wide markets, 160–161, 162
placemaking using virtual experiences
　　derivative placement, 168–169, 170
　　determining where your business is, 169–170
　　experience domains, 165–166, 170
　　flagship site, 163–165, 169–170
　　integrating the virtual with the physical,
　　　162–163
　　major platforms, 166–168, 170
　　World Wide Web, 169, 170
places, established, 128–129, 135–138
Plato, 18
podcasts, 20
Pohl, Mike, 70
polarity, real/fake, 220–224. *See also* exceptional
　　authenticity; influential authenticity; natu-
　　ral authenticity; original authenticity; and
　　referential authenticity
politicians and authenticity, 26–27
Pollard, C. William, 124, 135

Polonius, 96, 98–99, 239
Polonius Test, 97–98
Pope John Paul II, 28
pop-up stores, 65
Porras, Jerry, 139
Porsche, 197
Postman, Neil, 17
Postrel, Virginia, 93–94
Pour Your Heart into It (Schultz), 127, 135
Practice of Management, The (Drucker), 124
Premium/Personal polarity, 232–235
Procter & Gamble, 158–159, 165
Progression of Economic Value, the, 45–52
    commodities, 46
    commoditization, 47–48, 49
    customization, 48, 49
    economic offering concept, 46–47
    experiences, 46, 48
    goods, 46–48
    services, 46–48
    Theory of Everything, 45–46
    transformations, 46, 48–49
Progressive Insurance, 161
prosumer, 13
Purpose Driven Life, The (Warren), 75
purpose, sense of, 118, 123–125, 128–129, 204,
    216

QQ, 165
quality and authenticity relationship, 2, 5
Quasi-/Pseudo- polarity, 236–239
quasi-vegetarianism, 239
Quick, 67
Quinlan, Mary Lou, 59, 140

raison d'être, 29–30, 119, 123–124
Rasmussen, Steen Eiler, 83
raw-foodism, 54
Ray, Paul, 4
real (real-real), 112–113
Real Deal Expo, 244
Real/Fake Matrix
    assess your place on the matrix, 101–102
    create belief (fake-real), 107, 108–110, 224
    customer's determination of what is real, 99
    described, 97–98
    determine your dominant polarity and vec-
        tors, 244–246
    exceptional from Premium/Personal, 232–235
    explore multiple polarities, 247–250
    genre-based polarities overview, 219–220

get real (real-real), 107, 112–114, 224
go faux (fake-fake), 107–108, 224
influential from Other/Self, 239–243
juxtapose industry-specific vectors, 246–247
leverage your current position, 102–103
moving toward real-real, 113–114
natural from Un-/Re-, 226–229
original from Repro/Retro, 229–239
overcome the fake, 103
polarities examples, 220–222
polarities versus purity, 222–224
Polonius Test and, 96, 97–98
referential from Quasi-/Pseudo-, 236–239
retail venues places on the matrix, 99–101,
    104–106
reveal the unreal (real-fake), 107, 111–112,
    224
signify the real, 103
unreal rendered as real, 95–96
vectors alignment, 224–226
ways a business can talk about itself (*see* ele-
    ments of Is What It Says It Is on Real/
    Fake Matrix)
Real-real, 22, 97, 100, 102–103, 104, 112–114,
    117–118, 145, 220, 222, 224, 225, 226, 229,
    230, 233–234, 237, 240, 242, 243
Real-fake, 97, 100–101, 102, 103, 105–106,
    111–112, 113–114, 118, 222–223, 224,
    228, 230–231, 233–234, 235, 238–239,
    243, 244
Real Thing, The (Orvell), 221
reality TV, 15, 34–36, 89, 236
Real World (on MTV), 34
Rebel Rules, The (Conley), 21
Recreational Equipment, Inc. (REI), 112,
    154–155, 157, 162, 176–177
Red Bull, 66
reddit, 165
referential authenticity
    be realistic, 69–70
    creating a feeling of nostalgia, 71
    evoke a time, 709
    experiences seen as, 50
    make it matter, 68–69
    pay personal tribute,
    pick a place, 70
    polarity of Quasi-/Pseudo-, 236–239
    principles of, 71
    themed venues, 68
    Venice and the Venetian, 84
    video and computer games and, 69–70
religious organizations and authenticity,
    27–28

rendering authenticity
  authenticity paradox, 89–90
  business imperative, 2–3, 5–6
  economic Theory of Everything (*see* Theory
    of Everything)
  exceptional authenticity (*see* exceptional
    authenticity)
  influential authenticity (*see* influential
    authenticity)
  learning the discipline of, 250
  natural authenticity (*see* natural authenticity)
  original authenticity (*see* original authenticity)
  perceived authenticity (*see* genres of perceived
    authenticity)
  Real/Fake Matrix (*see* Real/Fake Matrix)
  referential authenticity (*see* referential
    authenticity)
Renner, Lois, 95
Replogle, John, 160
representations + perception, 141–143
Reproduction Movement, 231
Repro/Retro polarity, 229–239
resident trap, 51
retronyms, 14–15, 35
return on investment of placemaking experi-
    ences vs. advertising, 176–177
reveal the unreal (real-fake), 107, 111–112, 224
Revival of the Fittest (Sull), 215
Rhea, Darrel, 76
Rhodes, Sonia, 64
Rise of the Creative Class (Florida), 4
Ritson, Mark, 130, 197
Ritz-Carlton, 63–64, 139, 235
Robbins, Tony, 221–222
Rocky Mountain Soap, 49
Roddick, Anita, 226–228
Rollins, Kevin, 203
roots of place-based companies, 136–137
Rosedale, Philip, 17
Rousseau, Jean-Jacques, 87, 90, 93
Rubell, Jennifer, 228
Russert, Tim, 26

S1M0NE, 40
Sachs, Sid, 95
Saffo, Paul, 193
Sand Hills golf course, 53
San Juan Regional Medical Center, 208–210, 212,
    215
Sartre, Jean-Paul, 88
Sartwell, Crispin, 26
Saunders, Anne, 198

Scars of the Spirit (Hartman), 34
Schein, Edgar, 126
Scherr, Allan, 217
Schiphol Airport, 157
Schmitt, Bernd, 143–144
Schmitz, Jan-Patrick, 201
Schrage, Michael, 96
Schrager, Ian, 62–63
Schultz, Howard, 127, 135, 160, 174, 198
Schwartz, Jonathan, 135
scion.com, 13
Scott, A. O., 98, 246
Scott, Mark, 151
Scotti, Alberto, 83
In Search of Authenticity (Bendix), 5
Second Cup (coffee house), 242
Second Life (online world), 11, 17, 165–166, 223
Secret Service (DiJulius), 233
Segway Personal Transporter, 192–193, 194
SEI Investments, 95
Self-Help (Smiles), 240
self-help industry, 240
Selfhood and Authenticity (Anton), 88, 185
self-image, 5, 12, 21, 65, 75, 77, 94, 99, 127, 161,
    241
ServiceMaster, 124
services
  as economic offering, 46
  commoditization of, 47–48
  seen as exceptional authenticity, 49–50
  placemaking experiences and, 151–152
Sharp HealthCare, 64
Shaw, Bob, 132
Shedroff, Nathan, 76
Sierra Club, 24
Shelfari, 166
Simonson, Alex, 143–144
simulacra, 17, 31, 95, 109, 111
Sims Online, The, 165
Sincerity and Authenticity (Trilling), 87–88
Ski Dubai, 12
Slouka, Mark, 15
Slow Food/Cities movement, 66–67
Smiles, Samuel, 240, 241
Smith, Craig, 214
Snack Food Association (SFA), 244
social institutions and authenticity, 23–24, 29–30
social networking
  demand for authenticity, 16–18
  experience domains, 165
  how to render society more social, 18–20
  Internet and, 17
Soderstrom, Erick, 19

Solomon, Charles, 188
Sontag, Susan, 73
Sorkin, Michael, 109
Soul of a Business, The (Chappell), 125, 135
Soul of the Enterprise, The (Hall), 124–125
Soul of the Firm, The (Pollard), 124, 135
Soul of the New Consumer: Authenticity, The
    (Lewis and Bridger), 3
Sources of the Self (Taylor), 184
South Korea, 11
Southern Cross Experiences, 74
Southwest Airlines, 64
Spear, Joe, 137
Speare, Ellen, 239
Spessi (artist), 95
St. Joe Company, 55–56
Stagecoach Island, 166
standards of authenticity, being true to self. *See*
    True to Self standard of authenticity
standards of authenticity, being what it says it is.
    See What It Says standard of authenticity
standards of authenticity, establishing
    categories of ways a business can talk about its
        self (*see* elements of Is True to Itself on
        Real/Fake Matrix)
    elemental equations summary, 146
    expressions versus impressions, 143–144
    factors directly influencing customer percep-
        tions, 117
    forms of authentication, 134–135
    how to be perceived as acting authentically,
        145
    IBM's rewrite of basic beliefs, 115–117
    principles of acting at work, 144–145
Standing Bear, Luther, 85
Starbucks
    appeals to Other, 243
    dependence on authentic perception, 2
    focus on authenticity, 127
    influential authenticity use, 75
    position in placemaking portfolio, 160
    presented as an experience, 10
    the Starbucks guy, 90–91
    use of expressed statements, 133–134
Starizon, 139–140
Starobin, Paul, 26
Steak n Shake, 61
statements, expressed, 128–129, 132–135
Steiger, Reuben, 166
Steinway & Sons, 150–151
Stephens, Robert, 16, 161, 198–199
Stevens, Jim, 61
Stewart, Jon, 40

Stolk, Van, 76
Strat-O-Matic baseball, 69
Sull, Donald, 215, 216
Swarovski's Kristallwelten, 122

Target, 140–141
Taylor, Charles, 93, 184
Taylor, Fred Jr., 64
technology
    consumer frustration with, 13–15
    rendering more human, 15–16
theme restaurants, 195
Theming of America (Gottdeiner), 68
Theory of Everything (TOE), 45-46. *See also*
        Progression of Economic Value
theory of relativity, 180, 205
There.com (online world), 11, 165
theU.com. 25
Thomas, William H. and Judy, 72
Threadless, 19
Thum, Peter, 243
Tigrett, Isaac, 195
Timeless Cities (Mayernik), 83
Time Warner, Inc., 149–150
Toffler, Alvin, 13
Tolkien, J.R.R., 110
Tokyo Disneyland, 12
Tombstone, Arizona, 142
tourism
    boutique hotels, 62–63
    claims of "real" in, 37–39
    ecotourism, 56
    manufactured reality of the Netherlands and
        Disneyland, 81–82
    unreality of Venice versus the Venetian, 82–84
Tourist, The (MacCannell), 142–143
Tourneau, 51
Toy Machine Bloodsucking Skateboard Com-
        pany, 61
Toyota, 214
transformations, 48–49, 50
tribute bands, 41–42, 231
transformations
    as economic offering, 47–49
    inability to commoditize or customize, 48–49
    seen as influential authenticity, 50
    placemaking experiences and, 151–152
Trilling, Lionel, 87–88
True to Self standard of authenticity
    body of values, 118, 125–127, 128–129, 204,
        216
    categories of, 118

True to Self standard of authenticity (*continued*)
    easiest way to be perceived as phony, 190
    effects of heritage, 118, 121–123, 128–129,
        204, 216
    essence of enterprise, 118–119, 128–129, 204,
        216
    execution zone in Here-and-Now Space,
        182–184
    musician example, 179–180
    nature of offerings, 118, 119–121, 128–129,
        204, 216
    operating in Here-and-Now Space example
        (*see* Walt Disney Company)
    polarities and, 222–223
    sense of purpose, 118, 123–125, 128–129, 204,
        216
    space model (*see* Here-and-Now Space
        model)
    state your identity, 118
    strategic possibilities viewed through particle
        physics, 180–182
TST Engineerium, 153–154
Turkle, Sherry, 17

ubiquity and authenticity, 2, 160–161, 169
Ubisoft, 69
UNESCO, 50
Unilever, 133, 140
Union National Community Bank, 60
Universal Studios. *See* CityWalk
unreal (real-fake), 111–112
Unreal America, The (Huxtable), 96
Un-/Re- polarity, 226–229
USAA, 206–207

Vacant (retailer), 65
values, body of, 118, 125–127, 128–129, 204,
    216
Vance, Mike, 57
Vans Inc., 11, 59, 155, 162–163, 174, 177
Vans Skateparks, 11, 155, 163, 177
Vans Warped Tour, 155
Varni, Patrice, 166
Venetian, The, 82–84, 86, 223
Venice, 82–84, 86
Venice Observed (McCarthy), 83
venues + events, 135–138, 150
vintage, 15, 55, 122, 230–232
Viking Range Corporation, 155
virtual worlds, 11, 17–18, 165–166

VocationVacations, 11, 61

Wachholz, Rob, 132
Wachowski Brothers, 31
Walker, Rob, 121, 147, 221
Wallace, Rob, 142
Waller, Britta, 239
Wal-Mart, 5, 47–48
Walt Disney Company
    consequences of moving away from its
        heritage, 186
    debate on authenticity and, 1
    missed strategic opportunities, 187–188
    originator of theme park industry, 57
    Pal Mickey, 13
    PhotoPass service, 163
    placemaking and, 149–150, 163
    strategic redirection under Iger, 188
    success within its execution zone, 185–186
    use of fake-real authenticity, 81–82, 108–109
Walt Disney World, 9, 10, 69, 157, 185, 237
War of the Worlds (Slouka), 15
Warren, Rick, 75
Watson, Thomas J. Jr., 115
Webkinz World, 165
Web sites, 134, 143, 162–170
Wells Fargo's Stagecoach Island, 166
What's So Great About America (D'Souza), 90–91
What It Says standard of authenticity
    assigned names, 128–129, 130–132
    categories of, 128–129
    Chief Experience Officer and, 175
    declared motivations, 128–129, 138–141
    demand creation and, 148–149
    displayed appearances, 128–129, 141–143
    easiest way to be perceived as phony, 148
    established places, 128–129, 135–138, 150
    expressed statements, 128–129, 132–135
    identify your statements, 128–129
    placemaking portfolio and, 155–156, 163
    polarities and, 222–223
    Repro/Retro and, 232
Whole Foods, 53, 204
Williamsburg, 83
Winfrey, Oprah, 27
Winter Olympics (2006), 34, 247–249
Winter Olympics (2010), 249–250
Wipperfürth, Alex, 127
Wnek, Mark, 133
Wolfe, David, 14, 20, 94
Wolfe, Tom, 25

Woolsey, Mark, 246
world wide markets, 160–162
World Wide Web, 169, 170
Worner, Rick, 157
Worth, Sarah, 109–110
WPP, 134

Yahoo!, 13, 159, 165
Yokoyama, John, 152

Yosemite, 85
"You" Person of the Year (in *Time* magazine),
    19
YouTube, 17, 19, 165

Zafu, 192
zazzle.com, 13
Zengotita, Thomas de, 17
Zorbing, 12, 193–194

ABOUT THE AUTHORS

JAMES H. GILMORE and B. JOSEPH PINE II are cofounders of Strategic Horizons LLP, an Aurora, Ohio-based, thinking studio dedicated to helping enterprises conceive and design new ways of adding value to their economic offerings. They are coauthors of *The Experience Economy: Work Is Theatre & Every Business a Stage* (Harvard Business School Press, 1999). Mr. Gilmore is also a Batten Fellow and Visiting Lecturer at the University of Virginia Darden School of Business. Mr. Pine, who also wrote *Mass Customization: The New Frontier in Business Competition* (Harvard Business School Press, 1993), is a Senior Fellow with both the Design Futures Council and the European Centre for the Experience Economy, which he cofounded.